bettendorf public library
and information center

D1249757

WITHDRAWN

# A HISTORY OF IOWA

## BY DONALD L. KIMBALL

*Volume One*

1987

## Heritage and Settlement

## Antiquity - 1838

## LIMITED FIRST EDITION

Published by

Historic   Publications
(Division of The Trends & Events Publishing Company)
P. O. Box 158
Fayette, Iowa 52142

Other books by

DONALD L. KIMBALL

I REMEMBER MAMIE, 1981
   (The nation's only complete biography of
   Mamie Doud Eisenhower, late First Lady)

THE CHOICE---Freedom or Slavery, 1982

FREEDOM IS NOT FREE, 1983

THE MONEY AND THE POWER, 1984

THE REBIRTH OF POPULISM, 1985

IT CAN'T HAPPEN HERE, 1986

A HISTORY OF IOWA, Volume One - Heritage and Settlement, 1987

Forthcoming books by

DONALD L. KIMBALL

A HISTORY OF IOWA, Volume Two - The Territory of Iowa

ASSASSINATION --- The Murder of John F. Kennedy

Copyright 1988 by Historic Publications, Division of
   The Trends & Events Publishing Company.


Liberal permission is granted to reproduce anything published
in this volume provided that  credit is given but more especially
to those whom the author has quoted, cited or borrowed in the
research.

Library of Congress # 88-082296          ISBN # 0-942698-07-X

Iowa
R
977.7
KI

# Contents

# Dedication to

## MARIE FINCH

It is indeed a rare circumstance to be both a grandson and a grandfather at the same time in one's life. That is true of the author of this book. Therefore this first volume of "A HISTORY OF IOWA" is gratefully and lovingly dedicated to his grandmother, Marie Finch of Cedar Falls, Iowa.

Vivian Marie Garber was born at Deer Creek, Illinois, on 9 March 1894 in that small community's hotel which was built and managed by her father, Albert Garber who had married Lena Schertz. (The year 1988 is the centennial of Deer Creek and Marie Finch is listed in their centennial book as the town's oldest living native.)

The Garbers moved to Iowa and in 1913 Marie was united in marriage at Fairbank, Buchanan County, to Wilbur Wilson Finch, a descendant of pioneer Iowans who settled in Buchanan and Black Hawk Counties. (The Finch family came to America in 1630.) To Marie and Wilbur were born seven children: Katherine, Pauline, Kenneth, Charles, James, Joan and another son Gerald who died in 1945. All of her children live in Iowa today except son James of California.

Marie Finch celebrated the 94th anniversary of her birth in 1988 and sharing her long life with her in person or by messages were her six children, 20 grandchildren, 48 great-grandchildren and 17 great-great-grandchildren. At her age she is around 2/3rd's as old as the State of Iowa itself.

Marie and Wilbur Finch farmed near Fairbank, Iowa, and moved to Oelwein, Fayette County, Iowa, in 1938. In the early 1940's they removed to Waterloo, Black Hawk County, Iowa, where they remained. Wilbur Finch worked for the Rath Packing Company there and was fond of fishing, swimming and playing his violin. He died in 1975 at the age of 85.

Marie Finch was in the restaurant business for many years in Waterloo and one of her hobbies was playing her piano. She was very active in the Gold Star Mothers and was a particular friend of Mrs. Thomas Sullivan, mother of the five Sullivan brothers who died on the same ship in World War II. She was also very active in the Eastern Star.

Approaching 95, she remains in good health, plays her piano and enjoys the company of many friends. Constant visitors are her children, grandchildren, great-grandchildren and great-great-grandchildren. The dedication of this book to her is in appreciation of a long life, well-lived. We know she will enjoy it for she has lived through much history herself and there are many golden years to which she can look forward.

--- D. L. K.

*For*
*Don Kimball*
*Mamie Doud Eisenhower*

American author Donald L. Kimball is pictured above with the late First Lady, Iowa-born Mrs. Dwight D. (Mamie Doud) Eisenhower. Kimball is the author of the nation's only complete biography of her life. The above picture was taken at the entrance to the Eisenhower home on their farm at Gettysburg, Pennsylvania. The book "I REMEMBER MAMIE" is becoming rare in the Limited First Edition although some remain available.

# About the Author

He's walked with kings but never lost the common touch. That seems a fitting phrase with which to begin a biographical sketch of American author and Iowa statesman, Donald L. Kimball.

He's known more U. S. presidents than most living Americans, has served in high public office and is nationally and internationally known as an author, playwright, columnist and journalist. His has been a life of activity and achievement and he has received many honors both civilian and military. A descendant of pioneer Iowans, his major interests have always been in history, public concerns and writing.

Donald LeRoy Kimball was born in Fairbank, Buchanan County, Iowa, on 15 February 1933 the son of Donald and Katherine Finch Kimball. Both families arrived in America in the 1630s.

He was reared in Oelwein, Fayette County, Iowa, where both his father and grandfather worked for the Chicago Great Western Railroad. He was graduated from Stanley High School in 1951 and began working his way through college at Upper Iowa University in Fayette. He was active in politics at an early age and in Chicago in 1952 became acquainted with General and Mrs. Dwight D. Eisenhower. (His book, "I REMEMBER MAMIE" is the nation's only complete biography of the late First Lady.)

During the Korean War he was inducted into the army where he served for over three years rising from private to a commissioned officer. He volunteered for the paratroopers and served in the 11th Airborne Division, the 503rd Airborne Regimental Combat Team and was one of those who helped reorganize the famed 101st Airborne Division. He served from the company to the division levels.

In 1956 he entered the newspaper business and has been involved in publishing most of his adult life. He began writing a newspaper column in 1951. His writings, other than books, are too numerous to mention. He is the author of two plays, "A House Divided," the story of Lincoln's years as president, and "The Trial and Death of Christ."

He was elected to two terms in the Iowa House of Representatives and at one time was the youngest member of the legislature and is the one who served as the youngest chairman of a legislative committee in history.

He was graduated from Upper Iowa Univeristy and named to "Who's Who in American Colleges and Universities." He is an Honorary Citizen of South Dakota and both an honorary admiral and general.

He was married in 1957 to Mary Elizabeth the daughter of the late Frank and Ethel Moore. Mrs. Kimball is vice president for business affairs at Upper Iowa University. They have three married daughters: Dayna Marie, Mrs. Scott Baker; Ann Jeanette, Mrs. Thomas Joseph; and Katherine Mary, Mrs. Kevin Thomas. They have three grandsons. They are members of St. Mary's Episcopal Church, Oelwein, Iowa.

The author is not only qualified to write on historical subjects but he has been very much a part of both Iowa and American history.

--- K. M. T.

# Introduction

The history of Iowa is the history of a beautiful land. One could say "the" beautiful land. For it has so much to offer. It also has a long and colorful history, much of it recorded but a history taken for granted by so many of us. Many histories of Iowa have been written and there is little that is truly creative for an author who seeks to write of our early days, the times of the pioneer settlers.

And so another mere volume on Iowa history is not required. Yet time marches on and the story of Iowa as a State, the story of its people, the story of its accomplishments, the record of its contributions narrated in meaningful form have never been put in a chronological and comprehensive historical perspective. And that is the purpose of this book and the volumes that will follow.

There is truly something unique about Iowa and Iowa's people. There is a value in the hearts and minds of its folk that is found nowhere else on earth. Work, industry, thrift, culture and a singular friendliness are all part of the Iowa being, the character of Iowans.

The Iowa we find today, in 1988, is an outgrowth of all who have gone before us in creating the beautiful life in the beautiful land. We must know from whence we came to really know who we are. That is also an aspect of this particular series of volumes depicting the history of Iowa.

To accomplish this it is important to pick and choose from the wealth of material available that which has served to create what we have.

Iowans have a unique type of humility. They are down-to-earth folk with a friendliness known in few other places. They share common concerns and those are from the heart. In their history-long humility Iowans have never tried to be boastful or to be anything they are not.

As a result of this humility, this reluctance to wave their own flag, there still exists in many parts of the nation the image that we are really not much. No one from an eastern city would suspect that Iowa is a land of great culture, that we have huge art museums or that Iowans can go to an opera. And it is not particularly that we care to overcome whatever image may exist, for it is simply not part of our nature.

Fortunately the values Iowans have inherited are, for the most part, handed down from one generation to another in a State where the concept of family and belief in God still exist. All that in spite of a burgeoning government that would eliminate it in the most subtle of ways.

For us to know why we have these values that make us truly great requires a knowledge of where it all came from, where we came from and from whence came the Iowa spirit and Iowa values. Only a knowledge of history can teach us that. It is our duty to understand these things.

Iowa has rarely been looked upon as a place of great prosperity but it is said that while we don't reach the "highs" of economic heights neither do we hit the "lows" in times of financial stress, panic, recession or depression. Ours is a more even attitude, a more even economy.

Yet the true values survive.

A major purpose of this history is to dwell upon those values that made the beautiful land the great place it is. That cannot be done in one volume and several, perhaps ten or twelve, are envisioned. The central themes are extolling Iowa's greatness, recording significant history, sometimes even correcting history but mainly bringing history to life for those who read it, to graphically portray events and people of the past.

To do this we will use sketches and drawings and in some cases portray people of historic note as they may have looked and thereby assuming the traditional author-editor's license to do so. Available maps, portraits and actual pictures of people and places, from the time photography came into being, will be used when we can obtain them. After the advent of the camera this effort becomes easier for the historian. Yet much of that is predicated upon the willingness of those who have them.

The research, time and every human effort that goes into a monumental task such as this make it dear indeed. In the early history books banks, railroads and other businesses "advertised." This is an important subsidy to expensive undertakings. Because a history is permanent and will live for generations in the hands of individuals, in the public libraries and our schools and colleges, many want to be a part of it; part of the permanent record. Therefore, your publishers have created a type of "Sponsorship" whereby this can be done. Yet this not being a commercial venture, not more than 10% of any volume will be allowed to our sponsors. We are grateful to them and they are also listed in the back.

Another aspect of this volume, this series, is the recognition of living historic figures and other outstanding Iowans. We do not pretend to have them all here but we think it is significant to recognize great people while they're among us rather than see their names on a piece of granite.

Finally, we have selected this particular font of type and dubbed it the Iowa Historic font for its beauty and size; it's unique and it's easy for everyone to read. We hope you, our readers, enjoy it, too.

One thing we have learned in putting this first volume of "A HISTORY OF IOWA" together is that there's more history out there than we realize and there are more historians than we have heard about. It is their material and their recollections we seek. And we beg all to share.

By creating this encyclopedic series of volumes the aforesaid goals are our main ones. We feel that the central theme of Iowa's true greatness will show forth, literally become a reality for all who delve into them and discover what really does make Iowa "the beautiful land." For "beautiful land" means something far more than natural pulchritude.

Governor Branstad, in writing the forward to this first volume suggests that even "beautiful land" may not be "sufficient to portray the true beauty of Iowa." We agree. There is vast and undescribable beauty in all that is Iowa. In our people, our way of life, our humility, our tolerance, our profound beliefs, our determinations, our love of God and family and our optimism for the future even in difficult times.

We cannot know today or even ourselves unless we truly understand from whence we came. Absorb this volume and future ones; learn of Iowa's true greatness. Come to know your own "beautiful land."

--- Donald L. Kimball

9

# Forward

**TERRY E. BRANSTAD**
GOVERNOR

## OFFICE OF THE GOVERNOR
### STATE CAPITOL
### DES MOINES, IOWA 50319
515 281-5211

"Beautiful Land" is an appropriate description, if words can be sufficient to portray the true beauty of Iowa. Iowa's spirit is founded in her strong-willed and determined people. As the great new land, America, was settled, those pioneers who became known as Iowans planted their roots in our rich earth. They became stewards of the world's richest farmland, a resource ultimately more valuable than the gold in California or the oil in Texas.

Today, Iowa soil provides food for the world. But Iowa also is an insurance capital, a home to growing telecommunications companies, and a center of development in new technologies such as lasers and molecular biology.

If Iowa is truly to know itself and understand where it is going in the future, it is important to understand our past.

In a few years, Iowa will celebrate the 150th anniversary of statehood. The people who built a home in Iowa 150 years ago, brought with them profound religious beliefs, customs of their homeland cultures, and a commitment to freedom combined with a spirit of determination.

Those are the attributes of Iowans today.

The author of this book is a native Iowan and a descendant of the pioneers who built this great state. He has written a story of Iowa, a proud history of a place with a bright future.

Terry E. Branstad
Governor of Iowa

# The Government

## and

## Elected Officials

### of the

## State of Iowa

## 1987 - 1988

# The Governor of Iowa

## TERRY E. BRANSTAD

Terry E. Branstad was born at Leland in Winnebago County on 17 November 1946 and was inaugurated the 38th governor of the State of Iowa on 14 January 1983 at the age of 36. He is the youngest governor in the State's history and the only one ever elected from Winnebago County.

Governor Branstad was graduated from the Forest City High School in 1965 and the University of Iowa with a Bachelor of Arts degree in political science in 1969.

Following his graduation from the university he served in the United States Army from 1969 to 1971 and received the Commendation Medal for meritorious service.

He was elected to the Iowa House of Representatives in 1972 from the 8th district and studied law at Drake University in Des Moines and received a Juris Doctorate degree in 1974 and that year was also re-elected State Representative. He is involved in farming and began the practice of law in 1975.

He was elected to a third term in the Iowa House of Representatives in 1976 and in 1978 was nominated and elected lieutenant governor of Iowa. In 1982 he was nominated and elected governor. In 1986 he was elected to a second four-year term as the State's chief executive.

Governor Branstad is married and he and his wife, Chris, have three children, Eric, Allison and Marcus. The Branstads belong to St. Augustine's Catholic Church in Des Moines and are affiliated with the Republican party.

Governor Branstad is a member of the American Legion, the Farm Bureau, Lions Club, Sons of Norway, Knights of Columbus and Ducks Unlimited. Politically he has been a delegate to Republican state conventions from 1968 to 1986. In 1976 he was an alternate delegate to the Republican National Convention and in 1980 and 1984 a delegate. In 1984 he was chairman of the Rules Committee at the Republican National Convention.

By the appointment of President Reagan he is a member of the Board of Trustees of the Harry Truman Scholarship Foundation. He is a member of the National Governors Association and is involved with its committees on International Trade, Jobs, Growth and Competitiveness.

# The Lieutenant Governor of Iowa
## JO ANN ZIMMERMAN

Jo Ann Zimmerman was born on 21 December 1936 in Van Buren County, the daughter of Russell and Hazel McIntosh. The baby, Jo Ann McIntosh, was a descendant of early pioneer settlers and arrived in Van Buren County almost exactly a century after the first pioneers arrived there.

She was graduated from Keosauqua High School in 1954 and was the valedictorian of her class. In 1958 she was graduated from the Broadlawns School of Nursing.

In 1956 she was married to Tom Zimmerman and to them were born three sons and two daughters. Tom and Jo Ann Zimmerman are farmers and specialize in raising cattle. They are members of the Iowa Cattleman's Association and the Beef Breeds Council.

Married, rearing her children and engaged in many other public and political activities, Jo Ann Zimmerman found time to continue her education and was graduated from Drake University in 1973 with a bachelor of arts degree. She went on to do graduate work at Iowa State University in Ames and has met the requirements for a master's degree.

In 1982 she fulfilled another aspiration by entering politics as a candidate for public office. She was nominated and elected state representative on the Democratic Party ticket. In 1983 she took office and in 1984 was re-elected. In the House she served as vice chairman of the Human Services Committee and was on the Education and Agriculture standing committees. In 1984 she was cited as "Outstanding Legislator" by the Des Moines Register.

In 1986 Rep. Zimmerman became a candidate for lieutenant governor, was nominated in the June primary election and won the office in the autumn election.

On 16 January 1987 Jo Ann Zimmerman was inaugurated as lieutenant governor of Iowa, the first woman in the history of the State to hold that high office. Other than being first in line to the governorship, she presides over the Iowa State Senate as its president. Nationally, Lt. Gov. Zimmerman serves as chairman of the National Conference of Lieutenant Governors Task Force on Agriculture and Rural Development.

Lt. Gov. Zimmerman has led an active life serving her party, her church (she is a deacon of the First Christian Church in Des Moines), her community and her state.

As a descendant of pioneer Iowans, as a political activist and as Iowa's first woman lieutenant governor, Jo Ann Zimmerman has a secure place in the history of her state.

ELAINE BAXTER
SECRETARY OF STATE

MICHAEL L. FITZGERALD
TREASURER OF STATE

Elaine (Mrs. Harry) Baxter was sworn in as Secretary of State on 2 January 1987 to serve a four year term. Mr. and Mrs. Baxter are residents of Burlington, Des Moines County, Iowa. They are the parents of three grown children: Katherine, Harry and John.

Mrs. Baxter entered politics by running for and being elected to the Burlington City Council in 1973.

In 1980 she was elected to the Iowa House of Representatives on the Democratic Party ticket and was re-elected in 1982 and 1984. In 1986 she was elected Secretary of State.

Mrs. Baxter is a former history teacher and has served in several government positions including service in Washington, D. C. She was an appointee of President Carter serving on the Nominating Panel for the U. S. Court of Appeals.

Michael L. Fitzgerald was born in Marshalltown, Marshall County, Iowa, on 29 November 1951, the son of James and Clara Fitzgerald of Colo, Ia. He was graduated from the Colo High School in 1970.

His education continued at the University of Iowa from which he was graduated in 1974 with a bachelor of business administration degree. He spent the next eight years as a marketing analyst for the Massey Ferguson Company in Des Moines.

Treasurer and Mrs. Fitzgerald (the former Shari Wildman of Reinbeck) have two sons, Ryan, born in 1980, and Erin, born in 1983. They are members of Christ the King Catholic Church in Des Moines.

Treasurer Fitzgerald is a member of the Democratic Party and was elected State Treasurer in 1982 in his first try for elective office.

RICHARD D. JOHNSON
AUDITOR OF STATE

DALE M. COCHRAN
SECRETARY OF AGRICULTURE

Richard D. Johnson was born 3 February 1935 in Nebraska and has been a citizen of Iowa since the 1950s. He and his wife have four grown children.

He was graduated from Drake University in 1960 and became a CPA in 1963. He was employed by Peat, Marwick and Mitchell from 1960 to 1968 when he accepted work with the State of Iowa.

He has served as a city clerk and as Mayor of Sheldahl. He has been a member of the National Guard since 1955. The Johnsons are members of the Madrid Evangelical Free Church.

Richard Johnson was appointed State Auditor on 29 January 1979 by then Gov. Robert D. Ray to succeed the late Lloyd R. Smith. He was elected in his own right as a Republican in 1980 and re-elected to four year terms in 1982 and 1986.

Dale M. Cochran was born on 20 November 1928 at Fort Dodge and was graduated from the high school there later receiving a degree in agriculture from ISU at Ames.

Secretary Cochran has farmed for 33 years and was a member of the Iowa House of Representatives for 22 years. During that service he was minority floor leader for four years and Speaker of the House for four years. He was elected Secretary of Agriculture in 1986 and began a four year term on 2 January 1987. He is a Democrat in politics.

He is a director of the Iowa Soybean Assocation and the Iowa Rural Development Council. He is also a member of the Board of Trustees of Friendship Haven, Fort Dodge.

Secretary Cochran is married to the former Jeannene Hirsch and they have three daughters, Deborah, Cynthia and Tamara.

### TOM MILLER
### ATTORNEY GENERAL

Tom Miller was born in Dubuque on 11 August 1944 and was reared there, being graduated from Wahlert High School and Loras College. He went on to Harvard and received his law degree there.

He worked with VISTA 1969-70 and was a congressional legislative assistant. He worked in the Baltimore Legal Aid Bureau and taught part-time at the Maryland School of Law.

In 1973 he returned to Iowa and established a private law practice at McGregor in Clayton County and also served as city attorney.

In 1978 he was elected attorney general and was the only candidate of his party to win statewide that year; re-elected 1982, 1986.

In 1981 he married Linda Cottington; they have one son, are **Democrats and Roman Catholics.**

### JERRY L. LARSON
### JUSTICE, IOWA SUPREME COURT

Jerry L. Larson was born in Shelby County on 17 May 1936 and his home is there yet, at Harlan.

He received a BA degree from the University of Iowa and the juris doctor's degree from its Law School. In college he was editor of the Iowa Law Review and later a law clerk, U. S. Court of Appeals, 8th Circuit.

He returned to Harlan to practice law and was Shelby county attorney from 1964 to 1968.

In 1978 be was appointed a district court judge and served until 1978 when he was appointed to the Supreme Court of Iowa.

He is married to the former Linda Logan and they have four children, Rebecca, Jeffrey, Susan and David. They affiliate with the Republican party and are members of the Baptist church.

# The Supreme Court of Iowa

Arthur A. McGiverin, Ottumwa, Chief Justice

K. David Harris, Jefferson

Jerry L. Larson, Harlan

Louis W. Schultz, Iowa City

James H. Carter, Cedar Rapids

Louis A. Lavorato, Des Moines

Linda K. Neuman, Davenport

Bruce M. Snell, Jr., Ida Grove

James H. Andreasen, Algona

# The Iowa Court of Appeals

Leo E. Oxberger, Des Moines, Chief Judge

Allen L. Donielson, Des Moines

Dick R. Schlegel, Ottumwa

Maynard H. V. Hayden, Des Moines

Rosemary S. Sackett, Spencer

Albert L. Habhab, Fort Dodge

CHIEF JUSTICE ARTHUR A. McGIVERIN presides over the Supreme Court of Iowa having attained to that office in 1987. He was born 10 November 1928 in Iowa City, Johnson County, and was graduated from McKinley High School in Cedar Rapids, Linn County, in 1946. He served in the U. S. Army from 1946 to 1948 as a corporal and from 1951 to 1953 as a first lieutenant. He was graduated from the University of Iowa with BSC and juris doctor degrees. He was an alternate municipal judge 1960 - 1965 and a judge of the district court from 1965 to 1978 when he was appointed to the Supreme Court. He served as an associate justice until becoming chief justice.

# Iowa Legislative Leadership – 1987–1988

## The 72nd General Assembly

## The Senate

Lt. Gov. Jo Ann Zimmerman,
    Democrat, West Des Moines,
    President of the Senate

Sen. George R. Kinley,
    Democrat, Des Moines,
    President Pro Tempore
Sen. Bill Hutchins,
    Democrat, Audobon,
    Majority Leader
Sen. Emil J. Husak,
    Democrat, Toledo,
    Ass't Majority Leader
Sen. Michael E. Gronstal,
    Democrat, Council Bluffs
    Ass't Majority Leader
Sen. Wally E. Horn,
    Democrat, Cedar Rapids,
    Ass't Majority Leader
Sen. Calvin O. Hultman,
    Republican, Red Oak,
    Minority Leader
Sen. Edgar H. Holden,
    Republican, Davenport,
    Ass't Minority Leader
Sen. John W. Jensen,
    Republican, Plainfield,
    Ass't Minority Leader
Sen. John N. Nystrom,
    Republican, Boone,
    Ass't Minority Leader
Mr. John F. Dwyer,
    Secretary of the Senate

## House of Representatives

Rep. Donald D. Avenson,
    Democrat, Oelwein,
    Speaker of the House

Rep. John H. Connors,
    Democrat, Des Moines,
    Speaker Pro Tempore
Rep. Robert C. Arnould,
    Democrat, Davenport,
    Majority Leader
Rep. Florence D. Buhr,
    Democrat, Des Moines,
    Ass't Majority Leader
Rep. John Groninga,
    Democrat, Mason City,
    Ass't Majority Leader
Rep. Rod Halvorson,
    Democrat, Fort Dodge,
    Ass't Majority Leader
Rep. Bob Skow,
    Democrat Guthrie Center,
    Ass't Majority Leader
Rep. Delwyn Stromer,
    Republican, Garner,
    Minority Leader
Rep. Wayne Bennett,
    Republican, Galva,
    Ass't Minority Leader
Rep. Dorothy Carpenter,
    Republican, West Des Moines,
    Ass't Minority Leader
Rep. Kyle Hummel,
    Republican, Vinton,
    Ass't Minority Leader
Rep. Donald J. Paulin,
    Republican, Le Mars,
    Ass't Minority Leader
Mr. Joseph O'Hern,
    Chief Clerk of the House

# Membership, 72nd General Assembly

## The Senate

Boswell, Leonard L., (D) Davis City
Brunner, Charles H., (D) Ames
Carr, Robert M., (D) Dubuque
Coleman, C. Joseph, (D) Clare
Corning, Joy, (R) Cedar Falls
Deluhery, Patrick J., (D) Davenport
Dieleman, William W., (D) Pella
Doyle, Donald V., (D) Sioux City
Drake, Richard F., (R) Muscatine
Fraise, Eugene, (D) Fort Madison
Fuhrman, Linn, (R) Aurelia
Gentleman, Julia B., (R) Des Moines
Gettings, Donald E., (D) Ottumwa
Goodwin, Norman H., (R) DeWitt
Gronstal, Michael E., (D) Council Bluffs
Hall, Hurley W., (R) Marion
Hannon, Beverly A., (D) Anamosa
Hester, Jack W., (R) Honey Creek
Holden, Edgar H., (R) Davenport
Holt, Lee, (R) Spencer
Horn, Walley E., (D) Cedar Rapids
Hultman, Calvin O., (R) Red Oak
Husak, Emil J., (D) Toledo
Hutchins, C. W., (D) Audubon
Jensen, John W., (R) Plainfield
Kinley, George R., (D) Des Moines
Lind, Jim, (R) Waterloo
Lloyd-Jones, Jean, (D) Iowa City
Mann, Thomas, Jr., (D) Des Moines
Miller, Alvin V., (D) Ventura
Miller, Charles P., (D) Burlington
Murphy, Larry, (D) Oelwein
Nystrom, John N., (R) Boone
Palmer, William D., (D) Des Moines
Peterson, John A., (D) Albia
Priebe, Berl E., (D) Algona
Readinger, David M., (R) Des Moines
Rensink, Wilmer, (R) Sioux Center
Rife, Jack, (R) Moscow
Riordan, James R., (D) Waukee
Schwengels, Forrest V., (R) Fairfield
Scott, Kenneth D., (D) Clear Lake
Soorholtz, John E., (R) Melbourne
Sturgeon, Al, (D) Sioux City

Taylor, Ray, (R) Steamboat Rock
Tieden, Dale., (R) Elkader
Vande Hoef, Richard (R) Harris
Varn, Richard J., (D) Solon
Wells, James D., (D) Cedar Rapids
Welsh, Joseph J., (D) Dubuque

## The House of Representatives

Adams, Janet, (D) Webster City
Arnould, Robert C., (D) Davenport
Avenson, Donald D., (D) Oelwein
Beaman, Jack, (R) Osceola
Beatty, Linda, (D) Indianola
Bennett, Wayne, (R) Galva
Bisignano, Tony, (D) Des Moines
Black, Dennis H., (D) Grinnell
Blanshan, Gene, (D) Scranton
Brammer, Phil, (D) Cedar Rapids
Branstad, Clifford O., (R) Thompson
Buhr, Florence D., (D) Des Moines
Carpenter, Dorothy, (R) West Des Moines
Chapman, Kay, (D) Cedar Rapids
Clark, Betty Jean, (R) Rockwell
Cohoon, Dennis M., (D) Burlington
Connolly, Mike, (D) Dubuque
Connors, John H., (D) Des Moines
Cooper, James J., (D) Russell
Corbett, Ron J., (R) Cedar Rapids
Corey, Virgil E., (R) Morning Sun
Daggett, Horace, (R) Kent
De Groot, Kenneth, (R) Doon
Diemer, Marvin E., (R) Cedar Falls
Doderer, Minnette, (D) Iowa City
Dvorsky, Robert E., (D) Coralville
Eddie, Russell J., (R) Storm Lake
Fey, Tom, (D) Davenport
Fogarty, Daniel P., (D) Cylinder
Fuller, Robert D., (D) Steamboat Rock
Garman, Teresa, (R) Ames
Groninga, John, (D) Mason City
Gruhn, Josephine, (D) Spirit Lake
Halvorson, Rod, (D) Fort Dodge

Halvorson, Roger A., (R) Monona
Hammond, Johnie, (D) Ames
Hansen, Steve D., (D) Sioux City
Harbor, William H., (R) Henderson
Harper, Patricia, (D) Waterloo
Hatch, Jack, (D) Des Moines
Haverland, Mark A., (D) Polk City
Hermann, Donald F., (R) Bettendorf
Hester, Joan L., (R) Honey Creek
Holveck, Jack, (D) Des Moines
Hummel, Kyle, (R) Vinton
Jay, Daniel J., (D) Centerville
Jochum, Thomas J., (D) Dubuque
Johnson, Paul W., (D) Decorah
Knapp, Don, (D) Cascade
Koenigs, Deo, (D) McIntire
Kremer, Joseph M., (R) Jesup
Lageschulte, Raymond, (R) Waverly
Lundby, Mary A., (R) Marion
Maulsby, Ruhl, (R) Rockwell City
May, Dennis, (D) Kensett
McKean, Andy, (R) Anamosa
McKinney, Wayne, Jr., (D) Waukee
Metcalf, Janet, (R) Des Moines
Miller, Tom H., (R) Cherokee
Muhlbauer, Louis H., (D) Manilla
Mullins, Sue, (R) Corwith
Neuhauser, Mary C., (D) Iowa City
Norrgard, Clyde L., (D) Danville
Ollie, C. Arthur, (D) Clinton
Osterberg, David, (D) Mt. Vernon
Parker, Edward G., (D) Mingo
Paulin, Donald J., (R) Le Mars

Pavich, Emil S., (D) Council Bluffs
Pellett, Wendell C., (R) Atlantic
Peters, Mike, (D) Sioux City
Petersen, Dan, (R) Muscatine
Peterson, Michael K., (D) Carroll
Plasier, Lee J., (R) Sioux Center
Platt, Donald R., (R) Muscatine
Poncy, Charles N., (D) Ottumwa
Renaud, Dennis L., (D) Altoona
Renken, Bob, (D) Aplington
Rosenberg, Ralph, (D) Ames
Royer, Bill, (R) Essex
Running, Richard V., (D) Cedar Rapids
Schnekloth, Hugo, (R) Eldridge
Schrader, David, (D) Monroe
Sherzan, Gary, (D) Des Moines
Shoning, Don, (R) Sioux City
Shoultz, Don, (D) Waterloo
Siegrist, J. Brent, (R) Council Bluffs
Skow, Bob, (D) Guthrie Center
Spear, Clay, (D) Burlington
Stromer, Delwyn, (R) Garner
Stueland, Vic, (R) Grand Mound
Svoboda, Jane, (D) Clutier
Swartz, Tom, (D) Marshalltown
Swearingen, George R., (R) Sigourney
Tabor, David, (D) Baldwin
Teaford, Jane, (D) Cedar Falls
Tyrrell, Phil, (R) North English
Van Camp, Mike, (R) Davenport
Van Maanen, Harold, (R) Oskaloosa
Wise, Philip, (D) Keokuk

# Iowans

## in the

## Congress of the United States

## 1987 - 1988

# United States Senator

# CHARLES E. GRASSLEY

Charles E. Grassley was born at New Hartford in Butler County, Iowa, on 17 September 1933. He was born and reared on a farm.

He attended the public schools at New Hartford and was graduated from the high school there in 1951. In 1954 he married Barbara Speicher and they have five children: Lee, Wendy, Robin, Michele and Jay. He is a member of the Republican Party and the Baptist Church.

After high school he continued his education at the University of Northern Iowa receiving a Bachelor of Arts degree in political science in 1956 and a Master of Arts degree in the same subject in 1956. He later did work on a Ph.D at the University of Iowa.

In 1958 he was elected to the Iowa General Assembly as state representative from Butler County at the age of 25. He became an active and influential member of the state legislature and was re-elected in 1960, 1962, 1964, 1966, 1968, 1970, 1972 and 1974.

In 1974 he ran for and was elected to the United States House of Representatives succeeding the late Congressman H. R. Gross. He was re-elected by large majorities in 1976 and 1978.

In 1980 he won the Republican nomination for the United States Senate and was elected in the November balloting. In 1981 he took office and subsequently served on the Finance, Judiciary, Budget, Labor and Human Resources Committee as well as the Special Committee on the Aging.

Senator Grassley has received many awards and honors, almost too numerous to mention. Among them he is a seven-time recipient of the Watchdog of the Treasury award; National Taxpayers Union Best Friend Award; the Eisenhower Tribute Award for Defense Efficiency; Corn Growers Association; Ethanol Man of the Year award; four times the recipient of the National Federation of Independent Business' Guardian of Small Business award; American Legion Distinguished Service Award; three-time recipient of the Leadership Award from the Coalition for Peace through Strength; the Congressional Patriot Award; Honorary Member, National Association of Area Agencies on Aging; Mid-Continent Small Business United Political Advocacy Award; Honorary Member, Civil Air Patrol and the Americans for Constitutional Action Distinguished Service Award. He is rated with 100% approval by the National Alliance of Senior Citizens.

Senator Grassley is a member of the Farm Bureau, the Butler County and State of Iowa historical societies, Pi Gamma Mu, and Kappa Delta Pi International. Among his other signal honors he has an honorary Doctor of Laws degree from Upper Iowa University and serves on the Board of Trustees of that 131 year old institution.

Senator and Mrs. Grassley reared their five children on their New Hartford farm and the senator still farms the land when in Iowa. They have six grandchildren.

26

# United States Senator

## THOMAS R. HARKIN

Thomas R. Harkin was born on 19 November 1939 in the small Warren County town of Cumming which had a population of only 151. His father was a coal miner and his mother was an immigrant from Yugoslavia.

As a boy he attended the public schools in Cumming and Dexter working his way through high school. He was graduated from Dowling High School in Des Moines in 1958 and was active in 4-H.

In 1962 he was graduated from Iowa State University at Ames with a B.S. degree in government and economics. He worked his way through college as a construction worker and also won an ROTC scholarship.

He served in the Navy as a jet pilot from 1962 to 1967 and was in Vietnam. He was later one of the first Vietnam veterans elected to Congress. He is currently a commander in the Naval Air Reserve on inactive status.

In 1969 and 1970 he served as a staff aide to Congressman Neal Smith. In 1970 he was appointed a staff aide to the U. S. House Select Committee on the U. S. Involvement in Southeast Asia.

Harkin was graduated from the Catholic University of American Law School in Washington, D. C., in 1972. He was admitted to the Iowa bar in June of 1972 and later served as an attorney at the Polk County Legal Aid Society in Des Moines during 1973 and 1974.

In November of 1974 he was elected to the Congress from Iowa's 5th district and was re-elected in 1976, 1978, 1980 and 1982. While serving in the U. S. House of Representatives he was a member of the Committee on Agriculture and the Committee on Science and Technology.

In 1984 he was nominated by the Democratic Party for the United States Senate and in the November election he won the seat, taking office in 1987 as Iowa's junior United States Senator. In the Senate he is a member of the Agriculture Committee, the Appropriations Committee, the Labor and Human Resources Committee and the Small Business Committee.

Senator Harkin also serves as chairman of the Agriculture Subcommittee on Nutrition and Investigations; the Appropriations Subcommittee on the District of Columbia; the Labor and Human Resources Subcommittee on the Handicapped and the Small Business Committee on Competition and Anti-Trust. He is also a member of several subcommittees of the major committees upon which he serves.

He is a member of the Democratic Party and the Roman Catholic Church. He is married to the former Ruth Raduenz and they have two daughters, Amy born in July of 1976 and Jenny born in December of 1981.

**REP. JIM LEACH**
1st District of Iowa

**REP. TOM TAUKE**
2nd District of Iowa

Congressman Jim Leach was born and reared in Davenport, Scott County, Iowa and was educated in the public schools there.

His advanced education was at the London School of Economics, Johns Hopkins and Princeton Universities in political science.

He is married to Elisabeth (Deba) and they have two children, Gallagher and Jenny. They are members of the Episcopal Church.

Rep. Leach was elected to the 95th Congress in 1976 and has been re-elected every two years since. He is a Republican in politics.

He was a Foreign Service Officer for the State Department and a congressional staff assistant. He later was a delegate to the United Nations and the Geneva Disarmament Conference. He is chairman of the Ripon Society and serves on the Foreign Affairs Committee of the U. S. House of Representatives.

Congressman Tom Tauke is a native of Dubuque, Dubuque County, Iowa, born there 11 October 1950.

He was educated in the Dubuque schools, was graduated from Loras College with a BA degree and from the University of Iowa College of Law. While in college he worked as a political reporter for the Dubuque TELEGRAPH-HERALD and the New York TIMES.

He practiced law in Dubuque and was elected to the Iowa legislature in 1974 and re-elected in 1976.

In 1978 he was nominated and elected to the U. S. Congress and is a Republican. He has been re-elected to the Congress every two years since 1978. He is a trustee for Mt. Mercy College in Cedar Rapids and the Herbert Hoover Library.

He is married to the former Beverly Hubble and they have one son, Joseph, born 1986. The Taukes are of the Roman Catholic faith.

### REP. DAVE NAGLE
### 3rd District of Iowa

Congressman Dave Nagle was elected in 1986 and became the first Democrat in 52 years to represent the Third Congressional District.

He was born in Grinnell, Poweshiek County, Iowa, on 15 April 1943 and was reared in Toledo, Tama County, Iowa. He was graduated from Toledo High School in 1961. He was later graduated from the University of Northern Iowa and the University of Iowa College of Law in 1968. That year he began the practice of law in Waterloo.

He is married to the former Diane Lewis and they have one son, Ben, 17. They live in Cedar Falls.

Congressman Nagle is a veteran political activist in his party and was state chairman from 1982 to 1985. In Congress he serves on the Agriculture Committee and the Science, Space and Technology Committee. He has worked for reform of the Farm Credit System.

### REP. NEAL SMITH
### 4th District of Iowa

Congressman Neal Smith is serving his 15th term in the U. S. House of Representatives and is the dean of the Iowa Congressional Delegation. He is a Democrat in politics.

Rep. Smith was born on a farm in Keokuk County near Martinsburg and attended the Packwood schools. He was further educated at Missouri University of Liberal Arts and the Syracuse University Schools of Public and Business Administration.

He served in the Air Force in World War II winning nine battle stars, the Air Medal with four Oak Leaf Clusters and the Purple Heart.

In 1946 he married Beatrix Havens and in 1950 they were graduated together from Drake University Law School. They practiced in Des Moines until he was elected to the Congress in 1958; he has been re-elected every two years gaining great seniority.

**REP. JIM LIGHTFOOT**
5th District of Iowa

Congressman Lightfoot was born on 27 September 1938 at Sioux City, Iowa, and was elected to the 99th Congress in 1984 and re-elected to the 100th Congress in 1986.

He is married to the former Nancy Harrison and they have four children. They are members of the Republican Party and the Roman Catholic Church.

He has been active with the Federal Aviation Administration and is a Gold Seal Flight Instructor. He has belonged to the JayCees, Kiwanis, the Farm Bureau, Pork Producers and Cattlemens Assocation. He has received many awards both civilian and military including an "Oscar" in Agriculture, a Flight Safety Award, Agriculture Spokesman of the Year, the 4-H Alumni Award and in 1986 he was awarded the honor of being a "Taxpayers' Friend" by the National Taxpayers Union. He is from Shenandoah, Page County, Iowa.

**FRED GRANDY**
6th District of Iowa

Congressman Fred Grandy was born on 29 June 1948 at Souix City, Woodbury County, Iowa. After a career in theatre and television, his home is still in Sioux City.

He was graduated from Harvard University with a Bachelor of Arts degree in 1970 and pursued an interest in politics as a legislative aide and speech writer for former Congressman Wiley Mayne.

He is married to the former Catherine Mann and they have two children, Marya and Charles. They are members of the Republican Party and the Episcopal Church.

Fred Grandy was elected to the U. S. House of Representatives in 1986 and is a member of the Agriculture Committee and the Education and Labor Committee as well as the Select Committee on Children, Youth and Families. It is "almost unprecedented" (Cong. Bob Michel) for a new member to serve on both.

# Chapter One
# OUR NATURAL HERITAGE

"In the beginning God created the heaven and the earth."
Genesis 1:1

The history of Iowa is one of grandeur, glory, tradition, culture and above all the friendliest people in the world. It has made more than its share of contributions to society in all areas of human living. It is also, indeed, the "beautiful land."

There has always been much speculation about just what the Indian word "ioway" meant but most have concluded that it was meant to mean "the beautiful land." And for our purposes we shall assume that.

Inherent in the very name "beautiful land" one can find that definition fits in every way. From prehistoric times onward the fertile prairies, rivers full of fish and forests teaming with wild life have supported the needs of whatever race of man chose to live in that "beautiful land."

Iowa, therefore, has a natural heritage matched by no other geo-political comparable area on the face of the earth.

Within the borders of the State of Iowa there is 25% --one fourth-- of the Grade "A" farm land on the face of the earth. The hardy pioneers, blessed with freedom and finding opportunity cleared the lands and the prairies beginning slightly over 150 years ago and made Iowa the breadbasket of the world.

Iowa's natural heritage and the acts of God and His tool, nature, began many thousands of years ago. It is best told by others who have made the in-depth studies of the State's natural heritage.

Before man could occupy the earth as a home much change was required and many eons were to pass. There was at first no soil nor plants nor animal life. ("And the earth was.......void;") The soil was formed by the constant crumbling and powdering of the planet's rock crust. The soil was enriched by the growing of the early plant life as it died off and decayed into it.

Later, animals appeared and ate both the plant life and each other. Even their decaying flesh, blood and bones contributed to the later richness of the soil. Animals also came to be used by man as food and for the work man could make them do. It was after the earth had soil, plants and animals that it could become the home of man.

We are told that millions of years ago our Iowa lay under a huge sea and in it were millions of small animals which were trilobites, fishlike creatures that formed coral. Rivers from land masses very different from those we know today drained into this vast ocean and the silt, sand and mud they deposited hardened into layers of rock. Eventually the sea bottom was forced upward by the inner earth and it changed from sea bottom into dry land and it is reckoned that the climate became very warm.

On these new land masses there appeared heavy forests of trees that were fernlike and into which great dinosaurs came to roam. Later they once more sank into the seas and the forests formed new layers of rock which we now call coal. Mud and sand formed new rock strata over the coal beds. Many examples of the dinosaurs, the trilobites, fish that lived in the vast seas have been found in recent years embedded in the rock layers. The lands sank and rose many times over thousands of centuries and the layers of strata became thicker. Finally, the seabottoms rose and remained as the continents we know today. Thus we have a continent of North America and upon it and central to it is the Iowa with which we are familiar.

Still later, and for whatever indeterminable reasons, the climate became very cold. A veritable ice age! Huge galciers were formed by nature up in Canada and they continued downward across the continent and into the northern central part of what is now the United States. It is estimated that five times these gigantic ice sheets came down over Iowa and it is believed that twice the area of the state of Iowa was covered completely.

Between the ice ages there were long periods of warm climate during which many more forms of plant and animal life flourished. During the cold period biological life was restrained or there was often none at all. In the warm and thriving periods there were such animals as bears, horses, panthers and mastodons. As one glacial age after another descended upon the continent these animals either moved southward or died out.

The last three glaciers covered only part of the area that is the present state of Iowa. The last glacier was an estimated 50,000 years

© Chicago Natural History Museum

ago. After it melted in the warmer climes and receded to its northern origins, there were no animals such as the horse, dinosaur or mastodon. Thus it was for the Europeans to re-introduce the horse to North America.

The effect of the glaciers can be seen on the topography of the Iowa lands. Glaciers levelled the sur-faces of the areas over which they descended. They also left basins that filled with water and became lakes. On much of the surface they left huge boulders as evidence of their grinding and levelling existence. Hills were lowered and flattened, rounded off from their formerly rugged tors. Iowa's valua-ble gravel and clay deposits remained as gifts from the glaciers to the Hawkeye State.

Excellent examples of areas of Iowa missed by the most levelling of the great glacial movements can be seen among the beautiful hills and scenery in Clayton, Allamakee and some of Dubuque County. For those areas were passed by probably the later glaciers and remain moreso as they were well over 50,000 years ago preceding the final glacial flow. These pristine examples identify to us how all Iowa might have looked had there not been the glacial activ-ity or the "mighty frost giants."

Thus the land of Iowa as we know it with its gifts of nature, its topography and the beauty of it, has become our natural heritage.

"Iowa, in the symbolical and expressive language of the aboriginal inhabitants, is said to signify "The Beautiful Land", and was applied to this magnificent and fruitful region by its ancient owners, to express their appreciation of its superiority of climate and location. It is bounded on the north by Minnesota, and for small distances by Dakota, Wisconsin and Illinois; on the east by Wisconsin and Illinois; on the south by Illinois, Missouri and Nebraska; and on the west by Nebraska, Dakota, and with regard to the southeastern corner, by Missouri. It is on the right bank of the greatest river in the world, and near the center of a valley already admitted to be the richest cultivated by man.

"The general shape of the State is that of a rectangle, the northern and southern boundaries being due east and west lines, and its eastern and western boundaries determined by southerly flowing rivers--the Mississippi on the east, the Missouri and the Big Sioux on the west. The width of the State from north to

south is over 200 miles, being from the parallel of 43 degrees 30', to that of 40 degrees 36', or nearly three degrees. This does not include the small prominent angle at the southeast corner. The length is considerably more. It averages perhaps 265 miles. The whole surface is 55,044 square miles, or 35,228,200 acres. It is worthy of note that all this vast extent, except the small part occupied by our river, lakes and peat beds of the northern counties, is suceptible of the highest cultivation. We thus get some idea of the immense agricultural resources of Iowa. Too often the number of square miles in a county or State must be diminished by a third or a half, on account of mountainous or desert lands, to enable one to correctly estimate the real value to mankind. This State is nearly as large as England, and twice as large as Scotland; but when we consider the relative areas of surface which may be made to yield to the wants of man, those great countries will not compare with Iowa. It is almost idle to predict the future. Figures which

would be reasonable now, would only provoke a smile a few years hence. It may safely be affirmed, however, that under thorough cultivation, this one State could easily support the 50,000,000 of people in the United States.

Topography.

"All the knowledge we have at present of the topography of the State of Iowa is that derived from incidental observations of geological corps, from the surveys made by railroad engineers, and for barometrical observations made by authority of the Federal Government. No complete topographical survey has yet been made, but this will doubtless be attended to in a few years.

"The State lies wholly within, and comprises a part of, a vast plain, and there is no mountainous or even hilly country within its borders; for the highest point is but 1,200 feet above the lowest point; these two points are nearly 300 miles apart, and the whole State is traversed by gently flowing rivers. A clearer idea of the great uniformity of the surface of the State may be obtained from a statement of the general slopes in feet per mile, from point to point, in straight lines across it.

"We thus find that there is a good degree of propriety in regarding the whole State as belonging to a great plain, the lowest point of which within its border, the southeastern corner of the State, is only 444 feet above the level of the sea. The average height of the whole State above the level of the sea is not far from 800 feet, although it is a thousand miles from the nearest ocean. These remarks are, of course, to be understood as applying to the surface of the State as whole. On examining its surface in detail, we

Buffalo Museum of Science

**Former inhabitants of the Middle West** · Nobody yet knows why these great reptiles
became extinct.  Perhaps the climate changed faster than they
could become adapted to it.  Perhaps diseases exterminated them.

find a great diversity of surface by the formation of valleys out of the general level, which have been evolved by the action of streams during the unnumbered years of the terrace epoch. These river valleys are deepest in the northwestern part of the State, and consequently it is there that the country has the greatest diversity of surface, and its physical features are most strongly marked.

"The greater part of Iowa was formerly one vast prairie. It has indeed been estimated that seven-eights of the surface of the State was prairie when first settled. By prairies, it must not be inferred that a level surface is meant, for they are found in hilly countries as well. Nor are they confined to any particular variety of soil, for they rest upon all formations, from those of the Azoic to those of the Cretaceous age, inclusive. Whatever may have been their origin, their present existence in Iowa is not due to the influence of climate, of the soil, or of any of the underlying formations. The real cause is the prevalance of annual fires. If these had been prevented 50 years ago, Iowa would now be a timbered country. The encroachment of forest trees upon prairie farms as soon as the bordering woodland is protected from the annual prairie fires, is well known to farmers throughout the State. The soil of Iowa is justly famous for its fertility, and there is probably no equal area of the earth's surface that contains so little untillable land, or whose soil has so high an average of fertility. Ninety-five percent of its surface is capable of a high state of cultivation.

Lakes and Streams.

"LAKES. -- The lakes of Iowa may be properly divided into two distinct classes. The first may be called *drift lakes*, having had their origin in the depressions left in the surface of the drift at the close of the glacial epoch, and have rested upon the undisturbed surface of the drift deposit ever since the glaciers disappeared. The others may be properly termed *fluviatile or alluvial* lakes, because they have had their origin by the action of rivers while cutting their own valleys out from the surface of the drift as it existed at the close of the glacial epoch, and are now found resting upon the alluvium. By "alluvium" is meant the deposit which has accumulated in the valleys of rivers by the action of their own currents. It is largely composed of sand and other coarse material, and upon the deposit are some of the best, productive soils in the State. It is this deposit which forms the flood plains and deltas of our rivers, as well as the terraces of

their valleys. The regions to which the drift lakes are principally confined are near the head waters of the principal streams of the State. They are consequently found in those regions which lie between the Cedar and Des Moines Rivers, and the Des Moines and Little Sioux. No drift lakes are found in Southern Iowa. The largest of the lakes to be found in the State are Spirit and Okoboji, in Dickinson County, Clear Lake in Cerro Gordo County, and Storm Lake in Buena Vista County.

"Spirit Lake. -- The width and length of this lake are about equal, and it contains about 12 square miles of surface, its northern border resting directly on the boundary of the State. It lies almost directly upon the great water-shed. Its shores are mostly gravelly, and the country about it fertile.

"Okoboji Lake. -- This body of water lies directly south of Spirit Lake, and has somewhat the shape of a horse-shoe, with its eastern projection within a few rods of Spirit Lake, where it receives the outlet of the latter. Okoboji Lake extends about five miles southward from Spirit Lake, thence about the same distance westward, and then bends northward about as far as the eastern projection. The eastern portion is narrow, but the western is larger, and in some places 100 feet deep. The surroundings of this and Spirit Lake are very pleasant; fish are abundant in them, and they are the resort of myriads of water-fowl.

"Clear Lake. -- This lake is situated upon the water-shed between the Iowa and Cedar Rivers. It is about five miles long, two or three miles wide, and has a maximum depth of only 15 feet. Its shores and the country around are like that of Spirit Lake.

"Storm Lake. -- This lake rests upon the great water-shed in Buena Vista County. It is a clear, beautiful sheet of water, containing a surface area of between four and five square miles. The outlets of all these drift lakes are dry during a portion of the year, except Okoboji.

"Walled Lake. -- Along the water-sheds of Northern Iowa great numbers of small lakes exist, varying from half a mile to a mile in diameter. One of the lakes in Wright County, and another in Sac, have each received the name of "Walled Lake", on account of the embankments on their borders, which are supposed to be the work of ancient inhabitants. These embankments are from two to ten feet in height, and from five to 30 feet across. They are the result of natural causes alone, being referable to the periodic action of ice, aided to some extent by the action of the waves. These lakes are very shallow, and in winter freeze to the bottom, so that but little unfrozen water remains in the middle. The ice freezes fast to everything on the bottom, and the expansive power of the water in freezing acts in all directions from the center to the circumference, and whatever was on the bottom of the lakes has been thus carried to the shore. This has been going on from year to year, from century to century, forming the embankments which have caused so much wonder.

"Springs issue from all the geological formations, and from the sides of almost every valley, but they are more numerous, and assume proportions which give rise to the name of sink-holes, along the upland borders of the Upper Iowa River, owing to the peculiar fissured and laminated character and great thickness of the strata of the age of the Trenton limestone which underlies the whole region of the valley of that stream. No mineral springs, properly so called have yet been discovered in Iowa, though the water of several artesian wells is frequently found charged with soluble mineral substances.

"RIVERS. -- The two great rivers, the Mississippi and the Missouri, form the eastern and the western boundaries, respectively, of the State, receive the eastern and western drainage of it. The Mississippi with its tributaries in Eastern Iowa drain two-thirds of the State, and the Missouri with its tributaries drain the western third. The great water-shed which divides these two systems is a land running southward from a point on the northern boundary line of the State near Spirit Lake, in Dickinson County, to a nearly central point in the northern part of Adair County. From the last named point this highest ridge of land between the two great rivers continues southward, without a change of character, through Ringgold County into the State of Missouri; but it is no longer the great water-shed. From that point another ridge bears off southeast-ward through the counties of Madison, Clark, Lucas and Appanoose, which is now the water-shed.

"All streams that rise in Iowa occupy at first only slight depressions of the land, and are scarcely perceptible. These uniting into larger streams, though still flowing over drift and bluff deposits, reach considerable depth into these deposits, in some cases to a depth of nearly 200 feet from the general prairie level.

"The greater part of the streams in Western Iowa run either along the whole or a part of their course, upon that peculiar deposit known as bluff deposit. The banks even of the small streams are often five to 10 feet in height and quite per-pendicular, so that they render the streams almost everywhere unfordable, and a great impediment to travel across the open country where there are no bridges.

"This deposit is of a slightly yellowish ash color, except when darkened by decaying vegetation, very fine and silicious, but not sandy, not very cohesive, and not at all plastic. It forms excellent soil, and does not bake or crack in drying, except limy concretions, which are generally distributed throughout the mass, in shape and size resembling pebbles; but not a stone or a pebble can be found in the whole deposit. It was called "silicious marl" by Dr. Owen, in his geological report to the Government, and he attributes its origin to an accumulation of sediment in an ancient lake, which was afterward drained, and the sediment became dry land. Prof. Swallow gives it the name of "bluff", which is here adopted; but the term "lacustrine" would have been more appropriate. The peculiar properties of this deposit are that it will stand securely with a precipitous front 200 feet high, and yet is easily excavated with a spade. Wells dug in it require only to be walled to a point just above the water line. Yet, compact as it is, it is very porous, so that water which falls on it does not remain at the surface, but percolates through it; neither does it accumulate within it at any point, as it does upon and within the drift and the stratified formations.

"The thickest deposit yet known in Iowa is in Fremont County, where it reaches 200 feet. It is found throughout a region more than 200 miles in length, and nearly 100 miles in width, and through which the Missouri runs almost centrally.

"This fine sediment is the same which the Missouri once deposited in a broad depression in the surface of the drift that formed a lake-like expansion of that river in the earliest period of the history of its valley. The extent of the deposit shows this lake to have been 100 miles wide and more than twice as long. The water of the river was muddy then as now, and the broad lake became filled with the sediment which the river brought down. After the lake became filled with the sediment, the valley below became deepened by the constant erosive action of the waters, to a depth sufficient to have drained the lake of its first waters; but the only effect then was to cause it to cut its valley out of the deposits its own muddy waters had formed. Thus, along the valley of that river, so far as it forms the western boundary of Iowa, the bluffs which border it are composed of that sediment known as bluff deposit, forming a distinct border along the broad, level flood plain, the width of which varies from five to 15 miles, while the original sedimentary deposit stretches far inland.

"Chariton and Grand Rivers rise and run for 25 miles of their course upon the drift deposit alone. The first strata that are exposed by the deepening valleys of both these streams belong to the upper coal measures, and they both continued upon the same formation until they make their exit from the State (the former in Appanoose County, the latter in Ringgold County), near the boundary of which they have passed nearly or quite through the whole of that formation to the middle coal measures. Their valleys deepen gradually, and 15 or 20 miles from the river they are nearly 150 feet below the general level of the adjacent highland. When the rivers have cut their valleys down through the series of limestone strata, they reach those of a clayey composition. Upon these they widen their valleys and make broad flood plains, or "bottoms", the soil of which is stiff and clayey, except where modified by sandy washings. These streams are prairie streams in their upper branches and tributaries, but flow through woodland farther down. The proportion of lime in the drift of Iowa is so great that the water of all our wells and springs is too "hard" for washing purposes, and the same substance is so prevalent in the drift clays that they are always found to have sufficient flux when used for the manufacture of brick.

"Platte River belongs mainly to Missouri. Its upper branches pass through Ringgold County. Here the drift deposit reaches its maximum thickness on an east and west line across the State, and the valleys are eroded in some instances to a depth of 200 feet, apparently, through this deposit alone. The term "drift deposit" applies to the soil and sub-soil of the greater part of the State, and in it alone many of our wells are dug and our forests take root. It rests upon the stratified rocks. It is composed of clay, sand, gravel and boulders, promiscuously intermixed, without stratification, varying in character in different parts of the State.

"One Hundred and Two River is represented in Taylor County, the valleys of which have the same general character of those just described. The country around and between the east and west forks of this stream is almost entirely prairie.

"Nodaway River is represented by east, middle and west branches. The two former rise in Adair County, the latter in Cass County. These rivers and valleys are fine examples of the small rivers and valleys of Southern Iowa. They have the general character of drift valleys, and with beautiful undulating and sloping sides. The Nodaway drains one of the finest agricultural regions in the State, the soil of which is tillable almost to their very banks. The banks and the adjacent narrow flood-plains are almost everywhere composed of a rich, deep, dark loam.

"Nishnabotany River is represented by east and west branches, the former having its source in Anderson County, the latter in Shelby County.

Both these branches, from their source to their confluence, and also the main stream from there to the point where it enters the great flood-plain of the Missouri, run through a region the surface of which is occupied by the bluff deposit.

"The West Nishnabotany is probably without any valuable mill-sites. In the western part of Cass County, the East Nishnabotany loses its identity by becoming abruptly divided up into five or six different creeks. A few good mill-sites occur here on this stream. None, however, that are thought reliable exist on either of these rivers, or on the main stream below the confluence, except, perhaps, one or two in Montgomery County. The valleys of the two branches, and the intervening upland, possess remarkable fertility.

"Boyer River, until it enters the flood-plain of the Missouri, runs almost, if not quite, its entire course through the region occupied by the bluff deposit, and has cut its valley entirely through it along most of its passage. The only rocks exposed are the upper coal measures, near Reed's Mill in Harrison County. The exposures are slight, and are the most northerly now known in Iowa. The valley of this river has usually gently sloping sides, and a distinctly defined flood plain. Along the lower half of its course the adjacent upland presents a surface of the billowy character, peculiar to the bluff deposit. The source of this river is in Sac County.

"Soldier River. -- The east and middle branches of this stream have their source in Crawford County, and the west branch in Ida County. The whole course of this river is through the bluff deposit. It has no exposure of strata along its course.

bettendorf public library
and information center

"Little Sioux River. -- Under this head are included both the main and west branches of that stream, together with the Maple, which is one of its branches. The west branch and the Maple are so similar to the Soldier River that they need no separate description. The main stream has its boundary near the northern boundary of the State, and runs most of its course upon drift deposit alone, entering the region of the bluff deposit in the southern part of Cherokee County. The two principal upper branches near their source in Dickinson and Osceola Counties, are small prairie creeks within distinct valleys. On entering Clay County the valley deepens, and at their confluence has a depth of 200 feet. Just as the valley enters Cherokee County, it turns to the southward and becomes much widened, with its sides gently sloping to the uplands. When the valley enters the region of the bluff deposit, it assumes the billowy appearance. No exposures of strata of any kind have been found in the valley of the Little Sioux or any of its branches.

"Floyd River. -- This river rises upon the drift in O'Brien County, and flowing southward enters the region of the bluff deposit a little north of the center of Plymouth County. Almost from its source to its mouth it is a prairie stream, with slightly sloping valley sides, which blend gradually with the uplands. A single slight exposure of sandstone of cretaceous age occurs in the valley near Sioux City, and which is the only known exposure of rock of any kind along its whole length. Near this exposure is a mill-site, but farther up the stream it is not valuable for such purposes.

"Rock River. -- This stream passes through Lyon and Sioux Counties. It was evidently so named from the fact that considerable exposures of the red Sioux quartzite occur along the main branches of the stream in Minnesota, a few miles north of our State boundary. Within this State the main stream and its branches are drift streams, and strata are exposed. The beds and banks of the streams are usually sandy and gravelly, with occasional boulders intermixed.

"Big Sioux River. -- The valley of this river, from the northwest corner of the State to its mouth, possesses much the same character as all the streams of the surface deposits. At Sioux Falls, a few miles above the northwest corner of the State, the streams meet with remarkable obstructions from the presence of Sioux quartzite, which outcrops directly across the stream, and causes a fall of about 60 feet within a distance of half a mile, producing a series of cascades. For the first 25 miles above its mouth, the valley is very broad, with a broad, flat flood plain, with gentle slopes, occasionally showing indistinctly defined terraces. These terraces and valley bottoms constitute some of the finest agricultural land of the region. On the Iowa side of the valley the upland presents abrupt bluffs, steep as the materials of which they are composed will stand, and from 100 to nearly 200 feet high above the stream. At rare intervals, about 15 miles from its mouth, the cretaceous strata are exposed in the face of the bluffs of the Iowa side. No other strata are exposed along that part of the valley which borders our State, with the single exception of Sioux quartzite at its extreme northwestern corner. Some good mill-sites may be secured along that portion of this river which borders Lyon County, but below this the fall will probably be found insufficient and the locations for dams insecure.

"Missouri River. -- This is one of the muddiest streams on the globe, and its waters are known to be very turbid far toward its source. The chief peculiarity of this river is its broad flood plains, and its adjacent bluff deposits. Much the greater part of the flood plain of this river is upon the Iowa side, and continues from the south boundary line of the State to Sioux City, a distance of more than 100 miles in length, varying from three to five miles in width. This alluvial plain is estimated to contain more than half a million acres of land within the State, upward of 400,000 of which are now tillable.

"The rivers of the eastern system of drainage have quite a different character from those of the western system. They are larger, longer, and have their valleys modified to a much greater extent by the underlying strata. For the latter reason, water-power is much more abundant upon them than upon the streams of the western system.

"Des Moines River. -- This river has its source in Minnesota, but it enters Iowa before it has attained any size, and flows almost centrally through it from northwest to southeast, emptying into the Mississippi at the extreme southeastern corner of the State. The upper portion of it is divided into two branches, known as the east and the

west forks. These unite in Humboldt County. The valleys of these branches above their confluence are drift valleys, except a few small exposures of subcarboniferous limestone about five miles above their confluence. These exposures produce several small mill-sites. The valleys vary from a few hundred yards to half a mile in width, and are the finest agricultural lands. In the northern part of Webster County, the character of the main valley is modified by the presence of ledges and low cliffs of the subcarboniferous limestone and gypsum. From a point a little below Fort Dodge to near Amsterdam, in Marion County, the river runs all the way through and upon the lower coal-measure strata. Along this part of the course the flood-plain varies from an eighth to a mile or more in width. From Amsterdam to Ottumwa the subcarboniferous limestone appears at intervals in the valley sides. Near Ottumwa the subcarboniferous rocks pass beneath the river again, bringing down the coal measure strata into its bed; they rise again from it in the extreme northwestern part of Van Buren County, and subcarboniferous strata resume and keep their place along the valley to the north of the river. From Fort Dodge to the northern part of Lee County the strata of the lower coal measures are present in the valley. Its flood-plain is frequently sandy from the debris of the sandstone and sandy shales of the coal measures produced by their removal in the process of the formation of the valley. The principal tributaries of the Des Moines are upon the western side. These are the Raccoon, and the three rivers, viz.: South, Middle and North Rivers. The three latter have their sources in the region occupied by the upper coal measure limestone formation, flow eastward over the middle coal measures, and enter the valley of the Des Moines upon the lower coal measures. These streams, especially South and Middle Rivers, are frequently bordered by high, rocky cliffs. The Raccoon River has its source upon the heavy surface

deposits of the middle region of Western Iowa, and along the greater part of its course it has excavated its valley out of those deposits and the middle coal measures alone. The valley of the Des Moines and its branches are destined to become the seat of extensive manufactures, in consequence of the numerous mill-sites of immense power, and the fact that the main valley traverses the entire length of the Iowa coal fields.

"Skunk River. -- This has its source in Hamilton County, and runs almost its entire course upon the border of the outcrop of the lower coal measures, or, more properly speaking, upon the subcarboniferous limestone, just where it begins to pass beneath the coal measures by its southerly and westerly dip. Its general course is southeast. From the western part of Henry County, up as far as Story County the broad, flat flood-plain is covered with a rich, deep clay soil, which, in time of long continued rains and over-flows of the river, has made the valley of the Skunk River a terror to travelers from the earliest settlement of the country. There are some excellent mill-sites on the lower half of this river, but they are not so numerous or valuable as on other rivers of the eastern system.

"Iowa River. -- This river rises in Hancock County, in the midst of a broad, slightly undulating drift region. The first rock exposure is that of subcarboniferous limestone, in the southwestern corner of Franklin County. It enters the region of the Devonian strata near the southwestern corner of Benton County, and in this it continues to its confluence with the Cedar in Louisa County. Below the junction with the Cedar, and for some miles above that point, its valley is broad, and especially on the northern side, with a well marked flood plain. Its borders gradually blend with the uplands as they slope away in the distance from the river. The Iowa furnishes numerous and valuable mill-sites.

"Cedar River. -- This stream is usually understood to be a branch of

the Iowa, but it ought, really, to be regarded as the main stream. It rises by numerous branches in the northern part of the State, and flows the entire length of the State, through the region occupied by the Devonian strata and along the trend occupied by the formation. The valley of this river, in the upper part of its course, is narrow, and the sides slope so gently as to scarcely show where the lowlands end and the uplands begin. Below the confluence with the Shell Rock, the flood-plain is more distinctly marked, and the valley broad and shallow. The valley of the Cedar is one of the finest regions in the State, and both the main stream and its branches afford abundant and reliable mill-sites.

"Wapsipinnicon River. -- This river has its source near the source of the Cedar, and runs parallel and near it almost its entire course, the upper half upon the same formation-The Devonian. In the northeastern part of Linn County it enters the region of the Niagara limestone, upon which it continues to the Mississippi. It is 100 miles long, and yet the area of its drainage is only from 12 to 20 miles in width. Hence, its numerous mill-sites are unusually secure.

"Turkey River. -- This river and the Upper Iowa are, in many respects, unlike other Iowa rivers. The difference is due to the great depth to which they have eroded their valleys and the different character of the material through which they have worked. The Turkey river rises in Howard County, and in Winneshiek County, a few miles from its source, its valley has attained a depth of more than 200 feet, and in Fayette and Clayton Counties its depth is increased to three and four hundred feet. The summit of the uplands, bordering nearly the whole length of the valley, is capped by the Maquoketa shales. These shales are underlaid by the Galena limestone, between two and three hundred feet thick. The valley has been eroded through these, and runs upon the Trenton limestone. Thus all the formations along and within this valley are Lower Silurian. The valley is usually narrow, and without a well-marked flood plain. Water-power is abundant, but in most places inaccessible.

"Upper Iowa River. -- This river rises in Minnesota, just beyond the northern boundary line, and enters our State in Howard County before it has attained any considerable size. Its course is nearly eastward until it reaches the Mississippi. It rises in the region of the Devonian rocks, and flows across the outcrops, respectively, of the Niagara, Galena and Trenton limestone, the lower magnesian limestone and Potsdam sandstone, into and through all of which, except the last, it has but its valley, which is the deepest of any in Iowa. The valley sides are almost everywhere high and steep, and cliffs of lower magnesian and Trenton limestone give them a wild and rugged aspect. In the lower part of the valley the flood plain reaches a width sufficient for the location of small farms, but usually it is too narrow for such purposes. On the higher surface, however, as soon as you leave the valley you come immediately upon a cultivated country. This stream has the greatest slope per mile of any in Iowa, and consequently it furnishes immense water-power. In some places where creeks come into it, the valley widens and affords good locations for farms. The town of Decorah, in Winneshiek County, is located in one of these spots, which makes it a lovely location; and the power of the river and the small spring streams around it offer fine facilities for manufacturing. This river and its tributaries are the only trout streams in Iowa.

"Mississippi River. -- This river may be described in general terms, as a broad canal cut out of the general level of the country through which the river flows. It is bordered by abrupt hills or bluffs. The bottom of the valley ranges from one to eight miles in width. The whole

space between the bluffs is occupied by the river and its bottom, or flood plain only, if we except the occasional terraces or remains of ancient flood plains, which are not now reached by the highest floods of the river. The river itself is from half a mile to nearly a mile in width. There are but four points along the whole length of the State where the bluffs approach the stream on both sides. The Lower Silurian formations compose the bluffs in the northern part of the State, but they gradually disappear by the Upper Silurian, Devonian and subcarboniferous rocks, which are reached near the southeastern corner of the State.

Considered in their relation to the present general surface of the State, the relative ages of the river valley of Iowa date back only to the close of the glacial epoch; but that the Mississippi and all the rivers of Northeastern Iowa, if no others, had at least a large part of the rocky portions of their valleys eroded by pre-glacial, or perhaps even by paleozoic rivers, can scarcely be doubted.

Geology.
"Geologists divide the soil of Iowa into three general divisions, which not only possess different physical characters, but also differ in the mode of their origins. These are drift, bluff and alluvial and belong respectively to the deposits bearing the same names. The drift occupies a much larger part of the surface of the State than both the others. The bluff has the next greatest area of surface, and the alluvial least.

"All soil is disintegrated rock. The drift deposit of Iowa was derived to a considerable extent from the rocks of Minnesota; but the greater part of Iowa drift was derived from its own rocks, much of which has been transported but a short distance.

"In Northern and Northwestern Iowa the drift contains more sand and gravel then elsewhere. In Southern Iowa the soil is frequently stiff and clayey.

"The bluff soil is found only in the western part of the State, and adjacent to the Missouri River. Although it contains less than one percent of clay in its composition, it is in no respect inferior to the best drift soil.

"The alluvial soil is that of the flood-plains of the river valleys, or bottom lands. That which is periodically flooded by the rivers is of little value for agricultural purposes; but a large part of it is entirely above the reach of the highest flood, and is very productive.

"The stratified rocks of Iowa range from the Azoic to the Mesozoic, inclusive; but the greater portion of the surface of the State is occupied by those of the Palaeozoic age. The table below will show each of these formations in their order:

| SYSTEMS. AGES. | GROUPS. PERIODS. | FORMATIONS. EPOCHS. | THICKNESS IN FEET. |
|---|---|---|---|
| | Post Tertiary................ | Drift........................................ | 10 to 200 |
| Cretaceous....... | | Inoceramous Bed ....................... | 50 |
| | Lower Cretaceous........... | Woodbury Sandstone and Shales.. | 130 |
| | | Nishnabotany Sandstone............. | 100 |
| | | Upper Coal Measures................. | 200 |
| | Coal Measures .............. | Middle Coal Measures ................. | 200 |
| | | Lower Coal Measures ............... | 200 |
| Carboniferous... | | St. Louis Limestone ................... | 75 |
| | | Keokuk Limestone..................... | 90 |
| | Subcarboniferous........... | Burlington Limestone ................. | 196 |
| | | Kinderhook Beds ..................... | 175 |
| Devonian.......... | Hamilton...................... | Hamilton Limestone and Shales.... | 200 |
| Upper Silurian.. | Niagara...................... | Niagara Limestone ..................... | 350 |
| | Cincinnati .................... | Maquoketa Shales..................... | 80 |
| | | Galena Limestone ..................... | 250 |
| | Trenton ..................... | Trenton Limestone ................... | 200 |
| Lower Silurian.. | | St. Peter's Sandstone............... | 80 |
| | Primordial ................... | Lower Magnesian Limestone........ | 250 |
| | | Potsdam Sandstone ................... | 300 |
| Azoic.............. | Huronian | Sioux Quartzite....................... | 50 |

Azoic System.

"The Sioux quartzite is found exposed in natural ledges only upon a few acres in the extreme northwest corner of the State, upon the banks of the Big Sioux River, for which reason the specific name of Sioux quartzite has been given them. It is an intensely hard rock, breaks in splintery fracture, and of a color varying, in different localities, from a light to deep red. The process of metamorphism has been so complete throughout the whole formation that the rock is almost everywhere of uniform texture. The dip is four or five degrees to the northward, and the trend of the outcrop is eastward and westward.

Lower Silurian System.

"Primordial Group. -- The Potsdam sandstone formation is exposed only in a small portion of the northeastern part of the State. It is only to be seen in the bases of the bluffs and steep valley sides which border the river there. It is nearly valueless for economic purposes. No fossils have been discovered in this formation in Iowa.

"Lower Magnesian Limestone. --

This formation has but little greater geographical extent in Iowa than the Potsdam sandstone. It lacks a uniformity of texture and stratification, owing to which it is not generally valuable for building purposes. The only fossils found in this formation in the State are a few traces of crinoids, near McGregor.

"The St. Peter's Sandstone formation is remarkably uniform in thickness throughout its known geographical extent, and it occupies a large portion of the northern half of Allamakee County, immediately beneath the drift.

"Trenton Group. -- With the exception of the Trenton limestone, all the limestones of both Upper and Lower Silurian age in Iowa are magnesian limestones -- nearly pure dolomites. This formation occupies large portions of Winneshiek and Allamakee Counties, and a small part

of Clayton. The greater part of it is useless for economic purposes; but there are some compact, even layers that furnish fine material for window caps and sills. Fossils are so abundant in this formation that in some places the rock is made up of a mass of shells, corals and fragments of trilobites, cemented by calcareous material into a solid rock. Some of these fossils are new to science and peculiar to Iowa.

"The Galena limestone is the upper formation of the Trenton Group. It is 150 miles long and seldom exceeds 12 miles in width. It exhibits its greatest development in Dubuque County. It is nearly a pure dolomite with a slight admixture of silicious matter; good blocks for dressing are sometimes found near the top of the bed, although it is usually unfit for such a purpose. This formation is the source of the lead ore of the Dubuque lead mines. The lead region proper is confined to an area of about 15 miles square in the vicinity of Dubuque. The ore occurs in vertical fissures, which traverse the rock at regular intervals from east to west; some is found in those which have a north and south direction. This ore is mostly that known as Galena, or sulphuret of lead, very small quantities only of the carbonate being found with it.

"Cincinnati Group. -- The surface occupied by the Maquoketa shales is more than 100 miles in length, but is singularly long and narrow, seldom reaching more than a mile or two in width. The most northern exposure yet recognized is in the western part of Winneshiek County, while the most southerly is in Jackson County, in the bluffs of the Mississippi. The formation is largely composed of bluish and brownish shales, sometimes slightly arenaceous, sometimes clacareous, which weather into a tenacious clay upon the surface, and the soil derived from it is usually stiff and clayey. Several species of fossils which characterize the Cincinnati Group are found in the Maquoketa shales, but they contain a larger number than have been found any where else in these shales in Iowa, and their distinct faunal characteristics seem to warrant the separation of the Maquoketa shales as a distinct formation from any others of the group.

Upper Silurian System.

"Niagara Group. -- The area occupied by the Niagara limestone is 40 to 50 miles in width and nearly 160 miles long from north to south. This formation is entirely a magnesian limestone, with a considerable portion of silicious matter, in some places, in the form of chert or coarse flint. A large part of it probably affords the best and greatest amount of quarry rock in the State. The quarries at Anamosa, Le Claire and Farley are all opened in this formation.

Devonian System.

"Hamilton Group. -- The area of surface occupied by the Hamilton limestone and shales, is as great as those by all the formations of both the Upper and Lower Silurian age in the State. Its length is nearly 200 miles, and width from 40 to 50 miles. It trends in a northwesterly and southeasterly direction. A large part of the material of this is quite worthless, yet other portions are valuable for economic purposes; and, having a large geographical extent in the State, is a very important formation. Its value for the production of hydraulic lime has been demonstrated at Waverly, Bremer County. The heavier and more uniform magnesian beds furnish material for bridge piers and other material requiring strength and durability. All the Devonian strata of Iowa evidently belong to a single epoch. The most conspicuous and characteristic fossils of this formation are brachiopods, corals and mollusks. The coral "Acervularia Davidsoni" occurs near Iowa City, and is known as "Iowa City marble" and "bird's-eye marble".

Carboniferous System.

"Of the three groups of formations that constitute the carboniferous, viz., the subcarboniferous, coal measures and Permian, only the first two are found in Iowa

"Subcarboniferous Group. -- This group occupies a very large area of surface. Its eastern border passes from the northeastern part of Winnebago County, with considerable directness in a southeasterly direction to the northern part of Washington County. It then makes a broad and direct bend nearly eastward, striking the Mississippi at Muscatine. The southern and western boundaries are to a considerable

extent the same as that which separates it from the real field. From the southern part of Pocahontas County it passes southeast to Fort Dodge, thence to Webster City, thence to a point three or four miles northeast of Eldora, in Hardin County, thence southeastward to Sigourney, in Keokuk County, thence to the northeastern corner of Jefferson County, thence sweeping a few miles eastward to the southeast corner of Van Buren County. Its arc is about 250 miles long and from 20 to 50 miles wide.

"The Kinderhook Beds. -- The most southerly exposure of these beds is in Des Moines County, near the mouth of the Skunk River. The most northerly now known is in the eastern part of Pocahontas County, more than 200 miles distant. The principal exposures of this formation are along the bluffs which border the Mississippi and Skunk River, where they form the eastern and northern boundary of Des Moines County; along English River, in Washington County; along the Iowa River in Tama, Marshall, Hardin and Franklin Counties, and along the Des Moines River in Humboldt County. This formation has considerable economic value, particularly in the northern portion of the region it occupies. In Pocahontas and Humboldt Counties it is invaluable, as no other stone except a few boulders are found here. At Iowa Falls the lower division is very good for building purposes. In Marshall County all the limestone to be obtained comes from this formation, and the quarries near Le Grand are very valuable. At this point some of the layers are finely veined with peroxide of iron, and are wrought into both useful and ornamental objects. In Tama County the oolitic member is well exposed, where it is manufactured into lime. Upon exposure to atmosphere and frost it crumbles to pieces; consequently it is not valuable for building purposes.

"The remains of fishes are the only fossils yet discovered in this formation that can be referred to the sub-kingdom Vertebrata; and so far as yet recognized, they all belong to the order Selachians. Of Articulates, only two species have been recognized, both of which belong to the genus Phillipsia. The sub-kingdom Mollusca is also largely

represented. The Radiata are represented by a few crinoids, usually found in a very imperfect condition.

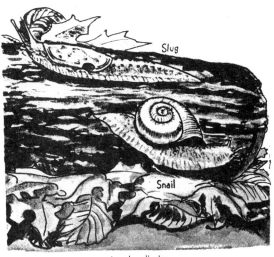

Land mollusks

"This formation is of great economic value. Large quantities of its stone have been used in the finest structures in the State, among which are the post offices at Dubuque and Des Moines. The principal quarries are along the banks of the Mississippi, from Keokuk to Nauvoo. The only vertebrate fossils in the formation are fishes, all belonging to the order Selachians, some of which indicate that their owners reached a length of 25 to 30 feet. Of the Aritculates, only two species of the genus Phillipsia have been found in this formation. Of the Mollusks no Cephalopods have been recognized in this formation in Iowa. Gasteropods are rare; Brachiopods and Polyzoans are quite abundant. Of Radiates, corals of genera Zaphrentis, Amplexus and Aulopora are found, but crinoids are most abundant. Of the low forms of animal life, the protozoans, a small fossil related to the sponges, is found in this formation in small numbers.

"The St. Louis limestone is the uppermost of the subcarboniferous group in Iowa. It occupies a small superficial area, consisting of long, narrow strips, yet its extent is very great. It is first seen resting on the geode division of the Keokuk limestone, near Keokuk; proceeding northward, it forms a narrow border along the edge of the coal fields in Lee, Des Moines, Henry, Jefferson, Washington, Keokuk and Mahaska Counties; it is then lost sight of until it appears again in the banks of the Boone River, where it again passes out of view under the coal measures, until it is next seen in the banks of the Des Moines, near Fort Dodge. As it exists in Iowa, it consists of three tolerably distinct sub-divisions: the magnesian, arenaceous and calcareous. The upper division furnishes excellent material for quicklime, and when quarries are well opened, as in the northwestern part of Van Buren County, large blocks are obtained. The sandstone, or middle division, is of little economic value. The lower, or magnesian division, funishes a valuable and durable stone, exposures of which are found on Lick Creek, in Van Buren County, and on Long Creek, seven miles west of Burlington.

"Of the fossils of this formation, the vertebrates are represented only by the remains of fish, belonging to the two orders, Selachians and Ganoids. The articulates are represented by one species of the trilobite, genus Phillipsia; and two ostracoid genera, Cythra and Beyricia. The Mollusks distinguish this formation more than any other branch of the animal kingdom. Radiates are exceedingly rare, showing a marked contrast between this formation and the two preceeding it.

"The Burlington limestone formation is to be seen only in four counties: Lee, Van Buren, Henry and Des Moines. In some localities the upper silicious portion is known as the Geode bed; it is not recognizable in the northern portion of the formation, nor in connection with it where it is exposed, about 80 miles below Keokuk. The geodes of the Geode bed are more or less masses of silex, usually hollow and lined with crystals of quartz; the outer crust is rough and unsightly, but the crystals which stud the interior are often very beautiful; they vary in size from the size of a walnut to a foot in diameter.

"The Coal Measure Group is properly divided into three formations, viz.: the Lower, Middle and Upper Coal Measures, each having a vertical thickness of about 200 feet.

"The Lower Coal Measures exist eastward and northward of the Des Moines River, and also occupy a large area westward and southward of that river, but their southerly dip passes them below the Middle Coal Measures at no great distance from the river. This formation possesses

greater economic value than any other in the whole State. The clay that underlies almost every bed of coal, furnishes a large amount of material for potter's use. The sandstone of these measures is usually soft and unfit, but in some places, as in Red Rock in Marion County, blocks of large dimensions are obtained, which make good building material, samples of which can be seen in the State Arsenal, at Des Moines.

"But few fossils have been found in any of the strata of the Lower Coal Measures, but such animal remains as have been found in these measures probably belong to the class Acrogens. Specimens of Calamites and several species of ferns are found in all the Coal Measures, but the genus Lipidodendron seems not to have existed later than the epoch of the Middle Coal Measures. The latter formation occupies a narrow belt of territory in the southern central portion of the State, embracing a superficial area of about 1,400 sq. miles. The counties underlaid by this formation are Guthrie, Dallas, Polk, Madison, Warren, Clarke, Lucas, Monroe, Wayne and Appanoose.

"Few species of fossils occur in these beds. Some of the shales and sandstone have afforded a few imperfectly preserved land plants, three or four species of ferns, belonging to the genera. Some of the carboniferous shales afford beautiful specimens of what appear to have been sea-weeds. Radiates are represented by corals. The Mollusks are most numerously represented. Trilobites and Ostracoids are the only remains known of Articulates. Vertebrates are only known by the remains of Selachians, or sharks, and ganoids.

"The Upper Coal Measures occupy a very large area, comprising 13 whole counties, in the southwestern part of the State. By its northern and eastern boundaries it adjoins the area occupied by the Middle Coal Measures. This formation contains a considerable proportion of shales and sandstone, but the prominent lithological features are its limestones. Although it is known by the name of Upper Coal Measures, it contains but a single bed of coal, and that only about 20 inches in maximum thickness. The limestone exposed in this formation furnishes good building material, as in Madison and Fremont Counties. The sandstones are quite worthless. No beds of clay for potter's use are found in the whole formation. The fossils are more numerous than in either the Middle or Lower Coal Measures. The vertebrates are represented by the fishes of the orders Selachians and Ganoids. The Articulates are represented by the trilobites and ostracoids. Mollusks are represented by the classes Cephalapoda, Gasterapoda, Lamellibranchiata, Brachipoda and Polyzoa. Radiates are more numerous than in the Middle and Lower Coal Measures. Protozoans are represented in the greatest abundance, some layers of limestone being almost entirely composed of their small fusiform shells.

Cretaceous System.

"The next strata in the geological series are of the Cretaceous age. They are found in the western half of the State, and do not dip, as do all the other formations upon which they rest, to the southward and westward, but have a general dip of their own to the north of westward, which, however, is very slight. Although the actual exposures of cretaceous rocks are few in Iowa, there is reason to believe that nearly all the western half of the State was originally occupied by them; but they have been removed by denudation, which has taken place at two separate periods. The first period was during its elevation from the cretaceous sea, and during the long Tertiary age that passed between the time of that elevation and the commencement of the Glacial epoch. The second period was during the Glacial epoch, when the ice produced their removal over considerable areas. All the cretacous rocks in Iowa are a part of the same deposits farther up the Missouri River, and in reality form their eastern boundary.

"The Nishnabotany sandstone has the most easterly and southerly extent of the cretaceous deposits of Iowa, reaching the southeastern part of Guthrie County and the southern part of Montgomery County. To the northward, it passes beneath the Woodbury sandstones and shales, the latter passing beneath the Inoceramus, or chalky beds. This sandstone is, with few exceptions, valueless for economic purposes. The only fossils found in this formation are a few fragments of angiospermous leaves. The strata of Woodbury sandstones and shales rest upon the Nishnabotany sandstone, and have not been observed outside of Woodbury County: hence their name. Their principal exposure is at Sergeant's Bluffs, seven miles below Sioux City. This rock has no value except for purposes of common masonry. Fossil remains are rare. Detached scales of a lepidoginoid species have been detected, but no other vertebrate remains. Of remains of vegetation, leaves of Salix Meekii and Sassafras cretaceum have been occasionally found.

"The Inoceramus beds rest upon the Woodbury sandstone and shales. They have not been observed in Iowa except in the bluffs which border the Big Sioux River in Woodbury and Plymouth Counties. They are composed almost entirely of calcareous material, the upper portion of which is extensively used for lime. No building material can be obtained from these beds, and the only value they possess, except lime, are the marls, which at some time may be useful on the soil of the adjacent region. The only vertebrate remains found in the cretaceous rocks are the fishes. Those in the Inoceramus beds are two species of squaloid Selachians, or cestracionts, and three genera of teliosts. Molluscan remains are rare.

Peat.

"Extensive beds of peat exist in Northern Middle Iowa, which it is estimated, contain the following areas: Cerro Gordo County, 1,500 acres; Worth, 2,000; Winnebago, 2,000; Hancock, 1,500; Wright, 500; Kossuth, 700; Dickinson, 80. Several other counties contain peat beds, but the peat is inferior to that in the northern part of the State. The beds, are of an average depth of four feet. It is estimated that each acre of these beds will furnish 250 tons of dry fuel for each foot in depth. At present this peat is not utilized; but owing to its great distance from the coal fields and the absence of timber, the time is coming when their value will be fully realized.

Gypsum.

"The only sulphate of the alkaline earths of any economic value is gypsum, and it may be found in the vicinity of Fort Dodge in Webster County. The deposit occupies a nearly central position in the county, the Des Moines River, running nearly centrally through it, along the valley side of which the gypsum is seen in the form of ordinary rock cliff and ledges, and also occuring abundantly in similar positions along both sides of the valleys of the smaller streams and of the numerous ravines coming into the river valley. The most northerly known limit of the deposit is at a point near the mouth of Lizard Creek, a tributary of the Des Moines River and almost adjoining the town of Fort Dodge. The most southerly point at which it has been exposed is about six miles,

by way of the river, from the northerly point mentioned. The width of the area is unknown, as the gypsum becomes lost beneath the overlying drift, as one goes up the ravines and minor valleys.

"On either side of the creeks and ravines which come into the valley of the Des Moines River, the gypsum is seen jutting out from beneath the drift in the form of ledges and bold quarry fronts, having almost the exact appearance of ordinary limestone exposures, so horizontal and regular are its lines of stratifications, and so similar in color is it to some varieties of that rock. The principal quarries now opened are on Two Mile Creek, a couple of miles below Fort Dodge.

"Age of the Gypsum Deposit. -- No trace of fossil remains has been found in the gypsum or associated clays; neither has any other indication of its geologic age been observed except that which is afforded by its stratigraphical relations; the most that can be said with certainty is that it is newer than the coal measures, and older than the drift. The indications afforded by the stratigraphical relations of the gypsum deposit of Fort Dodge are, however, of considerable value. No Tertiary deposits are known to exist within or near the borders of Iowa, to suggest that it might be of that age, nor are any of the Palaeozoic strata newer than the subcarboniferous unconformable upon each other as the other gypsum is unconformable upon the strata beneath it. It therefore seems, in a measure, conclusive, that the gypsum is of Mesozoic age; perhaps older than the cretaceous.

"The lithological origin of this deposit is as uncertain as its geological age. It seems to present itself in this relation, as in the former one, -- an isolated fact. None of the associated strata show any traces of a double decomposition of pre-existing materials, such as some have supposed all deposits of gypsum to have resulted from. No considerable quantities of oxide of iron nor any trace of native sulphur have been found in connection with it, nor has any salt been found in the water of the region. These substances are common in association with other gypsum deposits, and by many are regarded as indicative of the method of or resulting from their origin as such. Throughout the whole region the Fort Dodge gypsum has the exact appearance of a sedimentary deposit. From these facts it seems not unreasonable to entertain the opinion that this gypsum originated as a chemical precipitation in comparatively still waters which were saturated with sulphate of lime and destitute of life; its stratification and impurities being deposited at the same time as clayey impurities which had been suspended in the same waters.

"Physical Properties. -- Much has already been said of the physical character of this gypsum; but as it is so different in some respects from other deposits, there are still other matters worthy of mention in connection with those. According to the results of a complete analysis by Prof. Emery, the ordinary gray gypsum contains only about eight per cent of impurity, and it is possible that the average impurity for the whole deposit will not exceed that proportion, so uniform in quality is it from top to bottom and from one end of the region to the other. As plaster for agricultural purposes is sometimes prepared from gypsum that contains thirty per cent of impurity, it will be seen that this is a very superior article for such purposes. The impurities are of such a character that they do not in any way interfere with its value for use in the arts.

"Although the gypsum rock has a gray color, it becomes quite white by grinding, and still whiter by the calcimining process necessary in the quantities of oxide of iron not any trace of native sulphur have preparation of plaster of Paris. These tests have all been practically made in the rooms of the Geological Survey, and the quality of the plaster of Paris still further tested by actual use and experiment. The only use yet made of the gypsum by the inhabitants is for the purpose of ordinary building stone. It is so compact that it is found to be comparatively unaffected by frost, and its ordinary situation in walls of houses is such that it is protected from the dissolving action of water, which can at most reach it only from occasional rains, and the effect of these is too slight to be perceived after the lapse of several years. Hon. John F. Duncombe, of Fort Dodge, built a fine residence of it in 1861, the walls of which appear as unaffected by exposure and as beautiful as they were when first erected. Several other houses in Fort Dodge have been constructed of it, including the depot building of the Dubuque & Sioux Railroad. Many of the sidewalks in the town are made of the slabs or flags of gypsum which occur in some of the quarries in the form of thin layers.

54

Minor Deposits of Sulphate of Lime.

"Sulphate of lime in the various forms of fibrous gypsum, selenite and small, amorphous masses, has also been discovered in various formations in different parts of the State, including the Coal Measure shales near Fort Dodge, where it exists in small quantities, quite independently of the great gypsum of deposit there. The quantity of gypsum in these minor deposits is always too small to be of any practical value, usually occurring in shales and shaly clays, associated with strata that contain more or less sulphuret of iron. Gypsum has thus been detected in the Coal Measures, the St. Louis limestone, the Cretaceous strata, and also in the lead caves of Dubuque.

Sulphate of Strontia.

"This mineral is found at Fort Dodge, which is, perhaps, the only place in Iowa or in the valley of the Mississippi where it has as yet been discovered. There it occurs in very small quantities in both the shales of

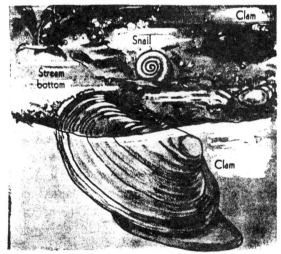
Fresh-water mollusks

the Lower Coal Measures, and in the clays that overlie the gypsum deposit, and which are regarded as of the same age with it. The mineral is fibrous and crystalline, the fibers being perpendicular to the plane of the layer; it resembles in physical character the layer of fibro-crystalline gypsum, before mentioned. Its color is of light blue, is transparent, and shows crystalline facets upon both the upper and under surfaces of the layer, those of the upper surface being smaller and more numerous. The layer is probably not more than a rod in extent in any direction, and about three inches in maximum thickness. Apparent lines of stratification occur in it, corresponding with those of the shales which imbed it. The other deposit was still smaller in amount, and occurred as a mass of crystals imbedded in the clays that overlie the gypsum at Cummins' quarry in the valley of Soldier Creek, upon the north side of the town. The mineral in this case is nearly colorless, and somewhat resembles masses of impure salt. The crystals are so closely aggregated that they enclose but little impurity in the mass, but in almost all other cases their fundamental forms are obscured. This mineral has almost no practical value, and is only interesting as a mineralogical fact.

"In Iowa this mineral has been found only in minute quantities. It has been detected in the Coal Measure shales of Decatur, Madison and Marion Counties, Devonian limestone of Johnson and Bremer Counties, and also in the lead caves of Dubuque. It is in the form of crystals or small crystalline masses.

Sulphate of Magnesia.

"Epsomite or native Epsom salts having been discovered near Bulington, all the sulphates of alkaline earths of natural origin have been recognized in Iowa; all except the sulphate of lime being in very small quantity. The Epsomite mentioned was found beneath the over-hanging cliff of Burlington limestone near Starr's Mill. It occurs in the form of efflorescent encrustations upon the surface of stones, and in similar small fragile masses among the pine debris that has fallen down beneath the overhanging cliff. The projection of the cliff over the perpendicular face of the strata beneath amounts to near 20 feet at the point where Epsomite was found. The rock upon which it accumulates is an impure limestone, containing also some carbonate of magnesia, together with a small proportion of iron pyrites in a finely divided condition. By experiments with this native salt in the office of the Survey, a fine article of Epsom salts was produced, but the quantity obtained there is very small, and would be of no practical value on account of the cheapness in the market.

Climate.

"The greatest objection to the climate of this State is the prevalence of wind, which is somewhat greater than in the States south and east, but not so great as it is west. The air is pure and generally bracing, -- the northern part particularly so during the winter. The prevailing direction of the wind during the whole year is easterly. Correspondingly, thunder-storms are somewhat more violent in this State than east or south, but not near so much so as toward the mountains. As elsewhere in the Northwestern States, easterly winds bring rain and snow, while westerly ones clear the sky. While the highest temperature occurs here in August, the month of July averages the hottest, and January the coldest. The mean temperature of April and October nearly corresponds to the mean temperature

of the year, as well as to the seasons of spring and fall, while that of summer and winter is best represented by August and December. Indian summer is delightful and well prolonged. Untimely frosts sometimes occur, but seldom severely enough to do great injury."

Thus Iowa has a vast and beautiful natural heritage, a rich agricultural land endowed with varied resources. The writer of the forgoing many pages cannot be determined and we would most gratefully give him or her deserving credit were it possible to do so. In-depth searches have not revealed the name of the eloquent writer.

It was into this land of fertile soil, mineral wealth, great forests and verdant plains that the first human beings came many centuries ago.

Indeed, they came to the "beautiful land" and they were to become known in our history as "Indians."

## Chapter Two

# THE INDIANS OF IOWA

The history and background of that noble race whom we call the (American) Indians goes back many centuries and its life and exploits are constantly under research and scrutiny. Unending "finds" and archeological discoveries bring more and more knowledge of them to date even in 1987.

Much of their history has been well-written by others and one informative account is found in the History of Clayton County, 1882, and was written by one to whom no credit was given in the book. He, or she, relates the following account:

"The history of this country and the races which held it before the advent of the Europeans, is shrouded in as deep a mystery as that which hides the past of the oldest nations of the East. There are just relics enough left us to prove beyond a doubt that there once existed here a remarkable race, but there has been wide speculation upon the nature and origin of the early races of America, especially those referred to as Mound-Builders. It is but lately that the researchers of science have enabled us to reason with much certainty. Though the divergence of opinion among scientists may for a time seem incompatible with a thorough investigation of the subject, and tend to a confusion of

Courtesy, Hist., Mem. and Art Department of Iowa

Musquakie squaw and papoose.
The Musquakies are a remnant of the
Sacs and Foxes.

ideas, no doubt whatever can exist as to the comparative accuracy of the conclusions arrived at by some of them. To solve the problem of who were the pre-historic settlers of America, it will not be necessary to go to ancient history. That this continent is co-existent with the world of the ancients cannot be questioned.    Every investigation instituted under the auspices of modern civilization confirms the fact. China, with its numerous existing testimonials of antiquity, claims a continuous history from antediluvian times; and although its continuity may be denied, there is nothing to prevent the transmission of a hieroglyphic record of its history prior to 1656, "anno mundi" (the date of Noah's flood), since many traces of its early settlement survived the deluge, and became sacred objects of the first historical epoch. That an antediluvian people inhabited this continent, however, will not be claimed, because it is not probable that a settlement of a country so remote from the cradle of the race as this, was effected until later times.

"The most probable sources in which the origin of the Indians must be sought, are those countries which lie along the eastern coast of Asia, and which may have been one more densely populated than now.    The surplus population pushed north and east in search of a new home, which was found at last by crossing the Behring's Strait, and then journeying sourthward. The number of small islands lying between the two continents tends to confirm this view; and it is yet further confirmed by some remarkable traces of similarity in the physical conformation of the northern nations of both continents.    The researches of Humboldt have traced the Mexican to the vicinity of Behring's Strait; whence it is conjectured that they, as well as the Peruvians and other tribes, came originally from Asia.

"This theory is accepted by most ethnologists, and there is every reason to believe that after the discovery of an overland route to a land of "illimitable possibilities," many bands of adventurers found their way from the Chinese or Tartar nations, until they had populated much of this continent. Magnificent cities and monuments were raised at the bidding of the tribal leaders, and populous settlements centered with thriving villages sprang up every where in manifestation of the progress of the people. For the last 400 years the colonizing Caucasian has trodden on the ruins of a civilization whose greatness he could only surmise.    Among these ruins are pyramids similar to those which have rendered Egypt famous. The pyramid of Cholula is square, each side of its base is 1,335 feet in length, and its height is 172 feet. Another pyramid, north of Vera Cruz, is formed of large blocks of highly polished prophyry, and bears upon its front hieroglyphic inscriptions and curious sculpture. It is 82 feet square, and a flight of 57 steps conducts to its summit, which is 65 feet high.    The ruins of Palenque are said to extend 20 miles along the ridge of a mountain, and the remains of an Aztec city, near the banks of the Gila, are spread over more than a square league. The principal feature of the Aztec civilization which has come down to us was its religion, which we are told was of a dark and gloomy character. Each new god created by their priesthood, instead of arousing new life in the people, brought death by the thousands; and their grotesque idols exposed to drown the sense of the beholders in fear, wrought wretchedness rather than spiritual happiness. In fact, fear was the great animating principle, the motive power which sustained this terrible religion. Their altars were sprinkled with blood drawn from their own bodies in large quantities, and on them thousands of human victims were sacrificed in honor of the demons whom they worshiped. The head and heart of every captive taken in war were offered up as a sacrifice to the god of battles, while the victorious legions feasted on the remaining portions of the bodies. It is said that during the ceremonies attendant on the consecration of two of their temples, the number of prisoners offered up in sacrifice was 12,210, while they themselves contributed large numbers of voluntary victims to the terrible belief.

"Throughout the Mississippi Valley are found mounds and walls of earth or stone, which can have had only a human origin, and their unknown constructors have been referred to as Mound-Builders. These mounds vary in size from a few feet to hundreds of feet in diameter. In them are often found stone axes, pestles, arrow-heads, spear points, pieces of flint, etc., showing that some of them, at least, were used for purposes of burial. Pottery of various designs is very common in them, and from the material of which they are made geologists have attempted to assign their age.

"One of the most famous of these relics is a stone fortification in Clark county, Indiana, known as the "Stone Fort." A place naturally strong for

THE MOUND BUILDERS
Between seven and fifteen centuries before the birth of Christ, "Indians" probably not long from far-off Asia built mounds. The one above is an old picture of a large mound in Illinois. They are said to be larger than the ones in Iowa. See the insert item in this chapter on the Effigy Mounds in Clayton and Allamakee Counties in northeastern Iowa.

purposes of defense, has evidently been used as a fort, and strengthened so as to become nearly impregnable. On one side the artifical wall is 150 feet long and 75 feet high. On the hill on which this is situated are five "mounds" of earth, in which the usual relics have been found.

"Some have thought that the Mound-Builders were a race quite distinct from the modern Indians, and that they were in an advanced state of civilization. The best authorities now agree that while the comparatively civilized people called Aztecs built the cities whose ruins are occasionally found, the Mound-Builders were the immediate ancestors of the Indians De Soto first saw, and little different from the Indians of today.

"Within a few years many discoveries have been made of remains of our predecessors. Together with many relics of the early inhabitants, the fossils of extinct animals have been unearthed in many places.  These animals roamed the forests and prairies long before the advent of dreaded man.  Among the souvenirs of an age about which so little is known, are 25 vertebrae, averaging 13 inches in diameter, and three vertebrae ossified together, which measures nine cubical feet; a thigh-bone five feet long and 12 inches in diameter; and the weight of all these is 600 pounds.  These are believed to have belonged to a Dinosaur (the literal meaning of which is "terrible lizard"), an animal 60 feet long.  When feeding in cypress and palm forests, it could extend itself to 85 feet, and feed on the budding tops of these tall trees.

"Other remains are found every year, and additional light thrown on America's early history.

"The origin of the Red Men, or American Indians, is a subject which interests as well as instructs. It is a favorite topic with the ethnologist, even as it is one of deep concern to the ordinary reader.  A review of two works lately published on the origin of the Indians, treats the matter in a peculiarly reasonable light. It says:

"Recently a German writer has put forward a theory on the subject, and an English writer has put forward another and directly opposite theory.  The difference in opinion concerning our aboriginals among authors who have made a profound study of races, is at once curious and interesting.  Blumenbach treats them in his classifications as a distinct variety of the human family; but, in the three-fold division of Dr. Latham, they are ranked among the Mongolidae.  Other writers on races regard them as a branch of the great Mongolian family, which at a distant period found its way from Asia to this continent, and remained here for centuries separate from the rest of mankind, passing meanwhile, through diverse phases of barbarism and civilization.  Morton, our eminent ethnologist, and his followers, Nott and Gliddon, claim for our native Red Men an origin as distinct as the flora and fauna of this continent.  Prichard, whose views are apt to differ from Morton's, finds reason to believe, on comparing the American tribes together, that they must have formed a separate department of nations from the earliest period of the world.  The era of their existence as a distinct and insulated people, must probably be dated back to the time which separated into nations the individuality and primitive language.  Dr. Robert Brown, the latest authority, attributes in his 'Races of Mankind,' as Asiatic origin to our aboriginals.  He says that the Western Indians not only personally resemble their nearest neighbors-the Northeastern Asiatics-but they resemble them in language and tradition. The Esquimaux on the American the the Tehukteis on the Asiatic side, understand one another perfectly.  Modern anthropologists, indeed, are disposed to think that

# Early Indian Mound Builders
# Left Iowa a Unique Heritage

Dr. R. Clark Mallam of Luther College in Decorah, Winneshiek County, Ia., was Associate Professor of Anthropology and Director of the Archaeological Reserach Center there. He had a profound understanding of the Effigy Mounds in Clayton and Allamakee Counties and did extensive writing about them. He wrote that "in approximately A. D. 650, the prehistoric cultures of the upper Midwest in North America underwent........ a change. ......... There, ......... a new culture developed along the western margin of the Eastern Woodlands culture area, in the region that today includes the four contiguous state of Illinois, Iowa, Minnesota and Wisconsin. This culture, known as the Effigy Mound Culture, existed from about A. D. 650 to 1200-1300. During this period various pre-historic peoples regularly constructed earthen mounds modeled on animal forms. ........ literally were constructed by sculpting the earth."

The "Marching Bear Mound Group" is pictured above. (Picture from the Effigy Mounds National Monument.) The picture is as Dr. R. Clark Mallam describes that they "are frequently found in association with other mound forms such as conical or round mounds; linear or elongated mounds; ............ surrounded by an earthen wall or embankment."

Above is a close-up aerial view of the northern portion of the Marching Bear Mound Group shown before. (Picture from the Effigy Mounds National Monument, South Unit.) A study to which Dr. Mallam referred in an article suggests that "Iowa had once possessed at least 54 effigy mound groups, distributed primarily along the bluffs and terraces of the Mississippi River and the lower reaches of its tributaries in northeastern Iowa. These 54 groups contained a minimum of 1,438 mounds."

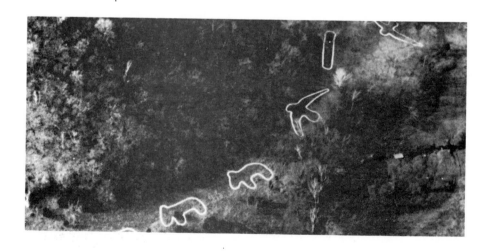

Bird, Bear and Linear Mounds from the Chantry Hollow Mound Group across the Clayton-Allamakee county line in Allamakee County. Dr. Mallam reports that the "mounds were divided into a series of catagories: 375 effigy mounds consisting of nine representative forms, 795 conical mounds .......241 linear mounds, two enclosures, and two mounds of indeterminate shape."

The "Woman" Mound Group in Adams Mill Hollows in the southern part of the Effigy Mounds National Monument in Clayton County is shown above. Smaller round mounds are shown near the effigy of a woman. In an article Dr. Mallam called for "an increased public awareness" of the mounds and their value. Many mounds in different parts of the country **have been** vandalized and destroyed.

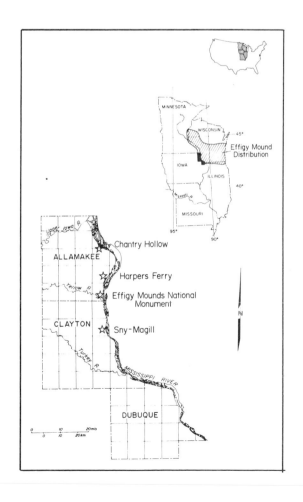

Relative location of the Effigy Mounds National Monument is shown at the left in this map provided by the U. S. Department of the Interior. It shows the area nationally, in its midwestern location and locally in the areas of Clayton and Allamakee counties in which the area of the national monument is covered. The mound builders were most active in the four midwestern States of Iowa, Illinois, Wisconsin and Minnesota.

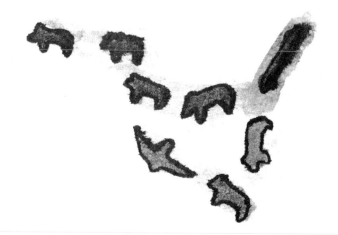

In a brochure put out by the National Park Service we are told that toward "the end of the last glaciation, about 12,000 years ago, Paleo-Indians, hunters similar to other early people east of the Rocky Mountains, came into northeast Iowa.

"The way of life of these early hunters was comparatively simple. Small groups pursued and killed huge elephantine mammals and now extinct forms of the bison. Their weapons were darts, tipped with ........... stonepoints......

"Remains of these Indians have not been found in the monument, but scattered evidence of their presence appears in the vicinity ............ Their part in the pre-history of the area is noteworthy, for it represents the beginning of the human story..............

"The early hunting tradition can be traced through several thousand years............ Archeologists have found the ax, adz, and gouge --- all attesting to changes in the adaptation of the Indians' way of life from the plains to the forest.

"............ The animals they hunted included the deer, bear, and bison ........ Implements and weapons attributed to these people have been found along the Mississippi River......... The discovery of numerous tools and weapons suggest a large population and a relatively prosperous life.

"Religious practices, magical in character, were important to these people. Shamans, who aimed at bending the forces of nature to man's will greatly influenced their actions......... These men conducted ceremonies ........ They also worked to prevent natural disasters and drive away sickness.

"The oldest mounds in the Mississippi Valley belong to the Red Ocher Culture. One mound excavated (was dated) ....... as being about 2,500 years old. Bundle burials had been placed on a floor covered with red ocher ......... offerings included large chipped blade, straight-stemmed and corner-notched spear or dart points, and spherical copper beads.

" ........... Their first pottery was crude, thick and heavily tempered with coarse pieces of crushed rock. Toward the end of the period, pottery became thinner and was decorated with wide, ...... incised lines.

"The next major cultural division .......... is called Hopewell ...... dating from 100 B. C. to A. D. 600 .......... Several mounds excavated in the monument are of the Hopewellian period. ............ the evidence was not as abundant as is usually found in similar centers of Illinois and Ohio.

"The Effigy Mounds people occupied the land now within the monument from a time overlapping the Hopewellian period until almost historic times. ............. Cultural remains indicate they differed from the Hopewellians chiefly in constructing mounds in effigy forms..........

" ...........the Effigy Mounds people were probably supplanted about 1300 or 1400 by Indians of the Oneota Culture (who) placed strong emphasis on agriculture and on life in larger villages. ........... Ioway villages were north and west of the present monument boundaries.........

"With the advent of the fur trade era, Indian occupation of the land now within the monument came to an end."

The Effigy Mounds were first mentioned in Jonathan Carver's "Travels Through the Interior Parts of North America in the Years 1766, 1767, 1768." They were later mapped in 1881 by T. H. Lewis and A. J. Hill.

64

Japan, the Kuriles, and neighboring regions, may be regarded as the original home of the greater part of the native American race. It is also admitted by them that between the tribes scattered from the Artic sea to Cape Horn, there is more uniformity of physical feature than is seen in any other quarter of the globe. The weight of evidence and authority is altogether in favor of the opinion that our so-called Indians are a branch of the Mongolian family, and all additional researches strengthen the opinion. The tribes of both North and South America are unquestionably homogeneous, and, in all likelihood, had their origin in Asia, though they have been altered and modified by thousands of years of total separation from the present stock."

"The conclusions arrived at by the reviewer at that time, though safe, are too general to lead the reader to form any definite idea on the subject. No doubt whatever can exist, when the American Indian is regarded as of an Asiatic origin; but there is nothing in the works or even in the review to which these works were subjected, which might account for the vast difference in manner and form between the Red Man, as he is now known, or even as he appeared to Columbus and his successors in the field of discovery and the comparatively civilized inhabitants of Mexico, as seen in 1521 by Cortez, and of Peru, as witnessed by Pizarro in 1532. The fact is that the pure-bred Indian of the present is descended directly from the earliest inhabitants, or in other words from the survivors of that people who, on being driven from their fair possessions, retired to the wilderness in sorrow, and reared up their children under the saddening influences of their unquenchable

griefs, bequeathing them only the habits of the wild, cloud-roofed home of their declining years, as sullen silence and a rude moral code. In after years these wild sons of the forest and prairie grew in numbers and in strength. Some legend told them of their present sufferings, of the stations which their fathers once had known, and of the riotous race which now reveled in wealth which should be theirs. The fierce passions of the savage were aroused, and uniting their scattered bands they marched in silence upon the villages of the Tartars, driving them onward to the capital of the Incas, and consigning their homes to the flames. Once in view of the great city, the hurrying bands halted in surprise, but Tartar cunning took in the situation and offered pledges of amity, which were sacredly observed. Henceforth Mexico was open to the Indians, bearing precisely the same relation to them that the Hudson's

Bay Company's villages do to the Northwestern Indians of the present; obtaining all, and bestowing very little. The subjection of the Mongolian race, represented in North America by that branch of it to which the Tartars belonged, represented in the southern portion of the continent, seems to have taken place some five centuries before the advent of the European; while it may be concluded that the war of the races which resulted in reducing the villages erected by the Tartar hordes to ruin, took place between one and two hundred years later. These statements, though actually referring to events which in point of time are comparatively

modern, can only be substantiated by the facts that, about the periods mentioned, the dead bodies of an unknown race of men were washed ashore on the European coasts, while previous to that time there is no account whatever in European annals of even a vestige of trans-Atlantic humanity being transferred by ocean currents to the gaze of a wandering people. Toward the latter half of the fifteenth century two dead bodies entirely free from decomposition, and corresponding with the Red Men as they afterward appeared to Columbus, were cast on the shores of the Azores, and confirmed Columbus in his belief in the existence of a western world and a western people.

"Storm and flood and disease have created sad havoc in the ranks of the Indian since the occupation of the country by the white man. These natural causes have conspired to decimate the race even more than the advance of civilization which seems not to affect it to any material extent. In its maintenance of the same number of representations during these centuries, and its existence in the very face of a most unceremonious, and whenever necessary, cruel conquest, the grand dispensations of the unseen Ruler of the universe is demonstrated; for, without the aborigines, savage and treacherous as they were, it is possible that the explorers of former times would have so many natural difficulties to contend with, that their work would be surrendered in despair, and the most fertile regions of the continent saved for the plow-shares of generations yet unborn. It is questionable whether we owe the discovery of this continent to the unaided scientific knowledge of Columbus, or to the dead bodies of the two Indians referred to above; nor can their services to the explorers of ancient and modern times be over-estimated. Their existence is embraced in the plan of the Divinity for the government of the world, and it will not form subject for surprise to learn that the same intelligence which sent a thrill of liberty into every corner of the republic, will, in the near future, devise some method under which the remnant of a great and ancient race may taste the sweets of public kindness, and feel that after centuries of turmoil and tyranny, they have at last found a shelter amid a sympathizing people.

"The art of hunting not only supplied the Indians with food, but like that of war, was a means of gratifying his love of distinction. The male children, as soon as they acquired sufficient age and strength, were furnished with a bow and arrow and taught to shoot birds and other small game. Success in killing a large quadruped required years of careful study and practice, and the art was as sedulously inculcated in the minds of the rising generation as are the elements of reading, writing and arithmetic in the common schools of civilized communities. The mazes of

forest and the dense, tall grass of the prairies were the best fields for the exercise of the hunter's skill. No feet could be impressed in the yielding soil but that the tracks were the objects of the most searching scrutiny, and revealed at a glance the animal that made them, the direction it was pursuing, and the time that had elapsed since it

had passed. In a forest country he selected the valleys, because they were most frequently the resort of game. The most easily taken, perhaps, of all the animals of the chase was the deer. It is endowed with a curiosity which prompts it to stop in its flight and look back at the approaching hunter, who always avails himself of this opportunity to let fly the fatal arrow.

"Their general councils were composed of the chiefs and old men. When in council, they usually sat in concentric circles around the speaker, and each individual, notwithstanding the fiery passions that burned within, preserved an exterior as immovable as though cast in bronze. Before commencing business a person appeared with the sacred pipe, and another with fire to kindle it. After being lighted it was first presented to heaven, secondly to the earth, thirdly to the presiding spirit, and lastly to several councilors, each of whom took a whiff. These formalities were observed with as close exactness as state etiquette in civilized courts.

"The dwellings of the Indians were of the simplest and rudest character. On some pleasant spot by the bank of a river, or near an ever-running spring, they raised their groups of wigwams, constructed of the barks of trees, and easily taken down and removed to another spot. The dwelling-places of the chiefs were sometimes more spacious, and constructed with greater care, but of the same materials. Skins taken in the chase served them for repose. Though principally dependant upon hunting and fishing, the uncertain supply from these sources led them to cultivate small patches of corn. Every family did everything necessary within itself, commerce, or an exchange of articles, being almost unknown to them. In case of dispute and dissension, each Indian relied upon himself for retaliation. Blood for blood was the rule, and the relatives of the slain man were bound to obtain bloody revenge for his death. This principle gave rise, as a matter of course, to innumerable and bitter feuds, and wars of extermination when such were possible. War, indeed, rather than peace, was the Indian's glory and delight, -- war, not conducted as in civilization, but where individual skill, endurance, gallantry, and cruelty were prime requisites. For such a purpose as revenge the Indian would make great sacrifices, and display a patience and perseverance truly heroic; but when the excitement was over, he sank back into a listless, unoccupied, well-nigh useless savage. During the intervals of his more exciting pursuits, the Indian employed his time in decorating his person with all the refinement of paint and feathers, and in the manufacture of his arms and of canoes. These were constructed of bark, and so light that they could easily be carried on the shoulder from stream to stream. His amusements were the war-dance, athletic games, the narration of his exploits, and listening to the oratory of the chiefs, but during long periods of such existence he remained in a state of torpor, gazing listlessly upon the trees of the forest and the clouds that sailed above them; and this vacancy imprinted habitual gravity, and even melancholy, upon his general deportment.

"The main labor and drudgery of Indian communities fell upon the women. The planting, tending and gathering of the crops, making mats and baskets, carrying burdens, -- in fact, all things of the kind were performed by them, thus making their condition but little better than that of slaves. Marriage was merely a matter of bargain and sale, the husband giving presents to the father of the bride. In general they had but few children. They were subjected to many and severe attacks of sickness, and at times famine and pestilence swept away whole tribes.

## EXPLORATIONS BY THE WHITES.

"In the year 1541, forty-nine years after Columbus discovered the New World, and 130 years before the French missionaries discovered its upper waters, Ferdinand De Soto discovered the Mississippi, at the mouth of the Washita. He, however, penetrated no futher north than the 35th parallel of latitude, his death terminating the expedition. De Soto founded no settlements, and produced no results except that of awakening the hostility of the red man against the white man, and of disheartening such as might desire to follow up the discovery with better aims. In accordance with the usage of nations under which title to the soil was claimed by right of discovery, Spain, having conquered Florida and discovered the Mississippi, claimed all the territory bordering on that river and the Gulf of Mexico. But it was also held by the European nations that, while discovery gave title, that title must be perfected by actual possession and occupation. Although Spain claimed the territory by right of first discovery, she made no effort to occupy

it; by no permanent settlement had she perfected and secured her title, and therefore she had forfeited it when at a later period, the Mississippi Valley was re-discovered and occupied by France.

"In a grand council Indians on the shores of Lake Superior, they told the Frenchmen glowing stories of the "great river" and the countries near it. Marquette, a Jesuit father, became inspired in 1669, with the idea of discovering this noble river. He was delayed in this great under taking, however, and spent the interval in studying the language and habits of the Illinois Indians, among whom he expected to travel. In 1673 he completed his preparations for the journey, in which he was to be accompanied by Joliet, an agent of the French Government. The Indians, who had gathered in large numbers to witness his departure, tried to dissuade him from the undertaking,

representing that the Indians of the Mississippi Valley were cruel and blood-thirsty, and would resent the intrusion of strangers upon their domain. The great river itself, they said, was the abode of terrible monsters who could swallow both canoes and men. But Marquette was not diverted from his purpose by these reports, and set out on his adventurous trip May 13; he reached first an Indian village where once had been a mission and where he was treated hospitable; thence, with the aid of two Miami guides, he proceeded to the Wisconsin, down which he sailed to the great Mississippi, which had so long been anxiously looked for; floating down its unknown waters, the explorer discovered, on the 25th of June, traces of Indians on the west bank of the river, and landed a little above the river now known as the Des Moines. For the first time Europeans trod the soil of Iowa. Marquette remained here a short time, becoming aquainted with the Indians, and then proceeded on his explorations. He descended the Mississippi to the Illinois, by which and Lake Michigan he returned to French settlements.

"Nine years later, in 1682, LaSalle descended the Mississippi to the Gulf of Mexico, and in the name of the king of France, took formal possession of all the immense region watered by the great river and its tributaries from its source to its mouth, and named it Louisiana, in honor of his master, Louis XIV. The river he called "Colbert," in honor of the French Minister, and at its mouth erected a column and a cross bearing the inscription, in French:

"LOUIS THE GREAT,
KING OF FRANCE AND NAVARE,
REIGNING APRIL 9, 1682."

"France then claimed by right of discovery and occupancy the whole valley of the Mississippi and its tributaries, including Texas. Spain at the same time laid claim to all the region about the Gulf of Mexico, and thus these two great nations were brought into collision. But the country was actually held and occupied by the native Indians, especially the great Miami Confederacy, the Miamis proper (anciently the Twightwees) being the eastern and most powerful tribe. Their territory extended strictly from the Scioto river west to the Illinois river. Their villages were few and scattering, and their occupation was scarely dense enough to maintain itself against invasion. Their settlements were occasionally visited by Christian missionaries, fur traders and adventurers, but no body of white men made any settlement sufficiently permanent for a title to national possession. Christian zeal animated France and England in missionary enterprise, the former in the interests of Catholicism and the latter in the interests of Protestantism. Hence, their haste to pre-occupy the land and proselyte the aborigines. No doubt this ugly rivalry was oft seen by the Indians, and they refused to be proselyted to either branch of Christianity.

"The "Five Nations," farther east, comprised the Mohawks, Oneidas, Cayugas, Onondagas and Senecas. In 1677 the number of warriors in this confederacy was 2,150. About 1,711 of the Tuscaroras retired from Carolina and joined the Iroquois, or Five Nations, which after that event, became known as the "Six Nations".

"In 1689 hostilities broke out between the Five Nations and the colonists of Canada, and the almost constant wars in which France was engaged, until the treaty of Ryswick, in 1697, combined to check the grasping policy of Louis XIV, and to retard the planting of French colonies in the Mississippi Valley. Missionary efforts, however, continued with more failure than success, the Jesuits allying themselves with the Indians in habits and customs, even encouraging intermarriage between them and their white followers.

1700 Ioway village. A replica natache (lodge) can be seen at Living History Farms, Des Moines, Iowa.

"Soon after the discovery of the mouth of the Mississippi by La Salle, in 1682, the government of France began to encourage the policy of establishing a line of trading posts and missionary stations, extending throughout the West from Canada to Louisiana, and this policy was maintained with partial success for about 75 years. The traders persisted in importing whiskey, which canceled nearly every civilizing influence that could be brought to bear upon the Indian, and the vast distances between posts prevented that strength which can be enjoyed only by close and covenient inter-communication. Another characteristic of Indian nature was to listen

*Indians Fishing, by John White, ca. 1585.*

The Granger Collection.

attentively to all the missionary said, pretending to believe all he preached, and then offer in turn his theory of the world, of religion, etc., and because he was not listened to with the same degree of attention and pretense of belief, would go off disgusted. This was his idea of the golden rule.

"The river St. Joseph of Lake Michigan was called "the river Miamis" in 1679, in which year La Salle built a small fort on its bank, near the lake shore. The principal station of the mission for the instruction of the Miamis was established on the borders of this river. The first French post within the territory of the Miamis was at the mouth of the river, and on one side by a deep ditch made by a fall of water. It was of triangular form. The missionary Hennepin gives a good description of it, he was one of the company who built it, in 1679. Says he: "We fell the trees that were on the top of the hill; and having cleared the same from bushes for about two musket

shots, we began to build a redoubt 80 feet long and 40 feet broad, to make our fort more inaccessible on the river side. We employed the whole month of November about that work, which was very hard, though we had no other food but the bear's flesh our savage killed. These beasts are very common in that place because of the great quantity of grapes they find there; but their flesh being too fat and luscious, our men began to weary of it, and desired leave to go a-hunting to kill some wild goats. M. La Salle denied them that liberty, which caused some murmurs among them; and it was but unwillingly that they continued their work. This, together with the approach of winter, and the apprehension that M. La Salle had that his vessel (The Griffin) was lost, made him very melancholy, though he concealed it as much as he could. We made a cabin wherein we performed divine service every Sunday, and Father Gabriel and I, who preached alternately, took care to take such texts as were suitable to our present circumstances, and fit to inspire us with courage, concord and brotherly love. ※ ※ ※ The fort was at last perfected, and called Fort Miamis."

"In the year 1711 the missionary Chardon, who was said to be very zealous and apt in the acquisition of languages, had a station on the St. Joseph, about 60 miles above the mouth. Charlevoix, another distinguished missionary from France, visited a post on this river in 1721. In a letter dated at the place, Aug. 16, he says: "There is a commandant here, with a small garrison. His house, which is but a very sorry one, is called the fort, from its being surrounded with an indifferent palisade, which is pretty near the case in all the rest. We have here two villages of Indians, one of the Miamis and the other of the Pottawatomies, both of them mostly Christians; but as they have been for a long time without any pastors, the missionary who has been lately sent to them will have no small difficulty in bringing them back to the exercise of their religion." He speaks also of the main commodity for which the Indians would part with their goods, namely, spiritous liquors, which they drink and keep drunk upon as long as a supply lasted." More than a century and a half has now passed since Charlevoix penned the above without any change whatever in this trait of Indian character.

"In 1765 the Miami nation, or confederacy, was composed of four tribes, whose total number of warriors was estimated at only 1,050 men. Of these about 250 were Twightwees, or Miamis proper, 300 Weas, or Ouiatenons, 300 Piankeshaws and 200 Shockeys; and at this time the principal villages of the Twightwees were situated at the head of the Maumee river, at and near the place where Fort Wayne now is. The larger Wea villages were near the banks of the Wabash river, in the vicinity of the Post Quiatenon; and the Shockeys and Piankeshaws dwelt on the banks of the Vermillion, and on the borders of the Wabash between Vincennes and Quiatenon. Branches of the Pottawatomie, Shawnee, Delaware and Kickapoo tribes were permitted at different times to enter within the boundaries of the Miamis and reside for a while.

"The wars in which France and England were engaged, from 1688 to 1697, retarded the growth of the colonies of those nations in North America, and the efforts made by France to connect Canada and the gulf of Mexico by a chain of trading posts and colonies, naturally excited the jealousy of England, and gradually laid the foundation for a struggle at arms. After several stations were established elsewhere in the West, trading posts were started at the Miami villages, which stood at the head of the Maumee, at the Wea villages about Oniatenon on the Wabash, and at the Piankeshaw villages about the present site of Vincennes. It is probable that before the close of the year 1719, temporary trading posts were erected at the site of Fort Wayne, Quiatenon and Vincennes. These points were probably often visited by fur traders prior to 1700. In the meanwhile the English people in this country commenced also to establish military posts west of the Alleghenies, and thus matters went on until they naturally culminated in a general war, which, being waged by the French and Indians combined on one side, was called the "French and Indian War." This war was terminated in 1763 by a treaty at Paris, by which France ceded to Great Britian all of North America east of the Mississippi, except New Orleans and the island on which it is situated; and indeed, France had the preceding autumn, by a secret convention, ceded to Spain all the country west of that river."

So much for the material extracted from the 1878 histories which give an account of the Indians, who they were, where they were and their early relations with the new white men coming into their lands. Let us now deal with the Indian populations as they affected our area that became Iowa and two of the more famous ones who left their names and influence on the Iowa we know.

The Indians that roamed the area of eastern Iowa around the turn of the century, 1800, were of several tribes. The ones with whom Julien Dubuque treated to obtain his settlement at the mines of eastern Iowa were the Sac and Fox tribes.

Farther down the area there were the Ioway Indians who dwelt along the Des Moines River. (The Oto and the Missouri Indians were in the western wilds of Iowa and the Sioux, really from Minnesota and the Dakotas, dwelt and roamed in northwest Iowa.)

Tribes such as the Potawatomi and the Winnebago were in Iowa and a part of its history but were not native, if you please, to the area but came in from other areas. They became a part of our history and were eventually made wards of the federal government.

It was the Sac and Fox tribes that claimed all of the area of Iowa from the Mississippi River to the Missouri River with a northern border that was the Upper Iowa River. Nor did the federal government question the claims of the Sac and Fox tribes. Rather it dealt with them and in a series of treaties and land cessions eventually obtained the control it wanted. The price paid to the Indians was little enough.

The Ioway Indians down along the Des Moines River and in that area were recognized by the national government as exercising a certain dominion over the area even while conceding the "ownership" to the Sacs and Foxes. Having no real conception of the vast area involved it is also certain that the Sac and Fox tribes realized little of how much they were supposed to "own."

Eventually all of the area that was to become Iowa was obtained by the general government and the Ind-ians were paid for it. It remains that the payment was usually small and the agreements unjust in retrospect but that is the way things were.

It was the "Ioway" Indians from whom our area and State eventually got its name. And, as with other Indian names that have come down to us, time and Anglicizing changed them to a degree but the essence was usually on phonetics.

Pere Marquette recorded a name for a tribe as the Pahoutet (pronounced Pa-hoo-tay) or Paoutet which would have been procounced similarly. Later Pere Andre wrote about the Aiaoua, pronounced as --- Ioway. In 1682 we are told that La Salle referred to the same Indians as the Aiounouea, procounced similarly but containing an "n." By 1700 Le Seuer, who made money by selling them firearms, called them the Aya-vois meaning "the Dusty Ones." And so there were many pronunciations and the Indian ones were probably phonetically correct but the White Man necessarily had to add his spellings!

The root spellings of "Iowa" are many but not too varied. The Sioux are reported to have called them the Ayubha. They found in their own language names such as Ayuvois and Ayuez both of which eventually became Ayauway, Ayouway, Iawai. Ioway and with a final dropping of the "y"..............Iowa.

Legends have early Indians giving meaning to "Ioway" for "beautiful," "beautiful land" and "this is the place." Cyrenus Cole, in "IOWA --- Through the Years" cites Frank Luther Mott as listing over 90 different pronunciations for "Ioway" and finds him giving favor to "Iuhwuh" with an exaggerated "I".

There was very little factual history of the Indians probably as a matter that it was not of great importance to them. They had no written records but legend was very much a part of their lives. Indian lore that was passed down from one generation to another got changed a little as it was transmitted.

As the white man came and the Indians lived among them and fought with them and engaged in commercial intercourse those native Americans became a part of the recorded history of the new settlers.

In Iowa's history two Indian chiefs stand out for their many exploits. They were Black Hawk and Keokuk, both strong and wise as leaders of their people. Black Hawk is the better known of the two and his place in Iowa history is secure.

Black Hawk was the stronger of the two in many ways. Keokuk was the wiser of the two leaders. Black Hawk was a Fox chief and Keokuk was a Sac chief. Black Hawk was prominent over many years as a leader, warrior, war-maker and in his late years as an honoree of the white man who came to dominate his lands.

More is known about Black Hawk and he even dictated the material for his own autobiography giving the year of his birth as 1767 and insisting that he was a descendant of the first chief, Nanamakee which was, of course, mythical. His own tribes never recognized him as a chief by descent. Rather Black Hawk is said to have become a chief because he was a natural leader, risto chieftainship by his own ability.

In 1804, as a young chief who had already made a name for himself, he went to St. Louis with some of his warriors to call upon the governor of Upper Louisiana whom he called "my Spanish father." That was after he had won a series of military vict-

MAKATAIMESHEKIAKIAK
(Black Hawk)

ories over the tribal enemies of the Sacs and Foxes and had established himself as a war leader.

It has been said that Black Hawk went to St. Louis to save some of his fellow tribesmen from prosecution for wrongs they had done.

Whether or not that was the reason for Black Hawk's journey to St. Louis what he did find was that his "Spanish father" was acting on the behalf of France to turn the entire area of the 1803 Louisiana Purchase over to the sovereignty of the United States of America. A company of soldiers under Major Amos Stoddard was present there to accept the vast area on behalf of the general government in Washington.

Chief Black Hawk averred that he had never heard anything good about the Americans and the story has it that as Major Stoddard was entering the governor's house Chief Black Hawk was leaving by a rear door. Cyrenus Cole suggests that: "The Americans soon helped to confirm his prejudices."

CHIEF BLACK HAWK
From a pen drawing by Charles A. Gray after the illustration in McKenny and Hall's "History of the Indian Tribes of North America" which is probably the one seen on the previous page.

———

Black Hawk not only had heard bad reports on the white man but he had cultivated an innate distrust of them; the future, to him, foresaw only trouble as the white settlers continued to move westward.

It happened that in the spring of 1804 a Sac Indian brave had slain a white man at a settlement above St. Louis. The killing was as a result of the white man dancing with an Indian maiden during which he "so shocked her primitive sense of modesty" that she sought to flee from him. Her father, under the influence of fire water came to the defense of his daughter and was ousted from the cabin of the white man. The disgruntled father awaited the white man just outside his cabin and when he left the Indian father murdered him. Father and daughter then fled to Saukenuk only to be pursued eventually by government soldiers who demanded his surrender. He relented and was taken to prison in St. Louis where he was held.

At Saukenuk a Sac council took place and five Indians including two Sac chiefs journeyed to St. Louis to assist the Indian prisoner who was a relative of one of the chiefs.

While they were there Governor William Henry Harrison arrived. He was the governor of Indiana Territory and Upper Louisiana had been attached to it temporarily. Governor Harrison had arrived to take over the area from Major Stoddard who had accepted it from its former owners.

Governor Harrison had instructions to negotiate a treaty for a cession of land along the Illinois River. He thought the presence of the five Indians would provide that opportunity although they had no authority from their tribes to act. Pierre Chouteau, a St. Louis trader and Indian agent, acted as an intermediary. One of the chiefs, Quashquame, later insisted that Chouteau had promised release of his accused relative if they would sell some of their lands along the Illinois.

Whatever took place finally, a treaty was signed. Historian Cyrenus Cole refers to it as "one of the most astounding treaties in the Indian history of America." In its terms the Sac and Fox tribes ceded all their lands east of the Mississippi River to the government of the United States. Also included was an "agreement" whereby 51,000,000 acres west of the Mississippi would also become the property of the United States. For this vast territory the Indian tribes would receive an annuity of $ 1,000 per year with payment to be made in goods with $ 600 going to the Sacs and $ 400 going to the Fox tribe. Astounding, indeed!

Whatever the parleying for the Indian prisoner amounted to, he was released and shot immediately.

The news of the treaty did not meet well with the Indian leaders up the river at Saukenuk and the five who signed it were denounced. It was with resistance to that "treaty" that Black Hawk came to the fore as the leader of those opposed to it and who refused to abide by it.

While Black Hawk entered into firm opposition to it Chief Keokuk was described as "passive." So "passive" in fact that he was denounced as a traitor and had to cross the Mississippi River to seek refuge and gain safety from his own people.

The other Indian chief mentioned heretofore was Keokuk, born in 1780 at the prominent Indian settlement known as Saukenuk. He became a rival of Black Hawk's and often disputed his methods. His mother was Lalott who is reckoned to have been either a daughter or a granddaughter of the French commander Pierre Paul Marin. He is described as having had blue eyes and his mental abilities were often given as proof of his white descent.

It was the disagreement over this treaty between Black Hawk and Keokuk that caused them to enter

into a feud that lasted for the remainder of their lives. Only old age would seem to pacify the two Indian leaders. And for 30 years the unjust treaty of 1804 caused much disruption of life along the Mississippi River.

British traders coming down into the Mississippi River valley from Canada used the treaty to fire antagonism against the United States by the Indians. Lt. Pike discovered this antagonism when he explored the upper Mississippi River valley and he warned his government about it. It would be a while before the government would act.

The U. S. government did act and sent Lt. Alpha Kingsley with a company of soldiers up the river to build both a fort and a trading post on the Iowa side of the Mississippi. He landed "about 25 miles above Le Moine" and began construction.

That was in 1808 and by 19 April 1809 the young lieutenant reported that he had accomplished his mission, completed the buildings and fortified them with a fourteen-foot palisade of sturdy oak logs set into the ground.

Fort Madison was the name Lt. Kingsley chose for his work in honor of James Madison who had become

CHIEF KEOKUK
As he appears in this picture  used
in many histories described as "Chief
Keokuk in all his finery."

the president of the United States only the month before.

While Black Hawk and the Indians who followed him could not prevent the construction of Fort Madison they determined that it should not exist for long. But in going to their winter hunting grounds below the Des Moines River they stopped at the fort-trading post and bought goods on credit.

Black Hawk and his band are reported to have plotted to destroy the fort the next spring but Lt. Kingsley learned of it and foiled it. He sent the Indians up the river with a warning. Black Hawk later admitted that he and his followers would have slain the entire unit at the fort had his plan succeeded.

Fort Madison, the original fort, finally fell to revenge-seeking Winnebago Indians in September of 1813. It was commanded then by Lt. Thomas Hamilton who escaped by night on the 4th of that month leaving the fort in ruins and with only the blackened chimneys in place.

The wars against white intrusion led by Black Hawk continued. In 1814 he led a large war party in response to a call from the British who had gained ascendancy over quite a lot of the Mississippi River valley. He and over 200 warriors drove a Lt. John Campbell from Fort Shelby near Prairie du Chien and carried away much loot in doing so.

In another such victory Black Hawk and his warriors, with the aid of the British and their big guns, defeated Major Zachary Taylor and the 334 men under his command. His British fire power was planted on the Iowa side of the river and fired effectively upon the boats carrying Major Taylor's troops. Among Black Hawk's many talents as a natural leader was a sense of military tactics which he often proved.

While Black Hawk won the affection of his British compatriots his efforts were not forgotten by the United States government. In 1816 and after the last war with Britain he was forced to sign a treaty in which he accepted the infamous 1804 instrument. He always regretted his touching "the goose quill to the treaty" and insisted that he gave away "my village."

When Black Hawk returned to Saukenuk he found the soldiers of the United States army building Fort Armstrong on Rock Island which would overlook his beloved village. A new friend, however, came to Black Hawk in the person of Colonel George Davenport who along with Antoine Le Claire, himself part Indian, befriended both white man and Indian alike.

Some years of peace prevailed up and down the great river. While Fort Madison was no more, other government forts had been erected to keep the peace. Concerning Iowa the two important ones were Fort Armstrong which guarded Rock Island and Fort Crawford at Prairie du Chien.

Black Hawk was peaceful but pensive. In his autobiography he tells of spending many hours on a high bluff above the Rock River smoking his pipe and contemplating the future of his people. Once he was beaten by three white men who intentionally accused him wrongly and he wondered how it was possible to "like such people." He lost a son and a daughter and felt the Great Spirit had come to dislike him. He mourned for his children by fasting on boiled corn and water for two years hoping thereby to regain any favor he had lost with the Great Spirit.

While the Indians were not in conflict with the white man, they did war among themselves. It is reported by Cole that some white settlers conjured up a massacre in which Pashepaho and Black Hawk and their warriors almost wiped out the tribe of Ioway Indians although there remains doubt about it.

In 1825 the United States government sponsored a large peace conference at Prairie du Chien at which representatives from Indian tribes from great distances travelled in response. They came from Wisconsin, Minnesota, Missouri and, of course, from Iowa. They finally formed a great multitude and their encampments covered a large area to include islands on the Mississippi. It is reported that the Sacs, the Foxes and the Ioways were the most conspicuous.

Chief Keokuk seemed to be the most outstanding of the chiefs always on a horse and described as "majestic and frowning."

Black Hawk was conspicuous by his absence.

The Indians were fed well and the peace pipe was smoked by Indian and white alike. The commissioners, William Clark of Missouri, and Lewis Cass of Michigan, drew boundary lines giving dominion over certain areas to certain tribes mainly the Ioways, Sacs and Foxes in the south and the Sioux in the north. Violations occurred almost at once and in 1830 another such conference was called at which a strip forty miles wide was established and this became the famous "Neutral Ground of Iowa." But it wasn't only the Indians who did not respect boundary lines, imaginary as they were. Neither did many white men.

All these years Black Hawk remained brooding in what was called his "Watch Tower." He could see the white man coveting his beloved Saukenuk and its rich cornfields. In 1827 the Indians returned from their winter hunting grounds to find that white squatters had taken possessions of Saukenuk and their fields.

When officials to include Indian agent Thomas Forsyth complained to General William Clark the squatters laughed at their orders to leave. Even the hated treaty of 1804 reserved those lands to the Indians.

Colonel George Davenport went to Washington and presented the grievances of the Indians to President Andrew Jackson himself. But "Old Hickory," one of America's great presidents and who consumed a quart of whiskey daily, was adamant. "If I remember aright this Indian chief, Black Hawk, and his band fought against us in the late war. Am I correct?" Col. Davenport had to agree with the president who retorted, "by the Eternal, every last one of them shall cross the Mississippi or be killed!" The president gave little comfort although he extended the removal of the Indians briefly. Col. Davenport, a friend to the Indians, even tried to buy Saukenuk and let the Indians remain but President

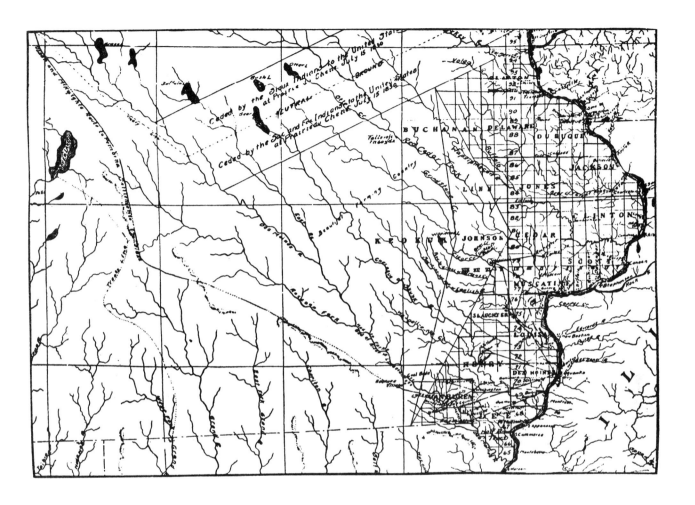

JUDSON'S 1838 MAP OF IOWA

This map of Iowa created in 1838 by Judson shows the Neutral Ground created in 1830 at the peace conference between the white man and the Indians in 1830. The diagonal strip of land had its base near Prairie du Chien and cut across the northen part of Clayton County and took in much of Fayette County. Both counties had by 1838 been created. Clayton County had some population but Fayette County had none. For further reference see Chapter XVIII, Clayton County, and Chapter XXIII, Fayette County. Other than having been placed on the maps of the period, the lines were nevertheless largely imaginary and were often violated by both the red man and the white man. Also note on this map of Judson's the extent of the surveying that had been done up to 1838. (See section surveys toward the end of Chapter VII, The Formative Years.) The above map also shows township lines as they had been surveyed. Note that Johnson County, designated for the capital, had hardly been touched. See a map in Chapter XXVI, Johnson County showing tracts that, in 1837, had delineated Indian lands. Linn County was only partially surveyed and Benton not at all up to this time in 1838.

Jackson would not hear of that.

The feud between Black Hawk and Keokuk continued anew. The passive Keokuk and the belligerent Black Hawk used different means to lead their peoples.

In 1830 Keokuk and his followers established themselves on the Iowa River but Black Hawk and his followers returned to Saukenuk to dispute the squatters' rights to live on their lands. Although the two races dwelt together for a while the tensions increased. The squatter Joshua Vandruff operated a still and sold fire water to Black Hawk's braves much to the dislike of their leader. After several drunken sprees and the quarrels between white and red that attended them, Black Hawk himself took a band of his young braves and poured many barrels of the stuff into the soil.

Vandruff was angered and went to Governor Reynolds who at first hesitated to act because Indians were wards of the federal government but when a second petition was laid before him he acted by calling for 700 mounted volunteers to remove the Indians. At that point General Edmund P. Gaines at St. Louis was brought into the situation with federal troops and he went to Fort Armstrong.

Gen. Gaines held a conference with the Indians including Keokuk, Wapello and Black Hawk who "came in a defiant mood." After much maneuvering by both state and federal units, Black Hawk was threatened with further military pursuit and forced to sign Articles of Agreement and Capitulation in which Black Hawk agreed that he and his followers would never again cross the Mississippi without permission of the president or the governor.

Black Hawk and his followers returned to Iowa and established themselves near the villages of Keokuk and Wapello. Defeated, impoverished and subdued, Black Hawk again believed all was gone for him.

In his dejected state he came under the influence of two who advised him to cross the river and make war. They were Neapope and Wabokieshiek the former a self-styled prophet and the latter a troublemaker. Their counsel to Black Hawk was that if he were to lead his braves across the Mississippi River in defiance of his latest agreement all the tribes in Illinois would rally to his cause and the British would send help from Canada. He could thereby regain the Indian lands and once again be a great chieftain.

Black Hawk liked what he heard and began to prepare for a great Indian crusade. Black Hawk was around 65 years of age at the time but the glorious visions of youth and a new greatness were still in his mind and in his heart. His first appeal was to the Foxes even while Keokuk was trying to convince him that he was being deceived.

In the spring of 1832 Black Hawk and his men, with them their women and children, journeyed along the Iowa River to Keokuk's village where he sought to gain more recruits. It has come down to us as "the War Dance on the Iowa" and is described by Cole as "one of the most spectacular episodes in the history of Iowa."

After "the Dance" Black Hawk attempted to whip his people into a frenzy for war upon the whites. Many of Keokuk's braves volunteered to follow the great Black Hawk who promised that ".....the British Father will send us not only guns....but he will also send us British soldiers to fight our battles for us."

In response to the belligerent

Indian, Chief Keokuk who was the great Indian orator of the time spoke and all listened. He agreed to follow Black Hawk on his proposed warpath on condition that "we first put our wives and children, our aged and infirm, gently to sleep in that slumber which knows no waking this side the spirit land. . . . . . For we go upon the long trail which has no turn. . . . . . This sacrifice is demanded of us by the very love we bear those dear ones."

Keokuk went on to try to persuade Black Hawk to abandon his "crooked path of ruin and destruction" and warned that his advisors were false. As Black Hawk stood in silence, Keokuk called his proposed venture "wild, visionary and desperate." Black Hawk's ears were deaf to Keokuk's logic and persuasion; his pride would not allow him to agree.

At dawn Black Hawk and his followers went down the Iowa River to the Mississippi and on 6 April 1832 the great river. It is supposed he had around 400 warriors on ponies and possibly 1,200 dependents in canoes. This was the beginning of what was to become "The Black Hawk War."

No one with a knowledge of the military would call it a "war." It has been well written that the "Indians blundered into it; and the white men blundered through it." It may have been as Theodore Roosevelt would say decades later: "It wasn't much of a war but it was the best we could get at the time."

Indeed, it wasn't much of a war but many prominent names in American and Iowa history were associated with it in one way or another. Two future presidents were involved. Zachary Taylor as a lieutenant colonel and Abraham Lincoln as a captain, later a private upon a re-enlistment.

General Winfield Scott finally commanded the army and almost became president. Jefferson Davis was a lieutenant in the regular army and saw service in Iowa; he later became president of the Confederate States of America. Albert Sidney Johnston served as adjutant to Brig. Gen. Henry Atkinson.

The greatest honors of the war were accrued to James D. Henry and Henry Dodge.

From the Black Hawk War the chief after whom it was named gained the most recognition, even fame. He is said to have "outmarched, outmaneuvered and outfought" the armies of the white man, both state and federal. Black Hawk's 400 warriors may have bested a total of 5,600 white soldiers.

The entire war was a series of hunt and chase, pursue and elude, escape and capture, more of a military hide and seek game. Something akin to army maneuvers, training. The casualties were not too great on either side until the end of the war. After the maneuvering up and down Illinois, through its rivers and forests the action moved into Wisconsin.

There was the Battle of Wisconsin Heights near the end of the "war" in which 50 of Black Hawk's men held off 600 well-equipped soldiers in what Jefferson Davis later called "one of the most brilliant military actions in history."

But the state and federal troops were better supplied with both food and ammunition and better weapons. At the same time Black Hawk's men were without good weapons, were poorly supplied and gleaned their food from the land. His men finally became a bedraggled outfit and the war turned against him after the Battle of Wisconsin Heights and prior to the Battle of Bad Axe.

Nor was the war a very long one. Black Hawk crossed the Mississippi in April and, after their many adventures, reached the river again at the mouth of the Bad Axe. His hungry and tattered band, which had often subsisted on roots and tree bark, were ready to cross when they were attacked by the steamboat "Warrior" under the command of Joseph Throckmorton. Black Hawk offered a white flag but his gesture was ignored. What happened next was one of the most ignoble deeds of the white man's war with the native Indians.

What became known as the Battle of Bad Axe amounted to a massacre.

Black Hawk and his people, many of them women and children, were trapped between the river and General Atkinson's 900 select volunteers who had crossed the Wisconsin River on 28 July 1832. Black Hawk's warriors and their women and children were entrapped. Those who got across the Mississippi were clubbed to death by Sioux Indians who had been brought to the aid of the white army. Others who got across were pursued all the way to the Red Cedar River. Their pursuers numbered the

warriors, women and children whom they'd scalped and killed at around two hundred.

Only around 150 of his warriors survived the Battle of Bad Axe. (It is marked today by monuments.) Black Hawk had been diverted from his main band in an effort to draw the army away from them. After the massacre Black Hawk and a small band of his followers fled up the great river. He found his way to a Winnebago village at Prairie La Crosse (Now LaCrosse, Wisconsin) where he made the decision to surrender himself to the "American war chief." Accompanied by several Winnebagoes Black Hawk journeyed to Prairie du Chien where he surrendered to the white victors.

There are many "accounts" of Black Hawk's "capture" but his own is substantially accurate. Others tried to claim credit for getting him. Both Jefferson Davis and Albert Sidney Johnston agreed that most were "false and fulsome." (Johnston)

Black Hawk was imprisoned at Fort Crawford and then taken to Jefferson Barracks near St. Louis where General Atkinson commanded. The chief was treated as a prisoner of war and a ball and chain were attached to his aged body. Cyrenus Cole says that Black Hawk "forgave the General for this indignity, but history has not been so lenient."

Black Hawk spent the next winter in prison under terrible circumstances but spring brought a visit from his wife and daughter who were accompanied by both Chief Keokuk and Colonel Davenport. In disgust at the horrible fate that had become his adversary, Keokuk asked President Jackson to release him.

President Jackson's response was to order Black Hawk brought to Washington and the two old men met face to face in the White House. The president then ordered Black Hawk taken to Fortress Monroe where he was finally well-treated by his new jailor, Col. Abram Eustis. When Black Hawk left Fortress Monroe the colonel put on a large dinner for the former Indian leader at which Black Hawk is said to have delivered a classical oration.

Col. Eustis appointed Major John Garland to accompany Black Hawk and the other Indians who had come with him back to Rock Island. On their return trip they went through Baltimore where Black Hawk is said to have made his good-bye to President Jackson and the cities of Philadelphia, New York, Albany, Buffalo and Detroit. All along the way and in every city crowds turned out to see the former "scourge of the frontier."

Black Hawk was feted to State dinners, theatre performances and other occasions where he soon became a celebrity. Great orators of the time, we are told, acclaimed him a hero and a martyr. Apparently even then many were disgusted with the treatment accorded the Indians, especially if they were aware of Gen. Harrison's infamous treaty of 1804.

What was scheduled to be merely an escorted journey home turned out to be a triumphal march. But the parades, receptions and accolades along the way did not match the final welcome he received at Rock Island.

Keokuk, his former adversary had become the great Chief of the Sac Indians and prepared a gigantic welcome for Black Hawk to include flags, decorations, great cheering and a throng of boats resting on the Mississippi carrying well-wishers. In a formal ceremony, Black Hawk was given his freedom. Major Garland gave a huge farewell party at which white and red man smoked the peace

CHIEF KEOKUK

pipe together and drank champagne. Many speeches praised Black Hawk as a genuine hero of his people and his aged eyes often filled with tears as he listened intently. Keokuk drank a wine toast to Black Hawk and "spoke in his happiest vein."

Black Hawk responded with humility, thanked everyone for their kindness and uttered forgiveness for his former opponents. His had been an adventurous life and his triumphal journey home had been the high point of it.

The next morning he arose to begin his final journey home, back to the Iowa River and his "little house."

Finally Black Hawk composed all his memories into what became his own autobiography. He had the assistance of Antoine Le Claire and a Rock Island newspaperman named John B. Patterson. The three men worked with Black Hawk remembering, Antoine Le Claire translating and Patterson doing the actual writing.

The book was published in Boston in 1834 and is called by Cole "a repository of the legends and and traditions, the myths, and even the fairy stories of his race." The book was reprinted several times and it may have been Iowa's first book.

Black Hawk didn't want to be remembered as a "bad Indian" and wrote to "give my motives and reasons for my former hostilities to the whites, and to vindicate my character from misrepresentation."

Black Hawk peacefully resumed his life along the Iowa River in the "little house" in which he'd planned what became the Black Hawk War.

He would spend some years of peace and harmony there and live to the allotted three score and ten, dying on 3 October 1838. He was suitably buried in the Indian tradition but not many were at his funeral as they were away. Even in death Black Hawk was not to have immediate peace. It is reported by historian Thwaites whom we quote elsewhere in this volume tht a travelling physician stole Black Hawk's skeleton and put it on public exhibit for a fee.

An indignant public demanded that the bones of Black Hawk not be so maltreated and there was a public outcry about the desecration. So much so that finally the old chief's skeleton was given over to the State of Iowa for safe-keeping. After a time the building in which Black Hawk's bones reposed was destroyed by fire and thus they, too, were burned beyond saving.

The Indians have been a part of the history of both America and Iowa. Yet Iowa has her own prominent Indian leaders. Among them were Keokuk, Wapello and Black Hawk who became the best known. His name is well remembered and it is appended to many sites and even a county was named for him after his death and upon its creation by the Territorial Legislature.

The Black Hawk Treaty and the Black Hawk Purchase, an integral part of the treaty, are discussed in several later chapters.

CHIEF WAPELLO
One of the prominent early Indian leaders. Both a city and a county are named after him, among others.

# After Bad Axe ---
# A Strange Story

Recall that after the Battle of Bad Axe, Black Hawk and the bedraggled remnant of his followers went northward to Prairie La Crosse. Only about 150 warriors remained and not near the women and children who started on the warpath with him. After Black Hawk decided to surrender himself by going to the "white chief" at Prairie du Chien, his warriors and other followers were leaderless and left on their own so to speak. Their longings, of course, were for their homelands down in Iowa and they started for them. They did not stay as a united group but divided into several groups.

The following information that is factually and historically correct was provided for this volume by a well-known historian from Monticello in Jones County, Mr. "Gus" Norlin, who obtained it from a reliable and historic source.

It seems that around 80 Indians who were part of the followers of Black Hawk at the time of his voluntary surrender journeyed back down into Iowa and located along the Maquoketa River which runs through Jones County. The area they had chosen was but a few miles east of the area that would become Monticello near Dale's Mill crossing.

One of their problems and the ones that excited the interest of the federal authorities was that they encamped on the north side of the Maquoketa and they should have settled south of it, that river being one of many such boundaries. There are two aspects to this encampment and the story that evolves from it.

While the former followers of Black Hawk remained there, some of them died. Some were reported to have drowned when the river flooded. The ones who died were buried in a burial ground chosen by the Indians.

Today's monument to Battle of Bad Axe between Prairie du Chien and La Crosse, Wisconsin. A monument to a massacre of Indians. (Photo by Susan Woodson.)

An early pioneer settler later learned of the small burying ground but kept it a secret telling about it to only his own family. After many generations the remaining descendant of that early settler imparted the location of the burial ground to Mr. Norlin only because he knew of the Norlin interest in history and also because he felt that knowledge of it should remain with someone. Mr. and Mrs. Norlin both found the grave sites just as it was explained to them. And they found the squares of stones Black Hawk's Indians had laid out around those early graves to mark them.

Today, in 1988, only three living persons know the exact site of that ancient Indian burial plot. The secret they keep allows the Indians to rest in peace, their graves undisturbed by anyone. Probably that is as it should be.

The other aspect surrounding that Indian encampment on the Maquoketa in Jones County centers about their settling on the north side of the river when the government wanted them on the south side.

It is a matter of record that one Jefferson Davis, who served in the Black Hawk War, issued orders to one Captain A. Lincoln to take his company of volunteers across the Mississippi River and go to Fountain Falls (now Cascade, Ia.) and drive the Indians across the Maquoketa River.

It was later learned that Captain A. Lincoln had been discharged nine days before. Records show there was only one A. Lincoln and only one Captain A. Lincoln in military service. So the "Captain A. Lincoln" can only have been the Abraham Lincoln who later became the 16th president.

Yet there is no record in history or in the annals of the Black Hawk War that Captain Lincoln ever did cross the Mississippi and drive the Black Hawk remnant across the Maquoketa River to its south shore. Legend may have it that he did but it has not been reported nor proven. That Jefferson Davis issued the order to do so to one "Captain A. Lincoln" is a matter of military record.

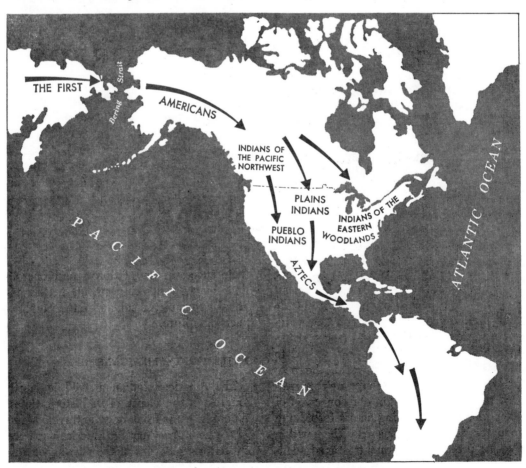

THE FIRST AMERICANS IN THE NEW WORLD

# Chapter Three
# UNDER SEVERAL FLAGS

Who can say who were the first white men to set foot upon the soil of what is now the state of Iowa? There is ample evidence in both legend and supposition plus some reasonably well-proven facts to substantiate that the Scandinavians explored the north central portion of the North American continent long before Columbus made his accidental discovery of the "novus mundus."

In 1898 a farmer near Kensington, Minnesota, found an unusual slab of rock with strange language-like markings carved into it. That while trying to uproot a poplar tree on the side of a hill formed by a glacier. It was 30 inches long by 17 inches wide and its thickness measured seven inches; it weighed 230 pounds. Upon the stone were inscribed what was subsequently determined by scholars to be Runic characters such as had been used centuries before by the Germanic and Scandinavian peoples. The piece became known as the Kensington Rune Stone, or just the Kensington Stone.

As later deciphered by those of learning there was a tale written into the stone telling of the slaying of ten of a party of "eight Goths (Swedes) and twenty-two Norsemen" which occurred while the remainder of their party were fishing for food.

It bears the date of the year 1362.

There is also the supposition that Norsemen made their way down into Iowa many centuries ago and especially into northwest Iowa. Much in the area of Peterson, Iowa, in O'Brien county suggests this possibility and that will be recorded in a later volume.

KENSINGTON RUNESTONE
AD 1362

That "Columbus discovered America" has been a theme of history teachers almost since education in America began. Over the years so much evidence has come to light that disproves that "Columbus discovered America" that it seems all but impossible to erase the supposition. Certainly Norsemen were on the North American continent long before Columbus was born and that evidence goes back to the ninth and tenth centuries. There is the Kensington Rune Stone discussed in this chapter. Out in northwestern Iowa and elsewhere in both Iowa and Minnesota cases may be made that Norsemen, or someone of European descent, traversed the rivers until they were deep inland. It is estimated that the Indians came over to the North American continent 12,000 years before the birth of Christ. And evidence prevails that they went all across the continent and down into Central and South America. Others try to make a case that the ancient Romans made it to Central America and use as support for their ideas the architecture and clothing depicted on ancient Mayan and other artwork. History tends to cloud much in oblivion but man's search for his past goes on and on and discoveries are constantly made. Perhaps Columbus' accomplishment was the timing for it is said that Europe was ready. His discovery did in most ways mean the beginning of Europe's interest in the New World. Legend has it that he finally proved the world was round but his real problem was his estimation of the width of the oceans. For what he did, Columbus is given his due credit. For being the first man to discover the "novus mundus" credit goes to the Norsemen and the Indians many thousands of years before them.

Regardless of legend and any other evidence it is certain that the first white men of record to set foot upon the soil of Iowa were Father Marquette and Louis Joliet (sometimes spelled in earlier histories as Jolliet) who came down the Wisconsin river in 1673. They first saw Iowa at the confluence of the Wisconsin and Mississippi rivers at the site of what is present day McGregor. It was on June 17th of that year that Marquette and Joliet and their party of five other men disembarked from their canoes and set foot at the base of (now) Pike's Peak in northeastern Clayton county.

As recorded earlier the explorers didn't stay long at McGregor. After landing on the flat area beneath what is now Pike's Peak, they made a meal from the provisions they carried or from wild animals killed for food. They ate their meals on the shore and slept in their boats with one of the party always awake and keeping the watch. They had been warned that there were savage Indians in the area and remained on alert.

Marquette and Joliet sailed down the Mississippi with their small party and are supposed to have disembarked

JOLIET

at the plains upon which now stand Dubuque and Burlington. They went inland at Toolesboro in Louisa County and inland again beyond where the town of Montrose is now located. At Burlington and Dubuque they found the flat pieces of prairie secluded on the west and above them by tall bluffs. They had been warned about unfriendly Indians but always seemed to find the ones they met agreeable.

Marquette and Joliet had once only heard of the great river they now explored. The French governor at Montreal in Canada had long been desirous of knowing what lay to the west and to ascertain certain verifications of what he had heard. He therefore decided upon an expedition.

To accomplish his goals the governor chose Louis Joliet, a fur trader who had been born in Quebec and was therefore a French Canadian. For Joliet's partner the governor selected Pere Jacques Marquette, a missionary priest born and educated in France. The pair spent the winter of 1673 at St. Ignace in northern Michigan making preparations for their journey. They made as good a map as was possible at the time, much of it from recollection and heresay.

MARQUETTE

Their "fleet" consisted of two birch bark canoes with a more sturdy spruce and cedar framework. They employed five trustworthy woodsmen familiar with living in the wilds. Joliet dressed in buckskin and Father Marquette wore his black cloth gown and carried his rosary. The canoes were loaded with corn, smoked buffalo meat, blankets, guns, eating utensils, other instruments and elegant trinkets for trading with the Indians or to be used for gifts.

The group of seven paddled out of the bay at St. Ignace and onto Lake Michigan. They went to Green Bay and ascended the Fox River. They carried their canoes and supplies over land and through woods to the Wisconsin River and then floated down it until, on 17 June 1673, they came to the great "father of waters," the Mississippi. Across it they got their first glimpse of Iowa, the beautiful land. It was of such beauty, Father Marquette wrote in his account of the voyage, that he "could not express it."

Thus the small expedition which had set out from the Straits of Mackinac a month earlier, on 17 May 1673, had reached the great river which was one of its objectives.

Certainly the French governor back at Montreal had other things in mind, other than exploration and knowledge to include converting the savage Indians to the Christian (Catholic) religion. It was a desire to extend the fur trade, to discover mines of gold, silver, lead and copper that was predominant. Four years earlier French representatives had counseled with the various Indian tribes at Sault Ste. Marie and agreement had been reached that all the regions were the possessions of King Louis XIV. It was then that the Indians gave accounts of the great river to the west the "great ware" or "Missipi". It was at first thought that the Indians meant the Pacific Ocean.

But Marquette and Joliet made the first journey and it was the Mississippi River that they found; the Pacific Ocean was half a continent beyond them. And so they floated downstream until they "safely entered the Mississippi on the seventeenth of June, with a joy that I cannot express," as Marquette recorded in his journal.

Marquette and Joliet floated down the Mississippi and their exploits and adventures are recorded elsewhere in this volume. Where they set foot upon Iowa soil will always remain a matter of conjecture. By habit and for reasons of personal safety they made fires on the shores of Iowa and possibly even Illinois to cook their meals. Not knowing the nature of the Indians but having heard they could be dangerous, they slept on the river in their canoes by night. Thus it might be presumed they set foot upon Iowa soil at many locations. Their inland trek within what is now Louisa County is recorded. Most of

The first sight of Iowa probably seen by Marquette and Joilet; a 1929 photograph from Julegranen as published in an early history by Dr. Thomas P. Christensen.

their short stops on the banks of the river were not recorded. It has to be presumed they set foot upon Clayton County soil first for no such expedition would come so far and not, hungry, tired and yet elated, not make such an effort. We see **Dubuque and other points as more than probably stopping-off places for meals and short exploration as probable of the plains that existed.** The group would never have tried to make camp where steep bluffs prohibited them. Yet all that remains speculation. Probable speculation?

The significance of the mission of Marquette and Joliet was to bring the interests of the Europeans into the area of the Upper Mississippi and the lands west of it.

From our "mystery writer" of the first two chapters of this volume we take up once more quoting as follows:

"In 1765 the total number of French families within in the limits of the Northwestern Territory did not probably exceed 600. These were in settlements about Detroit, along the river Wabash and the Neighborhood of Fort Chartres on the Mississippi. Of these families, about 80 or 90 re-sided at Post Vincennes, 14 at Fort Quiatenon, on the Wabash, and nine or ten at the confluence of the St. Mary and St. Joseph rivers.

"The colonial policy of the British government opposed any measures which might strengthen settlements in the interior of this country, lest they become self-supporting and independent of the mother country; hence the early and rapid settlement of the Northwestern Territory was still further retarded by the short-sighted selfishness of England. That fatal policy consisted mainly in holding the land in the hands of the government, and not allowing it to be subdivided and sold to settlers. But in spite of all her efforts in this direction, she constantly made just such efforts as provoked the American people to rebel, and to rebel successfully, which was within 15 years after the perfect close of the French and Indian war.

"Thomas Jefferson, the shrewd statesman and wise Governor of Virginia, saw from the first that actual occupation of western lands was the only way to keep them out of the hands of foreigners and Indians. Therefore, directly after the conquest of Vincennes, by Clark, he engaged a scientific corps to proceed under an escort to the Mississippi, and ascertain by celestial observations the point on that river intersected by latitude 36 degrees 30' the southern limit of the State, and to measure its distance to the Ohio. To Gen. Clark was entrusted the conduct of the military operations in that quarter. He was instructed to select a strong position near that point and establish there a fort and garrison; thence to extend his conquests northward to the lakes, erecting forts at different points, which might serve as monuments of actual possession, besides affording protection to that portion of the country. Fort "Jefferson" was erected and garrisoned on the Mississippi a few miles above the southern limit.

"The result of these operations was the addition to the chartered limits of Virginia, of that immense region known as the Northwestern Territory. The simple fact that such forts were established by the Americans in this vast region convinced the British commissioners that we had entitled ourselves to the land. But where are those "monuments" of our power now?

## HISTORY OF LOUISIANA TERRITORY
Louisiana Province.

The province of Louisiana stretched from the Gulf of Mexico to the sources of the Tennessee, the Kanawha, the Alleghany and the Monongahela on the east, and the Missouri and the other great tributaries of the Father of Waters on the west. Says Bancroft: "France had obtained, under Providence, the guardianship of this immense district, not as it proved, for her own benefit, but rather as a trustee for the infant nation by which it was one day to be inherited. By the treaty of Utrecht, France ceded to England her possessions in Hudson's Bay, Newfoundland and Nova Scotia. France still retained Louisiana, but the province had so far failed to meet the expectations of the crown and the people that a change in the government and policy of the country was deemed indispensable. Accordingly, in 1711, the province was placed in the hands of a governor-general, with headquarters at Mobile. This government was of a short duration, and in 1712 a charter was granted to Anthony Crozat, a wealthy merchant of Paris, giving him

the entire control and monopoly of all the trade and resources of Louisiana. But this scheme also failed. Crozat met with no success in his commerical operations; every Spainish harbor on the Gulf was closed against his vessels; the occupation of Louisiana was deemed an encroachment on Spanish territory; Spain was jealous of the ambition of France.

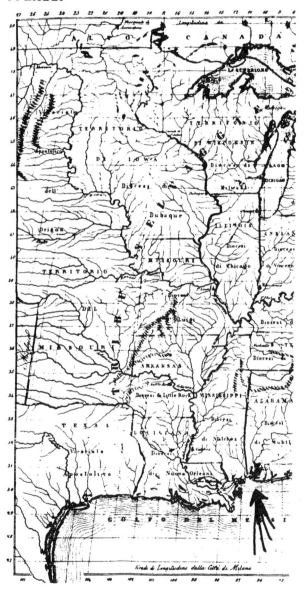

In the early 1700s the land that was to become Iowa was technically governed from far-off Mobile in Alabama from where Spain tried to make French encroachment difficult.

94

"Crozat failing to open the ports of the district, sought to develop the internal resources of Louisiana, by causing trading posts to be opened, and explorations to be made to its remotest borders. But he actually accomplished nothing for the advancement of the colony. The only prosperity which it ever possessed grew out of the enterprise of humble individuals, who had succeeded in instituting a little barter between themselves and the natives, and a petty trade with neighboring European settlements. After a persevering effort of nearly five years, he surrendered his charter in August, 1717.

ANTHONY CROZAT

"Another and more magnificent scheme immediately followed the surrender of Crozat's charter. The national government of France was deeply involved in debt; the colonies were nearly bankrupt, and John Law appeared on the scene with his famous Mississippi Company, as the Louisiana branch of the Bank of France. The charter granted to this company gave it a legal existence of 25 years, and conferred upon it more **extensive powers and privileges** than had been granted to Crozat. It invested the new company with the exclusive privilege of the entire commerce of Louisiana and of new France, and authorized to monopolize all the trade in the country, to make treaties with the Indians, to declare and prosecute war, to grant lands, erect forts, open mines of precious metals, levy taxes, nominate civil officers, commission those of the army, to appoint and remove judges, to cast cannon, and build and equip ships of war. All this was to be done with the paper currency of John Law's Bank of France. He had succeeded in getting His Majesty, the French king, to adopt and sanction his scheme of financial operations, both in France and in the colonies, and probably there never was such a huge financial bubble ever blown by a visionary theorist. Still such was the condition of France that it was accepted as a national deliverance, and Law became the most powerful man in France. He became a Catholic, and was appointed Comptroller General of Finance.

"The first move of the new company was to send 800 emigrants to Louisiana, who arrived at Dauphine Island in 1718. In 1719, Philipe Francis Renault arrived in Illinois, with 200 miners and artisans. The war between France and Spain at this time rendered it extremely probable that the Mississippi Valley might become the theatre of Spanish hostilities against the French settlements. To prevent this, as well as to extend French claims, a shain of forts was begun to keep open the connection between the mouth and the sources of the Mississippi. Fort Orleans, high up the river, was erected as an outpost in 1720.

"The Mississippi scheme was at the zenith of its power and glory in January, 1720, but the gigantic bubble collapsed more suddenly than it had been inflated, and the company was declared hopelessly bankrupt in May following. France was impoverished by it, both private and public credit were overthrown, capitalists suddenly found themselves paupers, and labor was left without employment. The effect on the colony of Louisiana was disastrous.

"Heretofore, Louisiana had been a subordinate dependence, under the jurisdiction of the Governor-general of Canada. Early in the year 1723 the province of Louisiana was erected into an independent government, and it was divided into nine districts for civil and military purposes.

"Notwithstanding the company had embarked largely in agriculture, and had established large plantations on the river, still it refused to abandon the idea of discovering boundless wealth in the mines of Missouri. They still believed that gold and silver mines were to be found in the Illinois country. Desire begets credulity; and the directory, ever ready to receive and encourage extravagant accounts of mines, offered rewards proportionate to the importance of the discovery. In this way the attention of the company was diverted to the search of mines in distant regions, as far as the sources of the St. Peter's, the Arkansas, the tributaries of the Missouri, and even to the Rocky Mountains, while they neglected the increasing hostile indications among the Chickasaws, the Natchez and other tribes immediately contiguous to their principal settlements.

In Chapter Eight of "THE MONEY AND THE POWER" by this author (c.1984) John Law's "money system" was treated at length. The following is a direct quotation from that book explaining John Law's money scheme.

"Renowned in the annals of early banking for showing what can be a miserable failure in the creation of "money" is the story of John Law. A Scotsman who had run through his inheritance, he arrived in France in 1716. John Law had what he regarded as a unique idea for a land bank that would issue paper notes to borrowers against the security of land. Before arriving in France he had proposed his plan in Scotland, Holland and Italy where it had been met without enthusiasm.

"France seemed to be wide open for such a scheme as his. Louis XIV (L'etat c'est moi) had died the year before after a very long reign. The government was in bad shape and its expenses were reported to be twice what it took in. The Duc de Saint-Simon had intelligently suggested the only straight forward solution: national bankruptcy! He was serving as Regent for the young seven year-old Louis XV.

JOHN LAW . . .                    Financial genius?

"Then John Law arrived on the scene. He reportedly had met Philippe, le Duc de Saint-Simon, some years earlier in a house of gambling where le Duc was supposed to have been "impressed with the Scotsman's financial genius." Whether or not "financial genius" shows forth in gambling houses is a matter of question; but, Law's willingness to gamble, especially with the money of others, is not in any doubt.

"On 2 May 1716, John Law and his brother were granted permission by nothing less than royal edict to start a bank with a capital of 6,000,000 livres equal to about 250,000 English pounds. The bank was further authorized to issue notes. It did exactly that and the first and main borrower was the government which used the notes to pay its expenses and to satisfy creditors. The notes were decreed to be legal tender for the payment of taxes.

"At the outset the notes were acceptable for anything, not just taxes. Law promised redemption in the currency of the weight of metal behind the notes at the date of their issuance. (As had been done so many times before in the history of money, the kings of France had reduced the metal behind the money with the fool idea in mind that less gold or silver would be to their financial benefit).

"Thus, the public perceived that Law and his banque were providing

LOUIS XV, the young king, too inexperienced to govern and surrounded by inept and corrupt advisors, allowed the fiat money practices of John Law to devastate France's economy.

security against royal debasement and for a while the notes actually commanded a premium! All assumed that a noble thing had been done. **The financial condition of the monarchy was better; prosperity reigned triumphant for a while.** The notes that were loaned to the government were put back in circulation paying for its (exorbitant) needs and much more was loaned to private enterprise which brought about the first real business revival in some time.

"So successful did the banque become that John Law was held in high regard for his "financial genuis" and he subsequently opened branch banques in Lyons, Tours, Amiens, La Rochelle and Orleans. The banque became a public institution, chartered by the crown, and was then the Banque Royale!

"**The first loans and the first notes issued were so successful that** Philippe the Regent suggested another issue. Like the first drink to a boozer; if the first is that good why not try another? John Law and the Banque Royale agreed and the second was like unto the first. Recognizing that there would have to be some means of backing up the growing volume of printed paper notes, Law went back to the original idea he had brought to France after unsuccessfully running it by the bankers of Holland, Italy and Scotland. That was to create a vast land development in America, the Mississippi Company, which was to mine and return to France the huge gold deposits under the ground of the Louisiana Territory. Part of the plan was to "go public," to place the stock of the company on the market. That was done and the French people gobbled up the issue. The stock rose so rapidly that many became millionaires within weeks. The Mississippi

Company (Campagnie d'Occident) was tied in with the Banque Royale in their mutual fates.

"In the spring of 1719, the banque had over 100 million livres in loans outstanding. By summer there were 300 million outstanding and by the end of the year, 800 million! The proceeds from the sale of the stock that were to develop the Louisiana wilderness didn't end up at the Mississippi at all; they went to pay for the excesses of the French government! Only some interest on the loans ever went toward that. John Law was making loans on notes of the Banque Royale to the government and other private borrowers who passed them on in payment of government debt and expense. Notes were used to buy stock in the Mississippi Company; the proceeds went to the government to pay creditors who used the money to buy stock in the company. Each cycle getting ever larger and repititious the more perceptive wondered which was the worst investment, the government or the Louisiana swamps.

"At the high tide of the thing, Law was regarded as the most important man in all France. He was regarded as a financial genius of the first order. In all his glory he even attempted to turn to social reforms. He was even made the Duc d'Arkansas! On 5 January 1720 he was made Comptroller General of France.

"But, as in all such efforts --- whether the pharoahs debasing the coinage or the U. S. Federal Reserve System --- the outstanding notes, the fiat money, continued to be the problem. Once the public perceived them to be irredeemable, John Law's house of cards began to fall. The first demands saw redemption; soon that was impossible. Finally it was necessary to restrict payment in

specie altogether. The big boom was over. Law tried to use his official capacity as Comptroller General and restrict the possession of gold and silver, even for jewelry, but that is always a last ditch effort. The crowds so jammed the Banque Royale to get their money and on more than one occasion people were squeezed to their deaths!

"Law suddenly ceased being a financial genius. The Regent who had first recognized his "financial genius" back at the gambling parlor sneaked the last Comptroller General out of France to save his life. He died in poverty in Venice, 'Decent poverty', we are told. His fiat paper money notes were put to 'the most **ignoble use to which paper can be applied,**' according to author Charles Mackay."

(THE MONEY AND THE POWER by Donald L. Kimball, pp. 65-69, Copyright 1984; pub. by Trends & Events Publications.)

"The year 1723 also witnessed the first outbreak among the Indians. This was by the Natchez, a peaceful tribe who were cruelly treated by the French. The Natchez were subdued for a time, but in 1729, with the Chickasaws and others, fell upon the

French village of St. Catharine and massacred the whole male population; two soldiers only, who happened to be in the woods, escaped, to bear the tidings to New Orleans. The colonies on the Yazoo and on the Washita suffered the same fate; more than 200 were killed; 92 women and 155 children were taken prisoner.

"This massacre and consequent war was disastrous in the extreme. The province had been in the most prosperous condition. The company had controlled it for 11 years, and raised it from a few hundred idle, indolent and improvident settlers around the Bay of Mobile, and along the coast west of that place, to a flourishing colony of several thousand souls, many of whom were industrious, enterprising and productive citizens. But now New Orleans and the other settlements presented for a time a scene of general commotion and consternation. They speedily recovered themselves, however, and at once took measures to completely crush the Indians, and prevent future trouble of the kind. This, however, was a difficult task, and required three years of constant war. The result was complete victory for the French. The Natchez were never more known as a tribe, the scattered remnants seeking asylum among the Chickasaws and other tribes hostile to the French. Yet no tribe has left so proud a memorial of their courage, their rights and liberties. The city of Natchez is their monument, standing upon the field of their glory. In refinement and intelligence, they were equal if not superior, to any other tribe north of Mexico. In courage and stratagem they were inferior to none.

"To the great joy of the whole province, a partial and temporary peace now succeeded. But the company had been involved in enormous expenses in this war. Their trade with the Indians, too, was diminished and less profitable. The state of things following upon the disasters consequent upon Law's failure, alarmed the directory, who, believing that they were not secure from similar disasters in the future, determined to surrender their charter into the hands of the crown, and abandon the further prosecution of their scheme. Their petition was readily granted, and on April 10, 1732, the king issued his proclamation, declaring the province of Louisiana free to all his subjects, with equal privileges as to trade and commerce.

"During the 15 years from 1717 to 1732 the province had increased in population from 700 to 5,000, and the improvement in character and prosperity had been equally marked. Settlements had sprung up farther inland. The Illinois and Wabash countries, comprising all the settlements on the Upper Mississippi, from "Fort Chartres" and Kaskaskia eastward to the Wabash, and south of Lake Michigan, contained many flourishing settlements devoted to agriculture and the Indian trade.

"From 1732 till 1764, the end of

French dominion in Louisiana, the province was was under royal governors. M. Perrier held this office for two years, and in 1734 Bienville, who had served before, and had been successful in his treatment of the Indians, was again commissioned governor and commandant-general of Louisiana. Bienville, though old, still thirsted for military fame, and desired to chastise the Indians who had sympathized with the Natchez. He demanded from the Chickasaws the surrender of the Natchez refugees. This being refused, he determined to punish the Chickasaws. Then ensued several years of war, with here and there a peaceful interval. At last peace was established, on terms unfavorable to Bienville and the French. Bienville, who for 40 years, short intervals excepted, had ably managed Louisiana was recalled in the spring of 1740. His public career ended under a cloud of censure, and the disapprobation of his sovereign. The Marquis de Vaudreuil succeeded Bienville as governor. During the latter's administration, in spite of the continual Indian wars, the province had gradually increased in wealth and population. About this time cotton, the fig-tree, the orange-tree, and other tropical products were introduced into the province.

"For the 10 years from 1741 to 1751 the settlements were comparatively free from Indian hostilities. Relieved from danger and apprehension of Indian violence, agriculture continued to flourish, and commerce, freed from the shackles of monopolies, began rapidly to extend its influence and to multiply its objects under the stimulus of individual enterprise. Sugar-cane was first cultivated in 1751.

"In 1752, the Indians, instigated by the English, began to be troublesome again. De Vaudreuil made a partially successful expedition against them, and the trouble was temporarily at an end. In 1753, De Vaudreuil was promoted to the government of Canada, and M. Kerlerec succeeded him as governor of Louisiana. The following year witnessed the beginning of long war between France and England for the possession of the Mississippi Valley. This contest was waged for eight years with varied success, until finally the tide of war set in favor of Great Britian, and France was compelled at length to surrender first one, and then another of her military positions in New France; and at last, driven by stern necessity, the king sought

North America after 1763.

peace at the expense of a treaty which confirmed to Great Britian the whole of Canada and the eastern half of Louisiana. Although Louisiana was thus concerned in this war, her remote situation secured her from the horrors of actual war, and she continued to prosper. She suffered, however, from another flood of irredeemable paper money.

100

"Hostilities between the great powers ceased in 1762, and a treaty of peace was ratified the following year, according to which France ceded all her territory east of the Mississippi to Great Britian.

"In the meantime, she had made a secret treaty with Spain, ceding all the residue of Louisiana, that is, all west of the Mississippi, to that power. So that from this time the valley of the Mississippi was virtually divided between the two great European powers of Great Britian and Spain. The dominion of the

DON O'REILLY . . . Spanish governor.

former was destined to be of short duration, and to be superceded by a new power heretofore unknown, a power which was ultimately to swallow up the dominion of Spain also. This new power was to be the United States of America, the land of freedom and the rights of man, the bulwark of human liberty and the asylum for the oppressed.

"The boundaries of Western, or Spanish, Louisiana, after the dismemberment, comprised, as we have already stated, all that vast unknown region west of the Mississippi River, from its sources to the Gulf of Mexico, and extending westward to the extreme sources of all its great western tributaries among the Rocky Mountains. It included also the island of New Orleans east of the Mississippi, and south of the bay of Iberville. The French inhabitants were so loath to be brought under Spanish rule, and manifested so much dissatisfaction, that his Catholic majesty did not insist on actual possession until two years after the cession. Even then, the prospect for disturbance was so alarming that Don Ulloa, the Spanish governor, deemed it best to withdraw to Cuba. Not until 1769, when a formidable army arrived from Spain, was the province formally occupied by the Spanish authorities, and the French flag lowered at New Orleans. Thus was Louisiana forever lost to France. During the 70 years of colonial dependence on France, it had slowly augmented its population, from a few destitute fishermen and hunters to a flourishing colony of 13,540 souls. The exports at this time were valued at $250,000 annually.

"The first act of Don O'Reilly, the new governor, was to order a complete census of the city of New Orleans. This showed an aggregate of 3,190 souls. The total number of houses was 468. The population at this same time of eastern Louisiana, now called under British rule, West Florida, was about 1,500.

"Up to this date but few settlements had been made on the west bank of the Mississippi above the mouth of the Ohio. The most important of these was St. Louis, begun in 1764.

"O'Reilly ruled with a despotic hand, and began by punishing some of the prominent citizens for the discontent they had manifested. Five were shot, others were imprisoned. He then introduced Spanish courts, laws, language and customs. Though his government was severe, it was on the whole salutary for the people. Confidence once restored, immigrants began to flock in large numbers from Spain. O'Reilly was recalled after one year, however, and was succeeded by Don Antonio Maria Bucarelly as Captain-General but the administration was supervised by Unzaga, Captain-General of Cuba, who was really an intermediate between the crown and the king's officers in Louisiana. Under his mild and judicious rule, Louisiana flourished and grew rapidly. St. Louis, at the end of his administration, was already an important town, with a population of 800.

"Unzaga was succeeded Jan. 1, 1777, by Don Bernard de Galvez. This was at the time when the colonies were making their great struggle for independence. As a Spaniard, De Galvez had no predilection for English rule, and his sympathies were enlisted for the colonies. The United States procured many military supplies through their agent in New Orleans. In fact, Spain and France recognized the independence of the United States, and joined in actual war with Great Britain. De Galvez, now General Galvez, in 1779 commenced by attacking the English posts in West Florida. In this he was successful, and before the end of the war, all of West Florida was in possession of the Spanish.

"During these Spanish successes in Florida, an attempt was made by the British commandant at Michilimackinac to invade Louisiana from the north, and he marched against St. Louis with 140 troops and 1,400 Indians. They encamped within a few miles of St. Louis, and began a regular Indian investment of the place, which had been temporarily fortified. During the siege the inhabitants sent a special request to Col. Clark, then commanding at Kaskaskia, to come to their relief. He immediately marched to the Mississippi, a few miles below St. Louis. He remained here until the 6th of May (this was in 1780), when the grand Indian attack was made. Clark crossed the river, and marched up to the town to take part in the engagement. The sight of the "Long-knives," as the Americans were called, caused the savages to abandon the attack and seek safety in flight. They reproached the British commandant with duplicity in having assured them that he would march them to fight the Spaniards only, whereas now they were brought against the Spaniards and the Americans. They soon afterward abandoned the British standard, and returned to their towns. Such was the invasion of Upper Louisiana in 1780 from the north.

"By the peace of 1783 all of East and West Florida were confirmed to Spain and thus terminated the last vestige of British power upon the Lower Mississippi, after an occupancy of 19 years.

"Relieved from the danger and privations of active warfare, the country began to prosper once more. Immigration once more set in. In the spring of 1785 a complete census was taken by order of Governor Galvez, which showed the population of Louisiana to be 33,000 exclusive of Indians.

"In the summer following, Galvez was promoted Captain-General of Cuba, and he left Don Estevan Miro as temporary governor until someone could be regularly appointed by the king.

## DON BERNARD DE GALVEZ
### Captain-General of Cuba

"In this year an attempt was made by the Catholic authorities to introduce the inquisition in Louisiana and a priest in New Orleans was appointed "Commissary of the Holy Office" in that city. Governor Miro, instructed by the king, forbade him to exercise the duties of his office. The Reverend Father, deeming it his duty to obey his spiritual rather than his temporal master, was then summarily seized at night, conveyed safely on board a vessel about to sail for Spain, and before daylight the next morning he was on his way to Europe. This was the first and the only attempt to establish the inquistion in Louisiana. The following year, 1786, Miro was confirmed as Governor by the king. Under his wise administration the province continued to enjoy a high degree of prosperity.

"It was about this time that the Spanish began to feel the encroachments of the United States. A portion of eastern Louisiana was claimed by the State of Georgia, as well as the Spanish. Then, too, the trade of the Mississippi was subject to various duties and annoyances by the Spaniards. For two or three years the Spaniards pursued a conciliatory course with regard to the Mississippi. They then began to vigorously enforce the revenue laws, and were only checked by a threatened invasion from Kentucky. From 1788 on, the Spanish government continually schemed to extend its possessions, and to hold its own against the rapidly growing United States.

"In the year 1792, Governor Miro was promoted to the Mexican provinces and succeeded in Louisiana by Baron de Carondelet. In 1793-'94 the French minister to the United States (France and Spain being at war) endeavored to arouse the west, and provoke a hostile attack on Louisiana, This attempt failed, and the minister, Genet, was recalled, at the request of the Federal Government.

"To conciliate the feelings of the Western people, Carondelet relaxed the restrictions upon the river trade, and peace and harmony ensued. The Spaniards continued to intrigue, however, with the Westerners, with a view to winning them over from the United States to Spain, and until 1795 were thus engaged. In this year all difficulties were settled by a formal treaty, known as the "Treaty of Madrid." This provided for the trade of the Mississippi, and fixed definite boundaries between the

United States and Louisiana. It turned out, however, that this treaty was only a measure of policy with Spain, and she still coveted the West. The fixing of the boundaries by survey and the surrender of certain posts, were delayed in such a way that the bad faith of the Spaniards became apparent to all. Troublesome negotiations and threats of war followed, and not until the middle of 1798 were the provisions of the treaty actually carried out.

"In 1797 Gayos De Lemos became governor-general of Louisiana. In the following year Daniel Clarke was received at New Orleans as American consul, though not regularly appointed. The first regular appointment was that of Evan Jones.

"Gayos died in 1799, and was succeeded by Don Maria Vidal. The province continued prosperous, and in particular Upper Louisiana, the population of which was now over 6,000.

"It did not require the spirit of prophecy to predict the speedy termination of Spanish power on the Mississippi. The rapid extension of the American settlements, the increasing trade from the Western States, and above all, the rapid immigration from the States, thoroughly alarmed the Spanish king. Rumor reached Louisiana to the effect that the province had been or was seen to be ceded to France, and the arbitrary acts of the Spanish governor again irritated the Western people.

"France had never been satisfied with the cession of Louisiana to Spain in 1762. This had been done in a time of weakness. Now France, under the guiding genius of Napoleon Bonaparte, was the greatest nation in Europe, and her emperor had resolved to secure Louisiana to France once more. This was effected in a treaty made Oct. 1, 1800, but which was kept secret for a long time.

"Ever since the alliance between France and Spain, it had been strongly suspected by the United States government that France intended to obtain the retrocession of Louisiana, perhaps with the addition of Florida, also. Our ministers at London, Paris and Madrid were therefore specially instructed to defeat this cession; but this cession had been already made by the secret treaty in October to take effect within six months after the complete execution of another treaty, concerning the then republic of Tuscany.

## DON MARIA VIDAL

Governor-General of Louisiana

"Even for Spain to command the mouth of the Mississippi, thus holding at mercy the trade of the Western country, now in so rapid progress of settlement, was a very uncomfortable thing. Out of this circumstance had heretofore grown intrigues, on the part of some of the leading politicians of Kentucky, to break the union with the States east of the mountains, and to enter into relations more or less intimate with Spain. Should an enterprising nation like the French--for which such partialities had been felt,--obtain the key of the Western waters, who could tell what might happen? This state of things, wrote Jefferson to Livingston, our minister at Paris, "completely reverses all the political relations of the United States, and will form a new epoch in our political course."

"We have ever looked to France as our natural friend—one with whom we could never have an occasion of difference; but there is one spot on the globe the possessor of which is our natural and habitual enemy: that spot is New Orleans. France, placing herself in that door, assumes to us the attitude of defiance. The day

NAPOLEON
.......... willing to sell.
(Unfinished portrait by David)

that France takes possession seals the union of two nations, who, in conjuction, can maintain exclusive possession of the ocean. From that moment we must marry ourselves to the British fleet and nation; we must turn all our attention to a maritime force, and make the first cannon fired in Europe the signal for tearing up any settlement France may have made."

"Much was added to the same effect, as reasons why the French government should consent to the transfer of Louisiana to the United States, suggestions which Livingston was instructed to make in a way not to give offense.

"Livingston, though he labored under a good deal of embarrassment at first in having no authority to offer any particular sum, opened negotiation for the purchase of New Orleans and the adjacent tracts on the Mississippi. Finding that nobody had any special influence with Bonaparte, or pretended to entertain any opinions different from his, he had managed to bring the matter directly to Bonaparte's personal notice, without the intervention of any minister. By way of additional motive to sell, he pressed the claims of American citizens, recognized by the recent convention, for supplies furnished to France, but upon which nothing had yet been paid.

"There seemed, however, to be little prospect of success till the application began to be seconded by the evident approach of a new European war. That made a great difference; and shortly before Monroe's arrival at Paris, Livingston was requested by Talleyrand to make and offer for the whole of Louisiana. That was an extent of purchase which had not been contemplated either by Livingston or by the administration which he represented. It had been supposed that the cession by Spain to France either included, or would be made to include, the Floridas as well as Louisiana; and the purchase contemplated by the joint instructions to Livingston and Monroe was that of the Floridas, or the western part of them, with the Island of Orleans. The highest amount authorized to be offered was 50,000,000 livres, or about $10,000,000. Should France obstinately refuse to sell, the ministers were authorized to enter into negotiations with Great Britain, with the view of preventing France from taking possession of Louisiana, and of ultimately securing it to the United States. Bonaparte presently suggested, as the price of Louisiana, 100,000,000 livres in cash or stocks of the United States, and the payment out of the American treasury of all claims by American merchants. This offer was made through Marbois, the head of the French treasury, instead of Talleyrand, who was suspected by Bonaparte of having mercenary motives in that and other affairs.

"Livingston and Monroe, after consulting together, offered 50,000,000 livres, minus the American claims. Marbois finally offered to take 60,000,000 livres, the United States to pay in addition American claims not to exceed 20,000,000 livres; and on this basis the treaty was finally concluded. This treaty, after setting forth the title of France as acquired from Spain, transferred that title to the United States, with a proviso that the inhabitants should be secure in their liberty, property and religion, and should be admitted as soon as possible, according to the principles of the Federal Constitution, to the enjoyment of all the rights of citizens of the United States. The ships of France and Spain laden with the produce of those countries or their colonies, were, during the next 12 years to be admitted at the port of New Orleans on the same terms as American vessels, and French ships ever afterward on the footing of the most favored nation. The payment of the 60,000,000 livres was to be made in six per cent stock of the United States to the amount of $11,250,000, to be redeemable after 15 years in annual installments of not less than $3,000,000. Claims of citizens of the United States on France were to be paid at the American treasury to the amount of $3,750,000, these claims to be adjudicated by a joint commission in France.

"The news of this arrangement was received with great exultation by the president and his cabinet. The assumption of power by the ministers in bargaining for the whole of Louisiana was cordially approved. At the same time Jefferson felt himself in an awkward predicament, for he had always insisted upon a strict construction of the constitution, and such strict construction

**THOMAS JEFFERSON**
He believed in a strict construction, i.e. interpretation of the Constitution. He gave way to vastly increase the size of the United States.

did not permit the United States to acquire territory by purchase. Jefferson privately admitted this difficulty, and proposed to get over it by amending the constitution. As the treaty required a mutual exchange of ratifications within six months, his plan was that Congress should go on, notwithstanding its want of power, and trust to a confirmation of their act under an amendment to be subsequently made. To hasten the matter, he issued a proclamation calling Congress together; but as the elections were not yet completed, the date fixed just preceded the expiration of the six months. When Congress assembled, the treaty and conventions with France were immediately laid before the Senate. After two days discussion their ratification was advised by that body, of which a strong majority were in political sympathy with the administration. Nothing was ever said about any amendment of the constitution to sanction this proceeding. The ratifications were immediately exchanged, the bargain was completed, and this vast territory from which Louisiana, Arkansas, Missouri, Iowa and other great States have been formed, was a part of the domain of the United States.

"This peaceful acquisition of Louisiana for so trifling a sum, securing to the rising settlements on the Western waters an uninterrupted river communication with the sea, the fear of losing which had been heretofore the occasion of so

many jealousies and such serious embarrassments, was celebrated at Washington by a public dinner, given by the administration members of Congress to the president, vice-president and heads of departments, and by similar festivals among the Republicans in different parts of the Union. This peaceful annexation so characteristic of Jefferson's policy, was exultingly contrasted with the violent method of seizing New Orleans by force, recommended by

the Federalists. The Federalists, however, were prompt to reply that the sum paid for Louisiana was just so much money thrown away, since Bonaparte sold what he could not keep, and what the breach of the Spanish treaty as to the right of deposit, and other claims on the nation for spoliations on our commerce, would well have justified the United States in seizing without any payment at all. It was, they averred, no policy of Jefferson's, but the war in Europe, that had brought the cession. The idea of obtaining the whole tract west of the Mississippi was, in fact, altogether too vast for Jefferson. Bonaparte had forced it upon him. Such an acquisition of territory seemed, indeed, to many, and Jefferson himself had serious doubts on the subject, to tend directly to the dissolution of the Union. The settlers west of the mountains had already more than once threatened to separate themselves from their Atlantic brethren, and to form an independent republic. Such threats, which had been very rife in Kentucky, and even in Pennsylvania, during the Whisky Insurrection, had made a deep impression on Jefferson's mind. The Federalists foretold, and he feared, that the removal of all external pressure on that side of the Mississippi would precipitate this danger, "an apprehension," says Hildreth, "which time has completely falsified, the crack having been proved to run in quite a different direction." Another objection, seriously felt by many, and especially by the New England Federalists, was, that the throwing open to emigration of such new and vast territories, tended to increase an evil already sufficiently felt, -- the stripping of the old States of their inhabitants, and the dwarfing of them in political importance.

"Nor were these considerations without their weight in the arrangements adopted for the newly acquired territory. By an act originating in the Senate, that territory was divided into two provinces by a line drawn along the thirty-third parallel of north latitude. The province south of this parallel, named the Territory of Orleans, already possessed a population of 50,000 persons, of whom more than half were slaves. Within the last 10 years the cultivation of the sugar cane had been successfully introduced in part by refugee planters from St. Domingo, and that together with cotton, had already superseded the production of indigo, formerly the chief staple. So lucrative were these new branches of industry--the decreased product of St. Domingo making an opening in the sugar market, and cotton, under the increased demand for it by the English manufacturers, bringing to the producer 25 cents per pound -- that the chief planters enjoyed incomes hardly known to landed proprietors anywhere else north of the Gulf of Mexico. Of the white inhabitants the greater part were French Creoles, descendants of the original French colonists, with an admixture, however, of French, Spanish and British immigrants. Under France the colonists had possessed hardly any political power; under Spain, none at all. With a cautious imitation of these models, in which Federalists would have been denounced as exceedingly anti-republican, the president was authorized not only to appoint the governor and secretary of the new Territory, but annually to nominate the 13 members who were to compose the Legislative council. This provision, though strongly objected to and struck out by the House as

contrary to democratic principles, was reinstated by the Senate, and on the report of a committee of conference, was finally agreed to.

"The laws of Louisiana down to the period of the cession to Spain, had been like those of Canada, the customs of Paris and the royal ordinances of France. The Spanish governor on taking possession, among other very arbitrary acts, had issued a proclamation substituting the Spanish code, and such remained the laws of the colony when it passed into the hands of the United States. This Spanish code, so far as it was not repugnant to the Constitution and laws of the United States, was continued in force, subject to such alterations as the new Territorial Legislature might make.

"All that region west of the Mississippi and north of the Territory of Orleans, was constituted by the same act as the District of Louisiana. It included one little village on the Arkansas, and several on or near the Mississippi, the principal of which was St. Louis. The white population of this region, embracing the present States of Arkansas, Missouri and Iowa, had been somewhat augmented of late by immigrants from the old French villages on the other side of the Mississippi; and by Anglo-American adventurers, who already outnumbered the French inhabitants. But the increase of this population, which did not exceed three or four thousand, was not considered desirable. It was proposed to reserve this region for the Indians; and the president was authorized to propose to the tribes east of the Mississippi an exchange of lands, and a migration on their part across the river -- a policy since extensively carried out. Meanwhile the jurisdiction over the few white inhabitants, and nominally over the whole district, was annexed to the Territory of Indiana, thus made the Ohio River and the thirty-third degree of north latitude, and west of the State of Ohio."

Our "mystery writer" tells well the story up to that point in time. The story will continue in sequence at a more logical time later in this volume for from the time Napoleon took the area of Louisiana from the Spanish throne which he controlled anyway new things were to happen to the people and the development of "the Louisiana Territory."

Our "mystery writer" observed that "under France the colonists had possessed hardly any political power; under Spain, none at all." Both Spain and France were absolute monarchies and, depending upon the personal strength of the king, the power of the throne was exercised by royal courtiers. The world of that time was for the few, and for the very few, as Winston Churchill would later suggest.

When the Louisiana Purchase area came into the ownership of the United States the entire way of life of the people residing in it would change dramatically. Now freedom would prevail and opportunity would be almost unlimited. The people would be sovereign citizens and no royal personage nor his appointees would rule over them. Provincial, Territorial or in Statehood status they would select their own leaders for the Constitution which was supreme in America guaranteed them a "Republican form of government" in the 4th Amendment of the Bill of Rights. Yes, it would be a new way of life. (See Chapter Five, Our American Heritage.)

Thus the area that comprised the Louisiana Purchase came under a new flag. President Jefferson knew that in many years hence all that area would also comprise new states in the American Union of States. New States that would be on an equal footing with even the original thirteen States. It is important that this "equal footing" term be perfectly understood.

The population of all white people west of the Mississippi River was very small in 1803 and there were not enough at that time to make up one state let alone the many that Jefferson envisaged. (By 1836, 33 years later the population of the District of Iowa, about to become part of the Wisconsin Territory, was only 10,531.)

But the newly purchased territory would go through the eventual requirements until the various sections of it were deemed qualified by the Congress for admission as States on that equal footing with all those theretofore in the Union.

The general government, as it was called, would preside over the governing of that vast wilderness area and the people would eventually decide their own manifest destiny.

# The Voyageurs

Usually, men build boats. In the case of the voyageurs who opened the way to the heart of North America, birch-bark canoes made the men.

Canoes built by squat, broad-shouldered men. The voyageurs averaged about five feet six inches tall. Few were more than five-eight because there wasn't room for tall men in canoes crowded with cargo and supplies. Their work developed thick arms and shoulders. When they portaged, the standard packs weighed about ninety pounds each. The voyageurs would take several at a time, to a total of 200 to 450 pounds. Despite the weight, they usually trotted across the portage.

This sort of natural selection makes sense. What's not so clear is why the voyageur was so merry as well as hardy and daring. "He could paddle 15 ---yes, if necessary, 18 --- hours per day for weeks on end and joke beside the camp fire at the close of each day's toil," wrote Grace Lee Nute in a publication of the Minnesota Historical Society.

Clearly, the voyageurs preferred the free life of the wilderness to grubbing rocks and stumps out of narrow farms along the St. Lawrence River. They could boast their independence of the petty annoyances concocted by the bureaucrats in Paris and Quebec.

Even with chains and lash it would have been difficult to make galley slaves work as hard as the voyageurs. Besides the drudgery of paddling and portaging, they were in constant danger of being drowned in a rapids, ambushed by the Iroquois or attacked by bears. If the food ran low, they stoically pushed on anyway. They not only worked voluntarily, they sang as they paddled.

The songs of the voyageurs covered a wide range of subjects and emotions, but probably the most popular was "A la claire fontaine" (The Clear Fountain). It carried through many verses about roses and nightinggales and a lost love --- oddly poetic for such a tough crew. These were the same men who looked down on stay-at-homes and gloried in being able to "live hard, lie hard, sleep hard, eat dogs."

French settlers learned to use birch-bark canoes as early as 1615 or

1616. A canoe light enough to be carried easily by one man could transport half a ton and be repaired anywhere in white birch territory, Maine to Alaska. The Indians went everywhere in canoes, bringing along wives, children, dogs, kettles, hatchets, bows, arrows, quivers, skins, tepee covers---whole villages. They didn't have kitchen sinks yet. Friendly Indians explained that it was easy to travel, paddling or portaging, hundreds of miles to the west via a network of streams and lakes. Voyageurs could take trade goods out to tribes in the far western wilderness and return laden with bales of valuable furs. Of course, the trip might take two or three years.

Proud of their strength and skill, the voyageurs decorated their canoes with bright colors and dressed themselves in gay costumes with colorful sashes whenever they approached a settlement. They usually got on well with the Indians, except for their implacable foes, the Iroquois. So well, in fact, that many of the first families in such cities as Detroit, St. Louis, Milwaukee and St. Paul can boast both voyageur and Indian ancestry. One exception was Etienne Brule, a noted early voyageur, who finally annoyed the basically friendly Hurons so much they boiled him and ate him.

Most voyageurs were unlettered and propertyless. Louis Jolliet, born in 1645, was an exception. He had studied to be a Jesuit and visited France. He spoke Latin, understood navigation and surveying instruments and could draw accurate maps. Joining his elder brother's fur business, he paddled and portaged like everyone else.

When the government of New France wanted to learn more about rumors of a great river in the West that flowed perhaps to the Pacific, they chose Jolliet to lead an expedition. He was to defray his expenses by trading furs as he went. He had no trouble signing up a crew of voyageurs for a share of the profits despite the dangers of a trip into unexplored wilderness never before visited by any European.

In October, 1672, they set out for the West from Montreal in two birch-bark canoes. Francois Chavigny, Jean Plattier, Pierre Moreau, Jacques Largilier, Jean Tiberge and Pierre Porteret were their names. Jolliet's younger brother, Zacherie, went along as far as Sault Ste. Marie. He stayed there to watch their hoard of furs and extra supplies when they pushed on into the wilderness the following spring after picking up Father Jacques Marquette at his mission 70 miles away.

Indians told them to paddle up the Fox River from Green Bay. A portage to the Wisconsin River took them to the Mississippi. They traveled down the Mississippi to the mouth of the Arkansas, where they encountered Spanish trade goods filtering up from the Gulf of Mexico and decidedly less friendly Indians, who had to be talked out of killing them. Certain that the great river flowed into the Gulf rather than the Pacific, they turned back. Other Indians showed them a short cut up the Illinois River to the Des Plaines with an easy portage to the Chicago River and Lake Michigan.

Jolliet spent the winter of 1673-74 back at the Sault. He had used the time not only to polish his journal and draw a map but to make extra copies of each in case anything happed to the originals. In the spring he started back for Quebec with two voyageurs, an Indian boy he had more or less adopted, a load of valuable furs and a chest containing his journal and map. After safely navigating 41 rapids, the canoe capsized in the 42nd just above Montreal.

Two fishermen found Jolliet unconscious and revived him. His companions, the canoe and its contents were never seen again. Jolliet's only consolation was the thought of the extra journal and map left at the mission at Sault Ste. Marie. He didn't know that the mission and all its contents had been destroyed in a disastrous fire.

Jolliet, who eventually became official hydrographer for New France, redrew his map of the Mississippi region from memory. For the story of the expedition, history has to rely on some notes by Father Marquette enhanced by interviews with Jolliet written down by Jesuit Father Claude Dablon. These circumstances inevit-

ably deflected some of the glory due to one of the greatest of the voyageurs.

When the British conquered Canada in 1760, the voyageurs continued the fur trade as usual. After all, it had been two of them---Pierre Esprit Radisson and Medard Chouart Des Groseilliers---whose illegal fur dealings had spawned the Hudson's Bay Company. While British names, like that of Sir Alexander Mackenzie, are attached to the later explorations of Canada on to the Pacific and to the Arctic, unsung---but singing---voyageurs paddled the canoes.

(The preceding was taken from the 1988 Marcquis Appointment Book, MCI, Wilmette, Ills., edited by Richard Frisbie with design and illustrations by Graziano, Krafft & Zale, Inc.)

# Chapter Four

# OUR SPIRITUAL HERITAGE

The overwhelming majority of those early pioneers settlers who came to Iowa were God-fearing and God-respecting and God-loving folk.

Basic to every other aspect of their being was their belief in God.

Even their American heritage, as we shall see, grew out of a deep religious and spiritual faith. For the Constitution of the United States of America and the Common Law it established were from the Bible.

It was religious freedom, among the desire for all other freedoms, that first impelled the pilgrims to set out for America. It was the tyranny of monarchies and often the national churches of several denominations that those who came to America were trying to escape. All they sought was the freedom to worship as they desired.

But it wasn't only the national established churches from which they sought to escape; it was to re-establish the principle that God is superior to human rulers. This great principle is made abundantly clear in the Old Testament and in the experience of the Hebrew people with their kings. Over many centuries that one principle had been lost among the rulers of the earth.

Indeed when the pilgrims landed at Plymouth Rock in 1620 and signed the Mayflower Compact the central core of their thinking was that the union among them was based upon the rule of God, not man.

Thus the principle of religious freedom was established.

Basic to that was that God is the creator and ruler of mankind. Those principles were firmly rooted in the hearts of all Americans and remained that way.

Yet most of the colonists coming to the new world were English and with them came the British State Church, the Anglican or Anglo-Catholic Church. After the Revolution it became known in America and to us today as the Episcopal Church. But the religious freedom that had been established prevailed and churches of many denominations were established in America. Indeed, many of the colonies had their emphasis on certain denominations of Christianity such as the Quakers in Pennsylvania and the Roman Catholics in Maryland. And there were religious disagreements but overall tolerance and respect were the practice. Yet there were the Salem witch trials and various examples of intolerance.

By the time of the American Revolution the principle of freedom of religion and religious tolerance was profoundly embedded in the hearts and minds of the colonial people. Indeed, so had the principle of the separation of Church and State. But that didn't mean then and doesn't mean today the separa- of God and State.

One of the issues with the religious establishment prior to 1776 was the paying of taxes some of which went to pay the clergy of the established Church, i.e. the Anglican Church. If you were a Catholic in Maryland, a Congregationalist in New York, a Unitarian in Massachusetts or a Quaker in Pennsylvania you would naturally object to paying taxes to support the English Church clergy in America.

An aspect of the American Revolution, therefore, was to sever the ties between the colonies and the English Church. The severance of all ties with the British Monarch was inherent. Every man became his own king; land titles became allodial. A man's home or farm was his and there was no higher owner such as the king. He became a sovereign citizen and was no longer a subject.

In other words, man's only sovereign was God. From 1776 government was the servant of man, not his master.

The colonies became States, sovereign States. They began to abandon the charters issued by the kings of England and wrote "constitutions" by which they would be governed.

Fundamental to those new constitutions was an expressed belief in "Almighty God."

The Magna Carta referred to "the will of God." That document is part of our spiritual heritage.

The first emphasis of the Mayflower Compact was "In the name of God........."

The Declaration of Independence is replete with reference to "nature's God" and the supreme "judge of the world."

No church and no religion were to be supreme over the religious or spiritual beliefs of the newly free American people, the sovereign citizens who owed their allegiance to God and nothing else in the world.

While the vast majority of the population of America professed the Christian religion even that faith was not the "official" faith of the nation. There was to be none and there was to be religious tolerance. Ideals cannot always be achieved in human society no matter how lofty or noble they are intended but the belief in a Higher Power or the Supreme Being was dominant in our foundations.

The Common Law, unwritten but essentially determining right and wrong, was a part of the spiritual heritage of Americans whether they lived in the cities of the east or on the frontier. It was established in the Bill of Rights and prevailed in the courts of the time which were very conscious of jurisdiction.

The Bible was one of the few books in the homes of the American people and many could not read. The knowledge of the Bible was one that was handed down and its precepts were a part of life.

Thus the spiritual heritage was very much a part of what those early pioneer settlers brought to Iowa. Churches of many denominations would bring their own concepts of that heritage with them across the great Father of Waters.

# At our nation's beginning --- a spiritual tone.......

by The Rev. Larry R. Johnson

James Russell Lowell, an American poet and statesman of the 19th century, was once asked, "How long do you think the American republic will endure?" Lowell replied, "So long as the ideas of the founding fathers continue to be dominant."

If Lowell was right and America can continue only as long as the concepts that created it, then we cannot afford to rest until we have exhausted all efforts to incorporate those same ideas into our present policy.

In the construction of any building, it is the foundation that demands the most attention. Aristotle said, "If you would understand anything, observe its beginning and its development." Applying that to the forming of a nation, we are reminded of the words of eminent historian Will Durant: "Once a civilization is cut off from its moral moorings, the result will be the actual demise of that civilization."

This year, as we observe the signing of the Declaration of Independence July 4, 1776, we ought to take as quick look to see what our forefathers had in mind when they began to lay the foundation stones of this nation. For it is the foundation which must continue to undergird and support the entire structure.

What then were some of the ideas of our nation's founders? Daniel Webster, in a discourse delivered at Plymouth on Dec. 22, 1820, stated: "Lastly, our ancestry established their system of government on morality and religious sentiment. Moral habits, they believed, cannot safely be trusted on any other foundation than religious principle, nor any government be secure which is not supported by moral habits."

Webster was not the only one to note the large amount of religious rock in the nation's foundation. John Quincy Adams, commenting on this country's conflict with Great Britain, stated: "The highest glory of the American Revolution was this: it connected in one indissoluble bond, the principles of civil government with the principles of Christianity."

The Supreme Court of the United States made much the same observation, when in 1892 the court completed an exhaustive study of the supposed connection between Christianity and the U. S. government. After reviewing hundreds of historical documents, the court asserted: "These references add a volume of organic utterances that this is a religious people, a Christian nation."

Why was it that these astute observers arrived at such conclusions, when so few today seem to be seeing these things? What did they see that we have missed?

Perhaps they read the words of the Mayflower Compact. On the night before that historic landing at Plymouth Rock in November of 1620, the Pilgrims crowded into the tiny hold of the ship to sign what many historians believe to be the birth certificate of the American Republic. The document reads: "In ye name of God, Amen. We whose names are underwritten, having undertaken for ye glorie of God, and advancement of ye Christian faith a voyage to plant ye first colony in ye northern parts of Virginia."

The Puritans who followed, establishing the Massachusetts Bay Colony, recorded much the same sentiments in the opening sentences of their New England Confederation: "We all came into these parts of America with one and the same end, namely to advance the Kingdom of the Lord Jesus Christ."

The first draft of the Declaration of Independence, written by Thomas Jefferson, included only a reference to "nature's God." For the vast majority of the men, this was not enough. Later, it was debated in committee by John Adams, Robert Livingston, Benjamin Franklin and Roger Sherman. They added words which have become significant stones in the support system of this nation. These men contended that not only were men created equal but "they were endowed by their (C)reator with certain inalienable rights."

Finally, when the Declaration was debated in the Congress, the phrase, "appealing to the Supreme Judge of the world for the rectitude of our intentions" was added. So were the important words, "with a firm reliance on the protection of divine Providence."

Beginning with our first president, George Washington, each successor has been sworn into that office with his left hand on the Bible open to the 28th chapter of Deuteronomy: "And it shall come to pass, if thou shalt hearken diligently unto the voice of the Lord thy God; to observe and to do all his commandments, that the Lord thy God will set thee on high above all the nations of the earth."

What ideas did our forefathers have in mind as they founded this nation? Perhaps the words of our Pledge of Allegiance say it best, "one nation, under God." But we must not forget their thoughts captured so well by Francis Scott Key in the last stanza of our national anthem: "Praise the Pow'r that hath made and preserved us as a nation."

(The preceding OUTLOOKS column was written for the Cedar Rapids GAZETTE and appeared in the July 4th, 1988 edition. It summarizes much with a vital message. It is reprinted here with permission.)

# OUTLOOKS

*. . . periodic observations from some thoughtful Eastern Iowans invited to express themselves here. The topics are unlimited. The views are theirs.*

## LARRY R. JOHNSON

*of Cedar Rapids is pastor of the Open Door Christian Church and president of Citizens for Decency of Cedar Rapids.*

OUTLOOKS --- A Note. OUTLOOKS is a unique feature of the Cedar Rapids GAZETTE, Cedar Rapids, Linn County, Ia., whereby a staff of selected OUTLOOKS columnists write their ideas on a number of topics. The columns appear ordinarily about once a month. The OUTLOOKS writings give an editorial divergence to that newspaper and those columns are evidently well read by many thousands of eastern Iowa folk.

# Chapter Five
# OUR AMERICAN HERITAGE

As white explorers, pioneers and settlers began to come westward and infiltrate the land that would eventually become the State of Iowa, they brought with them a rare heritage, one which few other migrating people in the entire history of the world had carried.

That was their American heritage!

America was, indeed, a young nation when Iowa's original counties were created from the first two. The very same year the Constitution of the United States was exactly fifty years old. It had been written and signed in 1787. In 1837 the Wisconsin Territorial Legislature divided Dubuque and Des Moines into many smaller counties.

The people who came to Iowa were from most of the States already in the Union. They were immigrants essentially from Europe, the English, the Scandinavians, the Germans, the Irish, the Scotch, the Dutch and many others.

In America they had freedom, were they already here living in earlier States. In America they found freedom, were they immigrants from across the great ocean. In America they sought but one thing more to add to that precious heritage of freedom.

That was opportunity!

Freedom and opportunity -- their American heritage!

Possessing freedom, what they would make of their opportunities was entirely up to them as individuals. Their American heritage was a unique one and many of them, especially the European immigrants did not exactly understand it.

It may be sufficient to note that the immigrants enjoyed a different status in America than they had in their European homelands. For in Europe they were in one way or another, wards of the government, subjects of the monarch, objects of control by the government. In the America into which they had come they were sovereign; the government was not "higher" than the people. It was not sovereign. The people, as individuals, were!

On July 4th, 1776, the American people declared their independence from the king of Great Britain in a unique action and by adopting a unique document which has become known in our history as the "Delaration of Independence." It thus became the first part of our organic constitution, a document that is part of what literally constitutes America!

Before 1776 the people of the colonies were the subjects of the king of Great Britain. After July 4th of that year they were no longer subjects but sovereign citizens.

The Declaration of Independence puts in its proper place and perspective what government is and should be.

Thomas Jefferson was the prime author of the Declaration of Independence and put in perspective exactly what government was supposed to be and do. He wrote into the Declaration that "all men are created equal" and that they are "endowed by their Creator with certain unalienable rights." Life, liberty and the pursuit of happiness! NOT gifts from government, but from each individual's Creator, from God. Those rights were those of the sovereign citizen by birth, just because he was born. Government did not bestow those rights and government could not take them away.

The only purpose of government was to secure those rights, to guarantee them, to protect and defend them for each individual!

And whenever government didn't function to secure those rights it was the right of the people to change their form of government. Not only their right, indeed, it was their duty!

And so the sovereignty of the individual was part of the American heritage that those early Iowa pioneers carried with them as they crossed the mighty Mississippi!

Thomas Jefferson was a political philosopher and genius and in his great mind was a pervasive knowledge of the world's history. He knew that every government that had ever existed in the history of the world had sooner or later oppressed its own people! And so in the great and immortal Declaration he sought to make it clear that government was to be the servant and not the master of the American people!

Some years following the Declaration it was clear that some changes would have to be made in what was evolving to be a national situation with several States and so they sent representatives to meet in a convention in Philadelphia to amend the Articles of Confederation that had bound them together since they had unified to resist British rule.

The result of that Constitutional Convention as we have come to regard it was that venerable document that literally constituted our general government.

It became known as the Constitution of the United States of America. And it was adopted exactly fifty years before the creation of Iowa's eastern counties.

In this year of 1987 as we observe the 150th anniversary of the creation of those original Iowa counties we in Iowa and all over America denote the 200th anniversary of the Constitution which was part of that American heritage brought to the shores of Iowa.

Along with the Declaration of Independence, then, the Constitution which established a framework of government became the second major part of the organic constitution of the United States of America. It is significant to remember that the "Bill of Rights" was not a part of the original Constitution but was added shortly after the American Republic was organized. The Bill of Rights was also the condition upon which many States agreed to ratify the Constitution. Indeed, the Bill of Rights has often been called "the price of ratification."

But our American heritage of freedom did not begin with the Constitution as we know it.

The struggle for freedom has been one that has existed since governments began. For every government that has ever existed in the history of mankind, has sooner or later oppressed its own people.

Part of our American heritage that the pioneer settlers brought with them across the mighty Mississippi was that claimed by freedom-loving people for thousands of years. That God intended man to be free is found in the Bible which has been called 80% political and 20% spiritual.

Probably the earliest date the "American" (or English) heritage of freedom if you will, tradition began was the year 1215 when King John of England was forced to sign at the point of a sword the Magna Carta. From that point on the "rights of Englishmen" began to grow in the hearts and laws of the British people. Subsequent acts of the British Parliament continued and expanded upon those rights. They were brought across the seas to America.

The first document signed in the new world that became part of our American heritage was the Mayflower Compact. That, too, can be justly regarded as part of our "organic constitution." Those who landed in America from 1620 on, had a justified and innate distrust of government and well they should have. That same distrust continued through the years of settlement and expansion and on through the great American Revolution. The early colonists soon learned that the farther government gets from the people the more tyrannical it becomes.

Such was not only one of the truths of history but they learned it the hard way as the mother country, Great Britain, became more and more oppressive over her colonies. King George III came to the throne of England in 1760 and he determined, unlike his father and grandfather, to not only reign but to rule. And rule he did. And as King George III and his government foisted an English banking system upon the colonists, increased taxation and trampled upon their "rights of Englishmen," the settlers in America began to object.

The English colonists thought they should be permitted to petition the king or the Parliament for a redress of their grievances but neither the king nor the Parliament would listen. Most in the colonies were loyal to their king as they believed he was their ruler "by the Grace of God." The more sagacious among the colonial leaders knew well the lessons of history and the story of kings and tyrants. It was under leadership that objection, resistance and finally revolution brought about a separation from the mother country.

Thus, an American spirit, an American heritage was becoming apparent and it was this heritage of freedom, as it developed, that would come across the Mississippi River into the land that would be Iowa.

Yet it is necessary to trace that spirit of freedom, that American heritage, in a little more depth to truly understand it. Perhaps the crux of the whole matter centered around how far government itself could go in ruling, as opposed to governing. As government grows larger and farther from the people a tyranny grows. In the case of the colonists and the mother country a whole ocean separated them.

To a degree the colonies of England in America were governed locally according to their charters and colonial legislatures enacted the laws. But as time went on the king supported by Parliament began to suppress the colonies and override the actions of the colonial lawmaking bodies. Tyranny set in.

Back in England one of the most ancient of laws was that even the king of England could not set foot in the most humble hut. But in the American colonies British soldiers were housed in homes without the permission of the owners. That was one, among many, of grievances Jefferson listed in the Declaration that impelled the colonies to separate from England.

There were many other such grievances. The Common Law right of trial by jury was ignored by the British when it came to the exercise of that right by the colonists. And the list went on and on. Finally the colonies organized a Continental Congress at which the representatives of the 13 colonies met to deal with their problems.

It was a Continental Congress, meeting in 1776, over a year after fighting against their British masters had broken out, that finally decided to declare independence from Great Britian and assume their separate station among the powers of the earth.

That same Continental Congress appointed a committee of three to write an instrument declaring the independence of the colonies from the mother country. Thomas Jefferson was the one of the three who was chosen to do the writing. The fruit of his sustained labor was his now immortal Declaration of Independence

The American heritage had begun to grow. The spirit of freedom had been implanted in the hearts of the colonists once again. Their forefathers had come to America seeking freedom. They had it for many decades until oppression set in. Then they had to fight for their freedom, their rights as Englishmen.

It must also be remembered that the freedom they sought in 1775 and after the Declaration of 1776 was not the effort of the whole of the population of Americans at the time. Indeed, not even a majority. It has been said that the whole effort was supported and sustained by 3 - 5 % of the entire population of the colonies. And that is very usual. The small and dedicated usually are the ones who fight for the freedom of the many. Because the "many" are ordinarily apathetic.

But loyalties are difficult to sever and the loyalty of most colonists to the king and the Church of England was one that did not wane easily. Indeed, for many years after Independence many remained sympathetic to the royal being.

The Declaration of Independence did two major things. One was that it made land titles allodial. Another was that it put every man in place of the king himself---it made the citizen the sovereign. Every man was his own king, so to speak. What that second change meant was that government was the servant of the sovereign citizen, and not his master as it had been under the king.

Prior to 4 July 1776 the king owned the land and his subjects worked it, or whatever the established relationship was; it varied. But when the sovereign citizen became the owner of the land, he did, indeed, own it. No one was over him. It was not a pretended title, granted, when he was a subject of the king and the title was with the king.

When the new sovereign citizen owned his land and their was no king over him there could also be no taxes without his consent. It was a "new birth of freedom" as Lincoln would say some four score and seven years later.

There is a difference between being a subject and being a sovereign citizen.

A subject is owned. A colonist, as a subject, was owned by the king of England. He owed fealty to the king. He was not his own. The foolishness of the idea that the king ruled by "the Grace of God" had been instilled in the subjects of the king to the extent that they believed it was God's will that the king rule over them. Now the idea of kings and nobility is gone; it disappeared on 4 July 1776. But it took some decades before the new sovereign citizens could adjust to the idea of their own sovereignty. But they did. (Government will always try to subject people to its own will; only oppression follows that same subjugation!)

So, if the king were no longer

General George Washington, who led the nation in its struggle for independence and who became thereby the "Father of our Country."

the "owner" of these former subjects, these now sovereign citizens, who was? That answer to that was then and must ever be, only God. Only God and no other power on earth can reign over the individual sovereign citizen. Government is a literal force created by the sovereign citizens to keep the peace and guarantee his rights. That is the only purpose for which government exists.

Thomas Jefferson made it all quite clear and very logical in his work. He referred to nature's God and suggested that governments are to govern with the consent of the governed. Those were perhaps radical thoughts in 1776.

But those who were emigrating to the "beautiful land" across the Mississippi River in the 1830s had a half century between themselves and the Declaration of Independence and they assumed those ideas as an integral part of their American heritage.

Those early pioneers settlers came to Iowa endowed with a freedom that few other peoples had enjoyed in all the history of mankind. They sought only opportunity and that was theirs, too. Very few were educated and only a handful could probably relate to the meaningful words to which we referred in the quotation on the opposite page. But the spirit of freedom and opportunity was their.......an American Heritage!

General George Washington led the rebellious colonies to independence and the final separation from the mother country. But it would take a few years to establish the republic that came to be another part of our American heritage. For once they were independent, the colonies were just that -- independent. They were sovereign states and independent of each other. Yet there were common bonds of union that held them together, as loosely bound as they were. The Continental Congress wrote the Articles of Confederation under which the new States lived for a few years until it was perceived that the national, or general, government was not as strong as it might have been to weld a mighty nation from the thirteen newly independent States.

A Constitutional Convention was called which met at Philadelphia in Pennsylvania and hammered out a document that was essentially a compromise between those who wanted an extremely powerful general government and those who wanted a weak one. The essence of the Constitution was a framework for a republic with democratic principles but it was in no way a democracy for those wise founding fathers knew that a democracy could be just a tyrannical as a monarchy or a dictatorship.

Many States refused to ratify

the proposed constitution because it did not contain a Bill of Rights. The colonies had fought for their rights which Great Britain had denied them and they were not going to see a government instituted that would not have those rights written into it and absolutely guaranteed. On the condition that a Bill of Rights would be added, the States ratified the Constitution. That was in 1787 and in 1788 our first elections were held. A Congress was chosen and a president was named in the person of George Washington who was apparently the natural and unanimous leader of his time. Together they organized a supreme court for which the Constitution provided.

The Bill of Rights were the first ten amendments to the now effective Constitution. After the Bill of Rights had been added to the Constitution the States themselves began to add Bills of Rights to their own constitutions.

(Later when Iowa's Constitution was written, it would contain that portion of the American heritage brought to Iowa by those who came to settle here.)

What the Bill of Rights involved was the English Common Law, now the Anglo-American Common Law and its many protections for the people, the sovereign citizens. It restrained government and legalism from oppressing the individual sovereign citizen. The Bill of Rights guaranteed those "unalienable rights" to which Jefferson referred in the Declaration of Independence.

Comfortable that the people of the States had a government properly chained down by the provisions of the Constitution and the Bill of Rights, the nation began to grow and prosper amid the freedom that it now enjoyed. At long last government would no longer have a claim upon the fruits of the labor of mankind nor tax away his substance.

What the Constitution did not do was the create any economic "system." It left people free to work and to earn and to enter into business, to do whatever each individual sovereign citizen considered was his own "pursuit of happiness." Man was free from the tyranny of government politically, socially, economically and in every other way. A person was a sovereign citizen. His rights were guaranteed. His land was allodial, not technically the king's property. He "owned" the government; it was to serve his needs for protection and the guarantee of his rights to that same life, liberty and the pursuit of happiness. Government and its agents could not interfere with anything he did as long as he did not trounce upon the rights and safety and well-being of others.

A free market economy was created and the free enterprise system brought to the new republic the greatest prosperity ever known in the history of the world. Indeed, there is a sort of a cruel justice in the marketplace but that is still far better than the dictates of government. Neither was there a nobility to sap the earnings of the people.

And so it was all the preceding and much more that went together to create an American heritage. And those who came to Iowa brought that heritage with them. Of course, there came, mostly in the 1840s and later, the immigrants from abroad, mostly from Europe, who sought the freedom about which they'd heard. Yet the same spirit was not yet engrained in them to the degree that it was in the native Americans. But it didn't take them long to learn what it meant to be free and possibly their appreciation of freedom exceeded that of those early native Americans who, after only half a century, were beginning to take their liberty for granted. That has been the norm in all of history's civilizations.

Thus into Iowa came the American heritage, brought to the beautiful land in the hearts and minds and in the will of those who came to settle it and create what might well be called an Iowa civilization. That American heritage soon became the Iowa heritage and it became an inheritance for all of us who were born upon this rich soil and for all who seek what Iowa has to offer even today.

Therefore, we have not only an American heritage but we have an Iowa heritage.

In recognizing this we must recall what another of our founding fathers said, namely Patrick Henry, who proclaimed that "eternal vigilance is the price of liberty." More than ever before in the history of our nation and our state we must be eternally vigilant over those liberties. In later years when Iowa became a State in the Union it adopted for its motto: "OUR LIBERTIES WE PRIZE AND OUR RIGHTS WE WILL MAINTAIN."

THE DECLARATION OF INDEPENDENCE was painted by one of our nation's early artists, John Trumbull and the figures in this work are portraits. This painting hangs in the Yale University Art Gallery and is a familiar scene to most Americans.

---

If every American of 1988 understood just this part of the seccond paragraph of the Declaration of Independence, ours would be a far better nation today:

"We hold these truths to be self-evident, that all men are created equal, that they are endowed by their Creator with certain unalienable rights, that among these are life, liberty and the pursuit of happiness. That to secure these rights, governments are instituted among men, deriving their just powers from the consent of the governed, that whenever any form of government becomes destructive of these ends, it is the right of the people to alter or to abolish it, and to institute new government, laying its foundation on such principles and organizing its powers in such form, as to them shall seem most likely to affect their safety and happiness................"

124

# Chapter Six
# OUR PIONEER HERITAGE

There was always a "pioneer heritage" in the hearts and minds of all who migrated westward from the 1600's to the late 1800's. One might even call it a "pioneer instinct." Whatever, it was there. And, to a degree, it remains.

That "pioneer heritage" had many characteristics, many attributes. It was in no way inherited by those who carved out the American widerness; it was something that was created within them.

It was basically spiritual. and out of that belief in and reliance upon a higher power or supreme being came a philosophy of freedom and a search for opportunity.

Survival, being the first law of nature, was one of the fundamentals of the "pioneer heritage." In carving out the new American civilization from the wilderness of North America those hardy pioneers always found that their efforts centered around survival first. This was especially true in the northern territories.

It was over a half century from that day when the pilgrims landed in Massachusetts to the time Marquette and Joliet first set foot upon the soil of what was to become Iowa. That was in Clayton County, near McGregor, in June of 1673.

It was more than a century later when Julien Dubuque settled to mine lead in the area of the great city that now bears his name. And it was nearly another half century before Dubuque and Demoine were created, on paper at least, as the first two counties west of the great river.

But, what of the pioneers? Certainly much is in recorded history of the more famous who came here. A civilization is much more than famous names and explorers who didn't stay for long. A civilization is made up of the people who venture to settle, raise families, build homes and buildings and seek to prosper in a new land.

And it was upon those pioneer foundations that the Iowa civilization, if you please, was established. Valuable elements of the pioneer spirit, the pioneer heritage, remain a century and a half later among the people of Iowa, a unique folk indeed.

They came across the mighty Mississippi River from almost every State in the American Union but mostly from the northeast. They came from many nations of the world but mostly, at first, from Europe and especially northern Europe.

With them they brought their beliefs, their desires for freedom and opportunity, their need to breathe free!

Most had very little. They came mostly in families. Often the father would come first seeking a place to settle or staking out an early claim to a choice piece of ground. He would then return and bring the family.

Transportation, the means of getting to the "beautiful land," was crude. They walked, they rode horses; they came in crude wagons or covered wagons. They had few belongings and little money. What they did have was the gold and silver coinage of the young Republic or, in the 1830's and 40's, the old large copper cents.

They often camped along the way. They fed off the land from berries and nuts and killed wild game as they journeyed across the States of Indiana, Illinois and finally the great river.

Once settled they began to raise their own food but that took a growing season and living continued to be from the wild land for sustenance.

Survival first. The women and the children were the first priority. It was they who rode the horses or were carried in the wagons. The men and larger boys walked. Likewise their first need was shelter when they found the place that was to be home.

The early shelters were crude indeed. The more permanent ones were, of course, the log cabins. En route to the place of settlement the immigrant pioneers stayed in caves, rough shelters of saplings and hides. Anything to be free from the elements. If a family were travelling in a covered wagon or some similar conveyance they would spend the night there.

Once "home" was located the house was erected. The log cabin was the usual home building. It was always built near a woods and a spring or stream. The trees would provides the logs for building and the fuel for the fire which provided heat for cooking and heat for warming the cabin. Often the floors were merely dirt which came to be packed down hard from constant use.

Often there was not glass available for windows and oiled cloth was used. In other cabins wooden windows were inserted in the walls and in good weather they could be opened to admit both light and fresh air. The earliest cabins were primitive enough and only one room was the norm.

As the land was cleared and a living made perhaps another room or more would be added. As families grew that became more and more of a necessity.

The possessions the pioneers brought with them were few also. Usually only the most valuable of family heirlooms if any. The necessities of life and living were first to be brought and those centered around tools such as hammers, saws etc. Agricultural equipment centered around the plow.

It wasn't long after a settlement was begun that entrepreneurs came to vend their wares and more modern conveniences were available for sale. Lumberyards and hardware stores came later. The general store preceded them. With a town with a store or stores the settlers could buy glass for windows, nails for building, cloth for sewing and an abundance of other goods.

The furniture the pioneers brought with them, if any, would have amounted to very little and would have necessitated the use of a wagon. Thus the furniture for early use in the original cabins was made by the man of the house with the help of his family. The eating table was of rough-hewn plank and the family sat on log benches.

The cooking was done over a large fireplace which was ordinarily built first with the cabin structured around it. It was large enough to emit heat into the area of the room meaning the cabin itself. The food was originally wild game and the nuts, fruits and berries indigenous to the area. Flower and other necessities soon flowed into the areas of settlement but they were, at first, scarce enough.

The first efforts of the man of the family was the clearing of land on which to plant the seed for food. The harvest the following autumn was intended to keep the family through the ensuing winter. Along with the father of the family went the help of all the others. If a man had sons they learned the work of the pioneer settlement at an early age. One of the true blessings of their lives was that the young learned quickly how to work. That was, and if it remains, part of the "pioneer heritage."

(In a different age than that of the 1830s and 40s, Iowans remain some of the best working folk in America.)

Thus the establishment of a homestead in very early Iowa was a family affair. Dad did the building, the farming, the tending of the animals, the butchering, the harvest and perhaps was even a blacksmith! Mom had charge of the house, did the cooking, the washing, the sewing and the mending. It was a sort of division of labor but not as we know it today for at times all pitched in to help with everything. In those early times survival was indeed the first law of nature.

Families lived together, worked together and learned together. It was a good life, a true family life.

The pioneer character was built upon hardship and achievement. Those were times when man was steeled by adversity. The rewards were great but they weren't always material rewards.

Their spiritual heritage, as we have noted, was a part of their day to day life. Their American heritage was their freedom and their awareness of it. Their pioneer heritage was a blend of both combined with their individual character, commitment to family and the community.

The Common Law was part of that pioneer spirit and in the absence of a written code they knew right from wrong and so theirs was a relatively moral world.

They worked hard and what they earned was theirs to keep. When part of their harvest went to help others it was a matter of true charity.

Part of the "pioneer heritage" was the realization that the family was the basic political unit in the new American Republic. They were or were becoming part of Iowa. It's motto would become: "Of all that is good, Iowa affords the best."

The pioneer family also struggled through many hardships together, as a family. There was sometimes the threat of violence from the natives of the area. And there were culprits among the pioneers, too. Nature itself was often an enemy. Many young died at birth or at an early age. Disease was a factor. And so the pioneer settler faced a multiplicity of threats, hardships and struggles. But they became close through adversity. They weathered the storms of nature, life and death always comforted by a deep faith. It was very true then that the family that prayed together, stayed together.

This pioneer spirit was not, of course, peculiar to the early settlers of Iowa alone. It had existed in one way or another since the pilgrims came in 1620 to seek release from the tyranny of Europe. But now it had come to Iowa.....and the new Iowans cherished it.

As the territory was settled by the pioneers particularly, as we have seen since 1833, there were few populous settlements and neighbors were often some distance away.

As someone said, maybe in jest and perhaps seriously, "as soon as you can see the smoke from your neighbor's fireplace, it's time to move on."

That feeling didn't apply to many early Iowa pioneer settlers for they were prone to settle and to stay. Nevertheless the early settlers often walked a long way to visit a neighbor if they didn't live in one of the many small communities.

Likewise there were no doctors close to most of the pioneers and were one needed it might have meant a trip of fifty or more miles. On the other hand, doctors made house calls in those very early days and often travelled within a fifty mile diameter of where they resided.

More often home remedies were used to heal most illnesses. Cow urine, because of its nitrogen content, was often used to cure what we today call "athlete's foot."

Herbs, wild roots, the leaves of certain bushes and plants were often used. Many had an herb garden after they settled onto their new homes.

Poultices, a soft and moist mass of bread, meal, herbs, etc., were often applied as a medicament to the body especially to draw out poisons.

In those ways the pioneers learned to treat themselves in the absence of professional medical aid. And perhaps those ancient home remedies were not so primitive for medicine is today learning new values in researching the oldtime cures.

The farms upon which those pioneer settlers lived became very self-sufficient. Their few needs centered around sugar, spices, salt and other things. These were later available in stores that sprung up in the small towns.

Someone always had to be the first to establish a claim and to "break ground" even before such little stores or trading posts could be opened. For certainly a market was needed for any business to thrive. It was usual for one early settler to make his claim not far from another. Neighbors were necessary to establish a sense of community and, indeed, for protection on the newly opened frontier.

Hard work consumed most of the time and efforts of the early pioneer families but there was the need of a social life. And many reasons were found for getting together. There were barn-raisings and quilting bees. When a church located in a community much of the social life centered around it. Eventually schools were established. But before the formal school was learning at home. While many pioneers could not read or write they passed on what they could to their children. As we noted in Chapter Four, ordinarily the Bible was the only book in a home.

Thus there was a "togetherness" that didn't prevail in more "advanced" societies. There was an equality that was unknown elsewhere. There was a neighborliness, too, that modern times has seen pass. Yet much of this "pioneer heritage" still prevails in Iowa!"

The Pioneer Heritage has come down to Iowans of today.

In relating to our "Pioneer Heritage" it is well to relate to the physical hardships of the pioneers as well as to try to capture that spirit of "pioneer heritage" that is still part of all native Iowans today.

History writer Barrows, cited elsewhere and at length in this text wrote the following prior to or around 1863:

"Well do the Old Settlers of Iowa remember the days and years, from the first settlement of 1840. Those were days full of sadness and often distress. The endearments of home had been broken up in another land, and all that was dear and hallowed on earth, the home of childhood and the scenes of youth were severed, and we sat down by the gentle waters of our noble river, and often 'hung our harps upon the willows.' But the bright prospects of the future led us on, and with hope as our sheet anchor, we lived upon the fruits of our labor, almost an exiled races, for many years. No splendid cottage was then our home. The rude cabin was our shelter, and we were scarcely protected from the rains of Summer or the snows of Winter. No luxuries crowned our board, but we rejoiced in that Providence, which shaped our destinies, and led us to the shores of the Mississippi. We loved the land of our adoption. We loved her soil, her climate and her majestic river, upon whose banks we often strayed and mingled our tears with one another. The Pioneers of Scott County, came as the vanguard of the great army that has flooded our land. They came to build for themselves and posterity a glorious destiny, amid the wilds of Iowa. They brought no sword, or battle-axe, but the plough share and pruning hook were their only weapons. They had no history to point them the way, no kind of friend to bid them welcome to these shores. The legends of the Indian could only tell them of the beauty of the land they came to possess, and instead of the smiles of welcome, they received only the smiles of savages."

We've discussed the history that preceded the coming to Iowa of the early pioneer settlers and determined how the area that was to become Iowa actually became a part of the United States of America. (Yet when the pioneers came often the land could not be "claimed" if an Indian title existed that kept the white man from it.)

We've discussed the spiritual heritage of the early pioneer settler and the foundations of his beliefs as they pertained to his daily life and his responsibility for himself.

We've discussed the American heritage that the early pioneer settlers brought with them to Iowa, barely a half century after Independence and the creation of the Republic.

It must be reckoned, therefore, that the "pioneer heritage" as we are to assume it to have been was a combination of everything that was a part of the lives of the early pioneer settlers. How the land came to be theirs, or their country's. The spiritual aspect of their lives, their spiritual heritage, was part of their pioneer heritage.

Freedom and opportunity and the right to choose who should govern over them was, too, a part of their pioneer heritage. Everything that went before them, then, became an integral part of the pioneer life they had chosen on the frontier across the Mississippi River.

Other than what they brought to it, theirs was a new land. It was rich and fertile, vast with beauty and opportunity. With such a "pioneer heritage" they would establish the foundations for a new culture, a new way of life: the Iowa civilization, if you please.

In this and forthcoming volumes we will view the land as more and more pioneer settlers arrived and the Iowa civilization took root and flourished, the veritable epic of its proud and unique development.

# Chapter Seven
# THE FORMATIVE YEARS

At the time of the American Revolution there was but wilderness beyond the Mississippi River and even, for the most part, east of the big river. The control of the large portion of North America did not include lands much farther westward than the Appalachian Mountains.

Many States in the new American Union had been granted charters by the English kings that often granted them more land than they had assumed up until 1776. For example, Virginia's charter granted her land that extended to the Pacific Ocean. After Independence it was necessary for the "Old Dominion" to give up any claim to land beyond its 1776 borders which, of course, at the time included what is now (and since the War between the States) West Virginia.

For Iowa, then, early government was a very vague matter for a half century. Very few white men had set foot upon the soil of the future state at the time it was acquired by the United States as a part of the Louisiana Purchase. Yet Julien Dubuque was safely settled in the area that was to later bear his name both as a city and a county.

In 1803 under the leadership of President Thomas Jefferson the infant Republic obtained the Louisiana domains from the French Emperor, Napoleon. Prior to that time there had been government under both Spain and France but very little as the population was so small.

When Jefferson and his diplomats secured Louisiana for the United States the size of the new and independent American nation was about doubled. The infant government had to find its way. The president had many ideas and the necessity for strong government was no more necessary under the United States than under the Spanish government. One of President Jefferson's ideas was that the vast new territory be explored. He could see into the future when many new Territories and States would be carved out of it all. That was in 1803 and the general government had half a continent to consider.

There was created by the Congress the District of Louisiana which existed as such for about a year and was annexed to Indiana.

In 1805 the Congress created a a separate Territory of the second class and the power of legislation was vested in a governor and the judges to be appointed. It is also significant that, at the time, a section of the act, by continuing in force until altered or repealed by the Legislature, all existing laws and regulations, provided tacitly for the system of slavery to prevail as it had already in certain settlements on the Arkansas and Missouri rivers.

The first military commandant

and civil governor of the "District of Louisiana" was Major Amos Stoddard described in early histories as "an intelligent and highly meritorious officer of the United States army, and author of a valuable work on the early history and resources of Louisiana."

From the vast area it was very early clear that two independent

MERIWETHER LEWIS
Explorer of the Northwest
Governor of Louisiana Territory
(Aquatint engraving, 1816, after C. B. J. F. de Saint-Memin; Granger Collection. From the book "The History of the United States" by Oscar Handlin. C. 1967 by Holt, Rinehart and Winston, Inc.)

States would be created but the remainder of the area was "an unknown savage wilderness of forests and prairies, traversed by a few roving bands of Indians, and explored only by a few French traders."

President Jefferson's yearning for knowledge of the "Purchase" saw its first results in the exploratory work done by Lewis and Clark in 1804 and 1805 when they went westward, found the source of the Missouri River and reached the Pacific Ocean by the Columbia River.

Lt. Zebulon M. Pike was the next to lead expeditions exploring the vast new area. He travelled up the Mississippi River and visited with Julien Dubuque and went farther northward into Minnesota along the great river. He went westward to explore the regions around the sources of the Arkansas and the Red Rivers. The principal object of those early explorations, we are told, was to establish friendly relations with the Indians preparing the way for the sale of the land for eventual settlement and government.

Early government over so vast a territory with so few people was a matter, most often, of paper work. No boundaries existed that were surveyed and if boundaries were drawn no one knew where they were unless the limits were fashioned by a river or other natural barrier.

In 1805 the "District of Louisiana" was remade to become the Territory of Louisiana in the first class with Territorial government but which would still be administered by a governor and appointed judges. The District of Louisiana was thereby severed from its relationship with Indiana and contained all the newly acquired land west of the Mississippi.

The first governor of the Territory of Louisiana was Gen.

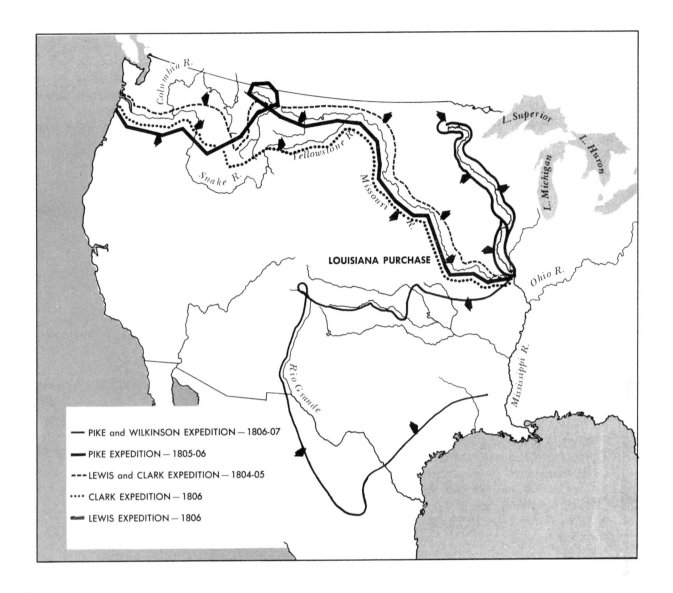

PIKE and WILKINSON EXPEDITION — 1806-07
PIKE EXPEDITION — 1805-06
LEWIS and CLARK EXPEDITION — 1804-05
CLARK EXPEDITION — 1806
LEWIS EXPEDITION — 1806

LOUISIANA PURCHASE

Various explorations brought back to President Jefferson knowledge of the vast lands encompassing the gigantic Louisiana Purchase which roughly doubled the size of the nation.   Note that Pike went up the Mississippi River to its source in Minnesota.  On the way he stopped and spent time with Julien Dubuque. Pike's Peak, overlooking McGregor, Iowa, in Clayton County is named after the explorer. From the Pike's Peak area can be seen far below the confluence of the Wisconsin and Mississippi Rivers where Marquette and Joliet first saw Iowa in 1673.   Both Lewis and Clark went up the Missouri River bordering Iowa on the west in their joint expedition and in their individual expeditions a year later, 1806.

James Wilkinson who was appointed in 1805 by President Jefferson and who served until the end of 1806.

Gen. Wilkinson was succeeded by Meriwether Lewis of expedition fame. Under Governor Lewis, who was assisted in his administration by territorial judges, the Territory of Louisiana remained a dependence of the United States until the year 1812. That year Louisiana became a State.

During its territorial status Louisiana was divided into six judicial districts, or very large counties. As in 1812 the "Territory of Orleans" became the State of Louisiana it was "deemed expedient" to change the name of the Territory of Louisiana.

By an Act of Congress passed on 4 June 1812 provision was made for "the organization of a representative grade of Territorial government upon the west side of the Mississippi, including all the settlements north of the western portion of the present State of Louisiana. (Louisiana is both east and west of the Mississippi and unrealized by many its capital, Baton Rouge, is actually east of the river.)

Regardless of the nature of the government the land that was to become Iowa remained a wilderness except for that part occupied by Julien Dubuque and his lead miners.

Thus the area that was to become Iowa became a part of the Territory of Missouri. In the entire vast territory there were few white residents. It is reported that in 1810 the entire population amounted to around 21,000 and 1,500 lived in the area of present day Arkansas. The remainder were in the present day area of Missouri as we know it.

On 4 June 1812 the Congress created the Territory of Missouri extending from 33 degrees latitude to 41 degrees north. The western limits would have been the Indian and Mexican lands far to the west, probably around 500 miles beyond the Mississippi River.

The capital was St. Louis.

The first governor was Gen. William Clarke and the Territorial Assembly consisted of a Legislative Council of nine members appointed by the president and a House of Representatives elected by the people. One representative could be chosen by every 500 residents who were free white males 21 years of age or older.

The first delegate to the Congress was Edward Hempstead.

Preparations began almost at once for the admission of Missouri as a State in the Union. The "Missouri question" was a long and debated one, now part of history.

On 10 August 1821 Missouri became a State and was regarded as a "slave State." The area between Missouri and Louisiana was created a Territory of the second class and organized as such.

With these acts Iowa remained relatively uninhabited and with little or no government. Nor had it much government ever.

From 30 April 1803 until 30 September 1804 it was merely part of the Louisiana Purchase.

From 1 October 1804 until 3 July 1805 "Iowa" was part of the

Congressional creation known as the District of Louisiana and attached to the Territory of Indiana for administrative and judicial purposes.

From 4 July 1805 our "Iowa" was under the Territory of Louisiana; it remained so until 30 September 1812.

On 1 October 1812 and until 9 August 1821 the lands of "Iowa" were a part of the Territory of Missouri until its admission as a State.

Then a seemingly strange thing happed. Iowa was left alone. No government and under no jurisdiction whatsoever. And it remained so for a little over 13 years. Congress and the national, or general government, seemed to have forgotten "Ioway."

Julien Dubuque had died in 1810 and the population was small. It would seem that those moving westward at the time preferred the warmer climes to the south. Other than Dubuque and his lead mining operations and other entrepreneurial pursuits, little activity abounded in the northeastern part of the area. Even the early Iowa pioneer settlers went, for the most part, to the "warmer" southern part of the lands of Iowa.

The people were self-governing, so to speak. Their knowledge of the Common Law and the Ten Commandments, their innate knowledge of right and wrong sustained them through those years when Iowa was under no jurisdiction and without government.

The period between 1821 and 1834 was one of "transition."

Chandler C. Childs of Dubuque wrote in the short-lived DUBUQUE DAILY REPUBLICAN in 1857 that the "state of society in the transition period, from the necessity of self-protection of individual interests until the application of territorial law could be

Gulf of Mexico

introduced in legal form, naturally produced many neighborhood conflicts between people and the selfish and vicious members of the community and against which there was no protection or remedy but the inherent right of self defense, or the union of the majority to suppress the daring intrusions or crimes of men who had no fear of anything but the execution of summary justice, though administered without the sanction of any legally constituted authority. Such punishments, usually inflicted by an excited populace often overstepped the rights and the authorized penalties inflicted by an organized community."

That era of "transition" or the absence of administrative or judicial jurisdiction continued until Congress acted in 1834.

On 1 October 1834 the area of Iowa was placed by the Congress under the jurisdiction of the Territory of Michigan. It remained so until 3 July 1836 and on the 4th of July 1836 "Iowa" came under the aegis of the Territory of Wisconsin. It was to remain in that status for two years before coming into its own. As a Territory itself.

Our mystery writer, to whom we allude from time to time, for his work in the 1878 histories of Iowa says: "In 1834, for the convenience of temporary government, the settlements north of the State of Missouri, and for 100 miles north of the Des Moines River, were erected by Congress into the 'District of Iowa,' and attached to the District of Wisconsin, subject to the jurisdiction of the Territory of Michigan. When the latter had assumed an independent State government, in 1836, the District of Wisconsin was erected into a separate government, known as the Wisconsin Territory exercising juris-

diction over the District of Iowa, then comprised in two large counties, designated as the counties of Des Moines and Dubuque. The aggregate population of these counties, in 1836, was 10,531 persons. It was not long before the District of Iowa became noted throughout the West for its extraordinary beauty and fertility, and the great advantages which it afforded to agricultural enterprise."

And so from under the jurisdiction of European monarchies to inclusion in the great Louisiana Purchase and then on under various governments, and indeed for a while no government at all, the vast lands that were to become "Iowa" were under several and various early governments.

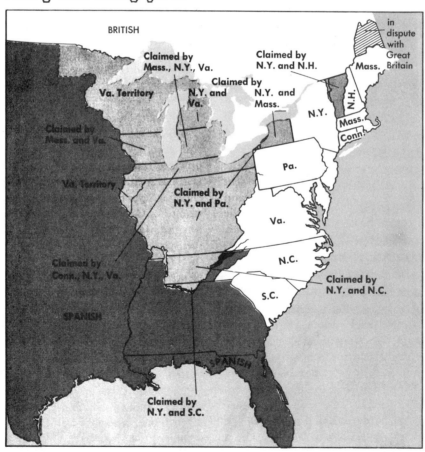

Conflicting claims by the former colonies to the lands of the northwest; some even claimed that their territories ran to the Pacific Ocean. Some colonies, by 1781, States, claimed lands claimed by other States.

136

This unpretentious wooden frame building was the capital of the Territory of Wisconsin when it was temporarily located at Belmont. As such it was, of course, the capital also for the District of Iowa.

So in 1836 the District of Iowa passed from the jurisdiction of Michigan upon its achieving Statehood. Thereupon the Territorial government of Wisconsin assumed the jurisdiction over the District of Iowa. The capital was located at Belmont although that town was always considered as a temporary capital until a planned one could be built and located at Madison in that Territory.

At the time Iowa's population, as we have noted, was only nearing the 11,000 mark. Most all of those inhabitants were in the Dubuque and Burlington areas in the counties of Dubuque and Des Moines. Iowans no more than became citizens of the Territory of Wisconsin than planning began in the minds of everyone for Territorial status for the "District." And, of course, Statehood was always the ultimate goal.

When the Wisconsin Territorial Legislature met at Belmont in October of 1836 it acted to create several counties out of the larger and southern Des Moines County in the District of Iowa. Those counties that were created were Des Moines, Lee, Henry, Van Buren, Muscatine, Cook and Louisa. Cook County a little later became Scott County.

When the Wisconsin Territory was created by the Congress on 20 April 1836 President Jackson subsequently appointed Henry Dodge as the governor. One of his first duties was to take a census and to make provision for the election of a legislature to include a Council (similar to a senate) and a House of Representatives. To guarantee a Republican form of government as guaranteed in the 4th Amendment. To give the people representative government which they had not had, as we have noted, under the monarchies of Europe.

The Wisconsin Territory had population on both sides of the Mississippi River. We've noted the population of the Iowa District at 10,531; on the east side of the river in Wisconsin proper there were 11,683. The figures were according to the territorial census and were as accurate as they could have been. No doubt some in the wilds or not contactable were not counted.

Governor Dodge issued a proclamation decreeing an election to be held; the decree was dated 9 September 1836. The election was to be held on October 2nd.

In the Iowa District "Demoine" County had the larger population there being a counted 6,257 residents and in Dubuque County there were 4,274 residents counted. Therefore each county was to have three members on the Territorial Council. "Demoine" would have seven members in the new Territorial House of Representatives and Dubuque would have five.

The election was held on 2 October as the governor had proclaimed and on 25 October 1836 the results were announced.

The Iowans elected to the Council and the House of Representatives were as follows from "Demoine" County: Elected to the Council (3): Arthur B. Inghram, Jeremiah Smith and Joseph B. Teas. The House members from "Demoine" were (7): Thomas Blair, John Box, David R. Chance, Warren L. Jenkins, Isaac Leffler, Eli Reynolds and George W. Teas. The Dubuque County members of the Council were (3): John Foley, Thomas McCraney and Thomas McKnight. House members from Dubuque County were (5): Hosea T. Camp, Peter Hill Engle, Hardin Nowlin, Patrick Quigley and Loring Wheeler.

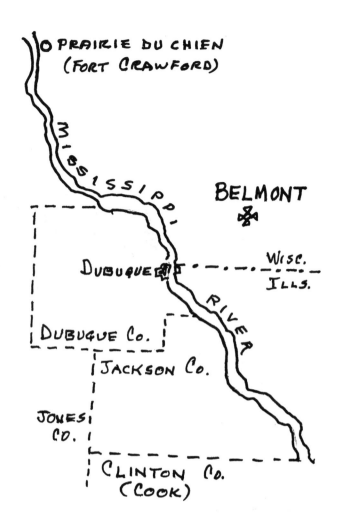

Different sources dispute the date of the first election; some say October 2nd and another insists upon October 10th. One way or another the list of the victors came out the same and later that month a legislature convened.

The Wisconsin Territorial Legislature convened on 25 october 1836 at Belmont, Wisconsin, in the frame building shown on the previous page. It selected Peter Hill Engle of Dubuque as the Speaker of the House and Henry S. Baird of Green Bay in Wisconsin as President of the Council. One of the acts of that Territorial Legislature was to establish the permanent capital of the Territory to be located at Madison.

As a result of some political maneuvering that session provided that the temporary capital should be at Burlington in "Demoine" County, the "District of Iowa." (See Chapter IX, Des Moines County.) Thus Burlington in Des Moines County, Iowa, became the temporary seat of government over a vast area that eventually became the States of Wisconsin, Iowa Minnesota and parts of North and South Dakota. Only a few other cities in our history, other than Washington, D. C. itself, had ever held even nominal jurisdiction over so vast an area. But, Burlington, Iowa, did! The action has been called a "master stroke" of political give-and-take on the part of the representatives from "Demoine" County. There were also conditions attached to the selection of Burlington as temporary capital.

The representatives from Burlington agreed that the young city would provide a place for the meetings of the legislature to include space for the officers of the government.

Jeremiah Smith, Jr., was one of the representatives from Des Moines County and, more especially as a resident of Burlington itself, with his own money he constructed a building where the legislature could hold its sessions.

The Wisconsin Territorial Legislature met for the first time in Burlington on 6 November 1837. It would remain in session until 30 January 1838 when it would recess until June 11th of that year.

But those sessions would be meeting in the same building, the one built for the lawmakers by Mr. Smith.

Sometime during the night of December 12th and 13th the temporary capital burned to the ground. The more accurate date is given as 13 December 1837 and that is the one

we accept as true for historical purposes. (See Chapter IX, Des Moines County.)

Other than meeting in Burlington both officers of the legislature were from Burlington. Arthur Inghram was elected president of the Council and Col. Isaac Leffler was elected as Speaker of the House. After the conflagration that destroyed the new house of government the two houses of the legislature had to find new homes.

The Council moved into McCarver's building which housed the newspaper and met in the west room on the second floor. The House of Representatives convened their sessions over the store of Webber and Remey.

About this time there was also convened in Burlington a sort-of Territorial Convention to which representatives from all the organized counties of Iowa came to express to the Congress their consensus and to send memorials thereto.

Those memorials to the Congress centered around their desire to become a Territory. A Territory of Iowa west of the Mississippi. That was paramount. Their two other memorials dealt with the settlement of an on-going boundary dispute with Missouri and pre-emptive rights for squatters. The Wisconsin Territorial Legislature formulated three similar memorials plus dividing Dubuque County into several smaller ones in a like manner as had been done with Des Moines County before.

GEN. GEORGE WALLACE JONES

George W. Jones was the delegate to Congress for the Wisconsin Territory. He was a resident of Sinsinawa in Wisconsin across the Mississippi River from Dubuque where he engaged in many activities to include lead mining and farming. His influence was national and it was almost a presumption that he would be elected the Territorial Delegate to the U. S. Congress.

He had been a personal friend of the presidents since James Monroe and in Congress was a personal friend of President Van Buren. Delegate Jones had much influence upon the naming of both Wisconsin and Iowa. He worked for Wisconsin Statehood and for Territorial status for the then "District of Iowa." He later moved across the river into Dubuque and became one of Iowa's United States senators after it became a State.

The portrait at the left is in oils and shows General Jones as he appeared when a younger man. The painting was done by W. L. McMaster and was at one time the property of the State of Iowa; it is presumed that it still is.

Other pictures of Gen. Jones appear in Chapter VIII, Dubuque County, and in Chapter XIX, Jones County, which was named to honor him even while he was a younger man which amounts to quite an unusual honor. Gen. George W. Jones achieved great wealth and power and even national influence in his long life. He always used it all for the good.

Thus Iowa had passed through its formative years. The full realization of its posterity was before it. Nature's God had treated it bountifully, giving it a rich natural heritage. Even the primitive dwellers and the more recent Indians had found sustenance and a good life in "the beautiful land."

The white man had found it and came to it, slowly at first, but by now in the thousands. It had been the property of monarchs of Europe but had finally come under the aegis of the United States of America.

A part of Louisiana and then of the Territory of Missouri it was left an orphan, a mere "waif," someone said. It lingered from 1821 until 1834 under no jurisdication. Then it was attached to the Michigan Territory in 1834 where it remained until 1836 when it became part of the Territory of Wisconsin.

In 1838 Iowa became a Territory and could look toward Statehood.

The article on the following pages is extracted from one entitled "The Earliest Days" by William Eldridge of Maynard in OUT OF THE MIDWEST - a Portrait. (See Ch. XXIII, book ad.)

## THE GREAT SURVEY

The next step in the movement of the white man across the Mississippi was the establishment, by the federal government, of some means of determining the boundaries of the new claims of land to be made into farms and town plats. In most of the eastern states the surveys were by "metes and bounds", using rocks, trees, and streams as identification points. These identifying points often tended to disappear through removal or erosion, and re-surveys were sought because of sales of property or disputes over local boundary lines. My grandfather was a surveyor in the rough terrain of eastern Ohio, a position of considerable importance in those days, and he was called upon to settle disputes over land rights. My father often told of how he "carried chain" for these measurements. My uncle, the eldest son, inherited the practice, which he turned over to his only son, who, even today, is called upon to make surveys. He says that most of the old surveys, made almost two centuries ago, check out very accurately, often to a fraction of an inch. These re-surveys sometimes resulted in the displeasure of one member of the dispute, if he coveted a few feet of his neighbor's land, and to the joy of the other member, who retorted, "I told you so."

The Congressional mills sometimes grind slowly, but in this case a system was evolved and passed; and the Surveyor General, who had his office in Cincinnati, Ohio, was instructed to create a procedure for making the surveys with the assistance of two deputies with offices in Dubuque and Burlington. The issuance of land titles was to be made from these offices and land sales headquartered there. It was estimated that there would be some 1,500 to 1,600 townships, each containing 36 sections of 640 acres, or a total of some 35 million acres. By the time the surveys were to commence, there were some 23,000 settlers already west of the Mississippi, clamoring for boundaries for their pre-emptions. The first letter from the Surveyor General's office in Cincinnati to the sub-office in Dubuque relative to the Iowa survey was dated August 16, 1836, and gave instructions for the beginning of the survey. The survey parties, who had been waiting for the word, immediately began the huge task.

I am certain that the readers of this history will not wish to be bored by a long account of the massive amount of corespondence and directions sent out by the Surveyor General's office. Anyone who wants to pursue the matter further will find details in a book entitled, "Original Instructions Governing Public Land Surveys in Iowa," published by Iowa State University. I shall here and only briefly attempt to relate how the surveys were made.

There must necessarily be a starting point for a project of this kind, and the government had established such a point. The survey of much of Missouri had already been completed, and so this starting base was extended up into Iowa. The east and west line, (called the "Base Line") beginning at the junction of the St. Francis and Mississippi rivers in Arkansas, would be a base for all surveys in Arkansas, Missouri, Iowa, North Dakota, and parts of Minnesota and South Dakota. The north and south line (called the "Fifth Principal Meridian") would begin at the junction of the Arkansas and Mississippi rivers, and extend northward from that point. The point of intersection was about 70 miles east and three miles south of Little Rock, Arkansas. The east and west tiers of townships were called "ranges," while the north and south tiers were called "township no. _____."

A geographical township, a 6-mile square containing 36 sections of 640 acres each, was to be the unit of measurement for determining the position of any parcel of land that needed to be described. It was planned that 24-mile units (east and west) would constitute the width of counties, which would be the next larger unit. The townships had already been surveyed and numbered north along the Fifth Principal Meridian as far as the planned Iowa-Missouri line, which would be near the 67th and 68th township north, except for the triangular tip of Iowa in the southeast corner.

There was a huge mass of detail in the survey that was made, which would only confuse anyone not acquainted with the technical procedure, so we shall keep to a minimum of description. The first survey that has any significance for us was made by a man named Orson Lyon. He was instructed to establish the Fifth Principal Meridian across the part of the state that constitutes the "belly" which lies to the east along the Mississippi. At the junction of the 78th and 79th townships north he was to survey a line at right angles to the Meridian, extending from the Mississippi west to the western border of the first Sac and Fox Purchase, a distance of about 50 miles, laying off the township corners. Then he was to continue the Meridian northward to the junction of townships 88 and 89, where another "correction" line would be established at right angles to the Meridian. Then the Meridian would be extended

north to the junction of the Mississippi, a distance of about 20 miles. Township lines would be established along these lines to accommodate the settlers who were establishing claims along the "Military Road" (which was to connect Dubuque with Fort Atkinson in the Neutral Lands). This was accomplished during the autumn of 1836, and the following year a surveyor named James Videto made the sub-division into sections and quarter sections.

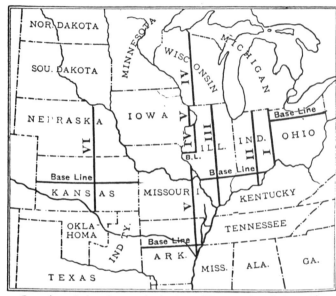

Location of six of the Principal Meridians and their Base Lines for Congressional Township Surveys.

One might ask what those "correction lines" were supposed to do. Unfortunately (at least for survey purposes) the earth is nearly round. A series of 6-mile square townships would soon run out of space, because the lines of longitude and latitude converge. To compensate for this a new line of townships (6-mile ones) was surveyed along these correction base lines and extended to the north. These townships along the base correction lines were given an additional 2 chain or 132 ft. in width to compensate for the irregularity of the curvature. The second correction line lies 21 miles south of

142

Maynard, and the Fifth Meridian lies 51 miles east. (Harlan township's description is Twp 82 N Range 9 west.) This second correction line coincides with U.S. Highway 20 through Buchanan County. All surveys start in the southeast corner of the township or section, and all errors or changes are thrown to the north and west. This is why many "forties" on these sides are "fractional", or more or less than 40 acres. The sections are subdivided into quarters and quarter-quarter (forties).

The work of platting the entire state was finished in 1859, ending with the establishment of township lines and subdivision in Lyon County over in the extreme northwestern corner of the state. Much of the labor was done by contract, although the most important lines were usually run by salaried men with experience. These men received from $100 to $150 per month and maintenance. The common laborers drew $15 per month and board. Most survey parties were composed of a minimum of six men, although seven or eight were considered more efficient in the difficult parts of the terrain. The minimum party consisted of the Chief of Party, who did the instrument work and calculation; two chainmen, who did the measurement; one or two ax men, who cleared brush, erected monuments, and cut firewood; one teamster, who hauled supplies and moved camps; and finally, one cook, who hunted game for the pot, purchased supplies, and did the cooking. Sometimes an extra man or two assisted with the instrument work and the hauling and clearing.

The transport consisted of two or three teams and wagons. One wagon, which was covered to protect the instruments, records, and supplies, served as headquarters for

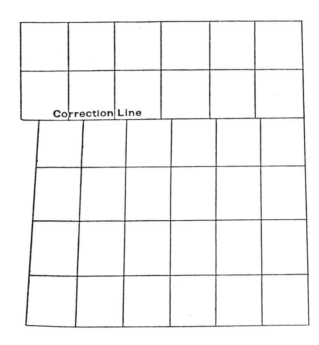

the party. The Chief slept in that wagon to protect the instruments and records. A second wagon was used to haul other supplies, such as a tent for the rest of the men, bedrolls, and a few personal items allowed for each man. The men slept out in the open or in the tent on bed-rolls laid out on the ground. The cook did all of the cooking over open fires. Food was limited to salt pork, beans, corn breads, and whatever game the cook or other men were able to shoot. One bit of information concerning a party that left Dubuque for a long trip into difficult terrain, gave the list of supplies as consisting of five barrels of pork, three bags of beans, and one bag of cornmeal, plus some grain for the horses and a little salt for both man and beast.

The work week consisted of six days, 12 hours each, and rain or shine. The regimen was tempered by leave on Sunday, if a settlement were handy. The Chief had his worries too. Many times he had to hunt up his help on Monday morning, often collecting the drunks and sobering

TOWNSHIP 89 N., RANGE 14 W., DIVIDED INTO SEC-
TIONS AND QUARTER SECTIONS.

| | | | | | |
|---|---|---|---|---|---|
| 6 | 5 | 4 | 3 | 2 | Sec. 1 |
| 7 | 8 | 9 | 10 | 11 | 12 |
| 18 | 17 | School 16 Land | 15 | 14 | 13 |
| 19 | 20 | 21 | 22 | 23 | 24 |
| 30 | 29 | 28 | 27 | 26 | 25 |
| 31 | 32 | 33 | 34 | 35 | 36 |

The darkened part of section 24 would be described as the N. W. ¼ of Sec. 24, Tp. 89 N., R. 14 W., of the 5th Principal Meridian.

The darkened part of section 25 would be described as the N. E. ¼ of the N. E. ¼ of Sec. 25, Tp 89 N., R. 14 W., of the 5th Principal Meridian.

The darkened part of section 28 would be described as the N. ½ of the S. W. ¼ of Sec. 28, Tp. 89 N., R. 14 W., of the 5th Principal Meridian.

NOTE.—A large map is published by the Federal Government, showing all the Congressional surveys in the United States. By means of this map, students may locate any city or village in his own or any other State where Congressional surveys exist. Smaller maps of Iowa can be purchased giving the surveys for Iowa, and a student should practice locating the towns of Iowa. We would suggest the location of the following cities: Atlantic, Boone, Burlington, Cedar Falls, Clinton, Cedar Rapids, Council Bluffs, Charles City, Creston, Des Moines, Dubuque, Fort Dodge, Grinnell, Indianola, Iowa City, Keokuk, Le Mars, Marshalltown, Oskaloosa, Ottumwa, Sioux City, Waterloo, Webster City, and Winterset.

(AUTHOR'S NOTE: This article on surveys was written by William Eldridge of Maynard, Iowa, and is extracted from a longer article by him which appeared in "OUT OF THE MIDWEST - A Portrait," a large book that was a Bicentennial project of Fayette County volunteers. See advertisement for purchase of the book on page 330, Chapter XXIII. The maps are from other sources. --- D.L.K.)

them with a rough trip in the bed of the wagon. Sometimes an employee would "go over the hill" during the week-end. So, often little was accomplished on Mondays. An almost military kind of discipline was maintained in camp because the men labored in close contact with each other, and there was not time for quarreling. Then, too, watch had to be kept at night to prevent a thieving Indian from taking horses or supplies.

One tale reveals how a team was stolen at night; and the cook, an old Indian scout, asked to be allowed to run down the culprit. He was gone three days and returned with the horses. He showed the Chief a bloody hank of hair and skin, then threw it in the fire saying, "That Injun ain't goin' to bother nobody again."

Another story tells how one of the wood-cutters was killed by a falling tree. The crew took an hour off to plant him with a proper burial service and erected a wooden monument close by a section cornerstone.

Life was rough in those days.

The surveying equipment consisted of a compass, a Gunter chainpins, and a field book. The compass was mounted on a tripod, levelled by thumbscrews. A telescope was mounted on a swivel above the compass so that angle degrees could be read. The Gunter chain, used in measurements, was composed of 100 links of steel chain, each link being 7.92 inches in length. A little pencil-work will show that 25 links would equal a rod, and the full chain length would equal four rods. Thus 20 chains would be a quarter-mile, and 80 chains would equal a full mile. The little steel pins would be stuck into the ground to mark chain lengths.

Calculation in survey work involves "triangularization," employing the prime law of trigonometry that if one knows two sides and the included angle of a triangle, or two angles and the included side, he can calculate the unknown sides or angles by the use of tables of sines, cosines and tangents. Thus, if one is surveying over rough terrain, he can make use of vertical, imagined triangles; or, if one cannot see a desired point, he can measure off another triangle using a common side and make his computations that way.

If one is driving along a highway or country road, he may sometimes see that the road ahead does some queer zig-zagging. This is usually because of careless or drunken instrument men who made the original survey. Sometimes the error was due to the difference between "true" or "polar" north and "magnetic" north, as denoted by the compass needle. If one were to stand facing "true" north (which can be determined by "shooting" the North

DIAGRAM TO ILLUSTRATE THE LOCATION OF LAND BY CONGRESSIONAL TOWNSHIPS.

| | | | | |
|---|---|---|---|---|
| Township 3 North | | | Township 3 North | |
| | | MERIDIAN | Township 2 North | |
| | | PRINCIPAL | Township 1 North | |
| BASE | | | LINE | |
| Range 3 West | Range 2 West | Range 1 West FIFTH | Range 1 East | Range 2 East |
| Tp. 2 S. Range 3 W. | | | | 6 5 4 3 2 1 / 7 8 9 10 11 12 / 18 17 16 15 14 13 / 19 20 21 22 23 24 / 30 29 28 27 26 25 / 31 32 33 34 35 36 |

Star at night), he would find that the needle of the surveying compass would point slightly to the right, toward the "magnetic" pole. The ensuing angle is called a "variation," which in our part of the country is approximately nine degrees. This variation must be taken into account in calculations.

A system of "monuments," or "markers," was used to identify points along the surveys. Various sizes and shapes of oak, elm, or some other long-lasting wood posts, were set and marked to establish township, section, or "quarter" corners. For instance, a section corner was marked by a small squared post, bevelled on top, set at 45-degree angles to the cardinal directions, and the section numbers carved or burned into the proper side. Township corners were shown by larger posts marked in a similar way with the township and range numbers. Other

145

identifying data were denoted by notches carved along the side of the post. The post was allowed to extend a few feet above ground and a "pit", or 4-sided ditch, dug a few feet away, with the dirt thrown into a mound around the post. The settler who was searching for a certain plot of land could easily identify any point. Having once secured the legal description of unclaimed plots, he had only to follow the line of monuments until he arrived at the correct place. It is unlikely that there are any of the original markers in place at present. If so, they are carefully protected. Sometimes in place of wooden markers, stones of various shapes and sizes were used for survey markers. When they were used, it was customary to place a charred post or shovelful of charcoal under the stone so that the spot could be identified if the stone were removed. Over the years, as the original markers were destroyed or removed, steel rods have been driven into the ground to serve as markers.

While the government made every effort to keep ahead with surveys, often a settler would choose a parcel of land that was as yet unsurveyed. In that case he "pre-empted" the claim, making known that he would buy it as soon as the survey was completed. Sometimes the competition for claims resulted in disputes, or even killings, but it was usually conceded that the first to declare and take possession was entitled to first opportunity for purchase.

After subdivision of a township, a land sale was usually held. Often land speculators would buy up large tracts of land, and the settler had to protect his rights. Usually a "committee" of "pre-emptors" was present to bid on the desired tracts,

and anyone who had the nerve to bid against the committee was unceremoniously escorted to a place where he could not bid. Any disputes not settled in this way were handled by a representative of the land office, often the engineer who had made the survey. His decision was final, not even being subject to court appeal.

In making the original survey, the 16th section of a township was leased to nearby settlers and the rent money deposited in the school fund.

Most land in the early days was sold for $1.25 per acre; but, as the demand grew, the price was advanced to $2.50 per acre. Large tracts were given for subsidizing the building of railroads. Some lands - "swamp" lands, for instance - were given to the states. There were some cases where land was not too desirable, and that was called "graduation" land and sold for less than the standard $1.25 per acre.

Payment for claims, and the issuance of titles, was made at either Dubuque or Burlington.

As segments of the great survey became available to the influx of land seekers, most were taken at once. Only the most undesirable plots remained unsold. The first areas to be filled up were near Dubuque and some of the other river towns. Settlement was illegal before June, 1833; but some traders and adventurers had quietly taken possession when the land became available.

By 1859 the entire state of Iowa had been surveyed. In the process much new territory became available to the hordes of land-hungry people from the eastern states who poured in from the east and the south, seeking new homes in our "Beautiful Land."

## Chapter Eight
# DUBUQUE COUNTY

Dubuque County may be regarded in many ways as the most historic of Iowa's counties to the extent that so much activity centered around that area long before the earliest of the pioneer settlers arrived.

Marquette and Joliet are supposed to have landed in the low level area below the bluffs where the City of Dubuque is now situated. If that is so then there is little doubt that they were the first white men to set foot upon the soil of Dubuque County, even the Norsemen, notwithstanding, for while they may have entered Minnesota, they likely meandered into Iowa at a farther western point, if at all.

It is also plausible that if Pere Marquette and Joliet did set foot on the shore at Dubuque it was their second stop on Iowa soil, for we know the first was at McGregor in Clayton County. Their river expedition, recall, landed for their meals and slept offshore in their canoes. Dubuque, therefore, is a reasonable distance to travel by canoe between repasts.

From 1673 and for over a century many white men probably passed the site of our present-day Dubuque in navigating up or down the Mississippi. Between Marquette and Joliet and

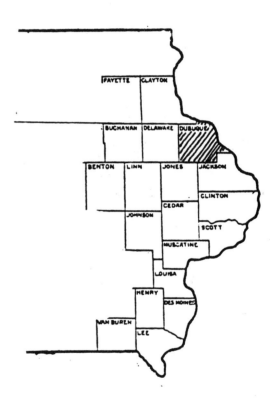

Julien Dubuque's permanent settlement many white explorers were at Dubuque.

From the earliest of known times the interest and activity in and around the area centered about the existence of the lead mines. Knowledge of the lead deposits long antedated the coming of Julien Dubuque. Following the expedition of Marquette and Joliet, the Mississippi soon became the great artery of trans-

147

portation in the central North American continent.

The Marquette and Joliet expedition marked the beginning of the westward movement in its own small way, at first, and stirred the interest of many others of many nations in what might lie across the great river.

The explorations of other white men following the first two Frenchmen are recorded earlier in this history.

JULIEN DUBUQUE

The first permanent white settler in what was to become the State of Iowa was Julien Dubuque.

The prime interest of the young Julien Dubuque was in the mining of lead. A magnificent lode was reputed to be in the area and they, when operated, became known as "the Mines of Spain." Dubuque first set foot upon the soil of the land that was to one day bear his name, probably in 1785. For it was in that year that he had arrived in Prairie du Chien where he headquartered while exploring for opportunities in the area. He had left his home in

Quebec in 1783. The adventurous Dubuque had also heard about the potential lead deposits down the river. He no doubt had visited the mining area before making efforts to settle there.

His first efforts to make any **kind of an intrusion into the area** had to be with the consent of the local Indians. By obtaining their permission he settled there in 1788 with a small group of miners who were in his employ. He also had the "permission" of the Spanish monarchy to mine the area.

While 1785 is reckoned to be the first visit to the area by Dubuque some suppose he could have been there as early as 1783.

Iowa's first permanent settler and the French-Canadian after whom both the city and the county of Dubuque are named, had a colorful and interesting background as well as ancestry.

**The history of Dubuque County (or city) is never complete without that of its (their) namesake, the Sieur Julien.**

The pioneer settler and founder was of Norman descent and for several generations before his birth the family had lived in Canada. The family name has been recorded as Dubuc, Dubucq and Du Buque and was spelled various ways until the name as we know it today was settled upon. In his signature (shown in this text) Julien himself spelled his name as we know it.

Jean Dubuque was the first of the family to come to the new world. He was born in Trinity Parish, the Diocese of Rouen, France, and married Marie Hotot at Quebec in 1668. They had a son named Augustin Dubuque who was born in 1707 and was the father of our Julien. Augustin married Marie Maillot in 1744 and the son, Julien, was born in 1762 on January

10th at St. Peirre-les-Becquets in Nicolet County in the district of Trois Rivieres on the banks of the St. Lawrence River.

On his mother's side it has been determined by R. G. Thwaites, Wisconsin historian, that Julien Dubuque's ancestors were distinguished officers in the Canadian army and members of the parliament as well as having been related to Jacques Polier who was a leading pioneer in Wisconsin and later a state official and judge.

Julien Dubuque was from a large family. There were 13 children and he was the youngest, there being six boys and six girls older than he.

Canada came under the rule of the British after 1763 and it wasn't until 1800 that Dubuque again lived under the French flag. (The treaty giving Louisiana to Spain had been a secret one and it took Napoleon to take back the area for France in 1800.) Then in 1803 France sold the entire area to the United States in what we know as the Louisiana Purchase. Thereby Julien Dubuque's citizenship was changed for a fifth time. And the last. For after 1803 he was a citizen of the United States.

All accounts say Julien Dubuque was well educated in the parish schools and at Sorel. Remaining documents written by him indicate he was more highly educated than most of the pioneer settlers. At a time when many could not write he penned a handsome signature.

Some of Dubuque's relation came to reside in the Mississippi River valley before he arrived in the area. There were Dubuques in Illinois and in the St. Louis area. Jean Baptiste Dubuque had settled in Cahokia, Ills., and had lived there when George Rogers Clark captured it for the British during the War for American Independence.

(Jean Baptiste's daughter, Caroline,

Julien's niece, married John Reynolds who later became a U.S. Congressman and Governor of Illinois from 1834 to 1837, and about whom more will be read later in this history.)

A cousin, Augustin Dubuque, became a naturalized citizen of the United States in 1787 -- the year the Constitution was written -- and took the oath of allegiance some sixteen years before Julien became a citizen as a result of the Louisiana Purchase.

Records show that Julien Dubuque's father died in 1783 and it is apparent that the young son, who would have been about 21 that year, soon departed the St. Lawrence area following his loss. He probably sailed the Great

Julien Dubuque's Signature

Lakes to Green Bay and into the Fox River, portaged to the Wisconsin River, and finally arrived at Prairie du Chien.

In a 1796 petition to Baron de Carondelet, then the governor, Dubuque averred that he had made "many voyages" before becoming the "peaceable possessor of a tract of land" among the Indians, according to the Rev. M. M. Hoffmann. (See Bibliography)

Having become the "peaceable possessor" in 1788, his voyages had to have been between 1783 and that year of his final settlement. At least one such voyage, we are told, was to see his relatives in Cahokia, Illinois.

The "mines" were relatively common knowledge and the adventurous young Dubuque was led on one of his trips to the Catfish Creek area where he reached an agreement with the Fox chiefs. Before that time the Indians were very protective of their lead mining resources and had usually, but not always, kept the white man away. Julien Dubuque knew what he wanted and he got it. When he entered into his agreement with the Fox Indians it is to be supposed that it was not the first time he had visited the area.

The Indians liked Dubuque as he was always fair with them and soon earned their lasting respect. They even gave him an Indian name which in French was "La Petite Nuit" meaning literally, the "Little Night" but more realistically it probably meant "Little Cloud."

THE DUBUQUE FAMILY COAT OF ARMS

The Dubucqs of Normandy in France carried as their heraldic insignia a coat which was silver with a bend azure, that is, a blue diagonal stripe on a silver shield. Jean Dubucq came from Normandy to Quebec in Canada in the middle of the seventeenth century, and his great - grandson Julien, who spelled the family name Dubuque, was Iowa's first permanent white settler and gave his name to both a county and a city.
(From Hoffmann's "Antique Dubuque", See Bibliography.)

Dubuque may have learned a lot about the mines from Marie Anne Cardinal, who was a prominent figure in Prairie du Chien and the widow of Jean Marie Cardinal. She was also a black Pawnee but when she was baptized in St. Louis along with her seven children the priest gave her the French name of Marianne. She took the name Marie Anne; her Indian name had been Careche-Coranche. (Her husband probably resided from time to time in antique Dubuque between 1763 and 1780 as is born out by land grants in the Upper Mississippi valley holdings issued during those years and also the confirmation of land grants to the successors of Jean Marie Cardinal in later years.)

From the widow of Jean Marie Cardinal, therefore, Julien Dubuque probably learned a lot about the area he was to inhabit. Dubuque's name also came to be associated with that of a man named Antaya and another resident of Prairie du Chien named Basil Giard about whom we'll read more later. (See Clayton County, Chapter XVIII.)

Having reached verbal agreements with the Fox Indian chiefs and gained a working knowledge of the area it was then time to formalize their understandings.

Dubuque's contract with the

Indians was signed at Prairie du Chien on 22 September 1788, with the representatives of the Fox Indians "of the branch of five villages." Upon the completion of the agreement Dubuque paid the Indians for his new grant in goods. An important part of the agreement was the permission of the Fox chiefs to erect monuments, markers, to establish the limits of the tract of land granted to Dubuque and over which he would exercise dominion. Such stone monuments were erected at the mouth of the Little Maquoketa River at the north of the mines and at the mouth of the Tetes des Morts to the south thus creating the upper and lower boundaries. It has been estimated the entire tract was 21 miles long from north to south.

Julien Dubuque moved almost at once to occupy the lands which had been granted for his domination and control. He settled there and began his work. In his hire were ten white men at first who were taken on as laborers removing from Prairie du Chien. Others later joined the growing community Dubuque had established. The only two names history gives us as being among those hired were G. Lucie and D'Bois the latter having arrived there with Dubuque himself in 1788.

Several of Dubuque's men eventually married Indian maidens from the local Fox tribes, and pioneer settlers as late as 1830 arrived at "the Mines of Dubuque," as they were by then known, to find the "graves of some of the children of these couples extant with the palings that had been placed around them still standing." (Hoffmann)

Julien Dubuque had lost his father, as we have noted, when but a young man of around 21. The tales of adventure and romance in the west had no doubt excited him. But he was an obviously courageous and intelligent soul as his life and adventures testify. He must also have possessed such talents and abilities as leadership, diplomacy, aggressiveness and the capability of managing a small business and farming "empire."

We think of Dubuque as a miner but he was also an expert farmer and a trader who rapidly became known up and down the Mississippi River. His diverse holdings, therefore, would have required some excellence of administration.

Many had tried over the years to deal with the Indians to gain a foothold in the rich lead mining area over which the Foxes had control. It was for Julien Dubuque to finally obtain the desired lands and develop them. He apparently knew how to deal with the Indians and to them trust was a major factor in a relationship. The Indians trusted Dubuque and he never gave them any cause not to. The friendship between

Dubuque and the Fox Indians became a firm one.

As is usual legends grew around Dubuque's genius for getting along with the Indians. Apparently Julien Dubuque was one of those colorful individuals around whom legends tend to grow. Some became the ones that made him bigger than life, more than reality. But as is also usual the venturesome Dubuque came to be portrayed by some in a lesser light than he deserves and also one demeaning to the Indians who, to Dubuque, were something more than noble savages.

Whatever his talents and abilities the mining, farming and commercial enterprises of Julien Dubuque prospered from the beginning. His mining operations spread to the entire area along the bluffs and extended where feasible several miles inland. It is also believed that Dubuque did not restrict his mining operations to the west side of the river. He not only enjoyed the confidence and cooperation of the Foxes on the west side of the river but evidently also that of the Winnebagoes on the Illinois shore. It is

known that he opened a lead mine near the present town of Elizabeth, Illinois, and in 1805 he was operating the old Buck and Hog leads on the Fevre River.

It is reported that in 1826 a heavy sledge hammer that belonged to Dubuque's miners was found under the ashes of an old furnace. That find was at Ottawa in Allenwrath's diggings only two miles from Galena.

R. G. Thwaites is quoted by M. M. Hoffmann again as saying:

"Dubuque appears to have largely employed his Indian friends in prospecting for lead mines. When their discoveries were reported to him, he would send some Canadians and half-breeds to prove the claims and sometimes to work them; although, in many cases, he was content with proving the claim and allowing the Indians to work it themselves, the product being brought to his large trading-house on the west side of the river. In this manner the entire region of the lead mines in Iowa, Wisconsin and Illinois became more or less occupied by Dubuque's men before any permanent American settlement."

It is evident that the Indians mined the lead long before Dubuque's arrival but in a crude fashion and certainly not for marketing or commerce. They needed probably only bullets for the musketry obtained from the French and English. It is presumed that the French taught mining skills to the Indians and that may have started with Perrot nearly a century before.

Dubuque "modernized" the operations and his workers had hoes, shovels, levers, crow-bars and other tools. The ore was usually brought to the opening of the mine shafts in crude but tough deerskin pouches. We are told that early writers observed the old men and squaws doing the mining while the young bucks worked at smelting. Other than those whom Dubuque brought with him from Prairie du Chien, most of the other workers who mined the lead were Indians.

The years passed and Dubuque became a very wealthy man. His mining operations yielded well and his farming and commerical ventures prospered also.

In his newly acquired station of wealth and prosperity it has been suggested that Dubuque "may have become doubtful of the thorough validity of his contract in 1788 with the Fox chiefs." (Hoffmann)

One way or another the Spanish authority had grown in the Louisiana district and the governors appointed by the king of Spain had been asserting themselves over the years since Dubuque arrived. He decided to rename his mining operations and decided in the 1790's to call them "Les Mines d'Espagne" or "the Mines of Spain" and at the same time decided to seek a formal recognition of his claims by and with the formal recognition of his claims by and with the formal approval of the Spanish governor who was, as we read earlier, Baron de Carondelet, who acted from his capital at New Orleans. Dubuque knew also that de Carondelet was anxious to grant titles to the vast lands and to have people settle upon them and populate them for the mother country. Wealth and defense were two of the baron's main reasons. (Spain was an ally of France and was at war with England.)

The subjects of France, Spain and England with warring with each other all over the globe and Spain sought the aid of settlers in the Upper Louisiana area. So the governor looked to Julien Dubuque, as a powerful leader who could support the Spanish lands.

In 1796, therefore, Julien Dubuque appeared before the governor-general or entered an appearance through an agent. His request was presented to the governor in the flowery language of the time: "Your excellency's very humble petitioner, named Julien Dubuque.....had bought a tract of land from the Indians.....and of his perseverance has surmounted all obstacles.....has come to be the peaceable possessor of a tract of land.....to which he has given the name of the "Mines of Spain".....the very humble petitioner prays your Excellency to have the goodness to assure him the enjoyment of the mines and lands.....to pardon me my style, and be pleased to accept the pure simplicity of my heart.....your Excellency's very humble, and very obedient and very submissive servant."

The governor-general sought the advice of one Andrew Todd who responded to the "Senor Governor" with his approval.

(Note that Dubuque told the governor-general that he had bought the land from the Indians.)

On 10 November 1796 Dubuque's petition was "granted as asked" by the baron de Carondelet with a restriction approved by the governor-general upon the request of "the merchant, Andrew Todd" who evidently had the ear of de Carondelet.

Dubuque's claim was now as strong as it could be for the time and under the temporal authority, then the Spanish Empire. Fr. Hoffmann called it a "princely claim." And whatever the restrictions and influence of "the merchant, Andrew Todd," he died of the yellow fever.

Dubuque grew and prospered and his only competition was from wandering trappers and traders or from Astor's American Fur Company which operated out of Mackinac far off in Michigan but which also had a representative who operated in what was to become Des Moines and Lee Counties. In the Dubuque area competition was carried on only on the eastern side of the Mississippi.

JULIEN DUBUQUE
Another picture of Julien Dubuque as he probably appeared. Note that the picture is "Copyrighted 1907" by, it would seem to read: C.L. Trudell who drew or painted it. (From SEED/HARVEST).

War broke out between England and Spain in 1796 as a part of Napoleon's expansionist efforts. Spain was controlled by Napoleon and he even put one of his brothers on the throne. Fr. Hoffmann tells us that "in the spring of 1797 English traders at Prairie du Chien were nearly pillaged by the Saques and Renards (Sacs and Foxes) headed by some traders from St. Louis with authority from the Spanish commandant of that place." It is quite evident that Dubuque, jealous of his monopoly rights, along with his Fox Indian chiefs and their warriors took an active role in at least one Spanish attack on Prairie du Chien.

Other than his vastly acquired wealth from mining, farming, commerce, peltries and other enterprises Julien Dubuque became a very wealthy man and with that wealth went both political and military power. His name was known up and down the Mississippi River valley. On the Catfish Creek was his home surrounded by stables, warehouses and cabins for his foremen and other workers. Truly Dubuque had created his own empire. It was once referred to as "a fortified settlement on the banks of the river." That because he had cannon and palisades built about his personal environs.

Julien Dubuque journeyed down the great river twice a year with his cargo boats of lead ore and furs referred to as "the riches argosies on the upper Mississippi during those years." While there he was entertained in high fashion by most of the leading citizens of St. Louis, to great dinners and formal balls.

After these trips he would return upstream with merchandise, wares, new tools and equipment, trinkets for the Indians and above all, gold and silver coin.

It has been accurately reported

that Dubuque's smelting furnaces were the largest in the west and he controlled the boats which carried his ore and various other products to market. He is said to have had absolute and supreme control over the lead industry establishing the market prices and fixing the price of the finished product. Hoffmann says: "By a hundred and twenty-five years he anticipated the policies of the Guggenheims and the American Smelting and Refining Company."

Julien Dubuque was described by the son of Dubuque's own business agent in St. Louis, James, son of Antione Soulard, as "a man below the usual stature, of black hair and eyes, wiry and well-built, capable of great endurance, and remarkably courteous and polite, with all the suavity and grace of the typical Frenchman. To the ladies he was always the essence of politeness."

Young Soulard also recalled that "on the occasion of one of Dubuque's visits, (to St. Louis) a ball was given in his honor, attended by all the prominent people of the place. It was held in a public hall, in the second story of a building.....at one point of the festivities the Sieur Dubuque took a violin from one of the performers and executed a dance to the strains of his own music which was considered a great accomplishment, and was received with tremendous applause."

Such was the life that Julien Dubuque carved out for himself. Year after year from 1788 on, his fortunes grew and his successes became legend. But somewhere along the way misfortune set upon him and his usual prosperity began to wane.

So great was his fame and wealth that by 1805 General James Wilkinson, in command of the American forces in Louisiana, sent young Lt. Zebulon Pike on an expedition up the Mississippi and part of Pike's instructions were to get acquainted with Julien Dubuque and examine his power and holdings.

President Thomas Jefferson himself gave the direction that Gen. Wilkinson instruct Lt. Pike to acquaint himself with and report upon Julien Dubuque's western empire.

It was on a Sunday, 1 September 1805, that Lt. Pike landed in front of Dubuque's river bank establishment. (The Dubuque Chapter of the Daughters of the American Revolution have commemorated Pike's landing with a monument on the exact spot.) Lt. Pike dined with Dubuque and received the hospitality reserved for important guests. The young lieutenant remained several days and found it impossible to see all of Dubuque's holdings. For example, the mines were six miles from Dubuque's home.

Supposition has it that Lt. Pike was introduced to Chief Raven of the Reynards (Foxes) and at the same time to a young Indian chief named Black Hawk. Hoffmann has B.F. Gue stating positively that "Pike met at Dubuque Mines the Sac and Fox chief, Black Hawk who had just returned from leading a war party against the Sauteurs (Chippewas). This may have been the second time Lt. Pike met Chief Black Hawk.

Zebulon Pike went on his way up the Mississippi and discovered its source. He scaled what is now known as "Pike's Peak" above McGregor in Clayton County which overlooks the very spot where Marquette and Joliet stepped foot on Iowa soil.

Back at the mines Julien Dubuque went above governing his personal empire but about 1804-1806 his fortunes began to change. Everything had come his way from the time he established himself at The Mines in 1788 and for two decades it seemed that everything he touched turned to gold.

Many reasons are advanced for the decline in Dubuque's fortunes. Was he too ambitious? Or were his speculations too risky. Did he challenge fate? Did he miscalculate the markets or economic conditions in the Mississippi Valley? Or, and this is quite well substantiated, was he too generous to the Indians?

Whatever the reason or reasons the year 1804 was the first one that saw Julien Dubuque unable to meet his obligations. He had become heavily indebted to Auguste Chouteau who is described as "that western prince of merchants and captain of finance at St. Louis....". The name of Chouteau would be connected with that of Dubuque in life and even in the years after the death of the fabulous mining entrepreneur.

Auguste Chouteau and his brother Pierre along with Pierre Ligueste Laclede founded the community of St. Louis in Missouri. The name of Chouteau was known all up and down the Mississippi River valley. Auguste Chouteau is described as "honorable as a gentleman as he was remarkable as a pioneer. Other than helping Laclede establish St. Louis he became famous and wealthy as a trader and merchant. His influence, social, economic and political was great and he eventually served as a U. S. government peace commissioner. In 1794 the Spanish Lt. Governor Delassus described him on 31 May of that year as "a man of incorruptible integrity." Hoffmann reflected that "Dubuque's close friendship with him (Chouteau) reflects nothing but credit upon the great Miner."

Thus to his friend Chouteau the miner Dubuque became indebted to the degree that he could not pay his obligations in 1804. It was on 20 October in 1804 that Dubuque conveyed to Anguste Chouteau seven undivided sixteenths of all the land included in his claim. The deed between Julien Dubuque, described as a mineralogist and Chouteau as a merchant read:

"That I, Julien Dubuque, by these presents, recognize and confess to have today sold, ceded and relinquished, now and forever.....to Auguste

Chouteau, the aforesaid merchant, who for the present time accepts and acquires for him, his heirs and assigns, to wit, a land containing 72,324 arpents to be taken from the south of a concession obtained by me, aforesaid Dubuque, from the Baron de Carondelet.....this present sale done by me, aforesaid Dubuque, for the price and sum of $10,848 and 60 sols, which by the present writing, I recognize to have received cash from the hands of the aforesaid Auguste Chouteau."

According to their understanding Dubuque was to enjoy his land and operations during his lifetime. Another part of their agreement assigns (by Dubuque) the "works, furnaces, buildings, improvements, & etc., done by me" to the heirs of Auguste Chouteau (after Chouteau, of course) and allows them to "take full and peaceful possession of it and enjoy it.....after my death."

The significance involved in the agreement/deed between Dubuque and Chouteau would end up in much litigation later.

An act peculiar to what the two men had done on 20 October 1804 would surface exactly two weeks later when a treaty was signed between the Sac and Fox Indians and General William Henry Harrison (Old Tippecanoe) who was plenipotentiary for the U. S. government in dealing with the Indians. The treaty, later denounced for several reasons as unjust, could have seriously affected the claims of three very powerful men. They were, of course, Julien Dubuque, Auguste Chouteau and Antoine Soulard whom we previously mentioned as Dubuque's business agent in St. Louis.

It was those three very influential men who prevailed upon General Harrison to add an ariticle advantageous to them to the the treaty. In

a certificate appended to the treaty which was submitted to the Indians it was agreed that the treaty did not affect claims obtained from the former Spanish governors. General Harrison further certified that the intention of the addition was to "embrace particularly the claim of Dubuque, the validity of which they acknowledged."

Courtesy, The New-York Historical Society, New York City

WILLIAM HENRY HARRISON *as a major general in 1813. After a painting by Wood.*

(Thirty-four years later, in 1840, William Henry Harrison was elected president of the United States and served one month, being the first president to die in office. That future U. S. president protected the claims of Julien Dubuque.)

Dubuque's occupation of the lands upon which he settled began in 1788 with an agreement from the Indians that he could mine the area. His possession rights grew and ownership was confirmed as just that by the Spanish governor of 1796. In his agreement with Chouteau he had bought the land from the Indians. In his request of the Spanish government he alluded to seven

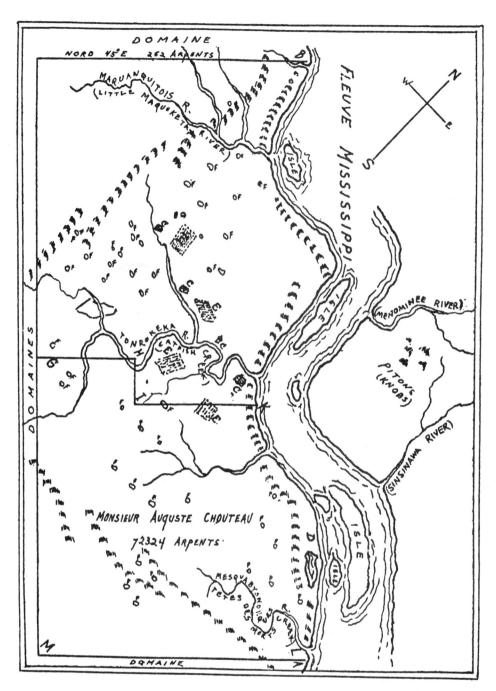

Map of the entire domaine (Fr.) of Julien Dubuque borrowed from Fr. Hoffmann's "ANTIQUE DUBUQUE." It is interesting to note that the word "domaine" in French, other than domain, also can mean: property, realm, province or sphere. The French definitions give added meaning to the "princely" holdings of Julien Dubuque. Note that the land ceded to M. Chouteau is measured in "arpents" which, in French, means acre. But, an acre by French reckoning is equal to only about a half an English acre. The line in the middle represents the agreed upon division line settled upon by the arpenteur (surveyor). Thus Dubuque "sold" to Chouteau roughly a little more than 36,000 acres as we know acres (English acres) to be. Dubuque's realm was, indeed, a princely one.

leagues of land but in actuality it amounted to 27 or 28 leagues.

Both Dubuque and Chouteau sought to have clear titles and Dubuque's grant from the Baron de Carondelet in 1796 was thought to be adequate. To further reinforce Dubuques ownership the Spanish grant was brought before the Board of United States Commissioners in St. Louis.

In October of 1804 Dubuque had transferred the larger part of his claim to M. Auguste Chouteau of St. Louis and on 17 May 1805 both Dubuque and Chouteau filed their claims jointly with the Board of Commissioners. On 20 September 1806 the Board decided in their favor and pronounced the claim to be a "regular Spanish grant, made and completed prior to the 1st day of October, 1800." One member of the Board, J. B. C. Lucas registered a dissenting vote.

When Julien Dubuque died on 24 March 1810 the Indians reclaimed all the land that he had operated and controlled. It was their understanding that the claim of Dubuque was ceded only as a permit to occupy the tract and work the mines during his lifetime. It was also their understanding that upon Dubuque's death the agreement expired and everything reverted to them, i.e., the Indians. They, therefore, took possession of the "Dubuque tract" and continued to operate the mines. They were sustained in what they did by the military authorities of the United States "notwithstanding the decision of the Commissioners."

Later when the Black Hawk Purchase was consummated the Dubuque claims then held by the Indians were absorbed by the United States "as the Sac and Foxes made no reservation of it in the treaty of 1832."

The heirs of M. Chouteau looked unfavorabley upon surrendering any claim to the Dubuque properties without resistance and late in 1832 employed an agent to look after their interests authorizing him "to lease the right to dig lead" on the lands. Here again the military compelled the miners who went to work to cease and abandon the operation under the agent and one of the claimant's reportedly journeyed to Galena, Ills., to institute legal proceedings. No court of competent jurisdiction could be found but he did bring an action to recover an amount of lead that had already been taken for the purpose of testing the title "being unable to identify the lead, however, he was non-suited."

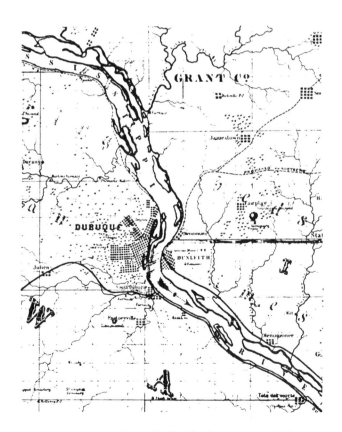

Detail from H. DeWerthern map, 1858.
*(Courtesy of the State Historical Society of Iowa.)*

So much for the fortunes of the first permanent white settler in Iowa. Julien Dubuque obtained from the local Indians permission to settle on the land and the area that would permanently bear his name, both the city and the later county.

Julien Dubuque never married but that, too, is a matter of permanent debate and research. Some suggest he married an Indian princess and other speculation remains.

The year 1988 marks the 200th anniversary of the year that Julien Dubuque came downstream from Prairie du Chien in Wisconsin to settle at "the mines."

The ownership and the titles to that lands of Dubuque remained in question for many years. Did the lands revert to the Indians? What about the claims of Chouteau's heirs. Was the land open to settlement following the Black Hawk Purchase and the June 1st, 1833, efforts by the early pioneer settlers to make claims. It's all an interesting part of history, indeed.

The death of Dubuque himself in 1810 did not stop the interest of many others over the years that followed. Settlers came and went and the continuing interest in the mining of lead never halted entirely.

In any event the interest of explorers and would-be settlers continued but new efforts would be made in the 1820s and the early 1830s. By the end of the third decade of the 19th century there would be established Dubuque County. By that time also the City of Dubuque would be for a while the major commercial center of the upper Mississippi valley.

Among the many who showed an early interest in the area of both Dubuque and eastern Iowa were the Langworthy brothers.

The Langworthys were prominent in many ways in the early settlement of Dubuque as we know it, i.e., after the earlier death of Julien Dubuque, and the permanent establishment of the city bearing the latter's name.

The Langworthys were from Vermont and came to the midwest in the early 1820's. James L. Langworthy was engaged in mining lead in the Galena area in 1823.

In 1829 James Langworthy crossed the Mississippi at the Dunleith crossing and tried to persuade the Indians to permit him and his company, probably his brothers, to mine lead in the area. He was refused that permission at the time.

JAMES L. LANGWORTHY
1800 - 1865

What James Langworthy did do following in the year 1829 was to explore eastern Iowa from the Maquoketa River northward to the Turkey River. He employed two young Indian men to accompany him and they trekked the entire area. (The community of Langworthy in Jones County is named for the miner and explorer.)

Later either in late 1829 or early 1830, James Langworthy did obtain permission from the local Sac and Fox tribes to mine lead in the Dubuque area.

Article IV of the 1904 treaty with the Indians stated: "The United States will never interrupt the said tribes in the possession of the lands which they rightfully claim, but will on the contrary protect them in the quiet enjoyment of the same against their own citizens and against all other white persons who may intrude upon them."

On that basis the Langworthys were not to mine lead for long at the Dubuque Mines, they having come to be called that in the years following Julien Dubuque's death in 1810. They had long ceased to be the "Mines of Spain."

White settlers were removed in 1830 by soldiers from Fort Crawford in Prairie du Chien by then Captain Zachary Taylor. (The later President of the United States was twice assigned to Fort Crawford once from 18 July 1829 to 4 July 1830 and again from 5 August 1832 until 18 July 1837.)

When the Langworthys and others began to mine lead in 1830 with the permission of the Indians the land which they worked was under no immediate jurisdiction. It had been under the Territory of Missouri until 9 August 1821 but was assigned no jurisdiction by the Congress of the United States until 1 October 1834, when it became part of and under the jurisdiction of the Territory of Michigan.

It was, then, in 1830 that James L. Langworthy obtained the permission to mine the Dubuque area that he had been denied in 1829. In June of that year, with his brothers and

Courtesy, Library of Congress

ZACHARY TAYLOR. *A picture from the Brady collection.*

other miners, he crossed the Mississippi and began to extract lead from the earth.

On 17 June 1830, in an act that has been favorably compared with the Mayflower Compact, the miners in a land without established law and no governmental jurisdiction enacted some of their own "legislation."

We are told that the "miners accordingly met by the side of an old cottonwood drift-log, stranded on shore, where the Jones Street Levee now offers such a commodious landing for steamboats (written in 1857), and appointed a committee to prepare such regulations as might be expedient."

Written by James L. Landworthy "upon a half sheet of coarse, unruled paper laid upon the old log" the document associated the miners together in their efforts and provided for a "referee" of sorts who would exercise some judical power in the settlement of disputes.

The "Cottonwood Accord" which survived in its original, at least until 1857 and may exist today stated:

"We a Committee having been chosen to draft certain rules and regulations by which we as miners will be governed: and having duly considered the subject, do unanimously agree that we will be governed by the regulations on the east side of the Mississippi River, with the following exceptions, to wit:

Article I. That each and every man shall hold two hundred yards square of ground, by working said ground one day in six.

Article II. We further agree that there shall be chosen by the majority of the miners present a person who shall hold this article, and who shall grant letters of arbitration on application being made, and that said letter of arbitration shall be obligatory on the parties concerned, so applying.

To the above we, the undersigned, subscribe.

> J. L. Langworthy
> H. F. Lander
> James McPheeters
> Samuel H. Scales
> E. M. Urn

In essence what they had done was to subscribe to the Common Law which was their heritage and enter into a jurisdiction created by themselves and upon their "application" as sovereign citizens.

The "Cottonwood Accord" was deposited with Dr. Jarrot who was evidently the choice of the miners to **exercise the judicial power they** had created and he was thus the first to have such a power granted to him by free and sovereign citizens in the territory, to "grant letters of arbitration."

On or about 4 July 1830, around a fortnight following the "Accord", Captian Zachary Taylor visited the area of the Dubuque mines and formally ordered the settlement and its mining activities to cease. He commanded the miners to go back across the river. They were under no jurisdiction, they reasoned. But "Old Rough and Ready" thought differently and acted upon orders from the War Department relying upon the treaty provisions heretofore cited. Captain Taylor gave them seven days to evacuate the area.

The miners unanimously refused to comply hoping to keep their valuable franchise, the lodes they had found and the lead they had mined.

Resolving to carry out his orders the future president sent a detachment of soldiers to Dubuque on a steamship which when sighted caused the miners to recross the great river into Illinois territory. From the eastern shore they watched the steamer land and the troops deployed.

They not only watched the troops land but saw the Indians take possession of the lead they had already mined. It has been stated quite accurately the the presence of U. S. troops in the area also served to protect the Indians from their **enemy, the Sioux. The army detachment remained in the Dubuque area** the rest of 1830 and during 1831. When the Black Hawk War started they were withdrawn to defend settlements in Illinois.

Chief Black Hawk was captured and another treaty written ending the war and purchasing Indian lands with their title to them being extinguished in 1833. Nothing referred to future white settlement.

Meanwhile some of the miners who had settled at Dubuque in 1830 joined in the war effort which lasted but a few weeks and ended with the Battle of Bad Axe.

Other miners recrossed the Mississippi in 1832 in an attempt to once again work the claims in which they had an interest, at least in their own eyes! It was but a part of the thirty or forty miners who had been evicted in 1830 who returned. That was in the fall of 1832. But, when they did return they were not long alone. For they were joined almost immediately by an estimated 200 other adventurers who sought their fortunes in the mines of Dubuque. Cognizant of the provisions of the Black Hawk Treaty they assumed that settling then, the fall of 1832, or later in 1833 (June 1st) would make little difference. They assumed they could either claim or purchase land on which to mine for the valuable lead.

And so to work they went and in the process mined large quantities of lead ore. Most of their work would prove to be in vain, however, as in January of 1833 troops from Prairie du Chien were once again dispatched to the Dubuque area and the miners were removed again. This time it was a more difficult hardship as the miners were forced to move in the midst of winter, leaving their cabins and crossing the cold or frozen river to the eastern shore. Many got to Illinois and never sought to return to Iowa. Others had moved their lead to islands in the river and built crude thatch huts and stick houses to keep them until spring and the river to St. Louis would once again become navigable.

Among those who had accumulated much lead and protected it were the Langworthy brothers, James and Lucius. At one time it is reported that they had on hand 300,000 pounds of lead or lead ore. Certainly they were among the more resourceful.

It was said of James L. Langworthy that he "was one of those energetic pioneers who would brave anything to command success. In the rivalry of cabin-building, there was an effort to see who would first build a house. He succeeded in having his cabin ready several hours before anyone else. It was situated in a ravine, soon afterwards called Langworthy Hollow." (C. C. Childs, see Bibliography.)

(The area which is Kaufmann Avenue, once Eagle Point Avenue was what was called Langworthy Hollow.)

The Langworthys, James and Lucius, were to become prominent figures in the early history and settlement of Dubuque County.

Although Julien Dubuque was long dead when the county began to populate and organize in the 1830s it was natural that his name would be appended to both the county and the new city.

The lack of organized law left the county to the general use of the Common Law. Being unwritten it merely bestowed upon the public the task of determining right and wrong and ordinarily through the use of a jury. Trial by jury. Judge Lynch, from whose name, we receive the ominous term "lynch law" presided over some strange cases. When early outrages were committed the enforcers of the "lynch law" seized the offenders and the people dealt out the punishments they thought befitted the crime. Sometimes offenders escaped justice entirely.

Such was the case of one Patrick Brennan who struck dead with a club a John O'Mara one night. He escaped the self-appointed policemen of the time and as far as we know never paid the price for the murder he had committed.

It must never be assumed that the frontier city of Dubuque, Iowa, was as the typical frontier community has been portrayed in some more violent western towns. For the immigrants to Dubuque and the area were essentially a religious, spiritual and moral people.

And with them to Dubuque came their American and spiritual heritage. The moral suasion of the early Dubuque folk was a part of their religious and spiritual lives and many churches and religious societies were organized early.

Yet there is always the small percentage who either seek or make trouble and every frontier county had those.

It is said that the first murder in the Black Hawk Purchase took place in Dubuque when one Patrick O'Connor shot and killed George O'Keaf, his mining partner. The two men slept in the same cabin and an early morning dispute over O'Keaf's seeking entrance, forcing the door open and subsequently being shot to death by O'Connor was the essence of the murder tale. The only reason ever found plausible was whisky.

O'Connor insisted the killing was his own business but the people thought differently. The Black Hawk Purchase was beyond the pale of civil government but the Common Law was the inherited law of the United States and the population insisted that justice prevail. Under the guidance of those who understood the Common Law the prosecution of O'Connor began.

The accused O'Connor did not deny his guilt and on the day after the murder he was allowed to choose a "jury of his peers." Twelve from a panel of 24. Woodbury Massey, a re-spected citizen, was elected foreman of the jury and a trial was held under a tree. Two men served as counselors and the jury found the accused O'Connor guilty and sentenced him to be "hung (sic) by the neck until dead."

The sentence was to be carried out on 20 June 1834. Appeals were made to the governor of Missouri and the president and neither claimed jurisdiction. Visitors came to Dubuque by hundreds mostly from Galena and Prairie du Chien. It is reported that 163 vigilantes were necessary to keep order.

O'Connor was taken to the tree from which he would be hanged riding on his own coffin with Father Fitzmaurice at his side. O'Connor's eyes were covered and the cart driven from under him. A collection was taken from the crowd to pay for a funeral.

In the year 1835 another murder was committed in Dubuque County. The victim was Woodbury Massey who had been the foreman of the jury that condemned Patrick O'Connor to death. It seems that Massey had bought a mining claim which came into dispute. His title had been proven but Massey finally had to serve notice upon the trespasser, one Bill Smith. He went with an officer to do so and as Massey and the officer neared, both Smith and his son fired simultaneously from ambush. Woodbury Massey fell dead with his own family as witnesses to his murder. The Smiths were arrested and taken to Mineral Point, Wisconsin, in Iowa County there, but the judge released them claiming he had no jurisdiction.

But, frontier justice was yet to prevail.

For a little later a brother of Woodbury Massey met the elder Smith on the streets of Galena, Ills., and killed him. Cyrenus Cole wrote that this "act of revenge was deemed to justifiable on the frontier" that the Massey brother was not even arrested for taking vengeance.

The vengeance exacted upon Bill Smith persuaded the son that he, too, must seek revenge and thereupon went to Dubuque resolving that another Massey had to be killed. Louisa Massey was by description "fair haired, blue eyed," a sister of Woodbury, "just verging into womanhood. When she heard of the younger Smith's intentions she decided, even if it meant her own death, to stop him.

With the guidance of a boy who knew the younger Smith, young Louisa Massey was taken to him and the boy pointed him out. Her face was partially hidden by a sunbonnet and in her clothing she carried a loaded pistol, stepped up to Smith and said, "If you are Smith, defend yourself." He was taken by utter surprise for within an instant the lass bared her pistol, fired into Smith and fled. Smith escaped death only when the bullet entered through a package of papers in his pocket.

Public opinion favored the young maiden who had sought to save her brother's life and end the chain of revenge.

Louisa Massey was reported secreted out of Iowa and into Illinois where she eventually married and was never heard from again.

But her name would find a place in history for when counties were being named one of them was gallantly named Louisa.

It is said that the murders of O'Keaf and Massey gave impetus to Congressional action to organize the Iowa area under new law. Senator Calhoun referred to the early settlers as a "lawless body of armed men" but that was not so as we have seen.

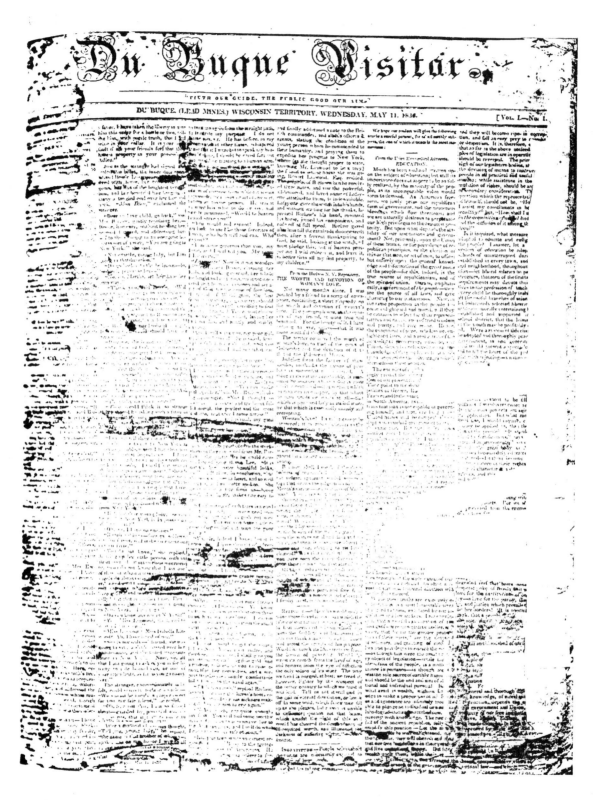

Reproduction of the first newspaper published in Iowa, The Du Buque VISITOR, which was the accomplishment of John King and issued the first time on 11 May 1836 with the motto: "Truth our guide --- the public good our aim." It was printed at "Du Buque Lead Mines, Wisconsin Territory."

Judge Lynch was reportedly the magistrate from whom posterity got the term "lynching" but there are other bases for it, also.

In one instance Judge Lynch took cognizance of a man who had abused his family; he was tarred and feathered and exiled back to the eastern shore of the Mississippi.

Except for the hanging of O'Connor there had been no capital punishment inflicted up to the period prior to the War between the States.

The moral suasion of religious societies began around 1836 and the first religious worship of a corporate and public nature was in the home of Patrick Quigley who was later receiver of the Dubuque Land District. (See subsequent article, this chapter, on the 150th anniversary of the Archdiocese of Dubuque.)

## MR. & MRS. PATRICK QUIGLEY

It was in their home on Bluff Street that the first Roman Catholic Mass was celebrated in 1833. In 1846 he lost the election to become the State's first governor by 247 votes.

Patrick Quigley was a native of Londonderry, Ireland, who came to Dubuque in 1833 via St. Louis, Mo., and Galena, Ills. He and Thomas McKnight laid out the town of Peru just north of Dubuque (about where the John Deere plant now sets) He was later Postmaster at Peru. He was also elected to the House of Representatives of the Wisconsin Terr-

itorial Legislature in the first election. It was thought at the time that the central location of Dubuque might make it the capital of the Wisconsin Territory were it never divided into two States.

Thomas McKnight was a prominent early pioneer settler of Dubuque who was the partner of Quigley in surveying Peru. Mr. McKnight was elected to the Territorial Council in the first election.

## MR. & MRS. THOMAS McKNIGHT

Mr. McKnight was elected to the first Wisconsin Territorial Legislature as a member of the Council (Senate).

Along with the Quigleys and the McKnights others of high character and excellent general repute rose to lead the infant city toward its destined greatness.

During the years 1833 - 1835 several hundreds immigrated to the county giving a rise in population. It is reported that there was a cholera epidemic in 1833 and one of "the fever" in the autumn of the year. (Cholera had first reached the United States in the spring of 1832.) After many deaths the hardy pioneers who had determined to make Dubuque and Iowa there permanent homes settled in to become a part of it.

In 1834 the first church was built on Locust Street and was known as the Centennary, or Methodist church. It was a log house built by the Methodist denomination and with the support of other non-

Methodists who were eager for a house of worship. Public meetings were often held in it and it was used as a school on week days for some years. A Mr. Whitemore, who later moved to Bowen's Prairie in Jones County, taught school there.

The first survey for the city of Dubuque was completed by George W. Harrison who laid out 30 blocks of land in what is today the southerly part of the city.

By 1834-35 the Roman Catholic population had determined to build in the new city and a building was first erected in 1836. It was St. Raphael's and was under roof by 1836 and in use by 1837 when the dedication took place on the Feast of the Assumption.

In 1835 Dubuque County extended northward up the Mississippi River to Fort Snelling in Minnesota which was a distance of about 400 miles. Nothing ever came of such vastness but it was on the map that way in the Michigan Territory and officials were so appointed. A commission to Patrick Quigley as a justice of the peace was dated 29 October 1835.

Once, under the aegis of the Michigan Territory the governor issued a call for a meeting of a territorial legislature. It was to have been held at Green Bay in Wisconsin. Dr. A. Hill and Captain John Parker were elected to represent Dubuque on the Council of the Territorial Legislature. We have two accounts of that "session." One relates that it was never held; another says it was held but nothing was done.

George W. Cummins was the first sheriff of Dubuque County. He received an appointment as such from Michigan Territorial Governor (Acting) John S. Horner on 5 April 1836. Michigan's control ended on July 3rd but on July 8th Governor

Henry Dodge of the new Wisconsin Territory gave Sheriff Cummins a second appointment. He was appointed a third time "with the advice and consent of the Legislative Council at Belmont, Wisconsin, on 2 December 1836. (The originals of these early documents are in the Research Center for Dubuque Area History at the Loras College Library according to Robert F. Klein, Editor of the Childs book. See Bibliography.)

STEPHEN HEMPSTEAD
As a young attorney and community leader; within in a few more years he would be elected governor of Iowa.

Another man rising to prominence in the growing community of Dubuque in 1836 was one Stephen Hempstead who "published his card" as a practicing attorney in the courts of Dubuque, Des Moines and Iowa counties." (Iowa County meant Iowa County, Wisconsin.)

The Dubuque VISITOR was published for the first time in May of 1836, the first newspaper in Iowa. It noted editorially that: "We have received no Washington news for upwards of a month." Yet the "Speech of Col. Jones on the Wisconsin Territorial Bill" was printed on page two in two columns. (George W. Jones was Territorial Delegate to Congress.)

New mineral (probably lead) lodes were reported discovered by Lockwood Wheeling and Coleman, Patrick O'Mara, the Langworthy Brothers, a Mr. Kelley and by James McCabe & Co. According to the VISITOR the Maquoketa Mines near Peru were "yielding large quantities of mineral.

The public was also given assurance in the first newspaper that "the rumor of danger from the Indians in the immediate vicinity was entirely unfounded."

Among the business cards published in the first VISITOR was one of Dr. F. Andross. (A Dr. F. Andros (sic) was the first to stake a claim up in Clayton County near Garnavillo. See Chapter XVII, Clayton County.) Two other doctors were also publishing their "cards" and they were Dr. R. Murray and a Dr. Stoddard. Of lawyers the editor noted:
"A good omen. We have but one lawyer at Dubuque."

H. L. Massey & Co. was a harness shop. John M. Davis was a tailor; L. Brady had a boot shop. Jeremiah Penix opened the "Dubuque Tavern." F. Gehon had a store at Peru and Dr. H. Newhall advertised drugs and medicines from his store at far-off Galena, Ills. as did Timothy Mason & Co. in Dubuque.

Those dealing in groceries and other provisions were quite a number to include John Regan & Co., Wm. Myers, Gartrell & Dougherty, R. C.

Bourne, Wheeler & Loomis, Quigley & Butterworth, Emerson & Crider, E. Lockwood, George L. Nightingale, C. H. Walcot & Co., O'Ferrall & Cox, Davis Gillilan and A. Levi & Co.

The second edition of the Du Buque VISITOR announced that the Territory of Wisconsin had been created by the Congress.

In 1836 there was not a brick building in Dubuque. The first one was built by Leroy Jackson and he operated a hotel briefly before moving to Delaware County. (See Chapter XX, Delaware County.) Nor was there a suitable building in which to hold court. But local residents had evidently solved that problem when they "established precedent" by having O'Connor's trail held out in the open!

The story of the first court seal, as related by Chandler Childs, is an interesting one. He tells that the "first official act of Judge Irwin" was to declare "That the seal, of which the following is a copy, be the seal of this court." The "copy" was a common wafer, he says, stuck to a page on which was a piece of coarse white paper and an impression made with a quarter dollar coin.

Gen. Lewis Warner was the clerk of the early court and had been made the registrar of deed in 1834 and also a justice of the peace. By the end of 1836 there were five attorneys in Dubuque.

In 1836 a library association was formed. Childs says that Dubuquers were evidently readers and one Thomas C. Fassitt published a notice that "Persons having books belonging to me are particularly requested to return them, as I have good chances of loaning again."

In an age of more religious tolerance and veritably ecumenism it would seem strange for us of the

1980s to think such religious cooperation existed in the Dubuque of 1836.

But Childs again relates that there was a subscription for funds to build a Presbyterian church with trustees being E. Lockwood, J. H. Swan and John King. And as it was the "united purpose of the several religious denominations to aid each other" Protestants donated funds for the erection of St. Raphael's Church and Catholics contributed funds to help the Protestant denominations. On 18 July 1836 a cornerstone was laid for the first Presbyterian church building in the territory. Chief Justice Dunn was present and a Baptist was the chaplain while Dr. Timothy Mason gave an address.

A few days later a meeting was held at the Tontine House to discuss a proposed canal through "the isthmus" Involved were such names as E. Lockwood, William Myers, James L. Langworthy, Hiram Loomis, James Cox and Thomas C. Fassett who was probably the "Fassitt" mentioned heretofore. They sought proposals for cutting a canal to connect the main slough with the bayou."

The post offices in the Iowa area were Dubuque, Peru, Burlington and Keokuk, the latter two being in (then) Des Moines County.

The first school house was erected in Iowa at Dubuque in 1833 and was opened in October of 1833. The costs of the building and expenses of maintaining it were donated by the Langworthy brothers, Thomas McCraney, Mathias Ham and several others to include some of the parents of the children in attendance. As many other children were admitted free as the house could

A part of Dubuque's History since 1847

Hoffmann Mortuary

1640 Main Street
Dubuque, Iowa 52001

Hoffmann — Schneider
Funeral Home

## A Great Tradition Faithfully Preserved

hold. Thus the citizens of Dubuque made an early educational commitment which has prevailed.

The 4th of July was a big affair in early Dubuque and an appreciation for freedom was prevalent. A long and involved program was part of it to include the reading of the Declaration of Independence itself! A meeting was held in the not-yet-completed St. Raphael's Church An oration was delivered and a procession formed to march to "the village green" where thirteen toasts were drank to honor the thirteen colonies that declared Independence. In 1836 an additional 20 toasts were drank which may or may not have made for some additional eloquence.

Significantly the oration in patriotism on that 4th of July 1836 by Stephen Hempstead. The future governor's remarks were basic and need to be both repeated and appreciated by Iowans of more than a century and a half later. He said:

"......it was the great example of Washington......which infused into the people that spirit of resistance which led them to cast off the yoke of oppression........

"As we look upon the history ....... of governments.....we are led to inquire the reason of their decay and downfall.

"....... the art of war was cultivated (in fallen civilizations) to the exclusion of commerce and useful knowledge, without which no republican government can be permanent or lasting. Then, how necessary it is that the whole body of the people in our republic could be enlightened and

competent to discuss and understand the great fundamental principles of government which they adopt, or under which they live."

Volunteer sentiments about the 4th of July were written and published by such prominent men of the Dubuque area at the time to include Dr. Stephen Langworthy, the Rev. Samuel Mazzuchelli, Patrick Quigley, John King, Leroy Jackson, Samuel McMasters, J. H. Swan, W. W. Chapman and many others.

Governor Henry Dodge visited Dubuque on 16 July 1836 and he indicated that Belmont in Wisconsin would be the capital as opposed to Dubuque which disappointed many.

It is said that the Mormons were seeking a homeland beyond New York and Ohio where they had been but the citizens of Dubuque made known in the VISITOR that the area was not their "promised land."

Congressional delegate George W. Jones continued to use his vast influence in Washington to do everything he could for the Territory he represented. He was at this time the delegate from the Wisconsin Territory. (Delegates then, as now, could not vote in the House of Representatives nor serve on committees of the House; other than those limitations they had all the other privileges of House members.) It was by his influence that a law was enacted by the Congress laying off the town of Dubuque for a survey to be made under the officers of the government.

GEORGE WALLACE JONES
Delegate in Congress
Another and possibly the best picture in existence of Gen. George W. Jones as the delegate in the U. S. House of Representatives from the Territory of Wisconsin. He was nationally influential before entering the Congress and while there used his friends and power to help develope the territory he represented.

Colonel W. W. Chapman was made colonel of militia, Paul Cain the lieutenant colonel and William S. Anderson, major.

The Miners Bank of Dubuque was chartered by the Wisconsin Territorial Legislature on 30 November 1836.

The village of Dubuque was incorporated in 1837 and its charter provided it be governed by a five-man Board of Trustees. T. S. Wilson was its president.

"The Iowa Thespian Society" was organized in 1837 and, among other cultural groups, led the way toward a growth-oriented and enlightened public. Its first drama was "The Glory of Columbia" put on at the Shakespeare House on 26 February 1837. George L. Nightingale, an attorney, was its leader.

In March of 1938 the following county officers were elected: James Fanning, P. A. Lorimer and Andrew Bankston, county commissioners. George W. Harris was elected recorder; Joseph L. Hempstead, coroner; C. J. Liest, J. Laflesh and Reuben Mayfield, constables.

The village trustees elected in April of 1838 were: John McKenzie, Benjamin Rupert, John Plumbe, Jr., and Philip C. Morehizer.

In May of 1838 Patrick Quigley and Lucius H. Langworthy were elected to the Territorial House of Representatives from Dubuque County.

It was highly important for a community to have a land office in its midst much as it was a courthouse. People coming to a city with a land office would engage in trade and commerce also and thereby promote prosperity. The location of the land office in Dubuque was another favor bestowed upon the young city by Gen. Jones, the delegate in Congress.

By 1838 when Iowa was about to become a Territory itself Dubuque County's population had been steadily increasing and the young city was growing ever attracting an immigrant wave. Such was the early history; from it Dubuque would grow.

# Dubuque County.....
## *Over the years*

OVER THE YEARS Dubuque County grew and prospered and became one of the larger counties of the state and the City of Dubuque one of the larger, also.

Over the years Dubuque County provided many leaders for Iowa and the nation in every area of human endeavor.

Gen. George W. Jones, about whom we've read so much, moved across the Mississippi River from his home at Sinsinawa, Wisc., to make his home in Dubuque. He subsequently served as United States Surveyor General, U. S. senator and minister to Columbia.

Patrick Quigley almost became our first governor and Stephen Hempstead did become our second governor.

Dubuque, city and county, would make many contributions to the new and growing State of Iowa. Set off somewhat apart from other large cities, legislators would wittingly refer to it as the "State of Dubuque."

It would become a stronghold of the Democratic Party and the Roman Catholic Church; later an archdiocese would have its capital in Dubuque.

By the 20th century it would be a city with a character of its own and what some called "a lot of old money" meaning established wealth. One priest of the archdiocese commented that in 1940 Dubuque never feared that Hitler's armies would ever invade it "for the Chamber of Commerce would never let them in!"

From perhaps a staid community, the city has grown and prospered and the county is a rich agricultural area. Yet Dubuque remains a city with a colorful history and there are many able historians who study it and preserve it.

September of 1988 will note two centuries have passed since Julian Du Buque made the agreement with the Indians at Prairie du Chien to occupy and mine the area. Volume II of this history will duly note the 200 years since he arrived here.

Today the U. S. Congressman representing the 2nd District of Iowa, Tom Tauke, is a native of Dubuque, born, reared and educated in that city.

In 1847, before Iowa was even a year old as a State, the Hoffmann Mortuary was established and it is today the oldest such business in the entire State of Iowa.

In recent years James L. Schneider returned to his native Dubuque to operate the historic Hoffmann Mortuary in the beautiful old home in which it has long been housed. While retaining the original name for obvious historic reasons, the business is also called the Hoffmann-Schneider Funeral Home.

(Msgr. M. M. Hoffmann who wrote several books especially "ANTIQUE DUBUQUE" from which we've quoted extensively, was a son of the founder of the Hoffmann Mortuary.)

Mr. Schneider was born, reared and educated in Dubuque. He is a graduate of Loras College and while in college he worked for the Hoffmann firm in the early 1960s. He went on to attend the University of Wisconsin and become a licensed mortician. He returned to Dubuque after owning and operating the Schneider-Mittnacht Funeral Home in Manitowoc, Wisconsin.

He is a Fourth Degree member of the Knights of Columbus, a member of Rotary and has been active in many civic and professional pursuits to include serving on the Board of Trustees of Silver Lake College in Wisconsin and a past president of the county Association for Retarded Citizens.

James and Sharon Schneider are so cognizant of the long history of the Hoffmann Mortuary and its part in Dubuque history that they reaffirm a "commitment to Dubuque area families to carry on the fine tradition." Mr. and Mrs. Schneider are also Sponsors of this history.

Jim and Sharon Schneider with their children: Shealah, Timothy, Connie and Jimmy.

On 5 June 1988 the Basilica of St. Francis Xavier at Dyersville, Dubuque County, Iowa observed its 100th anniversary. The structure at 104 3rd Street, S. W., in Dyersville is 76 feet tall with spires which reach 212 feet; they can be seen for miles in any direction. The term basilica comes from the Greek "Basileus" which mean kingly building. The number of churches holding the title of basilica is small; St. Francis Xavier holds it by Papal decree.

The public library in Dyersville is named the M. M. Hoffmann Library, the priest, author and son of the founder of Hoffmann Mortuary as we have noted.

# *Growing together . . . . .*
## Dubuque and John Deere

Begun in June 1945, the original John Deere Dubuque plant consisted of 600,000 square feet. Forty years later, it had expanded to more than five million square feet . . . . . the equivalent of 110 football fields under one roof . . . . .

An aerial view of the John Deere Dubuque Works in 1947.

An aerial view more than 40 years later.

## RUN WITH THE BEST®

**JOHN DEERE (1804-1886),** founder of Deere & Company.
The Moline, Illinois-based farm equipment maker marks its 150th anniversary in 1987.

# John Deere in 1837 . . . . . . .
## *Deere & Company - 150 years later*

Few corporations on the American business scene have the long and colorful history enjoyed by Deere and Company.

The business was started by John Deere who as a 33-year old blacksmith in 1837 developed a plow that would "scour" --- that is, rid itself of the sticky prairie soil so that a farmer could till his fields more efficiently.

When John Deere was smithing and experimenting in the little town of Grand Detour, Ills., Iowa was a part of the Territory of Wisconsin. Old Dubuque County was being considered for division into other counties. Iowa would not become a Territory for over another year.

One historic connection between Deere and Company is that while ol' John himself was developing a steel plow that would scour a little town was something of a settlement north of what we know today as the City of Dubuque. Its name was Peru.

Peru would not become a city but 150 years later a gigantic tractor plant would occupy its locale. For the 5,000,000 square feet of today's John Deere plant is where the town of Peru used to be.

Yes, John Deere, the blacksmith of Grand Detour, Ills., developed a steel plow that solved the farmer's sod-busting chore. With it the earth would no longer cling and need constant "scouring" as was required when using rough wooden or cast iron moldboards.

And, that's where it all started and today's world-wide corporate entity known as Deere and Company is the result. A century and a half of steady growth, through good times and even the rough ones, has made John Deere an international name. Deere started his work in Illinois and the headquarters became Moline.

Yet it seems that Iowa has always had a "claim" on Deere and Company probably because of its involvement in the economies of several cities in the state. Among them Waterloo, Des Moines, Ottumwa, Davenport and, of course, Dubuque.

Yes, from what one might call Dubuque's "pre-history" John Deere was working on the steel plow that would create a going business that would eventually end up with the tremendous investment in Dubuque and the area that is had today.

OVER THE YEARS the firm of Deere and Company bought out several Iowa companies in similar agricultural area and usually kept plants in the cities where they were. Waterloo firms experienced that type of merging and today that city has the world's largest tractor plant.

Drawing of a farmer scraping soil from his plow. John Deere ended that with his self-scouring creation.

John Deere carries a finished plow from his blacksmith shop to put on sale to farmers needing it to work.

John Deere's original blacksmith shop restored above. Below, farmer using early steel beam JD walking plow.

John Deere's business grew almost at once. Depicted above the early operation; in 1840 it went to Moline, Ills.

Even in art........Grant Wood's painting "Fall Plowing" once graced the cover of a book by Wayne Broehl entitled "John Deere's Company."

# Archdiocese of Dubuque Observes
# 150th Anniversary in 1987

"This diocese will have to be closed eventually." Those were the words used by Bishop Mathias Loras in a letter he penned in November of 1839 to Bishop Rosati in St. Louis, Missouri.

So discouraged was the first bishop of the diocese of Dubuque only months after arriving in Iowa. He had been created bishop in 1837 and the Diocese created at the same time. Many things saddened the bishop at the time and he set his discouragement to writing. But he did not quit and the diocese began to grow. Overcoming countless problems and the pains of growth his tiny 'diocese' of 1839 has grown to an archdiocese with a quarter of a million members. Even to the extent that in 1987 midwesterners refer to Dubuque, Iowa, as "little Rome."

It was in April of 1837 that the Third Provincial Council of the American Catholic Church met in Baltimore, Maryland, and recommended to the Pope that three new dioceses be formed in the west--- meaning the midwest to us---and that one of them be Dubuque. The other two were Mobile in Alabama and St. Louis in Missouri.

The Roman Catholic Church in America was small in membership at the time and its growth depended largely on immigrants especially from Germany and Ireland. It is said that "its congregations were poor and un-educated" and "its parishes were sparse and scattered." Most

THE RT. REV. MATHIAS LORAS
First Bishop of Dubuque

Catholics at the time were located in the "large" eastern cities while some were finding their way westward. In 1837 Dubuque was very far westward.

The Baltimore Council responded to the growth potential by acting what has been called "prematurely" by creating a diocese in the upper Mississippi River valley with little population and very few Catholics.

In "SEED/HARVEST" Thomas Auge says: "Most of the area it encompassed---the present states of Iowa and Minnesota---was Indian country, inhabited by roaming Indian tribes, fur traders and soldiers. Only in eastern Iowa, where the so-called Blackhawk (sic) Purchase had removed the Indians, were there any white settlements. In the four short years between the first settlement in 1833 and the formation of the Dubuque diocese, a few frontier villages had sprung up, located for the most part on the west bank of the Mississippi. These crude hamlets, inhabited principally by unlettered, poor settlers, were the only resource immediately available in the new diocese."

Prior to the creation of the diocese of Dubuque in 1837 pastoral oversight was exercised by Bishop Rosati from St. Louis, Missouri. It was he who sent priests to the area of Galena some years before. Recall that miners were in the rich lead mining Galena area many years before and that in 1823 miners took up in the Dubuque area where interest had dwindled for several reasons following the death of Julien Dubuque in 1810.

In 1832 Bishop Rosati assigned Father John McMahon to the Galena, Ills., area. To that area had come many Irish Catholics and Fr. McMahon was not only Irish but a dedicated priest. The problems he faced were many in the frontier mining town but he fought the good fight until he died in the cholera epidemic said to have been brought to the area by the soldiers of General Winfield Scott assigned there in the Black Hawk War.

In July of 1833 a small band of Roman Catholics in the Dubuque lead mining area met and laid plans for the building of a church. The minutes of the meeting survived the decades and a photocopy of them is

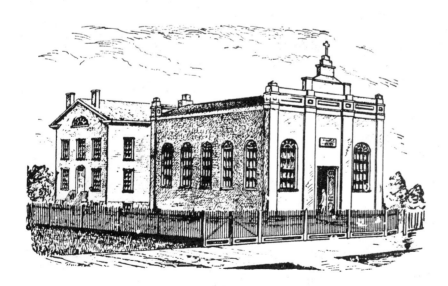

St. Raphael's Church. The first Catholic Church in Dubuque. Designed and supervised in its erection by Fr. Samuel Mazzuchelli. The cornerstone was laid on 4 August 1835 and its construction was complete in 1837.

printed here. The meeting was conducted by James Fanning. This is probably the group that worked with Fr. Mazzuchelli and the result was St. Raphael's Church.

Following the Black Hawk War and by provisions of the treaty "the purchase" was the result as we have noted elsewhere. The U. S. banned settlement on the western lands in Iowa until 1 June 1833. Bishop Joseph Rosati tarried not in sending more pastoral aid to the area. For on 10 June 1833 a Jesuit priest, Charles Van Quickenborne, arrived at Dubuque.

Fr. Van Quickenborne gathered the Irish Catholics into a congregation and thereby the sacraments were available to them. The first Mass was said by the new priest in the home of Patrick Quigley who was later receiver of the Dubuque Land District. Patrick Quigley came to Dubuque in May of 1833 and then went on to Peru, a few miles north. (Note that May was slightly before the June 1st date for settle-ment but activities in that area were always a bit different than elsewhere.)

He returned to Dubuque from his short sojourn to Peru and built a fine home for his family into which they moved in the autumn of 1833. It was on Bluff Street and it stood for many years. It was in that residence, then, that the first relig-ious worship of a public character was held, wrote Chandler Childs some years later. (Below on this page is an old picture of the Quigley home in a dilapidated condition taken from SEED/HARVEST; See Bibliography.)

In 1834 Bishop Rosati sent Father Charles Fitzmaurice to be pastor of the lead mining area. App-arently Dubuque was technically a part of the Diocese of Detroit at the time but the St. Louis bishop was interested in organizing the Church in the area and proceeded always to do what seems practical. Fr. Van Quickenborne succumbed to the same cholera and Fr. Fitzmaurice was left to carry on the missionary work,

*Memorandum left with James Fanning at Dubuque's*

*At an aggregate meeting of the Roman catholics living at the Dubuque mines, held on the 14 of July 1833. the following resolutions were unanimously adopted.*

*1 That as it is the general wish that a Catholic church be built in this vicinity, that the permit shall be obtained in the name of the Rt Rev. Dr Joseph Rosati Bishop of St Louis.*

*2 That, as a majority of 4 have declared the town of DuBuque or its vicinity, to be the most suitable neighborhood for the contemplated church, the designation of the precise spot, shall be left to the decision of the committee to be appointed, or a majority of them*

*3 That the following gentlemen do form the said committee. viz James Fanning, James McCabe, Patrick Omara, N. Gregoire, & Thomas fitz Patrick*

*Mr James Fanning was unanimously chosen treasurer, into whose hands the subscriptions & donations shall be paid: of which moneys received & expended an account shall be given by the Same treasurer to the clergyman appointed by the Bishop & to the Congregation*

*4 That the said committee shall have power to nominate a President out of their number & he or two of its members to have power to call for a meeting of the Committee & a majority of them to be a quorum to transact all the business relative to the building of the church*

*5 the building to be raised by the Subscription of the Catholics at this place & to be as follows a hewed log building 25ft by 20. and 10 or 12ft high. with a shingled roof & plank floor: with 4 windows each having 28 lights of 8 by 10 & shutters the door to be 8ft by 5.*

*Minutes from a meeting conducted by James Fanning, Dubuque.*

## MEMORANDUM LEFT WITH JAMES FANNING AT DUBUQUE'S

At an aggregate meeting of the Roman Catholics living at the Dubuque mines, held the ??/ July 1833 the following resolution were unanimously adopted.

That it is the general wish that a Catholic Church be built in this vicinity, that the permit shall be obtained in the name of the Rt. Rev. Joseph Rosati, Bishop of St. Louis.

That (?) a majority of 4 have declared the town of Dubuque or its vicinity to be the most suitable neighborhood for the contemplated church, the designation of the precise spot shall be left to the decision of the committee to be appointed or a majority of others.

That the following gentlemen do form the said committee, vis James Fanning, James McCabe, Patrick O'Mara, N. Gregoire, & Thomas (?) Patrick.

That James Fanning was unanimously chosen treasurer, into whose hands the subscriptions & donations shall be paid: of which moneys received & expended or allowed (?) shall be given by the same treasurer to the clergyman appointed by the Bishop (?) to the congregation.

That the said committee shall have power to nominate a President out of their number & he or two of its members to have power to call for a meeting of the committee & a majority of them to be a quorum to transact all the business relative to the building of the church.

The building to be raised by the subscription of the Catholics at this place & to be as follows a hewed log building 25 ft by 20 and 10 or 12 ft high with a shingle roof & plank floor: with four windows each having 28 lights of 8 by 10 shutters, the door to be 8 ft by 5.

---

serving Galena and environs as well as the Dubuque area.

While serving Galena prior to coming to Dubuque, Fr. Fitzmaurice had been in Dubuque in 1833 to say the first Mass in the community. The location of it was in the home built by Patrick Quigley that year and would be located at what is now First and Bluff Streets.

In 1835 probably the most active and most talented of the early clergy arrived in the area not only to serve Dubuque but parts of Illinois and Wisconsin. He was Father Samuel Mazzuchelli, OP, a young Italian who served the Catholic folk, designed church buildings and often worked side by side those who were erecting the religious edifices.

On 4 August 1835 Fr. Mazzuchelli designed the first St. Raphael's church building and supervised its construction. It was on that day that the cornerstone was laid.

Fr. Mazzuchelli was a Dominican who had spent some time in the wilds of Wisconsin as a missionary to both whites and Indians. He was coming down the river on his way to Cincinnati when he first stopped off at Dubuque.

The Catholics there prevailed upon him to stay and serve them. He finally agreed to do so and when the new diocese was formed shortly thereafter and the first bishop arrived, Fr. Mazzuchelli was well acquainted with the work that lay before them. It is well to note that when the diocese was created in faroff Baltimore, Fr. Mazzuchelli was the only priest working in it.

The choice to head the new diocese on the American frontier was Mathias Loras, a 45 year-old French priest who knew little about the Dubuque area.

Dr. Thomas Auge, who has written a manuscript on the life of Bishop Loras, writes on his background as follows:

"The son of a wealthy bougeois Lyons family, the childhood of Loras was spent in an atmosphere of piety, duty and discipline. His father, a prominent merchant, executed in 1792 by the anti-Catholic Jacobin Reign of Terror, died a martyr to his church and his king. Inspired perhaps by the sacrifice of his father, Mathias felt the call of a priestly vocation from an early age.

"The confusion arising from

the French Revolution and the Napoleonic Wars which followed it caused Mathias to have a variety of educational experiences. In the course of one of these, a school conducted by a parish priest in his rectory, a fellow student was Jean Vianney, the future Cure' d'Ars, a recognized saint of the Catholic Church. Despite the deep differences in family background---Vianney was the child of a poor, peasant family---the two young men became life long friends. The almost inhuman asceticism practiced by Vianney no doubt helped to form the notions of Loras on the spirituality of the Cross as the ideal of the priesthood.

FATHER SAMUEL MAZZUCHELLI, early clergyman in the Illinois, Wisconsin and Iowa area. An active and talented priest, his boundless energy kept the Church going in its formative years. He was later a valuable right hand for Bishop Loras.

"His priestly life began in 1814 when he benefitted from an early ordination because of a shortage of priests due to the murdersome character of the times. From the first the young priest became involved in education, eventually becoming the superior of the most important minor seminary in the Archdiocese of Lyons, located at L'Argentiere. In the course of his years in Lyons, Loras became a member of a religious order, the Fathers of the Cross. Restricted to the clergy of Lyons, the membership of this order consisted of the most influential and powerful priests in the Archdiocese.

"In 1827, after a dispute over a building project at L'Argentiere, Loras resigned his post as director. He spent the following year as the treasurer of the Fathers of the Cross before answering the call to the foreign missions, a vocation widely followed in post-Revolutionary France. Although he had considered Asia as a missionary field, the presence in Lyons of Michael Portier, the Bishop of Mobile, seeking clerical recruits for his diocese, led Loras to cast his lot with the Catholic Church in America.

"This thirty-seven year old missionary was an elegant, sophisticated, intellectual person who in many ways felt at home in the South. His family's business experience as well as his social graces helped him fit into the plantation-mercantile society of Alabama. Like many American Catholic clergymen, Loras felt no marked distaste for slavery accepting it as an integral part of Southern American society. At the same time, he found Americans too informal, particularly in regard to authority whether in civil society or in the family. His greatest problem as an American missionary was speaking English. While he quickly learned to read and write competently in this language, he spoke it with a heavy accent.

"The duties of Loras in Mobile once again placed him in education serving as the first president of the newly opened Springhill College; later he was pastor of the Mobile parish. These experiences, along with his travels throughout the South and to Washington, D. C., as well as his struggles with the English language, were his preparation for his new responsibilities as Bishop of Dubuque. Nothing in his background, however, equipped him for the burdens carried by a frontier bishop.

The diocese of Dubuque was organized, then, in 1837. Mathias Loras was consecrated a bishop, too, in 1837. The "diocese" was there but the bishop was not. For Bishop Loras went to Europe as previously stated and it was 1839 before he set foot upon the soil of his new realm. It was out of frontier Dubuque, the small towns around it and a veritable wilderness that, with many years of hard work, Bishop Loras did, indeed, create a diocese.

After his consecration as bishop in 1837, Loras traveled to Europe seeking priests and money, neither of which, aside from Fr. Mazzuchelli, existed in his diocese. Like so many American bishops, he benefitted greatly from the funds awarded by the Society for the Propagation of the Faith. This money, along with that supplied by the Leopoldverein, an Austrian missionary society, enabled Loras to establish the Catholic Church in Iowa." (Pages 3 & 4, SEED/HARVEST, Bibliography.) Establishing the See at Dubuque would require funding and the effort of many; those there anticipated the arrival of their new bishop.

It is from Bishop Loras' landing in Dubuque in 1839 that we shall narrate his tremendous effort in Volume Two of this series.

The first Mass is said to have been celebrated in the home of Patrick Quigley who, in 1833, built the first two-story frame house in the Michigan Territory. The Rev. Charles Fitzmaurice was reported as the celebrant and it took place in the south room. Mass was also said there by Father Mazzuchelli about whom we've read.

According to C. C. Childs there is dispute about it. He cites Msgr. Hoffmann as giving the credit for the first Mass to a Jesuit, the Rev. Charles Felix Van Quickenborne, who "offered up Mass in the home of a Mrs. Brophy on the waterfront, baptized numerous children and blessed several marriages. It was he who organized the present Cathedral parish of Dubuque. Before his arrival in Iowa, no priest or other minister of any denomination had ever performed a Christian ceremony within the limites of the present state."

Editor Robert F. Klein of the Childs' writings concludes: "It seems likely that the Fitzmaurice claim can be set aside in favor of Van Quickenborne who had visited both Galena and Dubuque in July of 1832 and 1833, and would very probably have said Mass on both occasions."

Wherever and whenever the first Mass was said is not as important as to note the historical facts relating to the establishment of the roots of the Roman Catholic Church in Dubuque. Many of the early pioneer settlers were from Ireland and Germany and they brought their religion with them. It was natural that they would want to see church buildings erected where they could worship in their own way and form congregations for other activities.

# C. W. FINCH

## The Mid-West's Railroad Historian

## Dubuque, Iowa

## Books by C. W. Finch:

OUR AMERICAN RAILROADS---The Way It Was
THE DEPOT AGENT
CGW WINSTON TUNNEL AND ITS GHOST
THE ROHNA
FISHING WITH CHUCK
CHESTER'S CAVE
THE HUNTED HUNTERS
THE RAILROAD AND ITS PROBLEMS
FINCH AND RELATIVES --- 1585 - 1985
THE HUMOROUS SIDE OF RAILROADING
FISHERMEN FIND FISHING FUN

(All of the above listed books may not be available but information about them may be obtained by contacting the author.)

## C. W. Finch, Author

1029 JUDY COURT
DUBUQUE, IOWA 52001

## Chapter Nine
# DES MOINES COUNTY

No one will ever know exactly who the first white man was to set foot upon the soil of Des Moines County although we agree that Marquette and Joliet went ashore among the Flint Hills. That may be more legend than fact but when one considers their interest in the west shore of the Mississippi River and their habit of preparing meals oon shore and sleeping on the river it seems likely that they were, indeed, the first white men to step onto the shores of Des Moines County.

Long known as Demoine and other similar spellings, Des Moines County was one of the original two counties created when Iowa, the land west of the Mississippi, was a large and unknown portion of the Michigan Territory. Des Moines and Dubuque Counties were created in 1834.

In the autumn of 1833 the formal attachment of the "district of Iowa" to the Territory of Michigan for judicial purposes was completed. Yet all of "the beautiful land" was a newly-acquired Indian territory.

Isaac R. Campbell was one of the first white men to explore the area that became Des Moines County. An account of his pursuits there was later published in the "Annals of Iowa." The year 1821 was an "early" year for going into the yet unsettled area which would not have been open

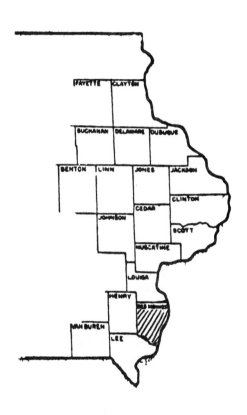

to public settlement until after the Black Hawk Treaty, meaning 1 June 1833. Campbell writes:

"I first visited this locality in June, 1821. It being then a wilderness and inhabited by the Sac and Fox tribes of Indians. The first marks I observed indicating the proximity of the white man was at Puck-e-seh-tuc, or 'Foot of Rapids,' now Keokuk. A log cabin had been erected here one year before this, under the supervision of Dr. Samuel C. Muir, a surgeon in the United States army, located at Fort Edwards, now Warsaw, Ills. The next settlement, and probably the first made by a white man in this country, was six miles above, at Lemoliese, now Sandusky, a French trader occupying this post, being engaged in traffic with the natives; his nearest neighbor, Blondeau, resided about one mile above.

"At the head of the Rapids was Montrose, an Indian village. The chief's name, in English, was 'Cut Nose.' Below the creek running into the river, on the lower side of the Indian town, were the remains of a deserted trading house, around which were growing a number of apple-trees.

"On the opposite side of the river (Nauvoo), was another village of the Sac tribe, Quash-quaw-me, was the chief. I have often heard it remarked that this dignitary originally sold all the land embraced in the State of Illinois to the United States Government. The Nauvoo mansion, formerly the residence of the prophet, Joseph Smith, occupies a portion of their grave-yard, where many a warrior's bones have long since moldered into dust.

"As we passed up the river, the next place of attraction was old Fort Madison, ten miles above the head of the Rapids, situated on the west side, half a mile below a sand-bluff, arising almost perpendicularly from the water's edge. This fort was constructed by Col. Zachary Taylor, and named in honor of James Madison, President of the United States.

"After leaving this old fort, on the second day we arrived, by keel-boat, at Shok-ko-kon (Flint Hills), now Burlington, situated on the west side of the river, about twenty miles above. Here was a trading-post, occupant's name I have forgotten, and at the mouth of Flint Creek, or River,

a short distance above, was located a Fox or Musquawka village. Its ruler and law-giver was the patriarch chief, Timea. Fifteen or twenty miles further up the river, on the east side, was Oquawka (Lower Yellow Banks)..........

(FOUR YEARS LATER, @ 1825)

"..............I next will refer you to my removal and settling at Commerce (Quash-qua-me Village), in the fall of 1825.

"..........residing here, I formed my first acquaintance with Black Hawk, the Mus-quaw-ke (or Sac Brave), by agreeing with him to erect a stonewall for the sum of $8, around the remains of his daughter, buried near my house, and the compliance with this contract, upon my part, engendered a feeling of friendship for me which I reciprocated. It resulted finally in the strongest ties of friendship, and lasted until the day of his death........"

It must be noted before going deeper into the colorful history of Des Moines County that Lt. Zebulon M. Pike, in his travels of exploration up the Mississippi River, landed at Burlington on 23 August 1805. Here he unfurled the flag of the United States of America. It may have been the first time in our history that our national flag had flown over the area that was to become Iowa. Indeed, the territory had become a part of the United States less than two years before Pike landed here.

We do not know for certain if Lt. Pike unfurled the Stars and Stripes over another area south of Burlington or not. What is important is that the almost exact spot where the young lieutenant landed in 1805 has been determined and the Stars and Stripes Chapter of the Daughters of the American Revolution has noted the place. The information is inscribed on a large boulder in the city's Crapo Park. On that boulder it says the following:

COMMEMORATIVE
OF THE FIRST UNFURLING
OF THE
STARS AND STRIPES
ON THIS SITE
BY LIEUT. ZEBULON M. PIKE
SON OF
A REVOLUTIONARY HERO
AUGUST 23rd, 1805
(Erected by the Stars and Stripes Chapter, Daughters of the American Revolution, on the One Hundredth Anniversary.)

Antiquity certainly bestowed upon Des Moines County its treasure of fossils and it is said that the real beauty of them lies in the marvelous state of preservation in which they are found. Reportedly even the digestive systems of some of them is plainly defined.

The first settlement in Des Moines County was in the vicinity of what is now Burlington and the site where the first cabin was built is aptly marked and pictured here. The city of Burlington was first known as the Flint Hills.

One early writer suggested that: "The history of a county is usually little more than the compilation of imperfect records, partial traditions and vague legends. Very few of the counties have preserved with proper care the archives of the earliest days of their existence......"

Much of the history of Des Moines County, unlike most counties, with the exception of Dubuque County, is quite well documented and many accurate accounts prevail. Much of it was gathered at a time when many of the pioneer settlers were still alive to recall for posterity the origins of the county.

As we have noted the area that was to become Des Moines County was entirely within the Black Hawk Purchase. The Indian title to the land was not extinguished until 1 June 1833. Until that time U. S. army troops were on alert to expel anyone who tried to secure claims before that date. The unsurveyed region meant that no government sales of land could be made for some years after formal occupancy. Early claims were made by "blazing" meaning that the marks of the axe or hatchet were made on tree trunks or stumps and/or the setting of stakes or rock monuments. A "code" existed that called for a mutual respect for claims and violators, or "claim jumpers," were among the worst of men.

In disregard of the Indian title which was to expire in 1833 many early pioneers were eager to get into Iowa and stake their claims.

One of that early band of eager would-be pioneer settlers was a Dr. William R. Ross who lived at Hamilton in Marion County in January of 1879 and had at that time attained to past 75 years of age. His recollections are of the 1832-33 period when many of the early settlers were looking to homestead in the Des Moines County area.

Prior to the activity toward settlement in 1832-33 there had been earlier pioneer exploration. For in 1829 Simpson S. White and Amzi Doolittle laid claim to the area upon which Burlington now stands. Theirs was, then, the first claims by white men in Des Moines County. They made their claims in anticipation of the day they could settle there permanently. Those dreams would not be realized legally until 1833. But in the fall of 1832 they made their first attempt at settlement.

Also in the fall of 1832 David Tethro made claim to the land that would become known as the "Judge Morgan farm" about three miles farther. Thus S. S. White, Amzi Doolittle and David Tethro were the original settlers of Des Moines County.

Dr. Ross recalled in 1879 that the original names of settlers in the time period of 1832-33 centered around the following: Maj. Joseph B. Teas, Joseph Morgan, William Morgan, William Stewart, John Ward, Isaac Canterberry, Lewis Walters, Isaac Crenshaw, Benjamin Tucker, Ezekial Smith and his sons Paris and Lineas, John Bullard, Richard Land, Thomas Dovrell, David Tethro, S. S. White, M. M. McCarver, Berryman Jenkins, William Wright, John Harris and

Charles Teas.

Mrs. Alexander Hilleary was Sarah the daughter of William Morgan and is regarded as the first white woman settler in Des Moines County. She came with her father in February of 1832 to do domestic work as her father, Col. Morgan, worked to improve his claim for bringing his entire family there when complete.

It was in that winter of 1832 that a detachment of troops, or perhaps hired dragoons, from Fort Armstrong on Rock Island descended upon the settlers and drove them off. The unit, commanded by Lt. Jefferson Davis, were under orders

to remove the white settlers and they did even to the extent of buning their cabins. Those early settlers were driven from the area of Burlington to what was known as the "Big Island" off shore and just below the present-day city.

Mr. Ross continued his recollections by stating: In February, 1833, before the Indian title was extinguished, William Morgan, son and daughter, Isaac Canterberry and family, Lewis Walters and family, Charles Teas, Joseph Teas, Benjamin Tucker, John Ward, son and daughter, Isaac Crenshaw and family, Morton M. McCarver and family, Simpson S. White and family, with perhaps, two or three other parties, whose names are not remembered now, made a venture on the Indian tract, within Des Moines County. The little company made claims, erected cabins, built rail fences, and, as soon as the season (which appears to have been an 'early' one) would permit, planted corn and sowed some grain. The troopers, under orders from Col. Davenport, rushed down upon the colony, destroyed cabins, laying waste the just-sprouting grain-fields, and driving the settlers from the claims they had made. The families took refuge in flatboats, and hastily conveyed what of their household goods and live-stock they could secure across the river to Big Island."

In June of 1839 a "Citizen of Burlington" wrote in that city's newspaper, the PATRIOT, some interesting recollection about the early claims of McCarver and White:

"In October, 1832, there were some twelve or fifteen individuals

who crossed the river in canoes, at the head of the Big Island, and landed at the claim of Smith, which extended two miles south of Burlington as it now is. The company made an excursion of a few miles around the edge of the timber, in the town prairie, laying claims for future settlement. But little was

done by them until February, 1833. At that time, they brought over their stock, and commenced building and cultivating the soil; but to their great detriment, they were driven by the Government soldiers, from Rock Island, across the river to the Big Island, taking with them their implements of husbandry and their stock. Their cabins and fences were set on fire and entirely destroyed. Notwithstanding all this, they held a council, and pretty unanimously agreed to hold on to their new homes. They built a flatboat, and resolved to watch for an opportunity to cross over the stream, and continue the cultivation of their claims. Many of those worthy individuals, after returning and making a small improvement, sold out, at a trifling advance, to such as were more able to carry on the work and preferred buying claims going back and taking up wild lands. Some of the original settlers remained and placed their farms under a high state of improvement.

"In regard to the improvements of 1834, we had some accessions to our village, of very good citizens, and several frame and log buildings were erected. But our farmers went far ahead, in improvement, of any people I ever saw who were laboring under such disadvantages. Every one was trying to excel in making the largest improvement and planting the most grain. I can scarcely remember one who broke less than thirty acres, and some broke even sixty and eighty. Those who had the largest improvements and who had to stand the brunt of the hardships in the new settlement were William Stewart, Richard Land, W. R. Ross, William Morgan, Lewis Walters, Isaac Canterberry, E. Smith, Paris Smith, P. D. Smith, Isaac Crenshaw, B. B. Tucker, E. Wade and father, and some few others who sold out and went further west, or left the country. A few of the pioneers died early; among them were John Harris and William Wright......"

Not long after the Indian title was extinguished and the land open to settlement we are told that "six or seven families from Indiana" arrived to settle near the mouth of Long Creek, northeast of Augusta, and about eight miles west of Burlington.

It has been well-stated that the history of Des Moines County and the settlement of Burlington are synonymous expressions. With the probable exception of Dubuque, city and county, the first activity in improving the lands of the Black Hawk Purchase were made "on the site or in the vicinity of the metropolis of Southern Iowa."

A "citizen of Burlington" stated that "Our commerce, from 1821 to 1832, did not increase in tonnage to any extent. I made several trips during this time on keelboats, from St. Louis to Galena, Ills. A number of these boats were owned by Capt. White, and navigated by him, as freighters, on the Upper Mississippi.

"Capt. James White informed me that his first voyage up the Mississippi on the steamboat Mandan, being forty days en route from New Orleans to the foot of the Rapids, which she attempted to ascend, but could get no higher than Filly Rock, on account of heavy draught and the want of a correct knowledge of the channel by the pilot ............ The next steamer that succeeded in ascending the Rapids was the Pike, which by many, has been considered the first steamboat that traversed the Upper Mississippi, which is correct so far being the first to go above the Des Moines Rapids."

The above is cited to show that early steamboat traffic was almost synonymous with what became the "Port of Burlington."

Dr. William R. Ross, as we've noted crossed the Mississippi in July of 1833 landing on the Iowa side about half a mile below the mouth of the Flint River. McCarver and White were already there. A Col. Morgan, as early pioneer settler, had around 50 acres of corn growing on his farm three miles southwest of the Flint Hills. Thus the early settlers overcame the ravages by government troops the year before and were now "settling in" lawfully.

The claims by McCarver and White were from the mouth of the Hawk-Eye Creek to the mouth of Flint River and they were half a mile in width. Within their claims was the remains of the early Indian post.

On 10 September 1833 William Morgan came back to the area bringing with him his family who had remained at their home in Sangamon County, Ills. One of his children was a daughter, Miss Matilda Morgan. The Morgan claim was below Hawk-Eye Creek and his cabin was complete in late September.

The first death in the settlement was that of William Ross, the father of Dr. William R. Ross, who died in October of 1833.

The first marriage was that of William R. Ross and the daughter of William Morgan, Miss Matilda. However the marriage was solemnized across the river on the east bank on 3 December 1833, under a sycamore tree, we are told. There has been speculation about its being the first wedding as it took place in Illinois but both the bride and the groom were residents of the Flint Hills area.

The first mill in the area was erected on the Skunk River near Augusta by Levi Moffit. Yet Donnel's Mill on Flint River may have been built first; it was three miles from present-day Burlington. A Mr. Hughes built another mill eight miles from Burlington and they are supposed to have been built in that order. It is said that "they were primitive afffairs and barely served the purpose designed."

Later in 1837 Mr. Donnel was authorized to establish a ferry across the Mississippi.

The winter of 1833-34 was reportedly a harsh one, lasting longer than most. It is said that the river was blocked by ice far into the spring. When the ice broke more settlers came but newcomers in winter found it easy to come across on the ice which was, however, especially dangerous if heavy wagons or livestock were involved.

Getting the county organized and establishing law and order and some semblance of government was no different in Des Moines County than in any other. No formal law existed but the early pioneer settlers had the benefit of the Common Law where precedent mattered little and an innate sense of right and wrong

JOHN B. GRAY

Born in Sheffield, Caledonia County, Vermont, on 9 April 1809, John B. Gray settled in the Black Hawk Purchase in January of 1834, seven months after it was open for white settlement. It was he who suggested the name of Burlington for the new city, after Burlington in Vermont.

ruled; meaning that a jury could decide about anything and law has not changed all that much for the better yet today.

"Laws were needed for the protection of the virtuous against the vicious, and when a band of men combine to do as nearly right as they can, a simple code suffices to regulate the lives of all," it was properly stated in an early history.

Consequently an "Association" was formed and one of their "rules" was the following: "Resolved, That any person or persons allowing the Indians to have whisky on any account whatever, shall forfeit all the whisky he or they shall have on hand, and likewise the confidence and protection of this Association."

The area of Burlington was under the Territory of Michigan when it grew to be a colony of early pioneer settlers big enough to require some political organization.

In 1834 instructions were sent, we are told, to Dr. Ross from the government at Detroit to organize De Moine County which ran from Rock Island down to the mouth of the Des Moines River and thence inland along the Missouri line for 50 miles. The Territorial government at Detroit sent Dr. Ross all the necessary laws and documents. As the organizing officer he duly called for an election.

The election was held in the autumn of 1834. Col. William Morgan was elected Supreme Judge with Henry Walker and Young L. Hughes as Assistant of District Court which was the highest court in the "District of Iowa" at the time.

Other officers elected were Col. W. W. Chapman as prosecuting attorney; W. R. Ross, clerk of the court, treasurer as well as recorder; John Whitaker, probate judge; Leonard Olney, supreme judge.

The governor of the Michigan Territory later appointed John Barker and Richard Land as justices of the peace

On 20 April 1836 the Congress created the Territory of Wisconsin and it was approved by President Jackson who, upon the recommendation of Delegate George W. Jones, appointed Henry Dodge as governor of the new Territory.

Governor Dodge issued a proclamation on 9 September 1836 for an election which was held on the second Monday in October. The Legislature elected then convened at Belmont in Wisconsin on 25 October 1836.

Representing Des Moines County were three members on the Territorial Council: Jeremiah Smith, Jr., Joseph B. Teas and Arthur B. Inghram. Representing Des Moines County in the Territorial House of Representatives were: Isaac Leffler, Thomas Blair, Warren L. Jenkins, John Box, George W. Teas, Eli Reynolds and David R. Chance.

The names of the new legislators were mentioned earlier but it is more significant in listing them here; note names of early settlers among those elected.

The 11th act of the new legislative body was to fix the site for a permanent capital at the new city of Madison in Wisconsin; but it also stipulated that Burlington be the temporary capital until suitable buildings could be erected at Madison. Dubuque was of a more central location and did make sincere efforts to have the capital located there but most realize that Wisconsin as a State would not have the same boundaries as Wisconsin the Territory.

The essence of the meaning of the art making Burlington the temporary capital was that once the two political entities, Wisconsin and Iowa, divided by the Mississippi, were divided, Burlington would remain in a positon of predominance with the aura of capital about it. And when the time came, Burlington did prevail and was, for some years, not only the capital of one, but two Territories. Something probably no other city in America could claim.

Act No. 21 of the Legislature provided in Section 3: "Be it further enacted, That the country included within the following limits, to wit: Beginning on the Mississippi River at the northeast corner of Lee; thence up said river to a point fifteen miles above the town of Burlington, on the bank of said river; thence, on a westerly direction to a point on the dividing ridge between the Iowa River and Flint Creek, being twenty miles on a due west line from the Mississippi River; thence a southerly direction so as to intersect the northern line of the county of Lee at a point twenty miles on a straight line from the Mississippi River; thence, east with the northerly line of the said county of Lee to the beginning, be and the same is hereby set off into a separate county, by the name of

### DES MOINES........."

Des Moines County came into being much the same as the other early counties; it had no Julien Dubuque who began activities a half century before nor the early activities of lead mining operations. But, it was to have its day in history as the temporary capital for the Wisconsin Territory and later of the Territory of Iowa. By 1838 the proud and colorful history of Des Moines County was just beginning to flower.

Opportunity was in flower and the many resources and advantages of the newly established Burlington beckoned a new and eager population. Pioneer settlers to join the earlier ones in creating a growing community. Their talents and opportunity itself assured success.

Ancient rock formations jut out along a bluff near Starr's cave at Burlington.

Des Moines County later became a widely known region among scientists due to its rich resources of fossils. Paleontologists became attracted to Burlington and at one time it claimed a resident known nationally and even internationally as an eminent authority on paleozoic crinoidea. Such fossils were found more frequently in the Burlington area than any other area in the world with over 400 varieties known.

Mr. Charles Wachsmuth had once collected around 800 varieties. His original collection was finally sold to Prof. Agassiz for $ 6,000 and later personally arranged at Cambridge by Mr. Wachsmuth himself.

As there was an early Roman Catholic influence at the Dubuque area, so there was an early Methodist influence in the Burlington area. Sometimes such influences center around that of one person and where the Methodists and Burlington are concerned it was the leadership of Dr. William R. Ross, a devout Methodist who led the way in that early settlement.

The Methodists were active in the early pioneer days and "circuit ridin' preachers" were usually the only clergy seen by most of the early pioneer settlers. Only two settlers were at Burlington, Flint Hills as it was early called, and Dr. Ross arrived to become the third one in the fall of 1833. He built a small cabin for both educational and religious purposes.

Not long after the Methodists were "on the ground" at Flint Hills the Baptists established themselves in Danville Township.

But the Methodists were the strongest and Dr. Ross was their lay leader, so to speak. At the time the well-known Reverend Peter Cartwright was the presiding elder of a large part of Illinois and the entirety of Iowa.

(Peter Cartwright ran against young Illinois legislator Abraham Lincoln for a seat in the Congress. The Reverend Cartwright asked Lincoln if he wanted to go to heaven and Lincoln replied that, at the moment, he was just trying to go to Congress.)

There were other Cartwrights in the Methodist ministry and several were connected with Burlington in some way.

When Dr. Ross asked the Elder Cartwright for a minister to come to Burlington, the Rev. Barton H. Cartwright was sent. He arrived at the home of Dr. Ross in March of 1834 with a team of oxen hitched to a wagon. Dr. Ross thereupon hired him to break ground and this the new minister did during the week and did his preaching on the Sabbath. He subsequently became known as the "Ox Driver Preacher." He reportedly broke 30 acres of ground for Dr. Ross in the spring of 1834 and filled the log cabin pulpit on Sundays.

We are told that the Rev. Barton's brother, the Rev. Daniel G. Cartwright, was really the first Methodist minister to come to Iowa. The Reverend Daniel had been sent by Peter Cartwright in 1835, the difference maybe having been that Barton H. Cartwright was only licensed and the Rev. Daniel Cartwright was ordained. This is an assumption, otherwise with Barton coming in 1834 and Daniel in 1835 the dates would tell a different story.

What eventually became known as "Old Zion Church" was started on 12 April 1834 under the leadership of Dr. Ross and when the Rev. Peter Cartwright formed a class of six at Flint Hills.

"Old Zion," the Methodist Meeting House, as it came to appear after 1850; nor was it called "Old Zion" then.

# A Capitol Enigma . . . . .

Readers, researchers, students of history and even historians have often been led astray in believing that "Old Zion" as so often pictured was the place where legislative bodies met. That the finished building with cupola and all was the "Old Zion" of historic significance. The first fact to be corrected is that the Wisconsin Territorial Legislature never met in the building. The riddle rests with the condition of the building and its cognomen when a legislative body did convene within its walls.

Your author is grateful to (Mrs.) Iona Dodds and (Mrs.) Susan Guest, both of Burlington, for "pointing him in the right direction" and aiding in rendering the actual facts in re this "capitol enigma."

First of all, the church of the Methodist Episcopal denomination was not completed, but only planned, in December of 1837 when the temporary capital building burned. That building had been built especially for the meetings at Burlington of the Wisconsin Territorial Legislature by Jeremiah Smith, Jr. It burned in the early morning hours of 13 December 1837. Jeremiah Smith, Jr., was a member of the House of Representatives and as a concession for getting the city as the temporary capital of the Wisconsin Territory, he built the building with his own funds.

When the legislature reconvened following the conflagration, it did not meet in the Methodist Meeting House. The Council met in McCarver's building which housed the newspaper offices on the first floor. It met in the west room upstairs where the editors resided. The House of Representatives met "over Webber and Remey's store" according to historian Cyrenus Cole.

The Methodist Meeting House was under construction early in 1838 and the only name it went by at the time was as aforesaid. When it was completed later, and when it was still just the Methodist Meeting House, the first Iowa Territorial Legislature held its first meeting there on 12 November 1838.

As to the Methodist Meeting House, it was made of a stone foundation with a brick facade on the top part. It looked as it is shown in the drawing on the next page. It did not have a cupola nor finished walls. Therefore, it has been a historic error for well over a century to depict it as the same-looking building in which the legislative body met.

As for "Old Zion" the cupola and the finished walls were not added until 1850 and it was between 1851 and 1857 that it started being called "Old Zion." Before that time it was in fact the Methodist Meeting House.

This enigma of history, this correlation of facts, is published here for the first time and with continuing appreciation to Mrs. Dodd and Mrs. Guest whose meticulous research clarified an age-old error.

"Old Zion" was not a term used in early Iowa history nor was the picture we have seen anything like its predecessor in architecture. We emphasize that the Methodist Meeting House b e c a m e "Old Zion" but it never was except as related above.

The Methodist Meeting House, the church building that eventually became known as "Old Zion" (in the early 1850s) is shown above in a drawing as it looked upon its completion in 1838.

The Territory of Iowa was created by the Congress on 12 June 1838 to take effect on the 4th of July that year. It was in this building on 12 November 1838 that the first Territorial Legislature met. While the capital of the Territory of Iowa was at Burlington from 1838 to 1841 all the legislative sessions were held there or in old St. Paul's Roman Catholic Church.

Pictured at right is the plaque placed at the site of the Methodist Meeting House by the Daughters of the American Revolution, Stars and Stripes Chapter, Burlington, in 1910. It refers to "Old Zion" but says "in which convened....." which was true enough at the time. The Guest-Dodds later research clarified the use of the name. (Photo by Eugene Kenneth Noah, 1988.)

198

# William Ross helped make North Hill Park reality

BY JONAN HASKELL

If any man on the early scene in Burlington and Des Moines County deserved the name Father of Burlington and Des Moines County, it was Dr. William Richard Ross. He was the right man in the right place at the right time for Burlington and Des Moines County.

He was the most versatile man in the early days of this community --- a medical doctor, a surveyor, a businessman, a government administrator, a devout religious leader, a real estate promoter, a believer and doer in education, a brick and stone mason, and a carpenter.

During the first years of settlement in the Black Hawk Purchase, the story of Ross and the history of North Hill Public Square (now North Hill Park) were the same.

Dr. Ross was the third man to stake out a claim in Flint Hills after Simpson S. White and Morton McCarver. His claim joined White's claim on the west for one mile from north to south and one-half mile from east to west. This claim included most of North Hill and included North Hill Park.

It was only two months after title to the land where the city of Burlington stands today was relinquished by the Indians (Jun. 1, 1833) that Dr. Ross came to the village of Flint Hills. He disembarked from his

Dr. William Ross

boat one-half mile below Flint Creek at the base of a 200 foot bluff; and, from this vantage point, he could see for miles up and down the Mississippi River. His gaze turned to the forest-covered hills circling a natural amphitheatre with its descending slopes reaching the valley below. In the distance across the valley, Hawkeye Creek meandered lazily on its way to the Mississippi River.

It was in this beautiful land that this stalwart pioneer carefully explored the northern most hill and stepped off his claim, blazed the trees, and set up four boulders on the corners of the claim.

Dr. Ross then returned to Quincy for workmen to assist him, for lumber and supplies to build two cabins, for stocks of merchandise for the first general store in Flint Hills which he planned to build soon. He brought dry goods, groceries and medicines and opened the store in September 1833. His customers were mostly Indians who paid for their purchases in fur pelts, the equivalent of money on this midwestern frontier.

During late August 1833, Dr. Ross returned from Quincy to Flint Hills with his father and three workmen. They built two small cabins as a part of working and holding the claim; they cut timber and split rails to fence the land; they broke a number of acres of virgin soil for cornfields, and a vegetable garden, and they finally cleared timber for pastures for the horses and cattle. Dr. Ross speaks of his pastures near the cabins; it may very well be that this was the area later known as North Hill Park.

According to a short biography of Dr. Ross: "In the fall and winter of 1833 I built two cabins on my claim for a dwelling and the other cabin for a school and preaching." The first cabin was southwest of North Hill Public Square on the place where Moir Hall stands. It was erected as a school house and was used as a church in inclement weather. In the spring and summer of 1834, the first school in the area met here with Zadoc Inghram as teacher to 16 students. It was supported solely by Dr. Ross.

William Ross was a devout Methodist who had a grove of trees on his claim (North Hill Park). It was in The Grove that circuit riders held revivals and camp meetings for days at a time; they preached there regularly once a month upon invitations from Dr. Ross.

At the request of the doctor, Peter Cartwright sent his nephew, Bruce Cartwright, to be the minister at The Grove. On April 27, 1834, Bruce Cartwright formed a class of six adults with Dr. Ross as the lay leader. This class was the genesis of the Methodist church in Burlington through the Methodist meeting house known as "Old Zion" to today's First United Methodist Church of Burlington.

The Michigan and Wisconsin territorial governments selected William Ross to perform some of the earliest governmental functions in Des Moines County and Flint Hills. He was appointed commissioner of elections (title used today). In this capacity, he advertised (mostly with posters on trees), conducted the elections, and announced the results for both county and town elections.

Dr. Ross was elected to three offices in Des Moines County which with Dubuque County covered the entire Black Hawk Purchase. His offices were recorder, treasurer and clerk of the district court. Much of the business of these three offices was conducted first in his family dwelling west of North Hill Park and from the two-story log cabin built in 1835 east of the park.

In addition to his county administrative and judicial offices, Dr. Ross served the federal government as a private carrier of the mail from Illinois postal stations to Flint Hills. He was made postmaster of the post office in Flint Hills and later of Burlington. He operated the post office for some time in his cabins near North Hill Park as well as from his general store downtown, and he often carried the mail with him wherever he went.

William Ross and Benjamin Tucker, private surveyors, were employed to survey the village of Flint Hills in November and December 1833. They were probably hired by those people who held the earliest claims--- Simpson White, Morton McCarver, Amzi Doolittle and Jeremiah Smith, Jr.

As first recorder in Des Moines County, Ross was involved in registering claims and many records which were made for the first time. As treasurer his duties were to levy taxes, collect taxes, pay the bills of the county, and hold the surpluses for the county if there were surpluses. Money was scarce on the frontier, this office must have had some grave difficulties. As clerk of the district court, he conducted all elections in the town and county until 1838 or 1839, was responsible for organizing routine business of the court and calling the court into session.

For some length of time, the court met in his home east of the North Hill Park.

Many social and community activities other than governmental functions took place in the Ross home for many years. The crowds, no doubt, overflowed the house into the park across the road.

Dr. Ross was a practicing physician from the time he came to Flint Hills. Much of his medical practice was conducted in his dwellings near North Hill Park and his general store in the lower town.

If any man on the early scene in Burlington and Des Moines County deserved the name Father of Burlington and Des Moines County, it was Dr. William Richard Ross.

(The forgoing article was written by Jonan Haskell, professor emeritus of Southeastern Community College now retired. It was published in the Burlington HAWK EYE Midweek Gazette on 16 February 1988. Professor Haskell is writing a history of that area.)

An unobstructed view of North Hill is evident in this Henry Lewis painting of Burlington about 1847.

# Today............
## ..... in Des Moines County

The Burlington Public Library is one of the most beautiful in eastern Iowa for its historic atmosphere. It might be rivalled by the public library at Clinton or Maquoketa for the uniqueness of its architecture.

When going into it for the purpose of researching Iowa history one finds Iowa history all around. For adorning the walls of that ancient structure are the paintings in gold gilded frames of many of Iowa's, and Des Moines County's, and Burlington's notables, One's mind literally marches through history.

Not to be overlooked is the friendliness of the staff and their willingness to be of help to patrons of the library.

Readers enjoy their hours in the atmosphere of history. Note in the picture above the old fireplace with the clock above it. A bust adorns the old wooden shelving at the right and at the left, above the shelves, is a painting with gilded frame.

Burlington's public library was started in 1868, 120 years ago, and is one of the oldest in Iowa. It dates back to a subscription library founded that year with the help of U. S. Senator James W. Grimes, a former governor of Iowa and a Burlington resident.

In 1885 it became a tax-supported institution and became, then, officially known as the Burlington Free Public Library. The present building is now 90 years old, having been completed in 1898 mainly through the munificense of Burlington philanthropist Philip M. Crapo. In 1975 it was placed on the National Register of Historic Places.

The Burlington Public Library also serves the entire of Des Moines County. An organization known as the "Friends of the Library" supports its goal and objectives and the dues are $3 for an individual, $5 for a family and $1 for students. The author of this volume of Iowa history is a "Friend of the Library" at Burlington.

# Chapter Ten

# LEE COUNTY

As with the other counties along the Mississippi, Marquette and Joliet probably set foot upon the soil of the area that was to become Lee County. For in Clayton County the act of setting foot upon the soil of Iowa seems so very logical. The same with the areas along the great river that were to become Prairie La Porte, Dubuque the city, Jackson County, Clinton County, especially Davenport, Muscatine County, especially Louisa where the trek inland seems to cohere with Marquette's journal moreso than anywhere else, the Flint Hills flat area that would seem inviting to explorers and finally in Lee County. And probably on down the Mississippi River beyond Keokuk and with which we are not really concerned in a history of Iowa.

Those men and their party were explorers; they weren't just making a pleasant trip down the river. They wanted to know what was on the shore; their needs dictated that it was necessary to go to shore from time to time for various reasons especially sustenance, food and fresh water. Yes, they carried some provisions but wild animals abounded and fresh springs could be found along the shore.

They could make fires on the shore and cook food which they could not do in their river craft. Histor-

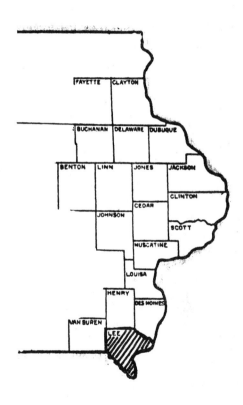

ians allude to Marquette's journal and his description of meeting the Indians inland. That was an event worth entering into a journal. But, would Pere Marquette merely record stepping ashore and having a cooked meal or marching a few feet into the wilderness that had never before been seen by white man? No. Nothing would have been eventful about that. But meeting friendly Indians and parleying with them, that was something different. Truly an event worthy of his journal. Worth the trouble of using valuable ink and scarce paper to make a written record. Thus our logic tells us we cannot rely upon Marquette's journal alone for he would have been very selective in what he took the time and effort with valuable writing needs to record. Every meal cooked on shore and every short excursion inland or stepping upon a flat area such as where Prairie La Porte came to be or the future Flint Hills for a short time would not have been, to him, a recordable event.

From their first sight of the Mississippi and on down the great river we trace the same logic and for whatever history decides it is our profound conclusion that Marquette and Joliet were onshore in Iowa many times and at many places.

There is little doubt, too, that white men explored Lee County long before there were any permanent settlements.

Apparently the first white settler in the area that became Lee County was a Frenchman who received a grant in 1796 and who built a home at the site of present-day Montrose in 1799 residing there until 1805 when the property passed into other hands.

But, we need to clarify the name of this Frenchman as it is given to us differently in different accounts. A knowledge of the French language is important to understanding the reason for the differences. (Here your author is grateful to have studied that language under the renowned Mme. Francoise Armande Du Puis from Paris, France, now Professor of Languages at Upper Iowa University.) And so, our conclusions.

The problem with different accounts is that the same man is given different names; in careless research one would think there were two such Frenchmen. Louis Fresson Honori and/or Louis Honore Tesson.

To clarify: Honore' is a traditional middle name for Frenchmen meaning honored or respected. It was not our man's last name nor was it properly spelled with an "i" at the end. Fresson, rather than being a proper name is really a nickname meaning "frisky" or "one with a little shiver of excitement" among others. Tesson is an old and proper French name and is likely our man's proper last name. The name of the fellow in question, we conclude, then, is properly Louis "Fresson" Honore' Tesson and that is the way we will use it.

It was in 1796, therefore, that Louis ("Fresson") Honore' Tesson was given a grant from the Spanish authorities governing Louisiana. One account says that on 30 March 1799 he obtained a permit to settle "at the head of the rapids of the De Moine River." On that day Tenon Trudeau, acting in his official capacity as lieutenant governor of Upper Louisiana, issued the order permitting M. Tesson to establish himself in the location cited heretofore and that "notice of it shall be given to the Governor General, in order to obtain for him the commission of a space sufficient to give value to said establishment, and at the same time to render it useful to the commerce of the peltries of this country, to watch the Indians and to keep them in fidelity which they owe to His Majesty."

Other privileges, we learn, were granted to M. Tesson so that he might trade with the Indians and possess the land, which he did do until 1805. Much like Dubuque he soon was heavily in debt. His obligation was to a fellow Frenchman, Monsieur Joseph

Robedoux, and when Tesson was not financially capable to meeting his debt to him, Robedoux took legal action to force payment. A judgment in favor of Robedoux caused the property to become subject to an execution.

On 14 May 1803 the land came into the hands of the plaintiff Roubedoux "in satisfaction of his claim." The property had been improved by Tesson to the extent that he built houses, planted orchards and had much land under cultivation. Except for the financial reverses Louis Honore' Tesson had lived up to the Spanish government's expectations in establishing commerce and getting along with the Indians, keeping them in the "fidelity which they owe to His Majesty."

Roubedoux was not to enjoy dominion over the tract for long. He died not long after acceding to ownership and in his will he appointed Auguste Chouteau as his executor. (Recall that he was also Julien Dubuque's creditor from St. Louis.) The appointment authorized Chouteau to dispose of Robedoux's property. In April of 1805 Chouteau sold the estate's land to Thomas F. Reddick. (Although the land became Roubedoux's in 1803, Tesson continued to occupy it even until after it was sold to Reddick.)

It should also be noted that the Spanish land grant to Tesson was for one league square but after the Louisiana Purchase and the area coming under the control of the United States, it was reduced to one mile square which would have lessened its area. A square league is larger than a square mile.

The Tesson grant was the area upon which the community of Montrose was eventually established and it was entirely within the limits of the (later) Half-breed Tract. A later

LOUIS ("FRESSON") HONORE' TESSON

controversy over ownership between claimants to the land and the Reddick heirs wasn't settled until 1839 and then only by the U. S. Supreme Court ruling in favor of the heirs.

It was some years later that another Frenchman who traded mostly with the Indians settled in Lee County. In 1820 it is known that a M. Le Moliese had established a trading post on the site of what became the town of Sandusky, six miles upstream from Keokuk. If the Le Moliese trading station was built before 1820, we cannot ascertain. From accounts it seemed likely it was there a year or two before.

Nor is it known for sure how long Le Moliese stayed in the Sandusky area. In 1829 Dr. Isaac Galland made a settlement on the "Lower Rapids" of the Mississippi River." That meaning the Demoine rapids, as they were called, and that would have been near the site of what was later Nashville. Yet history does not give Dr. Galland the honor of being noted as the first permanent white settler in Lee County.

Nor were the early Frenchmen Tesson, Le Moliese or Blondeau accorded that honor as each county has always searched to find its "first permanent white settler."

The first "permanent white settler" in Lee County is deemed by most historians to have been Dr. Samuel C. Muir. The Muir cabin is dated for historical purposes from 1820 although there are those who speculate that it was there before that date. 1819 is one popular assumption.

Yet in 1820 another Frenchman, other than Le Moliese, named Maurice Blondeau also opened a trading post about a mile north of Le Moliese. Blondeau is said to have become a favorite with the Indians who frequently called upon him to arbitrate disputes. It is said that as a mediator he would hear both sides of an issue, then give an opinion "with the wisdom of a modern Solomon." M. Blondeau became a trusted advisor of the Sacs and Foxes in negotiations in some of the early treaties with the United States.

So, if Le Moliese and Blondeau both established trading posts in 1820 and historians put Dr. Muir there before them, it is likely that the Muir cabin may have been built in the previous year or before.

---

WE ARE PROUD TO BE A SPONSOR
OF THIS HISTORY OF IOWA

We have a history of doing excellent work in these areas:

* Complete Auto Repair
* Front End
* Automatic Transmission
* Air Conditioning
* Sachs-Dolmar Saws
* Husqvarna Saws

*Dobson's Garage*
MONTROSE, IOWA

Dr. Samuel C. Muir, who has been given the distinction of having been the first permanent white settler in Lee County was a surgeon in the U. S. army and had been stationed at Fort Edwards later Warsaw, Ills. In 1819 or 1820 he built a cabin where the City of Keokuk now is. He was called "a man of strict integrity and irreproachable character."

While stationed at an army post on the Upper Mississippi River he had married an Indian woman of the Fox tribe. A romantic story is related that in her dreams she had seen "a white brave unmoor his canoe, paddle it across the river and come directly to her lodge." According to her Indian superstition she felt she had seen her future and went to the army fort. When she saw Dr. Muir she recognized him as the hero of her dreams. Her Indian name is forgotten to history but her "American" name became Sophie.

Dr. Muir was charmed by her beauty, innocence and devotion and he "honorably married her," so the story goes. For a time the doctor and the new Mrs. Muir had to put up with the "sneers and gibes of his brother officers." He even came to be ashamed of his dark-skinned wife. When his regiment was ordered to relocate down the big river to Bellefontaine he decided to leave her and never expected to see her again.

But Sophie, with their infant child, "this intrepid wife and mother," started out alone down the river in her canoe. After a laborious journey of around 900 miles, she found her beloved doctor commenting later that: "When I got there I was all perished away---so thin!"

Dr. Muir was extremely "touched by such unexampled devotion, that he took her to his heart, and ever after, until his death, treated her with marked respect. It was in 1819 that the derision of his fellow officers caused the doctor to resign his commission.

After building his claim he leased it to Otis Reynolds and John Culver from St. Louis, Mo. who sent their agent, Moses Stillwell, to take possession of the Muir cabin in 1928. Stillwell's brothers-in-law came with him and settled in the vicinity. They were Amos and Valencourt Van Ansdal. To Stillwell and his wife was born a daughter in 1831 "at the foot of the rapids" where Keokuk now stands and she, Margaret Stillwell who married a Mr. Ford, is regarded to have been the first white child born in the area that would be Iowa.

After leasing his property to Reynolds and Culver, Dr. Muir went to La Pointe (later Galena, Ills.) to practice medicine for the next ten years. His Indian wife bore him four children. After ten years of practice the doctor returned with his family to Keokuk.

Dr. Muir and Isaac R. Campbell bought the vacated buildings of the American Fur Company in 1831 and carried on a trade with the Indians and the Half-breeds. Campbell had explored Iowa back in 1821, was an entrepreneur who carried on an Indian trading business, ran a tavern and farmed, too.

In 1832 Dr. Muir died of cholera and it is said that his estate was wasted in "vexatious litigation" such that his wife and children were left penniless and friendless. Discouraged, Sophie, with her children, seemed to disappear and it is thought they returned to her own people up the Mississippi Valley.

Stillwell built two cabins in the winter of 1828 and his family became the first white family to take up residence at the foot of the rapids on

the Iowa side of the Mississippi. He cleared some ground and grew crops that year. He also built a stone building about 15 x 40 feet in area and used the stone bluff for the back wall. It was used as a warehouse for a short time by Culver and Reynolds and was destroyed by "the great ice gorge of 1832."

The American Fur Company built a row of five houses with Russell Farnham as the manager. They were log structures and later became known as "Rat Row." When the fur company abandoned them they were bought by Isaac Campbell who, along with 34 employees were "the entire male population."

Fearing Indian attacks a stockade was later built around Isaac Campbell's buildings at the suggestion of Maj. Jenifer T. Spriggs. The men were organized into militia and Campbell was elected lieutenant.

The Black Hawk War had ended in 1832 and after June of 1833 the town of Keokuk and the County of Lee began to populate.

In 1833 the first school in Keokuk was taught by Jesse Creighton in a tiny log cabin that had been built by John Forsyth. Mr. Creighton was also a shoemaker and when not teaching he repaired shoes for the settlers.

While Keokuk did begin to grow, its growth was retarded somewhat by the uncertainty of land titles due to the Half-breed Tract controversy.

The area that was to become Lee County was visited in 1832 by Captain James White who established a claim on the site of the future town of Montrose. As we've noted, others had been there many years before Captain White.

By 1834 a military post had been established there manned by a garrison of cavalry under the command of the later renowned Colonel Stephen Watt Kearney, soldier and explorer. (Kearney, Nebraska, is named after him.) By 1837 the soldiers had been removed from the post at Montrose to Fort Leavenworth, Kansas.

It was also in 1832 immediately upon the close of the Black Hawk War and before "legal" settlement was allowed that the following made claims: Zachariah Hawkins, Benjamin Jennings, Aaron White, Augustine Horton, Samuel Gooch, Daniel Thompson and Peter Williams. Their claims were made in the area of present-day Fort Madison. Some of those names extend into Lee County history and some may have removed.

However, their claims were purchased in 1833 by John and Nathaniel Knapp and in 1835 the Knapps laid out the town; in 1836 lots were being sold. The town was later surveyed by United States government surveyors who re-platted it.

Fort Madison, the city, seemed to have a more rapid growth than Keokuk for whatever reasons. It is about 25 miles north of the mouth of the Des Moines River. It is built on the site of the old fort erected many years before the area was open to immigration.

In 1805 Lt. Zebulon M. Pike journeyed upriver with orders to select a site for a military post "somewhere between St. Louis and Prairie des Chiens, and to obtain the consent of the Indians for its erec-

Drawing of the government post built at the site of present day Fort Madison in 1808, opened in 1809. It was named Fort Madison in 1809 by Lt. Alpha Kingsley, the commander in charge of its construction, in honor of James Madison, the reputed "Father of the Constitution" who had been inaugurated our fourth president the month before.

tion." In 1808 Lt. Alpha Kingsley settled in at the site of the future Fort Madison (the fort) for the winter with a small garrison of troops. He kept his men busy preparing white oak logs with which to build the fort. Early in 1809, as soon as the weather permitted, the logs were hauled to the site and building began. He also had heard that the Indians were making plans to attack and destroy the new outpost. He worked his men as hard as possible and on 14 April 1809 the fort appeared secure.

The previous month James Madison had been inaugurated as the fourth president of the United States and a month later the fort was named in his honor. Lt. Kingsley's letter was dated from "Fort Madison, near River Le Moin."

The Indians never liked the military outpost and threats against it were constant in either rumor or fact. Some years later, as we have related, it was burned during an Indian attack.

bettendorf public library
and information center

Some years later another fort was erected in the area and Lt. Col. Stephen W. Kearney was instructed to take three companies and "take up winter quarters on the right bank of the Mississippi.............near the mouth of the Des Moines." The captains of the three companies were Edwin V. Sumner who gained distinction as a general in the War between the States; Nathaniel Boone the son of Daniel Boone and Jesse B. Browne who stayed in Lee County after leaving the army and became a prominent attorney.

This latter fort, Fort Des Moines, was never intended to be permanent and on 1 June 1837 it was abandoned forever. Fort Des Moines had served its purpose.

In its brief tenure as a frontier outpost such distinguished persons served within its walls as Robert E. Lee, Jefferson Davis, Winfield Scott, Benjamin S. Roberts and Gen. William Harney.

As of 18 September 1836 Lt. Col. Mason, commanding, could write about Madison, the city, that "A town has been laid off at this place and lots have been sold, which takes in part of our garrison. This town has been confirmed by Congress to the heirs of Reddick . . . . . . . You will at once perceive, under the circumstances, how certain it is that we must come in collision with the citizens of this town, who have already commenced to build."

There is some question about how Lee County received its name and one historian says: "It is quite possible that the county was name for Lieut. Robert E. Lee." This could be but it might seem strange that a young lieutenat in the army might be the subject for whom a county would be named. Yet the possibilities may outweigh any arguments against it being any other.

At the time the county was being created by the Wisconsin Territorial Legislature, young Lt. Robert E. Lee of the regular army, West Point graduate, was engaged in making a survey of the Des Moines Rapids. The purpose of the survey was the improvement of navigation on the river.

Lt. Lee was "one of the most popular subordinate officers of the garrison at old Fort Des Moines and some authorities state that the county was named in his honor."

A Lee County Courthouse. Lee County has for much of its existence had not one, but two courthouses. Keokuk and Fort Madison have shared county government responsibilities. That is why we say "A" Lee County Courthouse and not "The" Lee County courthouse. This picture is used here to show the "Southern," Greek or Jeffersonian architecture; moreso to show its similarity with the Custis-Lee Mansion which sets atop the hill overlooking Arlington National Cemetary. Possibly because of the immediate popularity of Lt. Robert E. Lee when he was stationed at a fort in Lee County and possibly because of the national respect accorded the famous Lee family of Virginia, the county was named "Lee."

Robert E. Lee was a relative of George Washington and the scion of a famous old Virginia family. After the War between the States, General Lee retired to become a college president. He was a great humanitarian and has always been one of the most loved Americans. For whatever it means one of the Lee County court houses looks very, very similar to the Custis-Lee Mansion, Robert E. Lee's home that overlooks Arlington National Cemetary most of which was originally Lee property.

Others after whom Lee County might be named are Charles Lee, a New York land speculator, who was at the time carrying on operations in the Half-breed Tract and Albert M. Lea who mapped the shores of the Mississippi and explored the Des Moines River in 1835. The city of Albert Lea, Minnesota, is named after him. He also explored and mapped northern Iowa and southern Minnesota. The name would be mispelled.

Our choice is that the county was named for Robert E. Lee, general, college president, humanitarian and a most admired American.

THE CHIEF KEOKUK MONUMENT at Keokuk, Lee County, Iowa, erected to honor the Indian chief, Keokuk. Not born a hereditary chief he became a chief through cunning and subtle means. A compromiser he kept peace between the Indians and the white man mainly through appeasement. Perhaps he had no other choice. He was made a war chief in 1812 but as a leader presided over the continual relinquishment of the Indian lands to the immigration of the white settlers. The above monument was erected with funds from a popular subscription sponsored by the Keokuk Chapter of the Daughters of the American Revolution.

And so from its earliest times Lee County was taking shape as a county. White men had wandered by its beautiful shores and bluffs since 1673 when Marquette and Joliet first set foot upon its soil. Going up or down the great river which passes by Lee County many white men had been inland. It was not until Tesson that an attempt was made at settlement.

Then came the Indian problems and the forts; other settlements or attempted settlements. Fort Madison the community and the settlement at Keokuk became the most promising. There would later be disputes about the location of the courthouse and there were in many counties. The early history we have related constituted the beginning of permanent settlement.

We are told that Berryman Jenkins taught school at Galland in 1830 and that it was the first school in Iowa. Other sources give us 1829 for his school. (Jenkins later went to Oregon and became a millionaire.)

Many of the townships were not formally created until 1840-41 nor were the cities incorporated until later on.

The town of West Point sets on a site claimed by a man named Whitaker in 1834 who sold it to John Cotton and John Howell.

William and Isham Burton came from Indiana in 1835 and manufactured brick; it is reported that their brick was used in the Presbyterian church at West Point.

General John H. Knapp is said by some historians to have been the first white man to make a permanent settlement on the site of what is now the city of Fort Madison. Through various military experiences he became a brigadier general of militia in New York State. It was on a return trip up the Mississippi from New Orleans back in 1830 that he decided to locate at Fort Madison. He bought out the claim of one Augustus Horton, took possession and built a log cabin near what would be the foot of Broadway Street today.

In 1835 Gen. John H. Knapp built a hewed log house on the exact site of the old fort and even used one of the old chimneys yet standing He cleaned out the old well that had been used by the garrison and erected a new building to be used for a store. On 9 October 1835 General Knapp's wife, Harriet, arrived in Fort Mdaison with their two sons, John H. Jr., and Jonas along with a daughter, Elizabeth. Mr. and Mrs. Joseph S. Douglass arrived with two children; Mrs. Douglass was the daughter of the Knapps.

In June of 1835 John H. and Nathaniel Knapp who was the general's cousin hired Adolphus Allen to lay out and survey a town. The eastern limit would be the present day Oriental Street and its western boundary would be shortly above today's Pine Street.

Not long after the Knapps laid out their proposed town another group bought the claim of Peter Williams and laid it out with their plat continguous with that already surveyed by Allen. That group consisted of Dr. John Cutler the son of Judge Cutler, James D. Shaw and a Dr. Ferris.

The year 1836 was one of a large immigration into Fort Madison; many were passing through and many others had come to settle in Lee County. That year General Knapp built a large frame house at the site of the old fort and named it Madison House. It was used as a hotel and had accommodations, we are told, for fifty guests with a large room available for conventions and meetings.

At about the same time Cousin Nathaniel built a hotel, too. He called his Washington House. Both did a prosperous business and it has been said that sometimes as many as a hundred wagons were waiting on the Illinois side of the river to cross into Iowa by ferry.

According to one account Chief Black Hawk was a customer at General Knapp's store and his son, Nes-se-as-suk, who became a pal of the Knapp boys, John and Jonas. The boys were entertained in front of the store by old Chief Black Hawk sitting on a bench and telling them stories of his own adventures and exploits. The Indians were considered good customers and good credit risks but Chief Black Hawk is said to have left an unpaid bill for ten or twelve dollars at Judge Cutler's local store.

On the evening of 2 January 1837 General Knapp attended a ball and reception at his hotel, the Madison House, which was frequented by officers of the U. S. army dragoons stationed at what is now the site of Montrose, the old Fort Des Moines. Among the guests that evening was young Lt. Robert E. Lee. It was at that affair that General Knapp caught a cold which developed into quinsy and he died two days later.

Gen. Knapp was the first to be interred in the Fort Madison Cemetery. His hotel was taken over by son-in-law Joseph Douglass who died of typhoid fever. Mrs. Knapp leased the hotel business to Lorenzo Bullard for some years.

Nathaniel Knapp, the general's brother, was killed the following July at Bentonsport in Van Buren County in an incident fraught with question. (See Chapter XV, Van Buren County for complete story.)

With the sudden deaths of the Knapp brothers, both within a few months, Fort Madison lost two enterprising pioneers.

Questions eventually arose about clear titles to lots acquired under the Horton and Williams claims and Congress passed an act on 2 July 1836 providing for the platting of certain tracts within the Black Hawk Purchase for town sites. That was immediately prior to the "District of Iowa" becoming part of the Territory of Wisconsin. An act of 3 March 1837 provided for a re-surveying and those who had purchased lots from the original founders were granted land patents directly from the U. S. government.

These land patents were to become the best titles to land and became the closest thing to allodial title; they are rarely used today but the law affecting them is still in effect.

Fort Madison was incorporated by an act of the Wisconsin Territorial Legislature on 19 January 1838. On the first Monday in May, 1838, the first election was held for town officers and Philip Viele was elected president with Herbert Morris, Joseph S. Kennie, Charles McDill, John D. Drake and Isaac Atlee as trustees.

And so the County of Lee, with a colorful history, emerged as a county unit. Over the years it would become prosperous and provide many state figures and some of national influence and stature.

## VIEWS OF BLACK HAWK HEIGHTS
### in Lee County

(Borrowed from a 1914 History of Lee County. Author's name not available.)

## THE HALF-BREED TRACT

Before any permanent settlement had been made in the Territory of Iowa, white adventurers, trappers and traders, many of whom were scattered along the Mississippi and its tributaries, as agents and employees of the American Fur Company, intermarried with the females of the Sac and Fox Indians, producing a race of half-breeds, whose number was never definitely ascertained. There were some respectable and excellent people among them, children of men of some refinement and education. For instance: Dr. Muir, a gentleman educated at Edinburgh, Scotland, a surgeon in the United States Army, stationed at a military post located on the present site of Warsaw, married an Indian woman, and reared his family of three daughters in the city of Keokuk. Other examples might be cited, but they are probably exceptions to the general rule, and the race is now nearly or quite extinct in Iowa.

A treaty was made at Washington, August 4, 1824, between the Sacs and Foxes and the United States, by which that portion of Lee County was reserved to the half-breeds of those tribes, and which was afterward known as "The Half-Breed Tract." This reservation is the triangular piece of land, containing about 119,000 acres, lying between the Mississippi and Des Moines Rivers. It is bounded on the north by the prolongation of the northern line of Missouri. This line was intended to be a straight one, running due east, which would have caused it to strike the Mississippi River at or below Montrose; but the surveyor who ran it took no notice of the change in the variation of the needle as he proceeded eastward, and, in consequence, the line he ran was

bent, deviating more and more to the northward of a direct line as he approached the Mississippi, so that it struck that river at the lower edge of the town of Fort Madison. "This erroneous line," says Judge Mason, "has been acquiesced in as well in fixing the northern limit of the Half-Breed Tract as in determining the northern boundary line of the State of Missouri." The line thus run included in the reservation a portion of the lower part of the city of Fort Madison, and all of the present townships of Van Buren, Charleston, Jefferson, Des Moines, Montrose and Jackson.

### SKETCH MAP OF HALF-BREED TRACT

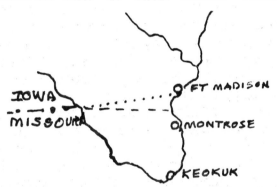

Dash line shows where boundary should have gone; straight east.
Dotted line shows where survey line did go; east northeast ending up below Fort Madison.

Under the treaty of 1824, the half-breed had the right to occupy the soil, but could not convey it, the reversion being to the United States. But on the 30th day of January, 1834, by an act of Congress, this reversionary right was relinquished, and the half-breeds acquired the lands in fee simple. This was no sooner done, than a horde of speculators rushed in to buy land of the half-breed owners, and, in many instances, a gun, a blanket, a pony or a few quarts of whiskey was sufficient for the purchase of large estates. There was a great deal of sharp practice on both sides; Indians would often claim ownership of land by virtue of being half-breeds, and had no difficulty in proving their mixed blood by the Indians, and they would then cheat the speculators by selling land to which they had no rightful title. On the other hand, speculators often claimed land in which they had no ownership. It was diamond cut diamond, until at last things became badly mixed. There were no authorized surveys, and no boundary lines to claims, and as a natural result, numerous conflicts and quarrels ensued.

To settle these difficulties, to decide the validity of claims or sell them for the benefit of the real owners, by an act of the Legislature of Wisconsin Territory, approved on January 16, 1838, Edward Johnstone, Thomas S. Wilson and David Brigham were appointed Commissioners, and clothed with power to effect these objects. The act provided that these Commissioners should be paid six dollars a day each. The commission entered upon its duties and continued until the next session of the Legislature, when the act creating it was repealed, invalidating all that had been done and depriving the Commissioners of their pay. The repealing act, however, authorized the Commissioners to commence action against the owners of the Half-Breed Tract, to receive pay for their services, in the District Court of Lee County. Two judgments were obtained, and on execution the whole of that tract was sold to Hugh T. Reid, the Sheriff executing the deed. Mr. Reid sold portions of it to various parties, but his own title was questioned and he became involved in litigation. Decision in favor of Reid and those holding under him were made by both District and Supreme Courts, but in December, 1850, these decisions were finally reversed by the Supreme Court of the United States in the case of Joseph Webster, plaintiff in error, vs. Hugh T. Reid, and the judgment titles failed. About nine years before the "judgment titles" were finally abrogated as above, another class of titles were brought into competition with them, and in the conflict between the two, the final decision was obtained. These were the titles based upon the "decree of partition" issued by the United States District Court for the Territory of Iowa, on the 8th of May, 1841, and certified to by the Clerk on the 2d day of June of that year. Edward Johnstone and Hugh T. Reid, then law partners at Fort Madison, filed the petition for the decree in behalf of the St. Louis claimants of half-breed lands. Francis S. Key, author of the Star Spangled Banner, who was then attorney for the New York Land Company, which held heavy interests in these lands, took a leading part in the measure, and drew up the document in which it was presented to the court. Judge Charles Mason, of Burlington, presided. The plan of partition divided the tract into one hundred and one shares and arranged that each claimant should draw his proportion by lot, and should abide by the result, whatever it might be. The arrangement was entered into, the lots drawn, and the plat of the same filed in the Recorder's office, October 6, 1841. Upon this basis the titles to land in the Half-Breed Tract are now held. (The foregoing information in re the "Half-Breed Tract" was taken verbatim from the history published by the Western Historical Company, Chicago, Ills., 1878.)

## LEE COUNTY AND THE STEAMBOAT

The possibility of harnessing the power of steam to do mechanical work was dwelt upon 130 years before the birth of Christ and was used then to make only toys function.

Later engineers such as Papin, Savery, Newcomen and Watt developed steam engines to the place where they were practical in the 17th and 18th centuries, A.D. To save funds mine owners put them to use pumping water out of coal shafts. To use steam for locomotion by ships or railways was something that didn't come about until the early 19th century.

The British claimed that William Symington's experiments on the Forth and Clyde Canal demonstrated the first practical use of steam power for a boat.

But Americans recognize Robert Fulton's voyage in the Clermont on the Hudson River as the true beginning of the use of steam power for river transportation. Fulton piloted the Clermont from New York to Albany in 1807 on a 32-hour cruise. The Clermont was a paddle-wheeled boat and Robert Fulton won fame for his exploit. Although the screw propeller was not yet developed and many other engineering advances would come, the economic use of high steam pressures could, with Fulton's success, be used with safety. His steamboat was a practical demonstration of man's coming mastery over water and wind.

The mighty and navigable Mississippi River merely flowed along awaiting the coming of the steamboat early known as "Fulton's Folly." Eventually vessels powered by steam would navigate up the great Father of Waters increasing trade and commerce. Valuable supplies for the new inhabitants of Iowa and a means of bringing and taking passengers would be part of the new steamboat lines.

River cities became ports and the first ones at which steamboats would stop were Keokuk and Fort Madison in Lee County in Iowa.

# A drawing by Robert E. Lee ?

THE KEOKUK LEVEE AT THE FOOT OF HIGH STREET --- The above depicted drawing is concluded to have been done at Keokuk in 1848, the date given, by Robert E. Lee, a regular army officer. It was discovered in the files of the Department of War by General W. W. Belnap after he assumed the position of Secretary of War. It is attributed to General Lee but the date given for the time of the drawing is 1848. It is known that young Lt. Lee was stationed at Fort Des Moines where the site of the City of Montrose now is in 1837. It is thought that young Lee probably of a higher rank by 1848 may have been stationed in the area a second time or perhaps assigned there on a temporary duty basis. Lee excelled in map reading and was known to have been artisitic in preparing military maps and drawings of installations. When he was at the Lee County area the first time he was doing work for the army in the prospects of navigation on the Mississippi.

# Chapter Eleven
# MUSCATINE COUNTY

It is again, with Muscatine County, our considered good historical judgment that the first white men to set foot upon the soil of that beautiful river county were Marquette and Joliet.

As with the rest of Iowa the area that is now Muscatine County endured as it had since antiquity in its beauty, woodlands and bluffs above the mighty river touched only by the moccasins of the Indian and a few white men for a century and a half. Then it all started.

Most agree that the Nye family were the first permanent white settlers in Muscatine County. The emphasis might be put on the words "first" and "permanent." As in many counties there is dispute. Several of a family named Thornton had settled in different places about both Louisa and Muscatine Counties.

One historian found that "the prevailing sentiment relative to priority was in favor of Benjamin Nye." But the same writer later came to the place of "grave doubt" finally concluding it to be a "mooted question" yet most historians of today give the distinction to the Nyes.

The writer cited above finds "evidence" that one Err Thornton was a settler in Muscatine County in the fall of 1833. Recall that the area

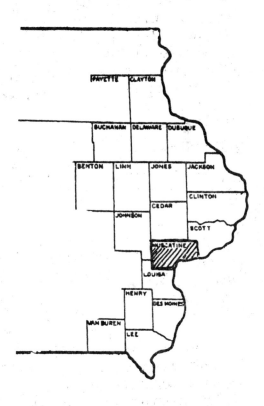

was opened for settlement after 1 June 1833 according to the terms of the "Black Hawk Purchase." The "evidence" cited is the writer's interview with Mr. Err Thornton some years later when he (Thornton) was in old age and living near Drury's Landing in Illinois. So much for the word "Permanent." Thornton came to the shores of Iowa with a brother named Lott. (See Chapter XIII, Louisa County.)

The Thornton's later said that they laid claim to land in Muscatine County in the fall of 1838. A Mr. J. P. Walton says that 21 February 1863 --- 30 years later --- Mr. Thornton referred to his "earlier claim" and that such was "no new one." Yet no positive evidence has ever been given. We also find the Thorntons prone to move about; it is likewise strange to find a "permanent settler" retired and living back on the eastern shore of the Mississippi River.

In 1834 Benjamin Nye crossed over the Mississippi River with his wife, Azuba, and their two daughters, Harriet and Laura. That year Benjamin Nye claimed land at the mouth of Pine Creek which is about 11 miles up the great river from where present-day Muscatine is located.

An enterprising man looking to the settlement and growth of the new lands west of the river, Ben Nye started a store and established a post office. He named the place Montpelier after his hometown back in Vermont. He then proceeded to build a saw mill which was followed shortly after by the erection of the first of three grist mills to be built on Pine Creek.

A year later, in 1835, James W. Casey arrived in the area that is now Muscatine the city. He established a wood yard on the shore of the Mississippi where he cut timber and sold it to the passing steamboats. His place became known eventually as Casey's Landing which may have been a bit more formal the the original name of Casey's woodyard.

James Casey dreamed of a great city that would someday occupy the site he came to love so quickly. His dream ended with his untimely death in 1836.

In 1835 Col. George Davenport had built a log trading post very near the Mississippi River at the foot of what would today be Iowa Avenue in Muscatine. A year later that log building was purchased from the illustrious colonel by John Vanatta who immediately carried out much bigger plans.

John Vanatta laid out a community one-half mile square which extended a quarter mile downstream meeting Casey's claim and another quarter mile upstream. This proposed city he called Bloomington. Vanatta continued to operate the trading post but invested in other interests to include a steam sawmill.

Bloomington grew and retained the name but after 1850 it became Muscatine, a name derived from the Indian name of Musquatine.

The log cabin trading post, we are told, was burned in a large bonfire on 4 July 1838, either to celebrate Independence Day or accidentally from the fireworks that were used. The story is not clear but perhaps the structure had merely outlived its usefulness and the burning was John Vanatta's contribution to that particular 4th of July.

Ben Nye, the early pioneer settler, continued on his land until 1852 when he died in March of that year as a result of stab wounds inflicted upon him by George McCoy, a son-in-law. The stabbing occurred in a bitter custody fight over McCoy's children, Nye's grandchildren.

Mrs. Nye, Azuba, also a hardy Vermont native and who became a sturdy and resourceful pioneer, continued to live on the property and rented out the land, we are told, until her death in 1879; she outlived her husband by 27 years.

Benjamin and Azuba Nye are buried in what is known as the Nye Cemetery near the mill at Wild Cat Den State Park. (The third mill which was built in 1850 is said to still stand in the Wild Cat Den State Park.)

Speculation necessarily arises about the infant twins of the Nyes who are buried beside them in the cemetery bearing their name. They were obviously not Harriet and Laura but probably twins born later, after their settlement at the mouth of Pine Creek. Either Harriet or Laura was most likely the wife of George McCoy with whom Ben Nye fought over the custody of the grandchildren. Or, as records are vague, the wife of McCoy could have been another daughter of the Nyes about whom we have no knowledge.

But, back to the beginnings of settlement in Muscatine County and back to the coming of the first permanent white pioneer settler.

Late in 1834, some months after the Nyes had arrived and built in what would become Muscatine County, there came to the area John McGrew. In a published statement of the date of 3 December 1874 McGrew recalled crossing the Mississippi River at New Boston and stopping at an Indian village named Blackhawk and hired an Indian guide. He was told that there were white settlers in the area and he followed a trail for "about twenty miles" when he found "the newly-erected cabins of Err and Lott Thornton who had made a claim about twelve miles below the site of

Muscatine." He reportedly stayed a couple of days with the Thorntons and went on to locate Col. Davenport's man, Farnham, who was running a trading post for the colonel near the mouth of Pappoose Creek. There were no other settlers until one reached the new settlement of Buffalo. (see Chapter XII, Scott County.)

It is significant but not unarguable that McGrew found the "newly-erected" cabins of the Thorntons in December of 1834. It is known that the Nyes had been in the county for several months. What does "newly erected" mean? Were the logs so freshly cut that they would indicate "newness?" All we have is the later recollection of Mr. Thornton and no one's recollection is infallible. Certainly not an older person desiring to a "first." We will never know for certain but we agree with most others that the Nyes were first and McGrew's finding the "newly-erected cabins" may tell a story.

McGrew returned across the river to New Boston but returned to Iowa in 1835 and cut rails for a living. In March of 1835 John McGrew staked out a claim and built a cabin near Lettsville which was the beginning of the first settlement on "High Prairie." A year later, in 1836, he married and remained on his claim until 1842 when he bought a farm in Township 76.

In the Old Settlers' Register, Err Thornton is recorded as coming in 1834 but that was entered into the record in 1865! Mrs. Nye's name is also recorded but the date is listed as 1833 yet the pioneer wife did not come to the county a year before her husband. Perhaps Benjamin Nye had "prospected" the area, as happened often, a year before coming here with his family. This can be noted in many other instances.

Yet McGrew reported no settlement at the mouth of Pine River in December of 1834 and a crop of prairie hay harvested by the Thorntons. Yet McGrew had to be wrong about a cabin on Pine Creek at the time and the facts about the hay are relative.

By 1835 there were three settlements in the Muscatine County area. There was the Davenport claim where Muscatine now stands; the Nye claim at the mouth of Pine River and the Thornton claim on the slough to the south. It was May of that year that James Casey arrived and made his claim just south of Davenport's and began at once improving "Casey's Landing" which subsequently became known as Newburg. Arthur Washburn came from New York that year and stopped there.

Dr. Eli Reynolds made claim of a tract of land about three miles up the river from Davenport's trading post and later, with Harvey Gillett as a partner, laid out a town and named it Geneva. He was the same Eli Reynolds who was elected in 1836 to the Wisconsin Territorial Legislature which met at Belmont. (See Chapter VII, The Formative Years.) He tried to get his town selected as the county seat but was unsuccessful as when the news of it reached Bloomington (Muscatine) the populace there got very excited and their pressure caused Governor Dodge to veto Reynolds' bill which got through the legislature but no farther. Today Geneva is but a name in the long history of similar towns.

Benjamin Nye's town of Montpelier met a similar fate and it is but a name in history; yet the township retains the name.

In 1836 a Colonel Vanater arrived in the area and purchased the Davenport claim in February, we are told. This was at the time Muscatine City and many newcomers made homes there.

Major William Gordon claimed some land near the Nye farm and opened a small trading post with Arthur Washburn acting as his clerk and shortly thereafter a post office was located there. Washburn was named Postmaster and the post office was called "Iowa."

Iowa, then, was once the name of a settlement's beginnings located, or perhaps better stated laid out, at the mouth of Pine River which would have been about 330 miles upriver from St. Louis, Mo. The Town of Iowa was once touted as a community with a great future because of its natural advantages of harbor and a mile and a half of shoreline along the Mississippi River where steamboats could land. Other than that its "advantages" were "fine sloping grounds, its good water, its water power, its timber and its building stone."

Perhaps because of its location and the natural advantages it truly had, the future might look promising to one of an early day. Iowa was predicted as the place for a county seat in its earliest of times. It was also suggested that "(s)hould the seat of government of the future state of Iowa be located on the Mississippi, it would probably be fixed at Iowa, owing to the central position and commercial advantages of that place and if it be on the interior it must be near the Iowa river, as the weight of population will be there and then the town of Iowa will be the nearest port on the Mississippi to the capital of the state." Had there been Chambers of Commerce in the mid-1830s one would surely think the previous quote to have been put together by the local chamber! So then Iowa (the town), too, is only a name in history.

As the county populated there came the need for modern conveniences and mills where grain could be taken in the more local areas.

Benjamin Nye's grist mill which he located at his little settlement at the mouth of Pine River was erected by him in 1837.

The first saw mill in Muscatine County was built by Weare Long in 1837 on Sweetland Creek but the changing water level of that creek made it impossible to run the machinery all year 'round. It soon fell apart and was later rebuilt but was never really successful.

In 1837 Eli Reynolds and John Lawson erected a steam saw mill at the mouth of Lime Creek next to Reynolds' little settlement of Geneva. It was the first steam saw mill ever built in Muscatine County. Robert Smith brought the machinery for it up the river from St. Louis and was

hired by Reynolds and Lawson as an engineer. A year later, in the spring of 1838, John Vanater bought Lawson's interest in the operation. Reportedly the mill was later taken down and the machinery taken to Muscatine where it was used in a stave factory.

In 1838 a third post office was opened in Muscatine County, located at Vanderpool with C. S. Comstock as the Postmaster. Amos Walton was his deputy and succeeded to the postmastership later in the year when Comstock resigned. The name of the post office was then changed to Geneva. Walton remained until his death in 1841 and the post office was then closed.

Gillett, recall, was one of the proprietors of Geneva and after it was platted he went east to sell lots in the town which was not really much of a town. That was something that happened often; a community might be "established" with perhaps a cabin or two and a promoter would go eastward seeking settlers by selling them lots to increase the size and population of the town.

Thus by 1838 Muscatine was well on its way to growth but many changes were to occur before it got on the road to becoming the important river county and city that we find it to be today. A proud history was developing early and many aggressive pioneer settlers had the future in mind as they planned, worked and strove for a mighty county.

Muscatine County was among the first ones organized out of Old Des Moines County but few actual records remain showing much of its early "official" history.

SAMUEL NICHOLS, JR.

Samuel Nichols, Jr., arrived in Muscatine County in 1838. The community of Nichols, Iowa, is named for him and his great-great-great grandson, Craig A. Meacham, is today (1988) the mayor there.

Sam Nichols came to Iowa on the advice of a friend, Robert Lucas who was about to become governor of the new Territory. Born in Virginia, he served in the War of 1812. He was 44, a widower with five children when he settled in Pike Township.

The county's earliest document records a marriage license issued to Andrew Starks and Merilla Lathrop. It is dated 13 February 1837.

The document shows that the old County Commissioners' court existed at that time and, again by recollection, two of the commissioners, or "Board of Supervisors" as Michigan law held them to be, were Arthur Washburn and Edward E. Fay. Washburn and Fay were recalled to have been the first members; there were probably three.

The United States District Court held its first session in Bloomington (now Muscatine) on 24 April 1837. That court's first act was to appoint John S. Abbott was its clerk. It has been noted by an early writer that here we find that Mr. McClaren was not confirmed, or continued, as the clerk of the court. Maybe he was county and only acting for a while in the U. S. clerk's position.

The only records extant of a County Commissioners Court was that for October of 1837; that is to say that the record is the first as it is supposed that it may have been the second or third or fourth meeting but only the first one where records were kept. Who knows?

The clerk of that session was one J. R. Struthers and the records are in the handwriting of S. Clinton Hastings who subsequently became the clerk of the court sometime after October 1837. So we conclude that our Mr. McCraney served as the clerk of two courts in their infancy during 1836 and 1837, but did not continue after others were appointed.

By 17 February 1838 the board was organized but not busy. It was composed of Err Thornton, John Vanater and Aaron Usher with Mr. Hastings as clerk. And so Muscatine County was becoming "organized."

# Chapter Twelve
# SCOTT COUNTY

Scott County is one of Iowa's eastern most counties, located on the Mississippi River with 35 miles of river shoreline. It has a long and colorful history.

Scott County was originally created as Cook County but did not retain that name for long and it was early changed to honor General Winfield Scott who, in old age, was commander of the nation's army yet when Abraham Lincoln became president. Scott County became a rich county both as a river port and as an agricultural area.

While it was Cook County it was larger than our Scott County is today extending farther up the Mississippi River. It was not much later that the legislative body changed the boundaries to where they are today.

It is bounded on the north by the Wapsipinicon River which traverses most of eastern Iowa. In the Indian language the "Wapsi" is derived from Wau-bessa-pinnecon Se-po interpreted meaning "the place of the white potatoes." Waubessa means white or swan-like; Pinne-ac meaning a potato. Se-po is the Indian name for river. In pioneer times there were great quantities of wild artichokes growing along the Wapsipinicon.

The Wapsi flows into the great

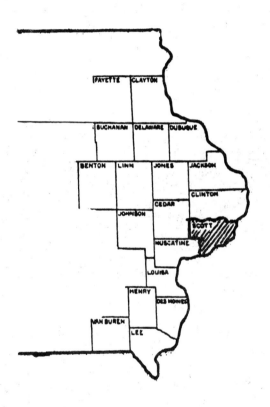

Mississippi and, in 1863 according to history writer Willard Barrows, was ten or twelve rods wide "with a swift current, and its banks generally skirted with timber." Along it were wide and rich bottom lands subject to spring flooding which made for excellent pasture but in those times the land was not dry enough to cultivate.

The western part of Scott County becomes flatter and more agricultural as one journeys inland. The rich rolling prairie is divided at the Fifth Principal Meridian which separates it from Cedar and Muscatine counties.

For many centuries we learn that the area upon which the present City of Davenport stands was once a well-populated Indian settlement, or village. A century and a half of discovering Indian artifacts testifies to this.

In his 1863 writing about the history of Scott County Willard Barrows is very insistent upon having Marquette and Joliet and their party land first at the site of Davenport. He insists that they could not have made it to the area of Toolesboro in four days from the time they left the Wisconsin River to join the Mississippi.

We understand that the first landing of which they made a record was the 21st of June 1673 but their bent to explore and their living habits dictate, we believe, that they set foot first in Clayton County. All historians, researchers and students of history may draw their own conclusions but Barrows is insistent:

"There could not have been sufficient time between the 17th and the 21st for the voyagers to have descended beyond this point, or to have reached the lower or Des Moines Rapids; which some historians claim to have been the landing places spoken of. There having been an Indian village here from time immemorial according to Indian tradition, fixes the fact most conclusively, that it was at this place, Davenport, that the soil of Iowa was first pressed by the foot of a white man."

Barrows relies upon Indian folk lore and tradition and about that there can be no doubt. Chief Black Hawk himself was interviewed by many and made known the settlement of his people in the Davenport area. But there were Indians and Indian villages all up and down the mighty Mississippi in the time of Marquette and Joliet. Dubuque and Jackson counties above Scott had Indian villages, too. The settlement of Indians does not give us historical evidence that the white man first set foot in Scott County but we cannot doubt, historically, that the Marquette and Joliet expedition did, indeed, set foot upon the shore near our Davenport. We believe they did, our logic being based differently than that upon which Barrows bases his. We believe Barrows correct in assuming that in June of 1673 Pere Marquette and Louis Joliet tramped the shoreline of the future Scott County at the site of Davenport or whatever site was convenient. Indians or not; they may have been seen or not. Perhaps the parley was not an unusual one and the explorers had several others but not worth recording to the extent that Fr. Marquette saw fit to record in his journal in re those at Toolesboro.

Who knows? This author has

formed his own logic about the matter and insists that Marquette and Joliet stood on the soil of Scott County, Iowa, in June of 1673!

Whatever Marquette and Joliet did in June of 1673 when they first saw the beautiful plain of Davenport and the area, Iowa stood alone for many decades. Rarely touched by the foot of the white men, the general activities of the day seemed to be in the east. Yet the frontier was slowly moving westward.

To show that Barrows never retreated from his ideas, he later wrote: "This mighty river which once bore to our shores the frail bark of a Marquette and a Joliet......"

Perhaps a significant date in Scott County history --- and, yes, for Iowa! --- was 15 September 1832 for it was on that day that General Winfield Scott parleyed with the Indians in Scott County (not called that then, of course) and the result of it was "the Black Hawk Purchase" which ended the Black Hawk War. For some time it was also called "the Scott Purchase" but the name of the Indian leader prevailed and it soon and forever became "the Black Hawk Purchase." General Scott dealt with the Sacs and the Foxes. Black Hawk himself was not present. A strip of land from the Missouri boundary line inland and up to the Neutral Ground and over to Prairie du Chien was involved in "the Purchase." At its widest it was but 60 miles yet it contained about six million acres. The Indians agreed to move off the land of the "Purchase" and their title in it would be extinguished as of 1 June 1833, some months later.

George L. Davenport, Esq., made the first claim in Davenport Township and it is significant to note that he did so immediately after the Treaty of 1832 (The Black Hawk Purchase) which provided for no white

*Geo. L. Davenport*

GEORGE L. DAVENPORT

George L. Davenport was the son of Colonel George Davenport after whom the city is named. The son became a leader in the growth of the city.

---

claims or settlement until 1 June 1833. But Mr. Davenport was a lifelong friend of the Indians and had been adopted into a Fox tribe while young; his only playmates as a child were the Indian children.

Other than growing up with Indian boys, he could speak the Indian tongue, was an expert archer and swimmer, speedy in running, generally athletic and a favorite with the entire tribe. All that enough to explain why his wishes for land claims were granted early by the Indians. Other emigrants who sought the same privilege had been driven away by force as we have seen.

225

COLONEL GEORGE DAVENPORT
After whom the city was named.

Earlier activity in the Davenport and Scott County area centers around the ferrying business. Reportedly Captain Clark established the first public ferry but as early as 1827 Col. Davenport had run a flatboat for ferrying purposes from Fort Armstrong (Rock Island) to the main shore. We are told Col. Davenport's ferry carried pack-horses, cattle and goods for trading with the Indians.

The land upon which Davenport now is located was first claimed by R. H. Spencer and one Mr. McCloud in the spring of 1833. They were soon in disagreement over their claim and to settle the dispute between them both their interests were bought by Antoine Le Claire for one hundred dollars. Such was the first real estate transaction in Davenport. Needless to say the value of that same ground has risen mightily. The land purchased was west of present-day Harrison Street and was not a part of "Le Claire's Reserve" about which we'll read later.

In the very early years the land lying below Western Avenue and between 2nd and 4th Streets was a quagmire, a slough at which today's Washington Square was the topmost portion; it was caused by springs and neither man nor beast could get through it. There are ancient tales of how cattle would get mired in it and even of their occasional death. The entire area was eventually filled in and the solid land developed.

Back in May of 1816 soldiers of the U. S. army, in command of a Col. Lawrence, ascended the Mississippi River and came ashore at the mouth of the Rock River. After exploring the area it was decided that the lower end of Rock Island would be an ideal site for a fort. They landed on the island on 10 May 1816. They began to build at once and soon Fort Armstrong became a reality. Col. George Davenport was the general superintendent

It is estimated there were around 10,000 Indians on both sides of the river and the purpose of the fort was ostensibly to keep peace.

Thus Colonel George Davenport came to the area and it was he after whom the later city of Davenport would be named. His son, George L. Davenport, was born on Rock Island at Fort Armstrong in 1817 and was the first white person born in the region. We have noted his relationship with the Indians; they named him "Musquake."

Colonel Davenport himself was a native of England and arrived in America in 1804 and was attached to the army from 1805 until 1815. His was an adventurous life. He was with General Wilkinson on the Sabine involving problems with Aaron Burr, former vice president of the United States, who had visions of his own western empire. He fought in the War of 1812 defending Fort Erie and was in the battle of Lundy's Lane. He came up the Mississippi with an expedition that sought to quiet the Indians and then selected the site and supervised the building of Fort Armstrong where he settled in 1816 and remained until his death.

It wouldn't be until 1836 that the city of Davenport was conceived. From the time of the Black Hawk Purchase until then several townships, mostly along and near the river, would receive those early pioneer settlers.

Possibly the first immigrant pioneer settler in Scott County, excluding the pre-emptive claim of George L. Davenport, was Captain Benjamin W. Clark who had been born in Virginia. He had served under General Dodge in the Black Hawk War and came to (now) Buffalo Township in 1833 where he made the first "claim," built the first log cabin, broke the first ground, planted the first corn and harvested the first crop in Scott County, Iowa.

A Mr. Lynde from Stephenson, now Rock Island, Ills., brought the first inventory of goods to Buffalo in Iowa.

Captain Clark planted the first orchard and discovered and mined some coal. "Clark's Ferry" was at one time the only one between Du Buque and Burlington and was the only place for a while to cross, bringing people, animals and stocks from Illinois to Buffalo. The entrepreneur Clark built a two-story public house in Buffalo in 1835 bringing the lumber from Cincinnati, Ohio, at, we are told, the cost of $60 per thousand feet.

In 1838 Captain Clark laid out the town of Buffalo in Buffalo Township and it was the first town formally laid out in the county. His settlement grew rapidly and in 1836 he built the first saw mill near the mouth of Duck Creek, that mill being the first in that region of Iowa.

Captain Clark claimed that his son, David H. Clark, had been the first white child born in Scott County. (Remember that George L. Davenport had been born on Rock Island.) The Clark child was born on 21 April 1834.

As with many other settlements that grew fast early, others were to be established and thrive in competition. Buffalo was later a controversial site as political maneuvering for future county seats left it hanging in the balance as to whether the legislature would have it in Scott or Muscatine County. It was referred to as "trickery and corruption" by Willard Barrows, history-writer and he said that: "This was the killing stroke to Buffalo."

CAPTAIN CLARK'S PUBLIC HOUSE
Or, hotel, was built in 1835 in Buffalo.

Coal, discovered by Captain Clark in 1834, was mined and sold to steamboats in 1835, 1836 and for some years. A James M. Bowling from Virginia settled at the mouth of what would become known as Bowling's Creek, arriving on 4 July 1835. He purchased the claim of Orange Babbett. It was at the mouth of Bowling's Creek that the coal was sold to steamboats.

Upstream about three miles Benjamin Wright and Captain E. Murray from Zanesville, Ohio, settled in and mined coal selling it to Davenport and Rockingham for 15 cents per bushel. The largest operation was that of Capt. W. L. Clark & Co. which produced about a thousand bushels daily.

For whatever reasons the Indians were not to let Mr. Bowling live in peace. In 1837 they numbered about 500 and loitered around Bowling's Creek finally setting fire to the prairie around him and burning his wooden fences. They then let their horses eat his small stalks of corn. He rebuilt his fences, replanted his corn and harvested a good crop. But the Indians were "a constant annoyance to him."

Other early pioneer settlers in Buffalo Township were Joseph and Matthias Mounts, Elias Moore and Andrew W. Campbell.

Rockingham Township was also one of the very early townships where the pioneer settlers came to seek new homes. In it the town of Rockingham was begun and it was at one time a rival for the county seat.

Settlement was started at Rockingham in the autumn of 1835. Directly opposite the mouth of the Rock River the claim that had been made upon Rockingham was bought by Col. John Sullivan from Zanesville, Ohio, James and Adrian Davenport, Henry W. Higgins and others. One of its advantages was that it would

"command the trade of Rock River."

In March of 1834 Adrian H. Davenport made a claim on Credit Island which is around 400 acres and near the Iowa shore, just a little above Rockingham and the mouth of the Rock River. It had once been the site of a French trading post. Adrian H. Davenport was soon joined by his father, Marmaduke Davenport, who had been the Indian agent at Rock Island. Mr. Davenport purchased the island from the government.

On 14 August 1834 a son was born to Adrian Davenport who may have been the second white male born in Scott County. A rival for that distinction might have been a son of Levi Chamberlain of Pleasant Valley. The Davenports become merchants in Rockingham.

In 1838 Adrian Davenport received the appointment from the new Territorial governor, Robert Lucas, to be sheriff of Scott and Clinton counties the latter being then attached to Scott for judicial reasons. He retained that office for 12 years.

By the 1st of August in 1836 Rockingham had but two cabins; in one lived the Davenports and in the other a Mr. Foster. It was then that Col. Sullivan returned from a trip to Ohio with his family and some emigrants seeking a place to settle. Among them were such names as Millington, Coleman, Lingo, Willis, Morehead, Brown, Mountain, Cale, Sullivan, Camp, Dutro, Higgins, Harold, Harrison, Shepherd and McCoy.

Dr. E. S. Barrows located there in the fall of 1836 and was the first practicing physician to locate in Iowa between Burlington and Du Buque. His practice eventually covered portions of Clinton, Muscatine and Cedar Counties.

A Judge Grant opened a large farm in 1838 at a spot called

"Picayune Grove" and introduced blooded cattle, the first in the county and possibly the state.

In the summer of 1837 the first steam saw and flouring mill was built and the early settlers had a place to refine timber and grind their grain.

The county was beginning to grow. After 1836 the settlement, or town at Davenport, began to gain an ascendancy as the center of activity. Buffalo had been the first town established in the county and for a time was the center of trade and commerce.

The first settlers of Davenport were Antoine Le Claire, Col. George Davenport, Maj. Thomas Smith, Maj. William Gordon, Philip Hambough, Alexander W. McGregor, Levi S. Colton, Capt. James May and a handful of others whose names we do not have or who weren't recalled for long by history.

Among the founders the one name that stands out as the most active in helping to found the community and get it established and going was Antoine Le Claire.

(Colonel Davenport claimed the first land and the city is named for him; he had many interests up and down the Mississippi River that included trading with the Indians, ferry traffic and land speculation. He became a wealthy man but was slain in middle age while living at Rock Island.

Antoine Le Claire was said to be the representative of both races of men who occupied the lands of Iowa in its very early times, meaning especially the 1830s. The city of Le Claire is named for him.

In a Centennial Address delivered upon the 100th anniversary of the Independence of the United States, the Honorable C. C. Nourse

*Antoine Le Claire*

expounded the virtues of Antoine Le Claire. He said:

"Antoine Le Claire was born at St. Joseph, Michigan, in 1797. His father was French, his mother a granddaughter of a Pottowatomie chief. In 1818, he acted as official interpreter to Col. Davenport, at Fort Armstrong (now Rock Island). He was well acquainted with a dozen Indian dialects, and was a man of strict integrity and great energy. In 1820, he married the granddaughter of a Sac chief. The Sac and Fox Indians reserved for him and his wife two sections of land in the treaty of 1833, one at the town of Le Claire and one at Davenport. The Pottawatomies, in the treaty at Prairie du Chien, also reserved for him two sections of land, at the present site of Moline, Ill. He received the appointment of Postmaster and Justice of the Peace in the Black Hawk Purchase, at an

229

early day.   In 1833, he bought for $100 a claim on the land upon which the original town of Davenport was surveyed and platted in 1836.   In 1836 Le Claire built the hotel, known since, with its valuable addition, as the Le Claire House.   He died September 25, 1861."

Antoine Le Claire had many attributes that made him "the right man at the right time in the right place" as far as the founding of Davenport and the development of the area were concerned.   His main talent was as a businessman and his activity in that area centered around promoting the growth of the city he'd helped to found.   His other major talent, among many, was his ability to speak and understand the Indians' language and to live peacefully with them.

W. Barrows

Willard Barrows, Esq., was one of those to whom we of 1988 owe much, for it was he, among others, who first recorded early historical material that was left to those of us today.

Willard Barrows was born at Munson, Massachusetts, in 1806 and was educated in the Common Schools and Academies of New England.   He taught school for a time in New Jersey and was married in 1832.   He selected the pursuit of engineering and surveying and by 1837 was occupied in the employ of the government in one of the first surveys of Iowa.   In July of 1838 he and his family settled in the newly established town of Rockingham about five miles below Davenport.

In the early 1840's he engaged in farming and held the offices of Justice of the Peace and Postmaster at Rockingham.   He later did surveying in Wisconsin and explored northern Iowa to gain knowledge of the area.   He visited the Mission School at Fort Atkinson and became a friend of the Rev. Mr. Lowry.

"Barrows' New Map of Iowa, with Notes" was published in 1854 by a Cincinnati company and was so highly valued that the state legislature ordered copies for all its members and the state officials.   He made a trip to California in 1850, returned by way of Cuba and Mexico and wrote of his exploits for the printed media.

Willard Barrows, who was living in 1863, wrote a considerable history of Scott County for the Historical Society's early publications.   It was said that his "suburban residence and ground are conspicuous to every person passing......" Scott County was in existence about 28 years when Willard Barrows wrote about its early history.   That was 125 years ago and much has changed in Scott County; his predictions have come true.

# Chapter Thirteen
# LOUISA COUNTY

Louisa County is named for Louisa Massey as we noted in an earlier chapter and selecting the name for the county was not as if it were being named for a famous river, person or event such as some of the counties.

It was Louisa Massey, you will recall, who sought revenge for the murder of her brother, Woodbury Massey, who had been foreman of a jury that found a murderer guilty. Woodbury Massey was a victim of vengeance and young Louisa set out to find the killer and bring him to a little "frontier justice." She shot him but did not kill him; yet he died of the wounds a little later. The incident became quite well known on the Iowa (and Illinois) frontier and the story probably grew as it was told and retold. Whatever, Louisa Massey gained both the sympathy and the respect of everyone.

No one knows anything of the later life of Louisa Massey. She is said to have married and possibly settled in Illinois and lived out her life as a housewife and mother.

Her first name will always be a part of history as it was attached to a new county in Iowa created down the river from her native Dubuque

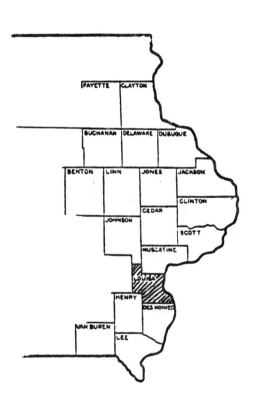

County. Some think there was good reason for giving the county her name as it brought attention to a lack of "law and order" on the Iowa frontier which was not really true. But such tales echoed through the halls of the Congress in Washington

and might possibly have been enough to help Congressional Delegate (Gen.) George W. Jones to get legislation enacted to further organize the area.

One way or another the county got its name from Louisa Massey of Dubuque. At the time and under the circumstances few disagreed with Louisa's harsh act. It would seem almost cruel to state that the county got its name from an "attempted murderess." Perhaps it would be more respectful, more noble even, to say it got its name from a "vengeful sister." Louisa County is probably the only county in America with that singular story behind its name.

LOUISA MASSEY
The Dubuque lass who gained lasting recognition in having a county named for her; as the result of a shooting.

---

The first of the early pioneer settlers in the area that was to become Louisa County was probably Christopher Shuck who is said to have "effected a settlement near the mouth of the Iowa River, and near the present village of Toolsboro (sic), in what is now Jefferson Township."

And as with most such early settlements the date of it later came into dispute; some thought it was a year later, 1835 instead of the 1834 that has been handed down through the years. We must recall that the lands of the Black Hawk Purchase were opened to settlement after 1 June 1833 and white pioneer settlers were crossing the river after that date. For a river county it might seem late for 1835 to be the year. We are certain there were explorers in the area long before and probably many possible settlers were in the area immediately after it was open to settlement. As with many such situations in history the researcher and writer of history itself should apply all logic and evidence where possible and arrive at plausible conclusions.

Ours is that Christopher Shuck arrived and "effected a settlement" in 1834.

But, here we must revert to our prior logic about who the first white men were to set foot upon the soil of the area that was to become Louisa County.

They were Marquette and Joliet in June of 1673.

In his writing and logic submitted in his writing about Scott County's history (See Chapter XII) Willard Barrows goes to lengths to bring Marquette and Joliet to the shores of Scott County. He reasons with some logic, and even with mathmatical suppositions, that the area Pere Marquette wrote about in his journal was the Davenport area and not Toolesboro as has been the general assumption. And we don't necessarily disagree with the fact that Marquette and Joliet did, indeed, set foot upon Iowa soil at the area of Davenport

What we do conclude is that there is no good reason to assume that the area of Toolesboro was the only place where Marquette and

Joliet set foot upon Iowa soil. We do conclude that the area of Toolesboro was probably, indeed, the place Pere Marquette wrote about in his journal and that Toolesboro in Louisa County should thereby keep that distinction. But to say that the area of Toolesboro was the only place where the French team landed would be equally illogical especially when one studies their habits, needs and probably daily routine. Our thoughts that even the use of pen, scarce ink and rare paper would preclude prolific writing is also valid. But the sustenance of life, the food along the shores to include hunting wildlife and the fact that it, and even the supplies they carried to some extent, needed cooking meant that they were on land quite often. You don't build a fire in a boat.

On the other hand we know they slept in their boats most of the time for fear of savage Indians about whom they knew very little. There was no way of knowing if they were friendly or not. And being attacked, killed or scalped in their sleep was not a means of finding out.

Our conclusion is that Marquette and Joliet first set foot upon the soil of Iowa at the area of McGregor in Clayton County. We further conclude, logically, that they went ashore at Prairie La Porte (now Guttenberg), Dubuque, Bellevue, Clinton, (and somewhere between Bellevue and Clinton), Davenport, Muscatine, Toolesboro, Burlington, Fort Madison and Keokuk. All those places can be reckoned to have been visited---their soil trod upon---by Marquette and Joliet in 1673.

And why? No logic would suggest that those early explorers landed at and scaled a cliff or a bluff above the Mississippi. But where a plain existed, as at the above mentioned places, it was easy and convenient to land their craft. And why not? They were, indeed, explorers! They needed to report upon what they were finding. Marquette kept the written journal; wouldn't it make more sense that he wrote onshore where a steady hand could do the writing rather than in a boat oared by more than one and giving no steadiness of hand for making entries into his journal? Where convenient, then, we can assume they went ashore and for many valid reasons.

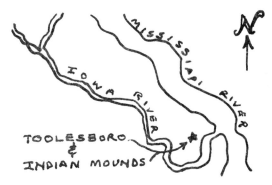

In Louisa County the Iowa River widens as it flows into the Mississippi and it flows in a north, northeasterly direction as it pours into the Father of Waters. Coming down an unknown river perhaps Marquette and Joliet and their crew automatically sailed into the Iowa River. We must also remember that sometimes the rivers were different in times past and that there were different channels. Change is the nature of things and the nature of things is change.

One way or another Marquette and Joliet and who knows who of their crew discovered tracks along the shore and went inland and found friendly Indians and parleyed with them. A chief is reported to have known enough of the French language to have visited with Pere Marquette calling him "black gown." As a missionary to the Indians the good father was also familiar with some Indian dialects. So communication was effected between the white man and the Indian. The other aspect to this is that any knowledge of the French by an Indian would indicate that men of that nation had been there before as we know, and have read.

Hence another conclusion of logic and that is that Toolesboro remains the place of the first real parley with the Indians by Marquette and Joliet. Toolesboro is proud of that distinction and justifiably so.

Returning to the first settler Christopher Shuck we find that he settled on his ground when it was in the control, legally, of the Indians as part of what was the "Keokuk Reserve." That special "reserve" covered quite a large area of what was to become Louisa County in 1834 and whites were not supposed to make claims there. The "Keokuk Reserve" was not ceded to the general government, i.e. the United States, until September of 1836.

Louisa County then, as now, was a beautiful area with fertile land and prospective pioneers were tempted by it even before it was open to settlement. As we mentioned when discussing the "Neutral Ground" in an earlier chapter, which was up in northern Iowa, both white men and Indians ignored the boundaries. It was a similar situation with the "Keokuk Reserve."

In 1834 Christopher Shuck evidently ignored the bounds. And so did others eventually for in 1835 a host of early pioneer settlers arrived in the area. Among them were Philip Harrison, John B. Snowden, Jeremiah Smith (we can't be sure if it were Sr. or Jr. Jeremiah Smith, Jr., was the future legislator.), William H. Creighton, Thomas Parsons,

James Irwin, William Kennedy, David Morgan, H. Parsons, Robert Childers, a Mr. Thompson and a Mr. Miligan.

In 1836 among the pioneer settlers who came were Abraham McCleary, Thomas Stoddard, Wright Williams, William S. Toole (after whom Toolesboro came to be named), G. Long, Levi Thornton and brother possibly Err about whom we've read for he was supposed to have been a pioneer of Louisa County, too, G. B. Williams, G. H. Crow, a Mr. Humphrey and a Mr. Stevens.

It was, as we noted, in November of 1836 that Keokuk and his followers gave peaceable possession of the "Keokuk Reserve" to the United States. Keokuk and his people then moved farther westward and eventually end up in Kansas. With Keokuk gone and his "reserve" available for white settlement, many came to stake their claims in 1837 and 1838.

The first white child born in Louisa County was not determined until 1888, according to one writer of history. It is related that a letter arriving from Dallas, Texas, dated 5 September 1888 from a W. M. Milligan (a publisher in that city) averred that he was born on 7 January 1836 in Elliott Township, Louisa County, Iowa. James Higbee who later became president of the Old Settlers' Society was probably the first born in the southern part of the county, the date given as 16 September 1836.

Thus another county in the new land across the river got under way: Louisa County. Unique in the selection of its name, rich in its land and scenic in the beauty of its hills and valleys, it was somewhat later than some of the other river counties in its start. Mostly because of the "Keokuk Reserve." But a new county was underway and it would be ................. Louisa County.

# Chapter Fourteen

# HENRY COUNTY

The Black Hawk War ended with a treaty and one of its provisions was the Black Hawk Purchase discussed earlier in this history. The land within the "purchase" was not to be opened to settlement until 1 June 1833.

The area that became Henry County, Iowa, had always been a tempting one to potential settlers and many had tried to enter upon the lands of the Black Hawk Purchase before the "official" opening. Hiram Smith built a log cabin prior to the legal time and it was taken by U. S. army Dragoons and burned. The government meant to enforce the "official day." Others were stopped, too, but many persisted in their attempts.

Hiram Smith was not to be deterred from settling in the land that was to become Henry County for he returned in May of 1833, still in anticipation of the June 1st opening date. He built another cabin near the site of what was to become Lowell, Iowa, and thereby became the first permanent white settler in Henry County.

The area of Mount Pleasant, early designated the county seat of Henry County, saw no permanent settlers there for a year after the opening date, until and after.

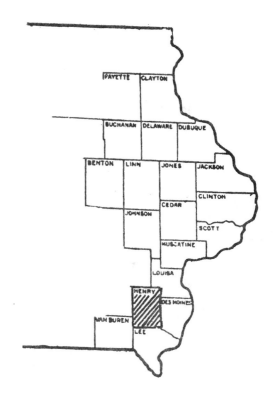

James Dawson arrived in the Mt. Pleasant area in the spring of 1834 and staked a claim west of where the city is today but shortly thereafter he removed elsewhere. Yet James Dawson is regarded in history to have been the first white settler in the vicinity.

Presley Saunders became a more permanent settler and is history's choice as the founder of Mount Pleasant, Iowa. He is accorded other honors for the pioneer he was.

Presley Saunders, along with Joseph Moore, Bartlett Williams and another Mr. Williams with a son, walked from their homes in Illinois to re-establish themselves along the Mississippi River on the Iowa side.

The Flint Hills area which is now Burlington was their original destination but a reported fear of the ague caused them to move on westward. The early pioneers, as we have noted, were always seeking a place to settle that had a good water supply, usually flowing springs, and a healthy stand of timber.

As Saunders and his associates travelled west to the center of what they perceived to be the next probable county, they discovered both natural resources. Other than such prime requirements they were struck with the awesome beauty of the place. Pleasant, indeed.

In fact, Presley Saunders was so impressed with all the qualities of the place they had found that he drove his own stakes at once and thereby made his claim to it. That was in 1834. Having done so he returned to Illinois and in February of 1835 returned with his family. Until he could build his own home, he and his family stayed with James Dawson whom, we recall, was already settled in what was to be Center Township.

Dawson and Saunders worked together to build a home for the Saunders family and it was located "at the foot of the present entrance drive of Saunders Park."

Later that same year of 1835 the farsighted Saunders laid out a plat for a community he envisioned and would name most appropriately Mount Pleasant. He the opened a store which was located "where our present Extension Office is now at the northwest corner of the central square." He engaged in that same business "with strict integrity" for the next 50 years.

Presley Saunders was born on a farm in Fleming County, Kentucky, on 11 July 1809, in the same state as and only five months after Abraham Lincoln. Presley was the son of Gunnell and Mary Saunders. He was reared on a farm and attended the primitive schools of that day but became mostly self-educated.

## Heidelberg Restaurant & Lounge

Bringing a touch of
### Gourmet
to Mount Pleasant

(319) 385-2002

**Highway 34 East**
**(319) 385 - 2002**

He later worked on a farm in Indiana for a brother-in-law and continued to hear stories of the vast agricultural west then about ready to open up for settlement and expansion. He removed from a farm in Indiana to another near Springfield, Illinois, and then came to Iowa. Other than his own family, his parents followed him to Iowa and spent the remainder of their lives in Mount Pleasant where they lived, according to Ruth Mallams, "in a low-built red brick house with an iron fence where the post office is now located."

Presley Saunders' brother Alvin was the first postmaster in Mount Pleasant and then removed to Nebraska. There he was appointed as the territorial governor and later became Nebraska's first United States senator after its admission as a State.

It was in 1828 that Presley Saunders and a Mr. Rogers had taken a drove of hogs to Galena, Ills., and after selling them hired a flatboat and took a trip downriver to St. Louis, Missouri. It was during this trip that the young Saunders became impressed with the land along and west of the river. He decided then that if he ever removed, it would be to such a region.

He took an active part in the Black Hawk War and became a captain in Moffet's Company. He saw action at the Wisconsin Heights and the

Battle of Bad Axe. He served until Chief Black Hawk was captured and the "war" ended.

Other than the first plat of 80 acres which was to become essentially the southwestern part of the new community, Saunders laid out two additional plats. When he did so he reportedly had but five dollars in cash as he continued to lay out the town of Mount Pleasant.

Presley Saunders had married in 1830 and had not lived in the community he founded very long when she died. He had met Edith Cooper in Springfield, Ills., and she was from one of the leading families of that young city. Her sudden death left him with one young daughter, Mary.

 **cornick realty, inc.**

RICHARD W. CORNICK
BROKER

209 E. WASHINGTON STREET    MT. PLEASANT, IOWA 52641

**319-385-4792**

AFTER HOURS BY APPOINTMENT

RESIDENTIAL
AGRICULTURAL
COMMERCIAL

PRIVATE & AUCTION SALES -- CERTIFIED APPRAISERS -- MULTIPLE LISTING SERVICE

Sometime later, in 1837, he married Hulda Bowen of the community and to that union was born four children. (In 1888 all were living in Mount Pleasant.)

Mr. and Mrs. Saunders lived in a two-story red brick house on the northwest corner of what is now the parking lot for Home Furniture on West Washington Street.

Presley Saunders, pioneer settler and founder of Mount Pleasant, died on 19 July 1889, in the city he had started and only a few days past his 80th birthday. He was one of many founders of Iowa communities who had seen his vision become a reality.

Presley Saunders and the earlier families of his descendants are buried in what is known as the "Saunders Circle" toward the south boundary of the city cemetery. From the street can be seen an elevated concrete wall a foot or so high marking the area of their graves.

By coincidence or whatever there is something "Lincolnesque" about the life of Presley Saunders. Both he and Lincoln were born in log cabins in the Kentucky countryside. Both went to Indiana and both removed from there to Springfield, Illinois. At about the same time both earned their living just outside Springfield. Both journeyed down the Mississippi as young men. Both operated stores although not at the same time. Both became self-educated men. Both married women from prominent Springfield families, the Coopers and the Todds. Both accumulated considerable wealth. Both left their marks on history although not in the same proportion and effect.

Here the similarities might be said to end for Abraham Lincoln eventually went east and his life ended

WE'RE PROUD
to be a part of
HENRY COUNTY
and
MOUNT PLEASANT

WE'VE BECOME A PART
of the history of
HENRY COUNTY
and
MOUNT PLEASANT

PIONEER HY-BRED
Mt. Pleasant Production Plant

PIONEER.
BRAND · SEED CORN

Pioneer Hy-Bred International, Inc., Des Moines, Iowa

Saunders' Little Town Grew at Once.

PRESLEY SAUNDERS

original counties of Des Moines and Dubuque. The early counties were "laid out" or "created" but many were not organized for some years. Often the newer inland counties were assigned to older counties on the river for the purpose of taxation, elections and judicial proceedings.

The Wisconsin Territorial Legislature which met at Belmont in the Wisconsin Territory in December of 1836 formed new counties from Des

there. And Presley Saunders went west and lived out his life there but he survived the martyred president by many years.

But even in death the two families came together in another way for some of the descendants of both men lie buried beneath the sod of Mount Pleasant, Henry County, Iowa.

The community that Presley Saunders founded flourished from the beginning and an influx of pioneer settlers soon made it the one prominent area of social, economic and political activity within an area of many miles but especially the area that was to become Henry County.

In 1836 the Wisconsin Territorial Legislature began carving up the two

# H. Eugene Smith
## *General Contractor*

"Build with Confidence"

Commercial, Industrial
and Agricultural

Pre-engineered metal
buildings for every need.

Concrete, Excavation
and Crane Service

# 319-385-3183   Ceco Buildings Division

**304 West Washington
Mt. Pleasant, IA 52641
(Residence Phone 986-6048)**

Moines County and the southern half of the Black Hawk Purchase. Those were Des Moines, Lee, Van Buren, Muscatine, Henry and Louisa. Scott County was originally created as Cook County but the name was later changed.

The official records of Henry County go back to 1837 and that year three commissioners were elected. From the very beginning Mount Pleasant was designated the capital, or county seat, of Henry County. That was done officially in 1836 and it has always remained so without dispute. (In other counties there have been almost vicious fights over the location of the county seat and thereby the county court house.)

The first county election was held on 13 January 1837 and three commissioners were elected. The commission form of government preceded

In the Collection of The Corcoran Gallery of Art

ABRAHAM LINCOLN
Contemporary of Presley Saunders whose life is compared in its similarities with that of the 16th president. Mt. Pleasant has a historic Lincoln tradition of which it is very proud.

the supervisor system with an aegis in between where a county judge presided over the affairs of the county as we shall see. Thus it was a very short time from its original settlement that Henry County had local (county) government. That probably had a lot to do with Saunder's early platting of a formal town that was the obvious site for the county seat. But other towns were considered earlier such as Oakland Mills and Trenton but there was never any real question about where the Henry County seat would be.

In 1836 Mount Pleasant had a population of a little over 100 to which it had grown in a very short

# We're Contel.
# We Bring People And Places Together.

## It's The Neighborly Thing To Do.

Wherever your next phone call is going—to a big city or just down the street—we'll be glad to get you there. And it's more than just a connection from your house to somewhere.

It's a mix of community service, community responsibility and community pride. Besides, it's the neighborly thing to do.

**CONTEL** Telephone Operations

**We're proud of Henry County History!**

# MEET THE COMPANY THAT SPAWNED THE BOOK!

## Mackay Envelope Corporation
### Mt. Pleasant, Iowa 52641

Long before he became a best selling author, Harvey Mackay made and sold envelopes. The secrets of success detailed in his book are not new ideas. They've been in daily use for many years at Mackay Envelope Corporation. They are the concepts that built our company into a leading envelope supplier to the business community and the direct mail and photofinishing industries.

**Harvey Mackay's book stresses these themes repeatedly:**
- **Concern for customers as people**
- **Anticipating their needs**
- **Attention to detail**
- **Excellent service and quality**

**At Mackay Envelope Corporation, these are the basics of everyday business.**

**SWIM WITH THE SHARKS**
*Without Being Eaten Alive*

OUTSELL
OUTMANAGE
OUTMOTIVATE
AND
OUTNEGOTIATE
YOUR
COMPETITION

**HARVEY MACKAY**
Called "Mr. Make-Things-Happen"
by *Fortune* magazine

We've become a leader in our industry through innovative ideas, consistent quality and exceptional service. We produce over 2,000,000,000 envelopes each year, serving our customers with efficient state-of-the-art equipment, envelope management programs, on-line imprinting systems, and storage/just-in-time delivery. And behind these capabilities are the unique ideas of Harvey Mackay.

You'll find them in his best selling book. And you'll find them in daily practice by all of us at Mackay Envelope Corporation.

Harvey Mackay, CEO, Mackay Envelope Corporation and author of the best selling new book "Swim with the Sharks Without Being Eaten Alive"

## (319) 385-9061

## HENRY COUNTY - 1836

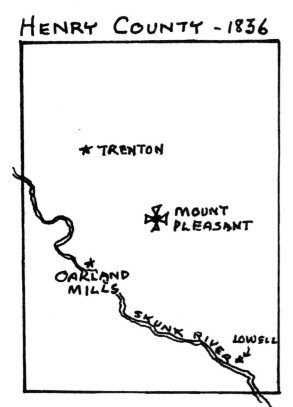

★ TRENTON

✠ MOUNT PLEASANT

★ OAKLAND MILLS

SKUNK RIVER

LOWELL ★

Other than Mount Pleasant, Trenton and Oakland Mills were considered very briefly as possible locations for the county seat. But in Henry County there was never any doubt that it would be at Mount Pleasant, as noted on the map at the left. It was not only the largest town but the most centrally located as shown.

time. And that was a respectable populace by the standards of the time.

The first Henry County Court House was built of logs and heated by fire places as were all of the original ones. They served their purpose until more permanent buildings could be erected of more solid substances.

# Marianne's Studio

**PORTRAITS WITH PRIDE**

**SERVING TO PRESERVE**

**HENRY COUNTY HISTORY**

**Videos ❉ Weddings ❉ Seniors
Family Portraits
Passports and Commercial**

117 South Jefferson          986-6573
Mount Pleasant

**ALVIN SAUNDERS**

There remain several stories about how Henry County got its

name. But the most plausible one, and the one we accept, surrounds its naming by Alvin Saunders, Presley's brother, about whom we have read earlier.

For whatever reason it appears from valid research that Alvin Saunders was given the honor of naming the county. Perhaps because he was the first postmaster and perhaps not.

It seems that Alvin Saunders was an admirer of one Colonel James D. Henry, whom he had known as a youth in Illinois and who gained fame as a soldier in the Black Hawk War. Col. Henry had become friend, mentor and idol of the young Alvin Saunders and so when it came time to decide upon whom the young county would honor in its name, that of Colonel James D. Henry was the choice. And Alvin Saunders is given the credit for projecting that name and its being accepted.

COLONEL JAMES D. HENRY

A hero of the Black Hawk War and an idol of Alvin Saunders, who was accorded the honor of naming the newly created county, Col. Henry was honored in the choice and the name was accepted readily by the people.

We're proud of the history of Mount Pleasant and Henry County . . . . .
We're proud to be a part of that history.

MOTOROLA INC.

PROUD TO BE A SISTER COMPANY

Mount Pleasant Production Plant - 1411 East Washington (Hwy 34 East)
Mount Pleasant, Iowa 52641

The tide of population was growing steadily as Mount Pleasant became the county seat for the new Henry County. The white man had broken his way through the rugged wilderness and homes, farms and villages began to appear upon the beautiful landscape of the area.

At Big Creek in Henry County the first grist mill was erected by a Mr. Z. Wilbourne who lived on the claim and operated the mill for many years. It was the only one around and a great convenience to the other settlers.

The first birth in Henry County occurred near the site of Lowell in the southern part of the county in December of 1835 and the honor was claimed by T. S. Box.

A settler who arrived early and "looked longingly on the site of Mount Pleasant" was one William Lusk but he is reported to have been too poor to buy the area and it was bought by Presley Saunders. But William Lusk was a hard worker and he went westward about three miles, staked out his claim, worked hard and in some years was a wealthy man, successful farmer owning many properties. His homestead amounted to a little over a thousand acres.

The first death in Henry County was considered accidental. A man named Pullman was found dead in 1835 with his rifle by his side.

No early census was taken, in the earliest years but the first one of 1838 showed Henry County with 3,058 souls and that was a considerable increase in those years.

Once established Mount Pleasant grew and its reputation for opportunity spread far and wide.

In 1835 it was anticipated that a new Territory of Wisconsin would be created by the Congress. Henry County was not yet even created on paper and the District of Iowa was a part of the Territory of Michigan. In 1835 there was a race for Territorial Delegate in Congress and the candidates were Duane Doty (a leader in Wisconsin and later its governor) and (then) Col. George W. Jones.

Presley Saunders, the leading power in Henry County, had a long chat with the candidate G. W. Jones and got from him a promise that he would use his influence if elected to obtain a post office for Mt. Pleasant. Col. Jones agreed and Presley Saunders used his influence with the voters of Henry County to favor Jones' election. Presley Saunders' influence must have been considerable for about 60 votes were cast and every one of them was for Jones.

Col. Jones was elected and went to Washington but he was

## MAIL PRODUCTION SERVICES

**Metromail**
CORPORATION

For quotes, background information, or technical data about any aspect of our **complete** Mail Production Services, including:

- Addressing
- Ink Jet
- Inserting
- Label Affixing
- Folding
- Forms Bursting
- Card Affixing
- Coin Affixing
- Detached Labeling

Metromail Corporation
P.O. Box 500
Mt. Pleasant, IA 52641

**CONTACT:**
Jim Hartman,
Mail Production Services,
Account Executive
319/385-2284

## We Know The Community...
## We're Building With You

**Ceco Buildings Division**

A Division of the Ceco Corporation
THE CONSTRUCTION PROFESSIONALS

unable to get a post office for Mt. Pleasant. Rather a compromise one was established at a place called Richland which was supposed to be between Burlington and Mt. Pleasant. The truth was that no such place existed and Mt. Pleasant had been passed over for a post office.

Before 1838 the mail went to Burlington and Postmaster William Ross, about whom we've read, agreed to try to forward it all to Mount Pleasant. But the pioneer folk were usually poor and there was very little money in circulation anyway. Letters cost 25 cents and postage could be paid in advance or sent to be paid for by the addressee who might not have had the funds and let the letter remain until they were obtained. When a post office was finally located at Mount Pleasant, Alvin Saunders got the commission as the Postmaster.

Mount Pleasant and Henry County grew and their foundations were solid. One historian wrote that "Churches and schoolhouses--- those edifices which proclaim the moral development of a country and represent the two greatest factors in the problem of civilization--- dot the prairie on every hand."

In 1837 Mr. John Lash was appointed Justice of the Peace for Henry County and he was the first to ever hold that office.

Mr. Lash recalled for history two incidents of interest to us who live in "the future." One very clearly showed the independence of the early pioneer settlers "when their isolation renders them a community unto themselves." The historian relates as follows:

"The first Territorial Legislature passed an act called the 'Claim Property Law,' which provided that such property as rails, when cut on a man's claim and not yet made into fence, were subject to execution and sale for debt. The settlers were violent in their opposition to this law, and even the traders, who supplied the poor pioneers with goods, were adverse to its enforcement,

**MIDWEST FEDERAL**

A good tree to come to......

..... for Shelter

With Offices

THROUGHOUT IOWA

deeming it an injury and injustice to those who were trying to redeem the wilderness. When the people of this section realized what the law really meant, they summoned all who were here and held a meeting in the memorable little log house on the public square. There they organized and observed the rules of parliamentary usage, and formally repealed a statute of the Territory! They voted that the law was an outrage and decided that it should have no force in Henry County. This summary proceeding was effective, for never afterward did any Justice dare to interfere with a settler's pile of rails. The law was soon after repealed......."

(The essence of the Common Law was at work here whether the justice of the peace or the people recognized what was going on. While a "meeting" cannot repeal a legislative act, a jury can for it is the judge of both the law and the facts. Had a Common Law jury made the decision to ignore---i.e. "repeal"--- the law, it would have had the full force and effect of its action; as it was, it was merely decided to ignore the law by the very strength of the numbers at their meeting. For example, this right of a jury still exists but is rarely used, mainly because the American people no longer understand their rights. This is not meant to be a lesson the Law but to note that essentially what those early pioneer settlers did in Henry County so many years ago was right and proper and its basis was, indeed, in the Common Law which was their inheritance and part of their Ameri-

can heritage.)

The other incident later recalled was that of the "indictment" of Presley Saunders. Now here was about as upright a citizen as there was in Henry County at the time but an incident occurred that led to a "court record" about which there was doubt in later years.

The basis of it was that of a fight involving physical harm or some such among several men.

Yet some decades later but before the death of Presley Saunders who lived to a ripe old age an abstract of a court record came to light; it was assumed there was none, according to Saunders.

The first District Court convened at Mt. Pleasant on 14 April 1837 and David Irvin was the judge. (This was probably the same judge who disclaimed jurisdiction when the Smiths, father and son, who had slain Woodbury Massey, were arrested and taken before him. See Chapter VIII, Dubuque County.)

W. W. Chapman was the district attorney of the United States. Jesse D. Payne was the clerk of court by appointment of Governor Dodge.

The first business of the court was the selection of a Grand Jury and some recognizable names appear on the list such as Clabourne Jones, Sr., Samuel Heaton, Marshall Saunders, Clabourne W. Hughes, D. C. Roberts, William W. Morrow, James McCoy, Keeland T. Maulden, Benjamin F. Hutton, Jacob Burge, Moses Shirley, Wilson Lowell, Thomas Clark, William King, David Minter, James Williford, Sr., George W. Lewis, Henry Snyder,

Proud of our history......

COAST TO COAST
H. A. Bezoni, Manager
Mount Pleasant

A part of our history..........

McWHIRTER CHEVROLET
Sales and Service
Mount Pleasant

Sr., Berry Jones, Litle Hughes, John H. Randolph, Warren L. Jenkins and Presley Saunders. John H. Randolph was the Foreman.

The record reads: "The Grand Jury aforesaid, after being duly sworn, were solemnly charged, and retired to their chamber to consider of presentments and indictments" and after due deliberation they declared to the there were none.

Succeeding records, we are told, conflict with that written above for it is said that a second jury was impaneled and excluded from it were Presley Saunders, Moses Shirley, Litle Hughes, John H. Randolph and Warren L. Jenkins. This second panel which excluded the grand jurors above then proceeded to return "indictments for assault and battery returned against John Mabee for assault on Bushrod Atkeyson; Jesse D. Payne for assault on Presley Saunders; William Morris, assault on Jesse D. Payne; Presley Saunders, assault on Jesse D. Payne; Zachariah Wilbourne, assault on William Morris; Asbury Porter, assault on Warren L. Jenkins; Bushrod Atkeyson, assault on John Mabee."

Presley Saunders, in later years, was unaware there had been a formal indictment but related the following story. When Henry County was organized its founding fathers agreed that Jesse D. Payne would be a good representative in the Territorial Legislature which would meet in Belmont. Other than representing the interests of the young Henry County, Payne returned with a commission as clerk of court.

"Mr. Payne established himself at Mount Pleasant, but did not altogether possess the faculty of making himself agreeable to Mr. Saunders," so the story goes. Payne thereupon merely helped himself to building-logs from Saunders' grove without asking permission.

The narrative continues as follows: "Such little informalities soon led to differences of opinion between the men, and one day, as Mr. Saunders was passing Mr. Payne's house, the latter called out to his uncle: 'John, go down into Saunders' grove and get me some wood!' Mr. S. overheard the remark and protested against the free use of his timber, whereupon Mr. Payne responded in a rather imperious manner. This led to still further words, and the words came to blows. Mr. Saunders admits that he was the assailant, and the

## Iris City Antique Mall

Where 27 antique dealers unite to serve you with the art and objects of southeast Iowa history. Come and see all the history we display for sale.

IRIS CITY ANTIQUE MALL
Highway 34 West
Mount Pleasant

inference is that Mr. Payne got the worst of the battle. At all events, Mr. S. at once repaired to a Justice and acknowledged his fault, and paid a fine of $5 voluntarily."

Presley Saunders in later years said he thought the whole matter ended with his voluntarily paying a fine. The record of the proceedings seemed entirely unknown to him and it has been decided that the handling of the matter was incorrect. The cases were never tried and that fact gives basis to questions arising in the entire matter. The persons accused admitted to a $55 bail but John Mabee was the only one fined and he paid a $5 fine.

It was a trifling incident and never brought to light until John P. Grantham was researching records many years later preparing a Henry County history paper.

It was certainly no poor reflection on Mr. Saunders whose fortitude in dealing with a timber thief may have been the better part of wisdom and immediate justice!

---

## Jerry's Restaurant
HWY 34 EAST
Mount Pleasant
385-4412

also

## Lori's Loft
986-9980

After dining out . . . . .
VISIT LORI'S LOFT

Antiques
Home-made Craft Items

# Over the years......
# in Henry County

Over a century ago a historian whose writing we have but whom we cannot identify said:

"Henry County ranks her neighboring counties in just the degree that her intelligence has progressed. The end is far away, for the improvements over the original settlement are significant compared with the possibilities of her resources. Nature has lavished abundant wealth upon her, and it remains for man to extract it from the earth. The farms are inexhaustible in productive qualities if rightly cultivated. The future promises much more marked changes in every branch of trade and commerce, and there remains for her inhabitants an enviable harvest of results.

"Pleasant for situation, rich in material wealth, peopled by intelligent men and abounding in an atmosphere of mental health, the county of Henry is destined to become a leading one in the Northwest, as it is to-day a leading one in the State. The responsibility of developing it is intrusted to good men and true, and the dawn of the twentieth century will behold in this fair region a source of constant pride."

Eloquent and prophetic, veritably true in its predictions, our ancient prognosticator couldn't have predicted the coming to town of one Ernest A. Hayes who has probably done more to promote the community than any single individual in its history. A "one-man Chamber of Commerce," he's featured in this volume as one whom history will honor even more adequately as times goes on.

# in Henry County

# E. A. Hayes is Mr. Mt. Pleasant

"When Ernie Hayes was hailed as 'Mr. Mt. Pleasant' at a gala surprise 80th birthday party on Jan. 20, 1984, the honor could not have gone to a more deserving gentleman." So wrote Jim Rose of the Mt. Pleasant NEWS in a special article about the Honorable E. A. Hayes in the paper's sesquicentennial edition in 1985. Known, loved and respected by the people of Mt. Pleasant and Henry County, the very apt subject of the Rose article is also well known all over Iowa and the rest of the nation.

Ernie Hayes was born in New London, Iowa, on 20 January 1904 and that was before the United States started inaugurating presidents on January 20th!

He was the son of Margaret Elizabeth Ferrell and Alonzo D. Hayes. There were three other sons who were James, Columbus, Harold and a daughter, Faye. Their father ran the A. D. Hayes Company in New London and later expanded into Mt. Pleasant with the business being located north of the junior high school. They dealt in grain, seed and the selling of cement.

Ernie Hayes was graduated from the New London High School in 1921 and from Iowa Wesleyan College in 1925. In 1985 his college graduating class noted their 60th anniversary. Young Hayes went on to obtain a Master's Degree from Washington University in St. Louis getting it in 1926.

With his formal education accomplished he returned to the family business and worked in it until 1929. That year he went out on his own.

It was in 1929 that he founded the Central States Mutual Insurance Association with two lawyers, F. S. Finley and Max Kinney. The firm prospered and in 1958 it was merged with United Fire and Casualty and the main headquarters was moved to Cedar Rapids. After that Ernie continued to operate the general agency in Mt. Pleasant.

He is listed in "Who's Who in the World" and is the only citizen of Henry County so honored. As of the publication of this book he is listed in "Who's Who in Iowa - 1987" and while it might not be apparent, E. A. Hayes was the first one chosen for that honor.

The remainder of this section about E. A. Hayes is direct quotes from the Mt. Pleasant NEWS article by Jim Rose.

".......with the Sesquincentennial celebration upon us a review of his accomplishments seems proper.

"For Hayes, a young 81 (in 1985), has done much down through the years in helping put Mt. Pleasant on the map. He has long been associated with the arrival of new industries in Mt. Pleasant and has traveled thousands of miles and put in countless hours in this pursuit.

"Hayes has been instrumental in encouraging all the major indus-

tries which have come to Mt. Pleasant since World War II to do so.

"Hayes said that in the 1950's he and other interested people realized the city could not continue to survive on agriculture alone. He said that he, A. M. Paterson, former longtime editor of The Mt. Pleasant NEWS, and others were of the opinion the city needed more industry. The only major industries here then were the Sheaffer Pen plant which came here in 1946 and the Staats Ribbon Co., which was started in 1896.

"We felt we needed new industry to broaden our economic base," Hayes said. "We also felt we needed to provide more housing and people to live in the houses, then providing them with the new industries we could encourage to come here."

"The Insurance Plan Savings and Loan (later Capitol) actively pursued promoting residential real estate development at that time, encouraging the securing and development of building sites."

"As a result the first major residential area was the purchase and development of Linden Heights by Insurance Plan. It covers 130 acres and has 100 lots with 50 of them with houses on them. The remaining lots are still available to buyers. (Those were 1985 figures.)

"Our group started a campaign to raise money for the Henry County Industrial Commission and had over 500 donors, including school children who brought a dollar each to help. Bob Dennis served as our executive on the fund raising project and help from chairman Edd King, George Rochefort and Harold Bainter.

"When we learned the acreage that Cargill Seed Co. later purchased was available, Rochefort and Leonard Close purchased the land, making it available later to Cargill at the cost,

Hayes said. 'This is typical of the fine cooperation by the people of Mt. Pleasant and surrounding area for later and current industrial development.'

"The first industry Hayes had a hand in locating here was the Sheaffer Pen Co. 'After World War II, Craig Sheaffer of Ft. Madison decided to locate his ballpoint pen (Fine Line) division here and purchased 36 acres in east Mt. Pleasant (now Sheaffer addition) for the plant site. However, he decided to cancel his building plans when he learned he could not get the necessary brick or brick masons for the construction.'

" 'I asked him what he needed and told him about the old canning factory the A. D. Hayes Co. owned on north Lincoln,' Hayes said. 'He bought the old factory and installed the ballpoint division in 1946.'

" 'The 36 lots that had been purchased by Sheaffer were developed and the land was given by Sheaffer to Iowa Wesleyan with the money from the lots sold by the college going to the college.'

"Mr. Sheaffer was later chairman of the Iowa Wesleyan board of trustees.

"When pen production dropped, the local plant was consolidated with the Ft. Madison plant and the local building was donated to Wesleyan.

"Emerson Electric then located in the building and filled space contracts for the government. The firm was here for 12 years, closing when the contracts ran out. Lee Deters was the plant manager. He is currently president of Smith and Wesson in Connecticut, according to Hayes. Then Motorola came here and continues to operate here. Some of the radio equipment is exported as far away as Japan.

"Garretson Industries and Mt. Pleasant Tool Works are two locally

On 16 July 1988, Mount Pleasant and the Henry County Development Committee welcomed and honored Sam Walton of Wal-Mart Stores to their city and county. Wal-Mart has a huge distribution center located at Mt. Pleasant from which many thousands of trucks come and go taking merchandise to their stores all over. Pictured above from from left to right are American author and Iowa statesman Don Kimball, Sam Walton of Wal-Mart Stores and Ernie Hayes of Mount Pleasant who is the prime mover behind the fourlane highway goal known as the "Avenue of the Saints." See article on page 256 for more information. (Photograph by Brad Hicks of the Mount Pleasant NEWS, Mount Pleasant, Iowa.)

owned and operated businesses developed successfully during that period.

"Hayes said before the decision by Blue Bird Midwest to come here in 1962, over 250 locations in seven states were considered. Hayes made many trips to Fort Valley, Ga., with Frank DeLucia, Wilson Ervin and Patterson to converse with the Luce brothers, Albert, Joe and George, owners of Blue Bird, about locating their midwest plant in Mt. Pleasant.

"Hayes, as a member of the Iowa Development Commission (IDC), traveled on trade missions to New York City, San Francisco, the Orient, Europe and South America.

"Besides the industries already mentioned, Hayes also has worked hard in encouraging the following industries to come here: Vega Industries (Heatilator Division); O. E. McIntyre (Metromail); Superior Cable (now Goodyear); Mackay-Iowa Envelope; Mitchell Engineering (now CECO Buildings Division) and more recently the Wal-Mart Distribution Center and Retail Store, City Carton Co., Mid-America Building Supplies and Pioneer Hy-Bred.

"Hayes has served on the Iowa Development Commission for 16 years. It was a member of that commission who first contacted Wal-Mart officials about the possibility of locating in Mt. Pleasant. When asked what he thought prompted Wal-Mart to come here he remarked, 'They liked us.'

" 'The decision of Wal-Mart to come here was based on the quality of the people in our area and their productivity,' Hayes said. 'They thoroughly approved of our lifestyle including our schools, churches and parks. Our geographical location is very beneficial.' (End of NEWS article by Jim Rose.)

Ernie Hayes is a very young 84 and longevity runs in his family, his genes if you please. Ernie's mother lived to be 103 and he points that out to guests in his home while directing them to a painting of her.

At an age when most men are retired Ernie Hayes puts in full days of work, none of which end with just eight hours. He continues to search for new business and industry for his hometown. He travels constantly to meetings all over Iowa and the nation where his persuasion and influence are felt among the wealthy and the mighty who can benefit his beloved Mount Pleasant.

Back home, however, he is the ordinary "Ernie" who has won the respect of an entire community and the county in which it is located. Few men enjoy such esteem in their lifetimes and fewer have contributed so much to their hometowns.

Ernie lost his wife in 1979 to whom he was married on 13 February 1937. She was the former Ruth Irons of Mason City and was an active member of the Episcopal Church. Just prior to the publication of this book, Ernie Hayes contributed a bell tower and steeple with chimes to the local church, St. Michael's Episcopal.

To Ernie and Ruth Hayes were born two daughters, JoAnn and Janet. JoAnn is now Mrs. Ed Farrell and she and her husband, a native of Mt. Pleasant, live in Austin, Texas. Janet is now Mrs. Richard Dougherty of Woodbury, Minnesota. JoAnn and Janet have blessed Ernie with six grandchildren with whom he visits often.

So blessed, also, as he is with the genes of longevity (at 84 he swims every night before going to bed !) that most guess Ernie Hayes will far surpass his mother's age. Who knows how many more industries he will bring to Mt. Pleasant in the next twenty or thirty years?

# Other books by Donald L. Kimball . . . . . . .

I REMEMBER MAMIE - The nation's only complete biography of the life of Mamie Doud Eisenhower, wife of General and President Dwight D. Eisenhower. Some unpublished stories and pictures. Hard cover with jacket; Some books still available in the Limited First Edition. $ 15.00 postpaid.

THE CHOICE - FREEDOM OR SLAVERY - American author Donald L. Kimball extracts some of the wisdom of the ages to analyse what's going on in America today. A truly thought-provoking book. Regular $ 13.95; Now $ 10.00 ppd.

THE MONEY AND THE POWER - A history of money, both real and false, and how governments have used the money power in the past. Soft cover. $ 7.00 postpaid.

(NOTE: All other books by Donald L. Kimball are out of stock)

# We publish books . . . . . . .

If your group, county or historical society is planning to publish a book perhaps it would be wise to get an estimate from our division, HISTORIC PUBLICATIONS, P. O. Box 158, Fayette, Iowa 52142. We think we have the lowest prices available. It doesn't cost to find out.

If you're an individual who has written a book or plans to publish, our IOWA AUTHORS PUBLISHING COMPANY (same address) has brought some prominent Iowans into print. This is subsidy publishing only; we do not finance any publishing but you'll find out prices and our means of payment reasonable and convenient.

VOLUME TWO of "A HISTORY OF IOWA" by Donald L. Kimball is in preparation. It will be entitled "The Territory of Iowa" and will cover the years 1838 - 1846 in 400 or more pages. Write us for pre-publication prices and save on Volume Two.

FOR MORE INFORMATION ON BOOKS BY DONALD L. KIMBALL OR PUBLISHING YOUR BOOK OR YOUR GROUP'S BOOK WRITE OR CALL:

Trends & Events Publishing, Box 158, Fayette, IA 52142 (319) 425 - 3375

# ERNIE HAYES . . . . We Salute You!

YES, WE THE UNDERSIGNED, among your many friends and neighbors, salute you for being a vital part of the modern history of Mount Pleasant and Henry County for these many, many years . . . . . for being "MR. MOUNT PLEASANT" . . . . . for all you've done to make our city what it is today . . . . . and, for just being you . . . . . THANKS, ERNIE, from all of us ! ! !

Marvin E. Day
**A & D MANAGEMENT**

Dick Benedict
**BLUE BIRD MIDWEST**

**CECO BUILDINGS DIVISION**
of The CECO Corporation

H. A. Bezoni, Manager
**COAST - TO - COAST STORE**

**CONTEL**
A Part of Mt. Pleasant History

Dick Cornick
**CORNICK REALTY, Inc.**

**HAWKEYE BANK & TRUST**
Also Salem, Hillsboro, New London

**HEIDELBERG HAUS**
Restaurant and Lounge

Ed Kiesey
**HOME FURNITURE**

Richard E. Elefson
**HOMETOWN PARTNERS REALTY**

27 Antique Dealers in the
**IRIS CITY ANTIQUE MALL**

Dorothy Boyd
**IRIS CITY REAL ESTATE**

Lori's Loft and
**JERRY'S RESTAURANT**

Also Saluting Ted Flacksbarth
**MACKAY ENVELOPE CORPORATION**

Portraits for Our History
**MARIANNE'S STUDIO**

Bob & Phyllis Overton
**MAIN STREET FRAME & ART**

**McWHIRTER CHEVROLET**
Sales and Service

Complete Mail Production Services
**METROMAIL CORPORATION**

**MIDWEST FEDERAL**
With Offices Throughout Iowa

**MOTOROLA, Inc.**
Mount Pleasant Production Plant

**PIONEER HY-BRED, International**
Mount Pleasant Production Plant

**RICHARD REALTY**
and Auction Service

**H. EUGENE SMITH**
General Contractor

Denny Oakes
**WALKER'S OFFICE SUPPLY**

Tom Weir
**WEIR FUNERAL HOME**

AND, THANKS AGAIN, ERNIE HAYES.....

# The Avenue of The Saints

"The Avenue of The Saints" is another project to which Ernie Hayes of Mount Pleasant has given of himself and his time. The Avenue of The Saints was some years ago but a dream, a goal of Ernie Hayes in his untiring efforts to bring progress to his hometown, Henry County and south eastern Iowa. Now it is not far from a reality . . . . but, as they say, still with a way to go.

The Avenue is ultimately a four-lane highway stretching all the way from St. Paul in Minnesota to St. Louis in Missouri. Much of the proposed area is already completed into four-lane highways. But it is still in parts and portions, with some miles of only two lane highways in between.

Ernie Hayes insist that The Avenue will bring to every city and community all the way through Iowa advantages it has never had before in easier transportation ingress and egress with the population centers involved. Personal travel for folk using the highway would be a tremendous help, Mr. Hayes says, in time and safety. But the commercial advantages should benefit every community along the way.

As a part of Ernie Hayes's promotion of The Avenue he has created stationery for writing letters, T-shirts for wearing and displaying one's support of the final four-lane goal and even "Avenue of the Saints" caps both of which he proudly wears from time to time.

(In fact, at the July 16th, 1988, visit of Sam Walton to Mount Pleasant and the activities honor Mr. and Mrs. Walton, who showed up in an "Avenue of The Saints" cap and T-shirt? You guessed it. Ernie Hayes! But that isn't the end of that story. Who else showed up wearing an "Avenue of The Saints" cap? You might guess that one, too. Sam Walton! Anyway, as the man said, "A good time was had by all!")

In his efforts to make The Avenue a reality Ernie Hayes is in constant contact with Governor Branstad, the Highway Commission and both state and federal officials and burueas that might be involved. Yes, and members of the Congress, too, from Iowa and other States, especially Minnesota and Missouri. Ernie Hayes, as has been said, is a "one-man Chamber of Commerce for Mount Pleasant and Henry County," and gives of his time and substance selflessly to achieve the four-lane highway goal that The Avenue involves.

The benefits to all the communities along the way, along The Avenue if you please, are self-evident. Easy access to the flow of transportation is vital to a prosperous economy. Such access would be available to many communities, both large and small, all the way from Saint Paul through Iowa down to Saint Louis.

The Avenue of The Saints is a project, a goal, on which Ernie Hayes has been working for many years. His investment in time and expenses is one he regards not only as a noble one, but his duty to his community, his county, his state and, verily, the great midwest.

Meanwhile, Ernie Hayes will put forth every human effort to achieve his goal. One thing is certain: the goal WILL be achieved. Ernie Hayes, Mr. Mount Pleasant, just won't have it any other way. In a later volume of this continuing history you can depend upon something being written about the completed "Avenue of The Saints" and you'll know who to thank.

# Chapter Fifteen
# VAN BUREN COUNTY

Van Buren County is another of the inland counties and is located on the Missouri border. It is named for Martin Van Buren, vice president of the United States when it was created. (See following page.)

Venturers were going inland as far as Van Buren County after the area was opened to immigration on 1 June 1833. Several communities eventually sprung up in the future county; some prospered and some disappeared. Today there are several communities and collectively they promote themselves as "the Villages of Van Buren" always emphasizing their colorful history.

Keosauqua is the county seat of Van Buren County and its settlement dates back to the mid-1830s. It is located on the Des Moines River which flows through the entire county from the northwest to the southeast. Originally, we are told, the town was two triangular pieces within the bend of the river. The south triangle was known as Van Buren and the north was called Des Moines. It is midway through the county that the Des Moines River makes a huge snakelike curve known as "the bend of the river." After

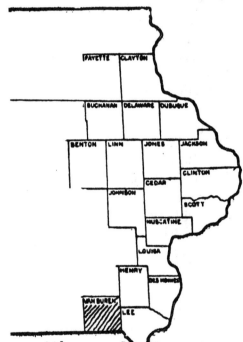

Pioneer settlers of Van Buren County, George S. McIntosh and Soloman McCracken, were direct ancestors of today's Lt. Governor of Iowa, Jo Ann (McIntosh) Zimmerman.

the two triangular sites were laid out another diamond-shaped one emerged and it was the third such to be named Keosauqua in the area. There the river runs northeast and the town of Keosauqua was platted by 1839.

Courtesy, Library of Congress

## MARTIN VAN BUREN

Van Buren County was named for Martin Van Buren of New York who was Andrew Jackson's vice president and who succeeded to the presidency in 1837. Iowa was then part of the Territory of Wisconsin and the county had been created but a short time before Van Buren became president. Both Jackson and Van Buren were close friends of Congressional Delegate G. W. Jones. Vice President Van Buren was also the last vice president to be elected president at the end of his term.

Farmington was the first town founded in Van Buren County and was the original county seat.

Edwin Manning came to the area of Keosauqua in 1837 and platted the village we noted was originally called Des Moines. He built a log house on the site where the Hotel Manning now stands.

Birmingham had venturers in its area early but was not platted until 1839. An early authentic log cabin stands yet today in its park. In the nearby Bethel Cemetery is the grave of Mary Ann Rutledge, the mother of Abraham Lincoln's alleged early love.

Bentonsport was named to honor U. S. Senator Thomas Hart Benton who always helped the area of Iowa on its way to Territorial and Statehood status. Benton's Port grew from the "Ross Settlement" that was started in 1836. A town across the river was called South Bentonsport but was originally Vernon.

The first murder in Van Buren County occurred at Bentonsport when a leading citizen of Fort Madison met his fate there.

"On July 13, 1837, accompanied by a friend named Doyle, he went to Bentonsport, in Van Buren County on some business connected with the court. Upon their arrival they registered at a hotel and engaged lodging, after which they went out on the town. Later in the evening another guest---Isaac Hendershott, of Burlington---arrived at the hotel and the landlord, assuming that Knapp and Doyle were out to 'make a night of it,' and all the rooms being taken, assigned Hendershott to the room engaged by the two Fort Madison men. Toward midnight Knapp and Doyle came in, took up a lighted candle and proceeded to their room to find the bed occupied. Knapp somewhat indignantly demanded to know what the occupant was doing in that bed, and, according to Hendershott's statement afterward, made a gesture as if to draw a weapon of some kind. Hendershott sprung from the bed, unsheathed a sword from the cane he carried and stabbed Knapp near the heart. The wounded man exclaimed, 'Doyle, I'm a dead man,' and sank to the floor still holding the candle in his hand. He lived but a few minutes and in the excitement which followed Hendershott made his escape. The following spring a steamboat stopped at Fort Madison and some one recognized Hendershott as one of the passengers. The news spread rapidly and in a short time an infuriated crowd headed by Thomas Fulton, a relative of Knapp, boarded the boat and gave the assassin a terrible beating. At the next term of the District Court in Van Buren County, Hendershott appeared at Farmington, relying upon his theory of self defense to secure an aquittal, but upon learning that an indictment for murder had been returned by the grand jury, he hastily decamped and was never seen in Iowa again."

The Iowaville-Selma area is a historic one. The "Iowaville Attack" is a part of its history. A combined Sac and Fox raiding party launched a sudden attack upon the peaceful white setlers. Both Black Hawk and Keokuk spent much time in the area and when he died in 1838 Chief Black Hawk was buried near Iowaville until his remains were disinterred and put on public display, a sad story that has been related earlier. The Iowaville-Selma area was inhabited by the Indians tribes for many centuries and relics are constantly found.

Famous artist Wendell Mohr has chosen the village of Vernon, across the river from Bentonsport as his home, moving from Des Moines. His line drawings depict Van Buren County history. He is well-known for his silk screens and watercolors.

**THE ALBERT KNEELAND FARMSTEAD**
The home of Albert Kneeland was built in the 1830s. Note that it was of finished lumber and not a log structure. It was rare in the 1830s to build anything but a log house. The picture was taken some years later after common photography was in everyday use.

The log cabin shown above is an exact replica of one built by the Morris family in 1838. It stands in Morris Park which was started as a private park by the Morris family.

# Bonaparte

An old riverboat port situated on the Hiawatha Pioneer Trail, Bonaparte has often been referred to as "the most fascinating of the Villages of Van Buren." It was first homesteaded in 1836 and in 1987 Bonaparte observed its 150th anniversary. It was in 1838 that the first steamship arrived at Bonaparte followed by an initial prosperity that saw a prosperous and "frolicking steamboat town."

In its early years Bonaparte became one of Iowa's most important commercial centers and was one of the largest towns in the territory. From it came flour, grist, lumber and woolen products. Those products were created by the power of large water wheels. Early settlers came from 200 or more miles away to have their grain ground into flour. So busy was this early town on the Des Moines River that early folk waited in line with wagonloads of grain to cross the river on Meek's Ferry.

A century and a half later only the lock walls and the dam shoulder can be seen today on the Des Moines River. The old iron rings to which the boats were tied remain in place. The old mill buildings and many beautiful homes still stand. They are made of brick and lumber after a modified Georgian style. Thus a sort of "Steamship Gothic" style of architecture makes Bonaparte a historically well-preserved community.

With its multitude of ancient structures the village continues to capture the spirit of the past. It has a museum which displays the essence of Bonaparte's prosperous past. The original lock wall can be seen in the Village Park and the Grist Mill is in the National Register of Historic Places. (W. Mohr artwork.)

THE BONAPARTE GRIST MILL – Built in 1836 by William Meek and his brother.

What was once a wilderness area occupied by the Sauk Indian tribes was visited in 1834 by Dr. Roger Nelson Cresap, Robert Coates and a Mr. Blackburn who came up the Des Moines River to the site of present-day Bonaparte. Dr. Cresap purchased 152 acres of land from the U. S. government. Included in his purchase was the eastern part of what became the town.

Robert Coates homesteaded there also and his land included the site of the town park and land to the west which was an area of timber not suitable for tilling. Coates sold his claim to Robert Moffett who in turn sold it to William Meek in 1836.

William Meek was a pioneer settler who came to Iowa from Michigan in 1836 and achieved early prominence as an entrepreneur. He came seeking, we are told, timber and water to build a mill. By clearing some land and building a primitive brush wing dam he had his grist mill which was the start of "Meek's Mills."

From a handful of pioneers the community saw many more arrivals and in 1837 the village was established. Dr. Cresap and William Meek donated land from their claims and the town was first named "Meek's Mills, Wisconsin Territory, U.S.A." It kept that name until 8 April 1841 when it was renamed Bonaparte after the French emperor of earlier years.

# Chapter Sixteen
# CLINTON COUNTY

Clinton County is Iowa's eastern most county and is named for De Witt Clinton once governor of New York and a national political figure. Because of its place on a map it has also been referred to as "Pompey's Nose." Clinton County's soil was first trod upon in June of 1673 when Marquette and Joliet and other members of their expedition exploring the Mississippi River sailing southward landed on its shores. It was much later when other white men would see the area that would be Clinton County.

The first permanent white settler in the area was Elijah Buell who arrived in July of 1835. He was a native of New York and had been in business or engaged in piloting boats on the Great Lakes, the Ohio River and finally the Mississippi. He had a yearning to settle somewhere permanently and chose the western shores of the Mississippi river.

A friend of Buell's, John Baker, settled at Fulton, Ills., Both came to what is called "the Narrows" and one settled in Illinois and one, Buell, ac-

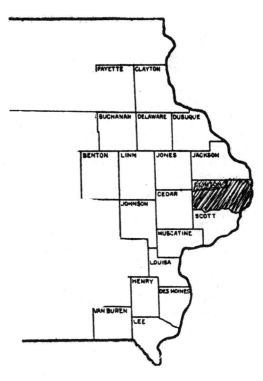

ross the river in Iowa. During August and September of 1835 Elijah Buell, along with a hired hand named Henry Carson, built a log house near the bank of the river. (That log house would have stood at what became Pearl and Second Streets in Lyons which is today the corner of Twenty-fifth Avenue North and Grant Street.) They cut their logs farther north and floated them down the river to the building site. Buell's son, Strong Buell, reports that some Indians helped them build the house which was a one-roomed affair size 16 x 16 feet with a puncheon floor and a shake roof.

## ELIJAH BUELL
### First Permanent Settler, Clinton County, who arrived in July, 1835

Elijah Buell went back to Illinois, to Cordova, and bought oxen with which to break ground and plow and some cows with their calves. He brought them to Clinton with the animals swimming the river to get across. They were probably the first domestic animals brought to Clinton County. That was in the autumn of 1835. After his cabin was completed Elijah Buell brought his wife and son Robert to Clinton County.

Robert Buell and his mother both became very ill with a fever and young Robert died. Elijah feared for his wife's life and walked to an Indian camp on Elk River where he got two squaws to return with him and care for her. They watched over her, then went out on the prairie and into the woods and dug roots, put them into water, cooked them and made a potion for the feverish woman to drink. In six days she was cured by nature's medicine and for the rest of her life gave credit to the Indian squaws who prepared the "yarbs" and roots that saved her.

Elijah Buell, early pioneer settler, became a friend of the Indians and even learned some of their landguage. A lot of wheat was grown in those days and Buell took wheat and pork into Chicago to sell.

About two miles below Buell's claim was a place called New York at which there was a trading post and store run by a Mr. Bartlett. The Indians could also get fire water there. Once Buell was threatened by a drunken Indian who had so much trouble loading his gun that the pioneer hit him over the head with an iron skillet. Fifteen of the Indian's companions who witnessed the scene wandered away meekly after their fellow "brave" was downed.

Elijah Buell prospered as the county's first permanent pioneer white settler. In 1837 he became one of the county's first commissioners and when he died it is said he was one of the wealthiest men in Iowa.

People came to settle in the area of Vandenberg in 1836; that was the original name of the city we now call De Witt which is surrounded by rich farm land. De Witt, too, is named for New York Governor De Witt Clinton. It is said that pioneer settlers were attracted to the area by the beautiful north-south stream running through it and they named it Silver Creek.

Another early settlement now forgotten and hardly a name in history was Independence Grove which was but a short distance from Vandenberg (De Witt) to the west.

Independence Grove got its name from John and George Elrod who settled there on the 4th of July in 1837. It was later named Eureka Mills because of the grist mill and the saw mills that were erected there. Once a settlement was made at Independence Grove some families arrived there and some cabins were built along Silver Creek.

One account refers to the Elrods and another refers to the Eldreds. We do not know which is correct. It is said that there was a cabin in the area before the Elrods (or Eldreds) arrived at Round Grove northeast of Vandenberg.

In 1836 A. G. Harrison came to Round Grove with Col. Doring Wheeler who had earned his rank in the Black Hawk War. He did not settle on his farm until 1841; Wheeler was later a clerk of court and a state senator.

In 1836 also to the De Witt area came a Dr. Ames and brother George W. Ames, Thomas Hatfield, D. F. Bly, Hiram Loomis and John Black. There came to be "Ames Timber" not far from Silver Creek and Crystal Lake.

It is significant that the first to come to Clinton County settled around the area of Lyons and De Witt (farther west where rich prairie was located) and Camanche. The area of the City of Clinton was a little later.

Recall that below the spot where Elijah Buell settled was a place called New York. It was New York that later became the City of Clinton. Joseph M. Bartlett kept a trading store there as we have related. Bartlett intended to promote his town of New York and had claims on land around there. It is said that he traded anything and would sell a lot in his new town for a harness, a horse or a wagon or whatever. In fact people didn't have much real money in those days.

In 1836 Joseph Bartlett sold his land to Captain C. G. Pearce, Col. B. Randall and a Col. Jennings. Col. Randall also had a store there in "New York" which would have been where the boat landing is today at the corner of Sixth Avenue South. Randall sold mostly pills, tobacco and whiskey. By 1837 there were but three houses in all of Clinton. One was Randall's, another the Perin home and another the Pearce home.

NEW YORK, IOWA
Which became the City of Clinton

The story is related by Strong Buell that (Mrs.) Nancy Perin Vosberg was 94 years old on 26 October 1929 and died the next June 1930 which would have meant she was born in 1836---but, evidently not at Clinton. For she tells of her younger sister (Mrs.) Mary Miller who was 91 in 1929. Here is her story:

"I was one and one-half years old when our family came to Iowa to live. Of course, I cannot remember landing at Rocky Point, but I do remember the hut in which we lived. It was a one room log hut with a dirt floor, packed hard, no windows, no chimney, no doors. My grandfather came with us and he at once began to cut the timber for a hewed log house and within six weeks the men had built that house for us to live in. It was in the hewed log house that my sister Mary, Mrs. Miller of Clinton, was born in 1838, the first white child born in Clinton county."

One of the oldest families in Clinton County is the Shaff family whose ancestor was Heman B. Shaff who arrived in September of 1837.

Heman Shaff lost his father when but a boy of five and he came west from New York with his mother, a brother and a sister. They first came to Illinois and stayed at Scott's Landing with the Adam family after whom Adam's Island was named; it was at the mouth of the Wapsipinicon.

Heman was young but the head of the family with intentions of establishing himself in the area. He learned soon that land in Illinois was $ 6.00 an acre and that immediately across the big river it was but $ 1.25 for land that could be obtained from the U. S. government. With that pioneering spirit about which we've read they decided to locate in Iowa.

Young Heman had heard good reports about the area and especially from one who had explored the area saying, "I know a good part of the country west of Camanche. The location is handy to wood and to water with a creek right through the land and a good spring near a level place for a house."

Upon hearing that Heman Shaff put his bid for land in Section 2, Township 81, Range 5 and returned to Illinois. He and his mother and the brother and sister spent the winter of 1837-38 with the Adam family.

In the spring of 1838 young Heman broke 90 acres of the claim of the original 240; later more ground was added and to this day a Shaff has worked some of that same land over a century and a half later.

The first log cabin was built in 1838 on "the left side of the road toward Follett's, going west from Shaffton. As of the early 1930s, nearly a century later, it is reported that there still stood three large cotton-wood trees which had withstood the storms of nature for over a century. Nearby the town of Shaffton was started which was named for the enterprising family. At one time four railroads were in the Shaffton area.

As to the purchase of the land Heman Shaff wanted to buy it in 1837 but it was not for sale until 1838 as the general government was marketing the land.

In the spring of 1838 three others whose names are prominent in the establishment and growth of Clinton County, and who were friends of Heman Shaff, accompanied him to Dubuque where he would make his purchase of the land he wanted; they were Follett, Wood and Ketchum.

They took with them gold for which they could buy all the land the four wanted. Gold was real money. But carrying gold was always dangerous as travellers were at risk of being robbed. There being strength in numbers the four decided to "guard" each other. They arrived in Dubuque and waited in line at the government land office for many hours. They were offered a place to stay by a friendly local citizen but even then, when the four were sleeping in a room together, one would stay awake.

With his purchase finally complete and his chosen land clearly in his possession Heman Shaff returned to Clinton County and it was then that he started breaking that first 90 acres. His friends returned with him and went about their pursuits.

On his land was a "heap of quarried rock" and Heman Shaff then built his home, a stone house which stood for a century---and may stand yet!---and which was eventually improved with boards and plaster thus losing its "primitive identity."

By the early 1930s it was the home of Heman Shaff, Jr., who would have been an older man by then.

Senator J. O. Shaff who served with distinction in the state legislature also resided in a home that was started of logs and stone by an early Shaff family entrepreneur. It was Sen. Shaff who led the fight in Des Moines for better roads, to "get the farmers out of the mud."

Other distinguished descendants of the pioneer Heman Shaff have served both Clinton County and the State of Iowa with distinction. In more recent times they were State Senators David O. and Roger Shaff.

Hickory Ridge is an old Indian gathering ground near Shaffton where the red man and his bands could fish and harvest the wild rice.

Goose Lake is a little town in Deep Creek Township which is fed by a creek of that name. It is not that the creek itself is so deep but that it is so far below its banks. It is supposed that the first settler in Deep Creek Township was a man named Boone who was a nephew of Daniel Boone. His claim is today known as Boone's Springs.

After the Indians gave up the area in 1837 they continued to come year after year to hunt, fish, camp or to visit. While those Indians were becoming fewer and fewer the population of whites were increasing and Clinton county was a growing area.

Wheat was a popular and profitable crop in the early years when the land of Iowa was being broken for the cultivation of the soil. In fact, considering the change in and inflation of our money supply wheat brought a better price in 1838 than it would in 1988. Of course, harvesting it was not the easier and mechanical task it is today.

# Over the years...... *in Clinton County*

The above picture shows James I. Meighan (left) and Art Blanche of De Witt (right). It was taken in the very early 1900s at De Witt. Jim Meighan estimates that he may have been 16 or 17 when the picture was taken. The city of De Witt still has a lot of relatives of Art Blanche living in the area. Mr. Blanche has passed on. Jim Meighan, pictured above, was born in Clinton County on 19 January 1886 when Grover Cleveland was president the first time. Clinton County was not yet fifty years old when Jim Meighan was born there on a farm between Charlotte and Petersville. He later lived in Bremer and Allamakee Counties. Today he is retired and living in Fayette County. He will be 103 years old in January 1989. He has attained to more than two-thirds the age of the State of Iowa itself.

# Chapter Seventeen
# JACKSON COUNTY

Jackson County was created by an act of the Wisconsin Territorial Legislature in 1837 and was named for Andrew Jackson the seventh president of the United States.

The Maquoketa River is the largest stream in the county and is usually shallow and peacefully meandering except during the spring and fall rainy seasons. It joins the Mississippi near Green Island. The Tete des Morts Creek is located in the northern part of the county nearer Dubuque County and flows into the Mississippi. The Elk Creek is a tributary of the great river but it joins it only after entering into nearby Clinton County.

Iron ore has reportedly been found on or near the shores of the Maquoketa River and along some of the smaller creeks but never in commercial quantities. In the very early years Dubuque found lead and mined it in the northern part of Jackson County but the supply of ore was limited. Float deposits of lead were found in early times but never in quantity.

Even gold and oil have been discovered in trace quantities but never enough for commercial use.

Timber was, from the beginning, a valuable resource in the county and there have been large groves of "white, red, black, and burr

oak and of hard maple." Scattered throughout are elm, basswood, black walnut, ironwood, butternut, cottonwood, gray ash, shellbark and birch. From the native woods Jackson County manufacturers at one time produced lumber, kegs, barrels, tubs, fence posts, siding for houses and other building materials at mills in Bellevue, Emeline, Iron Hill, and Monmouth. It has also been said that "the stand of timber between the forks of the Maquoketa is probably one of the finest in eastern Iowa."

The earliest settlers came to Jackson County in the 1830s and there was another influx in the 1840s. It was they who discovered the valuable natural resources of the new county and who began the development of it and its natural gifts. The earliest settlers were of French origin, then there was an influx of pioneers of German descent.

As with other eastern Iowa counties the Sac and Fox Indians roamed the area that is now Jackson County and erected their temporary homes there. Among their better known chiefs were Tama, Pienoskie, Poweshiek and Kishkekosh. Historians estimate that one or more of the above mentioned Indian chiefs were leaders at the site of Bellevue

and one account states that it was once the headquarters of Black Hawk himself. It is said that when the first white men arrived in the county the headquarters and council room at Bellevue were in perfect condition. Historians also know that there was another village that occupied the site of Sabula and that there were Sac and Fox tribes and Winnebagoes often camping along the Maquoketa and the other streams in the county.

The Black Hawk Treaty finally saw the Indian title to the eastern Iowa lands extinguished and the area of Jackson County available for settlement. As we note in the histories of other counties, the U. S. army often forcefully removed early settlers but such an incident hasn't been recorded in Jackson County's annals.

In 1833 most of the Sac and Fox tribes left the area of Jackson County but bands of Winnebagoes remained as they did in other counties. They merely wanted to live on their former lands and hunt, trap, fish and provide for themselves. They were reportedly both harmless and friendly but nevertheless feared by the women and children. They begged food from the pioneers and coveted the brightly colored cloth and clothing of the women and children. The pioneer settlers became protective of their clothing, cornmeal and flour while allowing the roving Indians to sharpen their knives and give them some food.

Levi Wagoner was an early resident who later wrote in the JACKSON SENTINEL that a remnant of the Black Hawk band occasionally came through the county to see their relatives or on their way to Wisconsin. They were nomadic and food always seemed to be their major problem. Wagoner says that "the braves did the hunting and stealing and the squaws did the begging, riding ponies and ranging the county for miles around. At night the braves would forage (steal) corn for their ponies."

Although no records, army or otherwise extant, it was formerly believed that a fort was once erected by the government at the site of today's Bellevue, named Fort Belle Vue and that a tribe of Winnebagoes destroyed it in 1812. The basis for this is laid in an early history of Jackson

County (1879) but historians have come to conclude that the "fort" was Fort Madison, built in 1808, and once named Belle Vue.

The day of 31 May 1833 was a hectic one on the eastern shore of the Mississippi for waiting to settle in the Ioway country. For it was there that hundreds, perhaps thousands, awaited the June 1st "land-rush" with the "Father of Waters" as the immediate barrier to settlers who waited to cross.

All awaited opportunity across the river. Sunset was the signal to get ready and at midnight the pioneers started fording the river to find sites for future farms and homes and opportunity in a new land.

Up and down the Mississippi were those who had been turned back, even as we have noted, forcefully evicted. History tells us that but two pioneers crossed the Mississippi that night of May 31 to June 1st 1833 into Jackson County.

James Armstrong and Alexander Reed obtained the first claims to land in Jackson County and apparently both entered the county on the same day, 1 June 1833. They probably crossed the river at Sabula.

James Armstrong staked out a claim on Mill Creek just south of the original Bellevue town plat.

Alexander Reed chose a site in Pleasant Creek valley which was a few miles to the south. He is said to have tilled the first Jackson County soil and reportedly killed 75 deer his first winter, 1833-34.

In the fall of 1833 other early pioneer settlers arrived and, among others, were David Segar, Thomas Nicholson and William Dyas who staked claims and became neighbors of James Armstrong. John and James White settled in Pleasant Creek valley near Alexander Reed's new farm probably in the spring of

Courtesy, National Gallery of Art, Washington, D.C.

ANDREW JACKSON
The seventh president of the United States after whom Jackson County is named is shown above in an oil portrait by Thomas Sully that is now in the National Gallery of Art.

1834. More settlers soon followed.

There is the tale oft told about some Indians who showed up at Dubuque in February of 1834 with some rich samples of lead ore. That in an area where lead was and had been an economic boon. Bribed with

Compliments of

MSB
MAQUOKETA
STATE BANK

Two Locations to serve You

203 No. Main
Maquoketa

MSB  112 Kinsey Dr.
Maquoketa

Phone 652-2491

269

gifts of blankets, tobacco, powder, cloth and trinkets by five local men the Indians were persuaded to lead them to where they had found the ore. The men were Ben Beardsley, Thomas Brazier, Jesse Harrison, William A. Warren and Leroy Jackson about whom we read later. (See Chapter XX, Delaware County.)

Over hill and dale and through the winter the Indians led them into the area of Jackson County. Their path even went through Sioux country, an enemy people. Some lead was found but there wasn't enough in the area to make mining worthwhile. They were finally escorted part of their way home by Sioux Indians. They ended up at Bellevue for a stay with pioneer settler William Jonas and then back to Dubuque.

It was in 1835 that John D. Bell crossed the great river and found a site in the beautiful bluffs along the river. He decided it would be an excellent spot for a community. Between the site he liked and the Illinois shore there was an island which was later named Seward Island.

That year, 1835, John Bell had a town platted naming it Bellview after himself. From the 250 foot elevation

General Grant slept here . . .

YOU CAN, TOO!

BED & BREAKFAST

at Kuhlman's Historic

DECKER HOUSE INN
128 No. Main St.   Maquoketa, IA
(319) 652 - 6654

above the river its valley can be seen for many miles. Later it took on the Gallic and was for a while called Belle Vue; a Gallo-Anglicizing finally gave us Bellevue. Settlers began arriving that very year of 1835 settling in Bell's town or staking claims to farms nearby.

Peter Dutell came in 1836 and built the first hotel in Jackson County. It was a two-story frame building and, unfortunately, eventually became the headquarters for a gang of thieves and counterfeiters.

By 1836 it was large enough for a post office and John Bell was the first postmaster. Meanwhile, six miles upstream Vincent Smith operated a ferry service with the Illinois landing near the Fever River.

J. K. Moss came to Bellview in 1836 and started the first store while a man named Kinkaid built a grist mill. Bell himself started the first saw mill and in 1836 Nic Jefferson opened a second store there.

It is said that the Sabula area, with its broad plains, was the only logical site for a town between Bellevue and Clinton. (We reckon that Marquette and Joliet probably shored at both sites.)

On his way up the Mississippi way back in 1805 Lt. Zebulon Pike and his expedition sailed past "the beautiful eminence on the west" the day of August 31st. That eminence was Leopold Hill near Bellevue in Jackson County.

Isaac Dorman and a man named Hinkley crossed the Mississippi River on a log in 1835 or 1836 and became Sabula's first pioneer settlers. In April of 1836 Dr. E. A. Wood, Charles H. Swan and W. H. Brown bought the interests of Dorman and Hinkley. The next year the three engaged Albert Henry to plat out a town and it was named Carrollport after a settler who arrived there in 1837.

After an incorrect address of "Carrion Point" seemed to bring derision to the place, the name was changed to Charleston but a town in Lee County already had that name. From the Latin, sabulum, for sand finally came the name of Sabula.

We must note in passing that Bellevue was once considered as the capital for the Wisconsin Territory. It was somewhat central and local folk pushed the idea. It is said that a capitalist in Galena, Ills., once offered to build the capitol building for the territory if he were allowed to buy half the town's lots. The honor that Burlington received in being named the temporary territorial capital might well have been Bellevue's.

Bellevue was on the Mississippi and by 1837 the population of the county was moving westward. In that year of 1837 settlements were made that were the beginning of three new towns with John Hendley settling at Andrew, Samuel Cotton at Cottonsville and the Farley Brothers, Andrew and Chris, establishing themselves at Preston.

The town of Andrew was destined to be the county seat and it would be the community which would provide the first governor for the coming State of Iowa. Preston would grow later when the railroad came. Bellevue was the original county seat when the county was first created.

Shadrach Burleson who was nicknamed "Shade" settled about six miles west of Maquoketa in the spring of 1837. Joseph Henry came to Jackson County that year, also, and built a grist mill in the Maquoketa area.

Governor Henry Dodge was to appoint the first sheriff for Jackson County and he received a petition signed by a host of leading citizens requesting the appointment of one W. Brown of Bellevue. The governor consulted about the appointment with William A. Warren who was the enrolling clerk for the territorial House of Representatives. Warren couldn't understand it as he had knowledge of Brown's involvement in cattle stealing and counterfeiting. The petition had Warren's own name on it and it was then that the governor and the clerk saw that the petition, too, was counterfeit— i.e. of forged signatures. It was Brown and his cohorts about whom we referred earlier! The governor finally appointed Captain Warren as the county's first sheriff.

Six voting precincts were established in Jackson County by 1838 and two outside; that is, one in Jones and one in Linn, two sparsely settled counties that were at the time attached to Jackson County for governmental reasons, mostly judicial and taxation.

## BANOWETZ ANTIQUES

### "Best In The Midwest"

Featuring American Victorian walnut, golden oak, country pine furniture. Also clocks, lamps, china, glassware, toys, banks, wicker, and much more.

THE MIDWEST'S LARGEST INVENTORY 35,000 sq. ft. of stock at Maquoketa.

### Two Locations:

Hwy. 61 North
Maquoketa, IA
319-652-2359
Mon.-Sat. 9 to 5
Closed Sunday

117 So. Main
Galena, IL
815-777-3370
Open Daily
9 a.m.-5 p.m.

271

In the spring of 1838 the county was surveyed by Colonel Thomas Cox and a Mr. McDaniel. Col. Cox had a brilliant background, civilian and military. (He finally was a leader of the posse that drove the Brown gang from the county about which we will read in Volume II.) It was Col. Cox's idea that an entirely new town be created and platted for the capital to be named Iowa City. He died suddenly in 1844 and the Jackson County Historical Society saw that his remains were interred in Maquoketa's Mount Hope Cemetery.

The first settlers on the site of what was to become the City of Maquoketa were John E. Goodenow and Lyman Bates who arrived in the spring of 1838 having crossed the ice bound Mississippi River on 9 March 1838. Following Goodenow and Bates were more early pioneer settlers to include Absalom Montgomery, Zalmon Livermore and Colonel Tom Cox. Six miles westward "Shade" Burleson's new neighbors were William Vosburg, Calvin Teeple and L. A. F. Corbin.

John Goodenow built the first cabin shortly after his arrival and set up a trading post where he had a stock of smithing tools, clothing, harnesses and other sundries he had brought from New York. He also had a small corn-cracker operated by horsepower with which he ground grain for others.

Maquoketa grew and prospered and is today the largest community in Jackson County. In June of 1988 the City of Maquoketa observed its Sesquicentennial, its 150th birthday, amid great fanfare, celebration and the "homecoming" of many former residents and their kin.

North of Maquoketa is the town of Hurstville which eventually came to have quite a history.

The first town to be surveyed and platted in the Maquoketa area was Bridgeport which was about two miles northeast of the future city. It was said to have been the "dream town" of Colonel Cox. A few houses were built there but it never "took."

Bellevue was the first county seat of Jackson County. Andrew later enjoyed that distinction and today Maquoketa is the county seat.

John W. Fagerland, president of the Maquoketa State Bank and a Sponsor of this history, urged the inclusion of information of Maquoketa's sesquicentennial.

# This book honors Grandmother of Maquoketa doctor

"Heritage and Settlement," Volume One of a several volume series entitled "A HISTORY OF IOWA" is dedicated to the grandmother of Maquoketa doctor, Jerry Bybee.

The volume is dedicated to (Mrs.) Marie Finch who will reach age 95 in March of 1989 and who is the great-grandmother of Dr. Bybee's children. (See picture and story at front of book following Table of Contents.) Mrs. Finch is the widow of the late W. W. Finch, a descendant of early Iowa pioneer settlers.

## *Osterhaus Snyder Pharmacy*

A FAMILY PHARMACY
in Maquoketa
SINCE 1965

652-5611
Proud of Maquoketa's History

# Maquoketa settled in 1838 . . .
## *Sesquicentennial observed in 1988*

About as many activities as one can imagine were part of the Sesquicentennial Observance in Maquoketa, Jackson Coutny, from June 8th to the 12th, 1988.

There were Indian talks and slides, music, flea markets, tours of historic homes, antique displays, potluck meals, historical parades, bike rides, horse drawn wagons, quilts on display, baking contests, a prairie walk, a Victorian tea, school tours, spelling bees, gospel and folk singing, a beard judging contest, square dancing, pleasure walks and runs, a tour of local industries, teen agers activities, classic car shows, a draft horse demonstration, an alumni social hour, concerts, a canoe float, an art in the park show, company reunions, a tug of war, a buckskinners rendezvous, a meeting of retired teachers, horse rides, ice cream socials, auctions, log sawing demonstrations, drawings and many more colorful activities.

There was the Great Maquoketa Sesquicentennial Parade which began at 2:00 p.m. on Saturday the 11th. It started downtown and went to the County Fairgrounds where the Jackson County Historical Museum was open. Presiding over the Great Parade was Carrie Gauld, age 106, who was the Grand Marshal.

"A good time was had by all" might be the trite old report. But, it would have reflected the many and varied activities. Over 800 attended an alumni banquet. Descendants of pioneers present were J. E. Goodenow and H. D. Keeley, age 91, both retired attorneys. The Sesquicentennial

Commitee was Syd Tubbs, Leighton Hepker, Dennis Voy, Bel Tubbs, Marcella Heneke, Michele Flagel, Leona Brock, Beverly Willey, Dottie Bayles, Gary Redling and Lucille Sorensen.

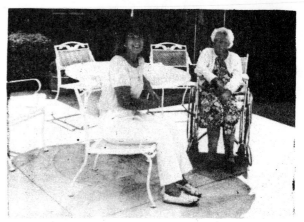

CARRIE GAULD, Grand Marshal of the Maquoketa Sesquicentennial Parade is shown above at Crestridge where she resides. At age 106, Carrie Gauld has lived more than two-thirds the life of the city itself. She is pictured with Holly Myatt who is the administrator of Crestridge. (Picture courtesy of The Sentinel-Press.)

# Banowetz . . . selling history
## . . . *is their part in history*

Their history is selling history! That may be an apt way of describing the meteoric rise from a small antique business to one of the largest and most active businesses that literally deals in history in the midwestern states.

A mere stroll through their estimated 35,000 square feet of area housing their historic antiques is more like roving through a museum than what one considers an antique shop. For the Banowetz operation is far more than an antique shop. It is history and that history is for sale to anyone, professional or novice, who wants to be surrounded by some of the past.

Located in historic Maquoketa, one can secure rare items that may well go back to the earliest days of Iowa, or Jackson County, or Maquoketa or............or, almost anywhere in the midwest.

It was an early dream of young Virl and Kathy Banowetz to some day own their own antique business and deal in history itself in the form of anything that portrayed out past.

Virl Banowetz became acquainted with antiques of history as he grew to manhood on a farm where his parents enjoyed preserving history with antiques and dealing in them on a "strictly wholesale" basis. Kathy and Virl Banowetz were married in 1967 and looked for a farm to buy but having in mind the antique business. Then they found the house and acreage of their first and present location at the intersection of Highway 61 and the Maquoketa Caves Road. There they had their beginning and there they have grown over nearly a quarter of a century.

Banowetz Antiques grew and the main business expanded. They are also now located in Galena, Ills., and have the largest antique business in that historic city.

In their dealing in history itself the Banowetz stock includes American furniture ranging from Empire to Victorian to Golden Oak to Mission and hundreds of clocks, lamps, a huge stock of china, stoneware, glassware, pottery, advertising items plus tools, dolls, toys, banks and country accessories. In fact, it is the largest inventory in the midwest.

Their customers come from every state in the nation and several foreign countries. Kathy and Virl Banowetz insist that the supply of high quality antiques is dwindling.

Owning and cherishing antiques from our past is also a way of preserving our history and our colorful heritage.

# Chapter Eighteen
# CLAYTON COUNTY

Clayton County's claim to historical fame will always be that upon its soil which, in 1673, the first white men set foot. That remains the first recorded such event west of the Mississippi River, the Kensington Rune Stone notwithstanding. Little is recorded of other white men stopping by while exploring up or down the great river in following years. It was many years before any settlers took an abiding interest in Clayton County or even in the area that was to become the State of Iowa.

**It is known for certain that Julien Dubuque was the first permanent white settler in what was to become Dubuque County, or Iowa for that matter.**

It is still a matter of some speculation as to who was the first permanent white settler in Clayton County, the historical assumption being only slightly marred by the early claims of Basil Giard. For it was he who once might have claimed that distinction. But in retrospect and in the opinion of credible historians Giard may not have been all he wanted to be.

Indeed, there remains to this day the small community of Giard and it

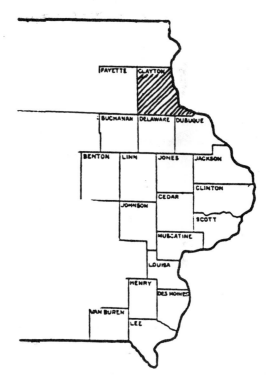

is duly marked and visible to highway travellers. There is also much in fact and legend that writers have perpetuated about Giard and the "Giard tract."

One way or another the name of Giard is indelibly written upon the map of Clayton County forever it would seem.

A dispute among area historians once centered around who was the first permanent white settler in

Iowa. Not merely white settler, but permanent white settler. History is clear that there were white settlers before either Julien Dubuque or Basil Giard but none were regarded as permanent. Those who early supported Girad's claims did so upon his own insistence.

On 15 October 1800, Basil Giard sent a petition to "the Governor of Upper Louisiana" who was at the time Carlos Dehault Delassus. Giard was asking the governor for a validation of his claim of ownership over a large tract of land westerly of what is now the City of McGregor, Clayton County, Iowa. Although the petition was sent from Prairie du Chien, in what became Wisconsin and in land belonging to the United States of America, Basil Giard nevertheless referred to himself as a "subject of the King of Spain." He claimed in his petition to the Spanish governor that he had occupied the tract of land "since fifteen years."

If so, Giard would have occupied the area from 1785 which would have been three years before Dubuque settled permanently at "the Mines."

But Giard's claim was not adequately supported by witnesses or contemportary evidence that he had, indeed, "occupied" the tract "since fifteen years" as he himself asserted. There were witnesses but they were weak in agreeing with Giard. The year 1796 is the year that government records indicate Giard's ".....Possession, Inhabitation and Cultivation" of the land. The year 1796 is also the earliest year that any of the witnesses supported the Giard claim to possession of the tract. Testimony rendered in 1808 found no witnesses who claimed for Giard any actual residence in Iowa. One insisted that Giard had "a farmer"

# The Newest and Latest

# 1984 History of Clayton County, Iowa

The new 1984 HISTORY OF CLAYTON COUNTY, IOWA, is the most comprehensive history of Clayton County families, past and present, ever published. Containing over 2,000 biographies and 918 pictures! The 864 page book is of top quality --- smyth sewn hard cased cover, 8 1/2 by 11 inches on acid free paper and easy to read 10 point type. Cost is now $ 60.00 for the book, with subsequent books at $ 50.00 each. For genealogical societies, groups and libraries the price is $ 50.00. Include postage of $ 4.00 additional.

ORDER FROM AND MAKE CHECKS PAYABLE TO:

Clayton County Genealogical Society
P. O. Box 846
Elkader, Iowa 52043

who cultivated the tract while another testified that it was a "hired man" who did the work. A third witness said that it was "some of the claimant's people" who worked the ground in question. One said that Giard had "lived as a trader at Prairie du Chien for twenty-six years."

None of the testimonial evidence substantiates that the claimant Giard had been a resident of Iowa for 15 years prior to the year 1800.

It was finally concluded that Giard was always a resident of Prairie du Chien and that no one during his lifetime ever considered him a resident of Iowa. Absentee landlord, possibly.

It was finally resolved, too, that a lot of land in Prairie du Chien, described as "Main Vil (lage), Lot 21, 174 ft. wide extending from the Mississippi river east to St. Friole Marias" was sold by Basile (sic) Giard on 13 April 1816. As testimony to the same, witnesses Michael Brisbois and Pierre La Pointe swore that Giard had occupied that property "thirty-two years ago; that he lived and died on said land....."

Basil Giard died in July of 1817. He "had lived" at Prairie du Chien. He died at Prairie du Chien. He is buried at Prairie du Chien. None of these facts serve to make Basil Giard an early settler of Iowa.

In 1800 Giard insisted he was a subject of the Spanish king and during the War of 1812, we find that he was befriending the British by selling them gun powder and rum.

Eventually Giard's claim was not to be proven valid. For on 5 June 1810 the Federal Board of Commissioners convened in St. Louis, Missouri, and tersely concluded that "Bazil (sic) Giard, claiming one league square of land, see book No. 3, page 200.....It is the opinion of the Board that this claim ought not to be confirmed."

For all that, there exists to this day the small community of Giard as well as Giard Township, Clayton County, Iowa, as evidence at least of Giard's interest of one kind or another in the area that now bears his name.

(Several accounts spell Giard's name differently, both first and last. Some accounts carry an extra "r" and make him Girard; for our purposes we have chosen Basil Giard. ---DLK.)

The first permanent claims of land and settlement thereon were made in 1833 on the Turkey River by William W. Wayman, Robert Hetfield and William D. Grant.

They established themselves and built log cabin homes about four miles upstream from where the Turkey River runs into the Mississippi, i.e., the mouth of the Turkey, and

# ELVERS

*Insurance & Real Estate*

Elkader

Phone 245-1121

INSURANCE COVERAGE OF ALL TYPES

Farm, Residential and Commercial
REAL ESTATE

on the north side nearly opposite what came to be Millville. Prior to establishing themselves there, a cabin had been erected at the mouth of the Turkey, it had not been a home but was rather used as a ferry house.

The areas upon which Wayman, Hetfield and Grant settled later became known as the Lander and Pierson farms. Of course, in 1833, there was yet no county seat or other place at which to register the land upon which they had settled and **made their claims. Few white men had attempted to make homes west** of the Mississippi up to that year. Yes, Dubuque had established a community and in the southern part of the territory, in the vast area that was Des Moines county, many were trying to settle. One historian ventured a guess that there weren't 50 white settlers in Iowa in 1832.

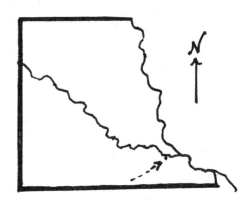

Sketch map of Clayton County, above, shows arrow pointing to Millville. It was directly across from Millville on the north of the Turkey River.

### JESSEN'S SUPER VALU, INC.
"Serving you is our goal"
Strawberry Point, Iowa
*"Home of Backbone State Park"*

Of those three first pioneer settlers in Clayton County, William W. Wayman is regarded as the first to come into the area that would become the new county with the full intention of becoming a permanent settler. Therefore, William W. Wayman may be regarded as the first permanent white settler in Clayton County, Iowa. And therein lies another story of historical significance.

The pioneer settler Wayman brought with him a housekeeper named Rebecca Clues who for a time was regarded as the first white women settler to come to the county. But it was later learned that "Aunt Becky" as she came to be known, was in reality a mullato and former slave.

In 1860 Judge Eliphalet Price, who wrote extensively on early Clayton County history, wrote of Rebecca Clues: "This woman who died recently, and who was for many years a county charge, always passed for a

𝕷𝖎𝖙𝖙𝖑𝖊 𝕾𝖜𝖎𝖙𝖟𝖊𝖗𝖑𝖆𝖓𝖉 𝕴𝖓𝖓

Bed and Breakfast

"It's a Taste of the Past"

Inquire Box 195, McGregor, IA 52157
or call
(319) 873-3670

white person. Formerly she was a dark mulatto and the slave of Governor Clark of Missouri who emancipated her after her change of color. This change of color from a mulatto to a white took place immediately after her recovery from a severe attack of bilious fever. She was the head or principal cook in the family of Governor Clark who lived in great style at St. Louis, and was the owner of many slaves. As a cook she had few superiors. When she first came to the mines (most likely at Dubuque, ---DLK.) she could speak the French and Spanish languages as well as the English, but in later years she lost all knowledge of the French and the Spanish, and began to speak the English with the negro dialect. Aunt Becky, as she was called, had experienced many of the vicissitudes of frontier life. She had been a slave and a free women; a mulatto and a **white woman; she could speak at one time three languages; she was the first white woman that came into** Clayton County, and, after a residence here of twenty-four years, she was the first woman in the county who died a pauper, after having attained the age of about eighty years."

As the year 1836 began a Dr. Frederick Andros arrived in the area farther north of where Wayman, Hetfield and Grant had settled and made a land claim for himself. It was on the edge of what was called High Prairie about one mile southeast of where Garnavillo stands today. On that land, Dr. Andros erected a log cabin and employed a man to take charge of his claimed property by

REBECCA CLUES

occupying it and also making rails out of the extensive supply of trees.

Dr. Andros made his claim in January of 1836 and shortly thereafter another pioneer settler arrived whose name was Loomis. He entered a claim adjoining the doctor's. Then a claim was made by John W. Gillet which encompassed a good share of the site upon which Garnavillo would eventually grow. He, too, built a cabin and moved into it upon its completion.

Settlers continued to come into the area of the county and later in the spring of 1836, William Correll established himself at what became Farmersburg and built a cabin. It is said that he spent that summer splitting rails and learning the French language. Shortly after Correll settled, one Allen Carpenter made a claim about three miles northwesterly.

The first prairie broken in Clayton County was done by Mr. Gillet who brought a breaking team and began plowing in June or July of 1836.

On 15 July 1836, Elisha Boardman,

Proud of Our County's History

**KLINE'S SUPER- VALU**
**Elkader, Clayton County, Iowa**

**GARNAVILLO MILL, INC.**
V.H., R.J. & PHIL BRANDT
FEEDS ● SEEDS
CUSTOM GRINDING, MIXING, PELLETING
GRAIN BANKING
Phone 964-2243
964-2063
GARNAVILLO, IOWA 52049

Horace D. Bronson and another man named Hastings set out from Green Bay, Wisconsin, and followed the usual route to get westward. That was to follow the Fox River and portage to the Wisconsin River. At the portage they found a Mackinaw boat belonging to the American Fur Company. It had been unloaded of its cargo of valuable furs and was about to return down the Wisconsin River to the Mississippi. The two Boardmans took passage on the boat and arrived at Prairie du Chien where they hired a half-breed to take the pair in his canoe to Cassville. It was there that they joined Bronson and Hastings who had arrived at the pre-arranged meeting place on horseback. They had followed the river after parting at the Fox River portage. The four of them crossed the Mississippi and soon arrived at the Hetfield cabin a few miles up the Turkey River. And they were in Iowa.

One might wonder what was drawing those pioneers from so far away to the western shores of the Mississippi and even farther inland. It may have had an element of adventure but the obvious reasons were opportunity and the freedom to do so.

About Clayton County we are told that the "surface of the upland is at an elevation of about 600 feet above the Mississippi. There is about one-third prairie (this description was written in 1882. ---DLK.) one-third openings or barrens, and one-third well timbered; mostly high rolling, well-watered with fine springs and streams of various widths, up to four chains. From the precipitous bluffs of the streams, the surface grows less rough to the highlands, which are gently undulating. The soil of the prairies is deep, rich, black loam, based upon a thick subsoil of yellow clay. The soil of the timberland is excellent for wheat. The streams afford an abundance of fish and power to propel a vast amount of machinery."

Thus the adventuresome four seeking opportunity in the new land arrived at the Hetfield cabin and were made welcome in the hospitable tradition of the early pioneer settlers. They left their own horses and obtained two other ones from Captain Grant and Eliphalet Price.

From there they set out on an expedition to explore the Turkey river. Captain Grant accompanied them and for protection they are said to have had but one small shotgun. For provisions they are reported to have carried 12 pounds of pork and a like weight in flour.

They journeyed up the river and camped at the fork in the river about eight miles below what would become the site of Fort Atkinson. During their first night there the Indians stole both their horses.

They searched through the wilderness for their steeds and their efforts yielded nothing. And so they decided to abandon their exploration and return downstream to Hetfield's. Their supply of food was running low and they had no success in killing wild game for nourishment although the woods in that area

*We're proud . . . .*

OF THE HISTORY OF

# Clayton County

And proud to be a Sponsor of this
NEW HISTORY OF IOWA

# HALVORSON

INSURANCE & REAL ESTATE
Connie and Roger
MONONA

along the Turkey River abounded in excellent food animals. What remained of their original supplies amounted to about a pound and a half of food for each man.

Then they mixed up the flour, baked it in hot ashes and divided it five ways. Captain Grant and Bronson decided to return on foot while the others took the time and effort to put together a small raft made of logs. With it they could then float down the river. Those who walked took the remaining pork.

(This same account is referred to generally in Chapter XXIII, Fayette County.)

Two other communities in Clayton County were to achieve growth and prominence as the county began to be settled and attained some growth.

Elisha Boardman is generally credited with being the founder or first permanent white settler in the Elkader area. With others he found the site upon which the city of Elkader was laid out. This was not to happen in the years covered in this history but that city would eventually become the center of commerce and trade for the middle portion of Clayton County. It would eventually, too, become the capital of the county or the county seat.

When this history coverage takes place Prairie La Porte was the seat of county government and Elkader was non-existent. Many prominent people would settle in Elkader. Governor Dodge would appoint John W. Griffith the first sheriff of Clayton County and his descendants still live there but in Elkader.

The future would hold in store a beautiful settlement on the prairie and be named for a hill covered with wild strawberries. That would, of course, be Strawberry Point which would become a colorful city with a colorful name. Accounts of the histories of those two communities will be related in Volume Two.

McGregor Building and Loan was founded in 1914 by a group of local businessmen to provide funds for home ownership. Receiving little or no salary they provided a public service incorporating the business on 30 April 1915. Between that date and 1935 the name was changed to Home Savings and Loan. As a mutual association all divisible surplus has remained in the business. In August of 1935 it became Interstate Federal Savings and Loan and today each account is insured by the FISLIC up to $100,000. Interstate Federal is the only locally owned and controlled association in Clayton County.

*Interstate Federal Savings*

.........and Loan Association of McGregor ....................

Since 1914

154 Main Street - Phone 319-873-3467 - McGregor

# Prairie La Porte
## ---City with a long history.......
## Now Guttenberg

In 1973 W. W. Jacobs of Guttenberg wrote "A HISTORY OF GUTTENBERG" that was done essentially in commemoration of the 300th anniversary of the landing of the Marquette and Joliet expedition upon the shores of Iowa. That same history was printed in The Guttenberg PRESS on 27 February 1974. Originally known as Prairie La Porte, the community could date its existence possibly to around 1832 It was a prominent community north of the earlier settled Dubuque. It was the first community of size or importance in Clayton County, Iowa.

W. W. Jacobs did a notable job of researching the history of Prairie La Porte, Guttenberg as we know it. The following is taken from the W. W. Jacobs history as published by The Guttenberg PRESS as noted above. (Copies may be purchased from the Guttenberg Public Library.)

"The banners of five nations have flown over a town site which through the passing of the years was successively a favorite camping ground of the Sac and Fox Indian tribes, a gathering place for the early French explorers and other adventurers from the East, the birthplace of the courts of Iowa, first administrative seat of an area much larger than the state itself, and finally a haven for an oppressed and freedom loving people. This is the background of the town of Guttenberg, Iowa, which since its founding a century ago has been the largest town in Clayton County. Situated in the famous "driftless area"---the land which the glaciers of old forgot or were unable to overwhelm, the area about Guttenberg appears as it did before the coming of the Ice Age, and we see the somber depths of forests and beetling crags in all their glory. It is built on a long, level flood plain, three miles long and thirty and more feet above the Mississippi River. Having the broad river to the east, and the high bluffs to the west, it combines the scenic beauty of both river and highland as does no other city on the far reaches of the "Father of Waters."

"Permanently settled by the Germans, it took the name of the Inventor of Movable Type, Johannes Gutenberg, who was born in Mainz, Germany, on June 24, 1397, and whose talents gave the world its first printed book, the now famous and rare Gutenberg 42-line Bible, printed in Latin.

"Originally the name of the community was spelled as was the inventor's with but one 't' and the original plats of the town carried this spelling, but when a second set of plats was made in 1848 by the G. A. Mengel Lithographing Company of Cincinnati, Ohio, the artist who embellished the plat spelled the name "Guttenberg" rather than in its original and correct form, "Gutenberg," and that spelling has been retained. There is one of these 1848 plats still in existence, the back of which is covered with notes, references, and affidavits, all of which carry the original spelling.

"Considerable research regarding the name of the Inventor has shown that in the few documents extant in Mainz and Strassburg, Germany, no less than six different spellings of the name appear in these records. The inventor, however, preferred the spelling "Gutenberg" and the carelessness on the part of the early city authorities in not adhering to the original spelling is indeed unfortunate, for the idea of naming a community after a man so eminent, and then dishonoring his memory by perpetuating his name with improper spelling, is so inconsistent that it has excited comment in the press all over the nation.

"As far as is known the first written mention of the town site was made in the private papers of an ostracized Italian attorney, found in a library in Venice. It appears that this man was supposedly cast out of Italy, and being of a roving nature, joined an expedition which crossed the Atlantic Ocean to the Gulf of Mexico and came up the Mississippi River. In the papers it is mentioned that "about fourteen leagues above the lead mines (evidently now the City of Dubuque) there existed a large flat area, on which many Indians were encamped." This statement seems entirely reasonable when we consider the number of Indian relics and skeletons which have been unearthed during construction on the town site. Then too, many of the "old timers" were wont to tell of the many Indians who were here after the coming of the whites.

"We know, too, this was the domain of the Fox and Sac tribes, and that they were here until after the Black Hawk War and the treaty which followed. The Black Hawk Purchase and the treaty were completed at Davenport on Sept. 2, 1832, and ratified on Feb. 13, 1833, after which the land was open for settlement.

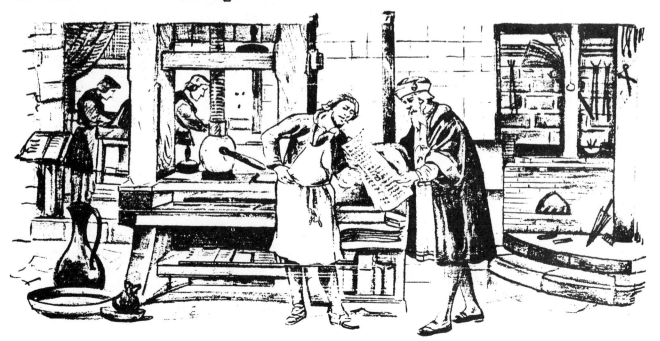

283

"The last Indians here after the coming of the white man finally drifted from the town site proper, and spent their time in the valleys both north and south of town, after which they moved farther westward in the state.

"Mention of the town site was also made in the log of the Steamer "Virginia," which was the first such steamboat to make the trip up river from Saint Louis in 1823. "A deserted Fox village was seen on the banks of the Turkey River. Eight miles further upstream the boat passed the old Village 'de la Porte.'"

"The town site was originally called "Prairie La Porte," meaning "the door of the prairie," so named by the early French missionaries who covered the area and who saw how the open prairies to the north and south were easily accessible through the valleys from the flood plain along the river.

"This area has had an extremely interesting history since that day in June, 1673, when Joliet and Marquette paddled down the Mississippi. The next white traveler along our waterfront was Father Hennepin, who under the direction of LaSalle, explored the upper reaches of the Mississippi in 1680. It was not until 1689 that Nicholas Perrot took formal possession of the area in the name of the King of France. The succeeding years were those of French exploration, and the building and establishing of their forts in strategic places.

"With all this naturally came the fighting with the Indians and the resultant hatred and mistrust of the Indian for all white men. The British, too, had been doing some exploring, and as early as 1758 the French were watching the growing English settlements with alarm. When the struggle for supremacy in the New World finally came, France made a secret treaty after the fall of Quebec in 1763, ceding the City of New Orleans and all the land west of the Mississippi River to the Spanish crown. Spain used a heavy hand on the settlers of this section during the ensuing forty years, and when Napoleon came into control in France he realized his dream of securing once more for France the land which she had ceded to Spain by the Treaty of Paris. But after securing possession, he found it was too far away to control, and because he felt that he might again lose the newly secured land to the British invaders, he offered it to the new government of the United States, who bought the area and on April 30, 1803, it became an integral part of the United States.

NAPOLEON

284

"This vast area, some 1,171,931 square miles, was divided into two parts, the 33rd degree north latitude being the dividing line. The part south was known as the Territory of Orleans; and the north portion as the District of Louisiana. This was attached to the Territory of Indiana, and the laws of Indiana governed it.

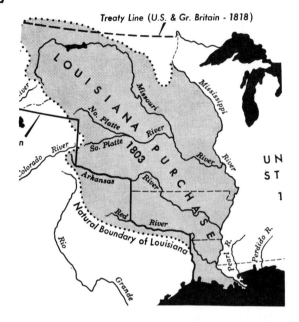

"In 1812 the Territory of Orleans was admitted to the union as the state of Louisiana. It was then called the Territory of Missouri, with its boundaries remaining as before. Missouri was admitted as a state in 1821, and from that date until 1834 this area existed as an unorganized territory without government, except of the most general nature. In fact both Presidents Monroe in 1824 and Jackson in 1829 urged that all the Indian tribes east of the Mississippi River be moved into this territory."

We are proud of our history...... of Strawberry Point & Clayton County

**STRAWBERRY POINT DRUG**
Strawberry Point, Iowa

Out of Old Dubuque came Clayton County to which the new Fayette County was "attached."

In fact, the area over which Clayton County had jurisdiction included most of both North and South Dakota, almost the entire state of Minnesota, and about one fourth of the land in Iowa.

(But, see Chapter XXIII, Fayette County, which was given the area discussed above in its creation of boundary lines: because there was no population in Fayette County at the time, it was assigned to Clayton County for taxation and judicial purposes. Other than that it was Fayette County that was the largest county unit ever created in the history of the world. The purpose in naming that vast area was to honor the Marquis De La Fayette.)

The history of Prairie La Porte will continue based upon the W. W. Jacobs accounts in Volume Two of this history of Iowa.

# We're proud........

Of The Long History Of

### CLAYTON COUNTY

And we're proud to have been a part of Clayton County history for over three-quarters of a century. Your............

## Monona Co-op

# Historic McGregor
## ---in Clayton County.........
## 1837 - 1987
## 150 years on the Mississippi

Sometimes known as the "Port of McGregor" this historic community in northeast Clayton County observed its 150th anniversary in 1987 amid great celebration and a host of activities. The Honorable "Bud" Jameson was the mayor during that historic year and the official host to the thousands who joined the community in its observances.

1987 was the 150th anniversary of the founding of what is now McGregor, Clayton County, Iowa.

In 1837 young Alexander McGregor crossed the Mississippi River from Prairie du Chien, Wisconsin, and established a ferry boat landing. Known at first as McGregor's Landing a city grew.

In 1785 Alexander McGregor's family migrated from Scotland to New York. In 1835 Alexander left his family to seek his fortune in the fabled American west. The lead mines of Galena, Ills., and Dubuque held little interest for him. Going north he settled for a while in Prairie du Chien. Soon thereafter he bought some land across the great river in a valley then known as Coulee de Sioux.

It was upon his newly acquired property that the city bearing his name would be established and grow for a time into a very important city.

Alexander McGregor first began operating his real estate as a ferry boat landing and the first one was powered by men using poles. As the interest in Iowa's land and resources grew, four years later saw the need for a larger ferry to accommodate the growing business.

The new and larger ferry was operated by horse power. That is, four horses, or mules, trod a circular wheel in the middle of the boat.

Records from 1840 show the following charges for riding across the river on the ferry. One person, 25 cents; man and horse, 75 cents; wheeled carriages, 25 cents per wheel; horned cattle or horses, 50 cents a head; sheep and goats, 6 1/4 cents per head; mules, jacks and jennets, 50 cents per head and freight not in wheeled carriages, 6 1/4 cents per 100 lbs.

Commerce and trade followed Alexander McGregor to "the other side of the river" and a settlement soon grew around his operation. In fact it grew to heights not initially dreamed.

Many active and eager enthusiasts of McGregor history put together a celebration of celebrations to denote their sesquicentennial.

On June 13th there was a re-enactment of Alexander McGregor's crossing the Mississippi and his landing on the Iowa side. Professional actors with formal scripts put on the show that recreated the birth of a community. The June 13th, 1987, event was the major "kick-off" for the sesquicentennial program.

Many hundreds gathered in old McGregor for the Old Fashioned Town Reunion where anyone with ties to McGregor gathered for a week-long event that began the 4th of July.

August 2nd featured The Great River Revival which was held at Pike's Peak Park overlooking the city. This was a celebration of the River with a variety of live music to suit all tastes. Amid the musical sounds were displays of river life and culture.

On August 8th and 9th McGregor's streets were lined with antique cars as a part of its Sesquicentennial "Antique, Classic and Collectible Car Show." It was truly a "stepping back in time" experience to observe the ancient vehicles from all over assemble there.

Later in August around two dozen hot air balloons assembled at McGregor and participated in a sanctioned competition especially involving flights around the beautiful McGregor terrain and that on both sides of the great "Father of Waters." There was also a balloon parade down the main avenue of the ancient river city.

October 3d and 4th saw the colorful "Fall Art Show" which was set in the Triangle Park mentioned earlier. The brilliant hues and tints of the artists' works were in unison with the colors of autumn that were just beginning to make themselves known on the high bluffs above the show of human talent.

A week later, on October 19th the community presented "GRRR......" as a part of its sesquicentennial. The "GRRR......" stood for the Great River Race Run which was a 5K and 10K run through Pike's Peak State Park. The fall colors on the trees were by then becoming more vivid and added color to the event......"an extra exhiliaration to the race," the local Chamber of Commerce boasted.

McGregor's Sesquicentennial year's events concluded on October 10th and 11th with the city's "Wild West Shoot Out" popularly known as the "Hole in the Sock Gang Strikes Again!" The "Shoot Out" has been enacted in previous years and was three times its former size in 1987. The spectacular "Shoot Out" let the many onlookers observe what it might have been like when early McGregor was a part of the "wild west." Amid the fall colors overlooking the final events of the city's sesquicentennial there was food, live music and a beard judging contest.

Thus the ancient river city, the Port of McGregor, observed the 150th anniversary of the crossing of the Mississippi by Alexander of the same name and the beginning of its existence. The port city remains literally alive with 19th century buildings and much pride is taken in them as they are restored and kept in good repair.

Interstate Federal Savings and Loan Association and the Jamesons' Little Switzerland Inn (Bed and Breakfast) are two businesses that take great pride in their 19th century architecture. They are two of the sponsors of this history and their sponsorship space can be seen herein.

# Monona.....
## *The Garden City*

Monona is called "The City on The Hill" and also "Iowa's Garden City." Either describes a beautiful community located in the heart of a very rich farming area to which the town owes much of its commercial success. Located in the northeast section of Clayton County due west of the Mississippi River, the town occupies a commanding position. The highest point is 1,212.85 feet above sea level and is the second highest such elevation in the state of Iowa. That point is found on the Wendell Baskerville farm west of Monona.

Early residents of the town called the highest elevation "Pigeon Mound" because large flocks of passenger pigeons lit there. In the area the passenger pigeon was considered a menace because the over abundance of them caused the seeds sown by area farmers to become food for those birds while it was not yet covered with soil. The passenger pigeon was hunted much for food by the pioneer settlers and is extinct today.

The Winnebago Indians under Chief Whirling Thunder had a village northwest of Monona and it probably influenced the early history of the white man's settlement. It is said that in the earliest days, prior to the town's establishment meaning in the late 1830s, the Indian village was one of the nearest and most convenient points for traders and illicit whiskey dealers to make contact with the Indians. Until more civilized people arrived that relationship made the area one with a wild and rough reputation.

The name, Monona, was originally spelled "Mononah." It is thought to have been the name of an Indian maiden who had leaped from a high rock overhanging the Mississippi River drowning in the deep waters below when she learned that her father refused to permit her to marry the Indian brave with whom she was in love.

It was later learned that the name of the maiden in the Indian legend was Winona and not Mononah. But the community had its name and it has always remained Monona! Also, Monona is the only town in Clayton County to have an Indian name.

This history ends around 1838 as a matter of chronology and the first permanent white pioneer settlers didn't arrive until 1840 and it is from that year we shall continue the history of Monona and its founding in Volume Two of this series.

## *Spirits & Things*

Wine was important in the past.

We have the best selection in

Northeast Iowa for your future.

*John Rohde, owner*          *539-4422*

WE TAKE PRIDE IN

THE HISTORY OF MONONA

## Monona Pharmacy
RIC FOREMAN, R. Ph.

## LIFE'S SEASONS

Life is like the four seasons, which we all must go through,
Ending mostly as we are old, and sometimes young or new.

Winter is like the start of new birth, still, but starting to grow,
Warming up towards the end, but sometimes ending in a snow.

Spring is like the young, as into adults they mature,
Budding youth turning to love, as the young face the future.

Summer is like the fullness of time, as adults reach their prime,
Struggling to make their living, soon to the end of their time.

Fall is like the waning of life, as if we're lucky to get real old,
Yearning for life with every day, and yet longing for days of gold.

We hasten through life's years, and rarely take the time,
To count all the blessings that He gave us along the line.

I wonder if we ever take the time, as we journey thru life's day,
To thank God and our Savior,  for everything He's done for us this way,

And now as our seasons are ending, we accept it with grace and serenity,
We pass on, we meet our Maker, and love God for all eternity.

Harold C. Dohrer

# HAROLD DOHRER

INVESTMENTS
All stocks, bonds and
Mutual Funds
Money Market Accounts

*Registered*
*Representative*
Offerman & Co.
Elkader, Iowa
Ph. 245-1121

Harold C. Dohrer is a lifelong resident of Clayton County, Iowa, and takes an unusual interest in its history, having lived through three quarters of a century of it. He once farmed near Chicken Ridge and has since been successful in the investment business. A consuming interest in his life has been the Barber Shop Chorus; he is also a sometime poet and we are proud to publish the above verse. He is also a partner with former Senator Adolph Elvers in the real estate business.

# Over the years.......
## ....... in Clayton County
# Adolph Elvers, Elder Statesman

Adolph Elvers may legitimately be referred to as Elkader's, or perhaps Clayton County's "elder statesman." He is pictured on the page at the left with the late President John F. Kennedy while he was a senator from Massachusetts and a candidate for the presidency. Elvers was, at the time, chairman of the Democratic Party in Clayton County.

Senator Elvers, as he remains known by many, is retired somewhat at the age of nearly 80. He is known by most as "Ade" and is a familiar figure around his hometown. He goes to his office everyday where he still engages in his real estate and insurance business other than watching Cubs baseball games on his office TV. (The author refers to him as "Uncle Ade" because their paths have crossed so often over the years in many different ways.)

"Ade" Elvers' life was not all a life of politics but a life of service to his community and his fellow citizens. Many honors have come his way and his office is adorned with but a few of them with plaques, pictures, numerous awards, trophies and even autographed books!

A lifelong resident of Clayton County, Adolph W. Elvers was born on 4 August 1911 at Elkader. He was graduated from the Elkader High School in 1929 and spent his active life in operating a dairy farm and engaging in the insurance business both of which proved successful for him. In 1934 he was married to the former Lola Hanson at Elgin, Fayette County, Iowa.

Over many years he has been recognized for his industriousness and other activities locally, statewide and nationally. In a long and active career he has been president of the Elkader Co-op Feed Company, president of the Clayton County Telephone Company, president of the Volga Co-op Creamery Company and president of the Iowa Creameries, Ames, Ia. He served for some years on the board of directors of the National Milk Producers Federation, Washington, D. C. He was for six years county chairman of the Clayton County Democratic Party. He was elected to the State Senate in 1962, took office in January of 1963. He became a powerful force in the State Senate, gained a committee chairmanship where most senators wait to do so. He was a close associate of Governor Hughes. He never surrendered his high ideals and always voted in the statesmanlike interests of his senatorial district and his state.

Today, in Clayton County, Senator Elvers enjoys his semi-retirement and has truly earned the cognomen of "Elder Statesman."

# These Clayton County Merchants, Businesses and Professional Persons

## ARE PROUD OF OUR COUNTY'S HISTORY AND ARE PROUD TO SPONSOR THIS HISTORIC WORK

ELVERS INSURANCE AND REAL ESTATE
Elkader

HAROLD DOHRER INVESTMENTS
Elkader

MONONA COOPERATIVE COMPANY
Monona

STRAWBERRY POINT PHARMACY
Strawberry Point

HALVORSON INSURANCE AGENCY
Monona

GARNAVILLO MILL, INC.
Garnavillo

CLAYTON COUNTY
GENEALOGICAL SOCIETY
Elkader

MONONA PHARMACY
Ric Foreman, R. Ph.

KLINE'S SUPER-VALU
Elkader

SPIRITS & THINGS
Monona

BED & BREAKFAST
McGregor

JESSEN'S SUPER-VALU
Strawberry Point

THEIS CLOTHING
Elkader

INTERSTATE FEDERAL
SAVINGS & LOAN
McGregor

# Chapter Nineteen
# JONES COUNTY

Jones County, Iowa was among the early counties inland from the Mississippi that was settled, the first date for a new settler in its history being 1834.

With the colorful history of Jones County comes also the very colorful background of the man for whom the county was named, General George Wallace Jones.

Recall that the Wisconsin Territorial Legislature created Jones County out of that original large county that was Dubuque until 1837. The territorial legislature also formed the boundaries of Jones county and the others. In some cases it also named the county seat.

It is significant that the boundaries of Jones County, once established, were and are so accurate they never required changing or re-surveying. There are **sixteen townships within the county** and each is exactly six miles square and each has exactly 23,040 acres or 36 square miles. This fact is unique and those townships in Jones County are "true" townships.

Hugh Bowen was the first settler in Jones County although some white men had ventured into the county earlier. James Langworthy had been in the area as early as 1829 and others explored it as late as 1834.

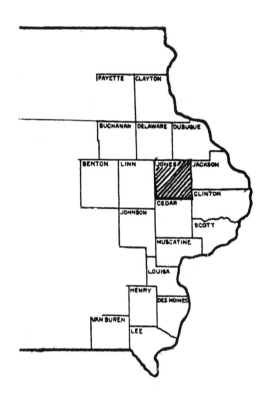

But the first permanent white settler was Hugh Bowen, as a matter of historical record.

Not long after Bowen came J. Flinn, Mose Collins, Joshua Johnson and Alfred Weatherford. That was in 1835.

The new settlement in which those families found themselves soon became known as Bowen's Prairie.

Thus Bowen's Prairie was the first area of settlement within Jones

County. It is today Richland Township which was organized formally later on 5 July 1842 and at that time included what became Cass, Wayne, Castle Gove and Lovell the latter becoming essentially the City of Monticello.

The first child born in Jones County was given birth at Bowen's Prairie and she was Ava Johnson, probably the daughter of Mr. and Mrs. Joshua Johnson.

Monticello in Lovell Township saw its first permanent settler in Daniel Varvel who built his first cabin on the east bank of Kitty Creek in October of 1836. When he found that the site was subject to heavy flooding from the creek, he built a second cabin in April of 1837.

Daniel Varvel was followed by Mr. and Mrs. Richard Smith who located in the area that is Monticello in the spring of 1837 and they were probably the first married couple to settle there.

The Varvel home soon became the stopping place for both the mail and travelers.

In Fairview Township there was also the village of Fairview that showed great promise in its early years. It may be called the "fore-runner" of Anamosa. No white man had settled in Fairview Township before July of 1837.

Clement Russell arrived in July of 1837 and settled on and owned the whole town of Fairview. Russell erected a cabin 18 x 24 feet which was large for that time. John G. Joslin came to Fairview in 1838.

At one time Ulysses S. Grant owned property in Fairview and peddled leather in the area around Fairview, Iowa.

Dr. Clark Joslin was the first medical doctor in Jones county and served an area of a sixty mile radius for over 40 years.

James Spencer was the first settler at Langworthy although we've noted that white men had explored the area several years before he arrived and made his permanent settlement.

Anamosa had its beginnings in 1838 and will observe its sequicentennial in 1988. Its history is dealt with seperately later in this volume.

As Bowen's Prairie grew in numbers there was established **Bowen's Prairie Cemetery and most of the original settlers of that** community and Jones County are buried there. The first recorded death in Jones County was that of a young lad named Alfred Denison who got lost in the tall prairie grass about which we've told earlier. Two days after his disappearance he was found frozen to death. But there is no record of where the young boy was buried.

Scotch Grove also has a fascinating background and it was founded by the sturdiest of pioneers, Scotsmen and their families who walked a thousand miles, it is said, to finally settle there. The first settlers came in 1837 after Alexander McLean had scouted the area.

It is recorded that the Scotch settlers walked a thousand miles with two wheeled ox-drawn carts of wood carrying their belongings and occasionally carrying the women and children. They journeyed from Selkirk settlement in Canada to locate a permanent home.

In 1837 came John Sutherland with his wife and ten sons and two daughters. With the large family were also Alexander Sutherland, Joseph Bremmer, David McCoy and, returning to the area he had earlier explored, Alexander McLean.

In 1838 David and Ebenezer Sutherland joined the settlement. Christina, a daughter of John Sutherland, died soon after their arrival.

As early as 1837 a black man who had served in the U. S. Army claimed land in Hale Township. He was a free man and his claim was a military benefit. Neighbors often referred to the place of his claim as "Nigger Point." In today's era of sensitivity politics that would be a misnomer indeed. It is today called Pleasant Grove.

Few counties are named for more colorful or legendary figures as Jones County in receiving its name from General George Wallace Jones. Gen. Jones was a quiet and unassuming individual but was a friend of every president from Monroe to Cleveland.

He was born in Vincennes, Indiana, on 12 April 1804 and was educated at Transylvania University of Kentucky. He studied law and was a schoolmate of Jefferson Davis; they became lifelong friends. Jones was graudated in 1825. In 1824 he was selected as chief of a bodyguard for the Marquis d'LaFayette at Lexington.

George W. Jones was admitted to the bar and was a little later clerk of the U. S. District Court at Ste. Genevieve, Missouri. The climate bothered his health and he moved northward to Galena, Illinois in 1827.

In 1824 he was honored with an appointment as sergeant of the guard for General Andrew Jackson when he was elected to the United States Senate. Jones and Andrew Jackson became lifelong friends, too.

Other than honors and new friends, while at the University of Kentucky he made the acquaintance of Henry Clay who had been asked by Jones' father to be guardian for the young man.

During the Black Hawk War, Jones was aide-de-camp to General Dodge and was appointed Colonel of Militia. Later Jones succeeded General Dodge. He was also for a short time Chief Justice of the Michigan Territory.

He settled at Sinsinawa, Ills., not far from Galena and was a farmer, miner and merchandiser. In 1835 he was elected Delegate to Congress. He later moved across the Mississippi and became an Iowan. After Iowa became a State, Gen. Jones was elected to the United States Senate where he served with great distinction.

295

### GEORGE WALLACE JONES

General and Senator George W. Jones, after whom Jones County is named, is shown in his later years. It was rare for a county to be named after a man so young.

COMMENT about Jones and his politics which is quoted here verbatim from the Anamosa JOURNAL-EUREKA of 5 July 1888 - one hundred years ago; it says:

"General George Jones, of whom Jones County is named after, has repented his ways and abandoned the Democratic Party and enrolled himself under the Republican banner. This is of great comfort to the people of Jones County."

# Monticello was 150 years old in 1986 - Daniel Varvel was the first settler

The City of Monticello observed its 150th anniversary in 1986 pre-dating the conception of this new history of our State. Not many communities in the State can boast of having reached 150 years by 1986. Few communities have observed their Sesquicentennial in such an elaborate manner. A tremendous volume about the city was published to note what had been done. Understandably not a lot was written about those very early years but C. L. (Gus) Norlin wrote an incisive piece about Daniel Varvel, the first settler and founder.

The book, "MONTICELLO - 1836 - 1986" was edited by Leigh Clark, Editor in Chief; Dr. L. C. Perkins, Co-Editor; C. J. (Jim) Matthiessen, Copy Editor; Virginia Rummmel Bone, Typist and Word Processor Operator. (See Bibliography) Marcia Gabiel and C. J. (Gus) Norlin were co-chairmen of the Monticello Heritage Sesquicentennial and were assisted by a Board of Directors consisting of Mary Ellen Yeoman, Cindy Hall, Dr. D. W. Kaiser, Sue Burrichter, Jerry Jasa, Jim Holt, Rudy Monk, Vera Schoon and Loretta Tuttle and a host of other local enthusiasts.

For our purposes we want to note the life and activity of early pioneer settler Daniel Varvel for which we should give appreciation to the author of the following article for his historical research and thanks for permission to use it. (We hope to draw heavily on their excellent volume in this series.)

## DANIEL VARVEL
### by C. L. "Gus" Norlin

(Ed. Note. Eighteen years of research into the life of Daniel Varvel brought me little more information than what was already available from the 1879 History of Jones County, Iowa. Just where Varvel had come from prior to his short stint of working in the Galena, Illinois, lead mines after his "Black Hawk War" discharge, remained a mystery as did the question of where he went after leaving the Monticello area about 1867! - C. L. N.)

For 15 of the 18 years of my research, I dogged various western Historical Societies seeking information and had a number of inquiries printed in various national publications. Finally, I found where he had gone, and where he was buried, but I could find no family descendants. There were none left in the Correctionville, Iowa, area, Varvel's final resting place.

Finally, while researching some information for the Sesquicentennial Calendar I came across a very old scrapbook in my collection in which a yellowed piece of newsprint carried the announcement, "Margaret Varvel, widow of Daniel Varvel died yesterday at Gordon, Nebraska, in the home of her daughter Mary Stauffer. Mrs. Varvel's husband was the first settler of Monticello, Iowa."

A phone call to the Editor of Gordon, Nebraska's newspaper assured me that the neewspaper would print my letters of inquiry about the Stauffers. My first letter brought an immediate reply from a very young descendant of the Varvels, and also told me that my inquiry was being forwarded to Beavercreek, Oregon, where a great-granddaughter of the Varvels, Thelma J. Green, lived. She is 86 years of age --- and she

DANIEL VARVEL
First Settler of Monticello

has the Varvel family Bible in her possession. The trail led on to Long Beach, California, and College Station, Texas.

When the trail ends, going forward and backward, more is learned of Daviel Varvel, his ancestors and descendants than could be hoped for...........their history in the colonies begins about 1741. The Varvels were of French extraction.............

None of the Varvel descendants were aware that Daniel Varvel was Monticello, Iowa's first settler. All were delighted and surprised however to know their ancestor had left an indelible mark on the pages of our city's history.

I believe Daniel Varvel was born in Franklin County, Kentucky, in a log cabin nestled in the foothills of the Blue Ridge Mountains. It is possible, however, he was born in Rowan

County, North Carolina, and as a very small child made the journey from there to Franklin County (where) ... most of his young life was spent.

Daniel's father was a farmer, and Daniel grew to manhood helping on the farm......

It appears young Varvel left home at about the age of 15 .... (and) ..... set out and crossed the border into Ohio...........

We all lose track of the young man Varvel for the next few years ...... until we learn he is a volunteer in the Army during the "Black Hawk War" as that disgraceful affair has become known.

Immediately after hostilities ceased, Daniel was mustered out at Dunlieth (East Dubuque, Ills.) and found work in the lead mines around Galena, Illinois.

Early in October of 1836, Varvel found himself on the northeast bank of the Maquoketa river, across from the mouth of Kitty Creek. Kitty Creek was nameless at the time and we can suppose the name "Kitty" was the white man's pronunciation of the Indian word "Gitchee," a name used by Chippewa, Fox, Sac, and other Indian tribes, for streams.

We know he crossed below the mouth of Kitty Creek, for here is a broad flood plain, and the surge of water is allowed to spread giving a somewhat shallower depth...........

If Varvel had in mind to move further west when he left Galena, Ills., he changed his mind at this time.

Varvel picked a site upon the east bank of Kitty Creek, just a short distance from its mouth with the river, and began building a log cabin. The date was October 6, 1836 and from that date our heritage is measured. While Monticello did not become a governmental subdivision until some years later, almost from Varvel's first day here it became known as Varvel's Place, then later, Varvelstown. A few years later it was named Monticello. ........ A week after varvel's arrival, his friend William Clark joined him; then in the spring of 1837 Mr. and Mrs. Richard South erected a small cabin and started farming............by 1839, the area resembled a small ..... village.

Daniel Varvel and Margaret Beardsley were married on December 13, 1839, and to this union were born five children. ...................

Varvel himself became a pillar of the growing community, and in at least two instances was instrumental in having areas platted to enlarge the growing village. He was a prime mover in founding the first school.

(After an unpleasant situation caused by political disagreements the Varvels moved to Correctionville, Woodbury County, Iowa. This will be related in Volume II of this series.)

After this move by Daniel Varvel and his family there were no more ties to the Monticello area by any Varvels or descendants.

--- C. L. Gus) Norlin

ANAMOSA IOWA
1838
1988
JULY 1-2-3
SESQUICENTENNIAL

# ANAMOSA....named after an Indian maiden-----
## Observed its Sesquicentennial in 1988

As noted elsewhere in this history the county seat of Jones County was established at the little town of Lexington. That was before the "city fathers" found out that there was already a community in Iowa named Lexington. It was, therefore, incumbent upon them to find another name for their county seat.

An informative brochure about Anamosa printed by the local Chamber of Commerce states as follows:

"Ana-mo-sah, a charming Indian maiden, and her father happened to spend a night at the Ford Inn here. The local leaders were meeting at the Inn and heard the young girl called 'Anamosa.' They thought the name was so appealing that they chose it to replace 'Lexington.' ANAMOSA is said to be Indian for 'White Fawn'."

(A stone, marking the site of the old Ford Inn, is located at the far end of South Main Street and was placed there by the local chapter of the Daughters of the American Revolution.)

Anamosa's Public Library even looks "historical" with its seemingly ancient stone architecture.

## THE LEGEND OF ANAMOSA

According to legend, ANAMOSA was an Indian maiden whose father was chief of a tribe which camped at the joining waters of the Buffalo and Wapsipinicon Rivers. Indian lore has it that the point where the two rivers meet is a protected and favored spot in the eyes of the Great Spirit.

While here, ANAMOSA became infatuated with Wapsipinicon, a brave from another tribe. When he spoke to the chief and made known his desire for ANAMOSA, he was denied her. In his grief he ran to the wooded bluffs bordering one river and jumped from a high cliff into its waters and drowning. Thereafter the river was called Wapsipinicon and later the Jones County seat took the Indian maiden's name.....ANAMOSA. The Wapsipinicon River runs through the southwest edge of Anamosa and it is suggested thereby that "ANAMOSA" is eternally embraced by Wapsipinicon! (Material extracted from Anamosa Chamber of Commerce brochure.)

OVER THE YEARS Jones County grew and prospered. Its county seat was early established at the little town of Lexington where the first log courthouse was erected to house the handful of county officers then needed to govern the area. The name was later changed as is noted in the section included herein on the City of Anamosa.

(On the second floor of the Jones County Courthouse there hangs today a large painting of the "Courthouse at Lexington" which was done in 1979 by the author of this book. From the west window opposite where the painting hangs can barely be seen the site of that original courthouse. The author painted six smaller versions in oil of the "Courthouse at Lexington" which are rare and valuable and are in the hands of local Jones County residents.)

From Anamosa came the famous American artist, Grant Wood, whose painting "American Gothic" is certainly one of the nation's most famous. The Grant Wood story will appear in a later volume. He is buried in the cemetery at the southwest edge of Anamosa, his grave marked by a plain stone.

The Honorable Warren J. Rees, who "read law" has been a part of Jones County history for well over a half century. Warren Rees was later appointed a district judge and then a member of the Iowa Supreme Court where he served with distinction

## DEDICATED ANAMOSA CITIZENS WORKED HARD TO MAKE 1988 SESQUICENTENNIAL A SUCCESS

A Sesquicentennial Committee of dedicated Anamosa citizens and editors worked long and hard to make the city's 150th celebration a success. They produced the events of the July 4th, 1988, weekend and a beautiful and large book to note the occasion.

Chaired by (Mrs.) Anna Parham, others on the Sesquicentennial Committee were: (Mrs.) Charlene George, (Mrs.) Nita Heurter, (Mrs.) June Eggers, (Mrs.) Helen Gerst and Miss Betty Stover, Al Bierbrodt, David Odeen, Mike Payton and Kathryn Ortgies.

The sesquicentennial book, "ANAMOSA - 1838-1988 - A Reminiscence" was published and its editorial staff was: Bertha Finn, Editor-in-Chief; Pat Worden-Sutton, Co-Editor; Jo Ann McRoberts Walters, Business Editor; Mildred Barker Brown, Photographic Editor.

# Justice Rees salutes the city's Sesquicentennial

ELLEN FRASHER portrayed the Indian maiden, Anamosa, during a pageant performed two evenings of the Sesquicentennial. She acts the part as a poem by Jay G. Sigmund is read by Kay Dougherty. (Photo by Gail Eschen, Anamosa Journal-Eureka.)

WARREN J. REES, retired judge of the Supreme Court of Iowa and Anamosa's most distinguished citizen, is shown above reflecting upon the city's past and remarking optimistically about its future. Affectionately known as "the judge," Warren Rees has had a long and colorful career.

SESQUICENTENNIAL CANCELLATION was a special one-day affair whereby cards and letters could note the day. (Pictures of Justice Rees and Cancellation by David Winger of the Anamosa Journal-Eureka)

JOHN D. MILLER
John D. Miller of Anamosa is ending a long and distinguished career of service to Jones County. A Navy veteran, John Miller spent many of his years as a Jones County Deputy.

# Stone City.....
# historic and serene

Many tourists are attracted each year to historic Stone City which is located five minutes away from Anamosa by paved road to the northwest. This little town, nestled in the folds of the Wapsipinicon valley, has a rich history which began with the quarrying of the famous Stone City limestone. Then in the late 1930s, Jones County was the residence of an internationally known artist, Grant Wood. He taught painting there as the students used brightly colored ice wagons for shelter. Grant Wood's well-known painting "Stone City" was created there and visitors can stand on the exact site. Members of the arts have a fond memory of Stone City. Famous poet Paul Engle, also a writer and director of the Creative Writing Workshop at the University of Iowa, Iowa City, lived there summers to write until 1963 when the historic Green Mansion in which he lived was destroyed by fire. Stone City is a place of beauty and serenity with a history all its own, especially in the arts. (Material extracted from a booklet originally produced by the Anamosa chapter of the Business and Professional Women's Club and revised and distributed by the Anamosa Chamber of Commerce.)

(Many early Iowa buildings were erected of native stone extracted from state-owned quarries such as the prison shown at the right. This institution is located at Anamosa and many have erroneously believed that the material came from Stone City which it did not.)

# Keeping the peace

JOHN W. COOK

Jones County's popular and highly respected sheriff has now served many years in that office being elected and re-elected several times. Personable but firm Sheriff Cook has shown many initiatives while serving as the chief law enforcement officer of Jones County. It was by his efforts and the rehabilitative use of incarcerated personnel that the Jones County Courthouse was painted and redecorated.

# Chapter Twenty
# DELAWARE COUNTY

Among all the inland counties Delaware received many early white adventurers probably because of its proximity to and immediately west of Dubuque County.

As early as 1829 James Langworthy explored the territory between the Maquoketa and Turkey Rivers. Upon attempting a later return to the area with his brother, Lucius, soldiers from the army fort at Prairie du Chien, Fort Crawford, stopped them and drove them back across the Mississippi. The land was not officially open for settlement and soldiers were regularly used to keep settlers from entering and building.

When the land was opened for settlement James Langworthy and others established themselves at Dubuque and continued the mining of lead that had flourished there years before.

William Bennett and his very young wife, Elizabeth, were probably the first settlers to come to Delaware County. Belle Bailey, who wrote a history of the county, estimated that the Bennetts came and settled in either 1834 or 1835. Either year would be realistic but in retrospect 1835 would seem the most probable, all other information considered. The Bennetts built a small

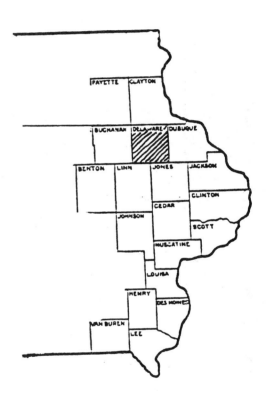

log cabin in what is today Honey Creek Township, the southeastern part of it.

Elizabeth Bennett is usually regarded as the first settler in Delaware County of a permanent nature. For her husband was a rover and an adventurer and didn't stay in any one place for very long. He is even reported to have been an associate of some sordid characters from the Missouri hills far south of their cabin site. He was away from his home for weeks and months at a time. But his young wife remained at home and lived in the small cabin which had but a heavy quilt for a door. It was there that she became enured to the hardships of the frontier.

Elizabeth Bennett became a sturdy pioneer settler. Living alone on the edge, more than the edge it would

seem, of civilization she developed a frontier resourcefulness and became a good shot with a gun often surviving by killing small game for nourishment and defending herself against the more ferocious beasts such as the wolf and the bear. Both were plentiful in those early days and were known to attack human beings.

During the winter of 1837-38 she gave birth to a child which would ordinarily have relieved her of much of the loneliness she bore. In the cold of that winter and due to the other conditions which were hardly conducive to survival on the Iowa frontier the baby lived but for a few days.

Nor are we told whether it was a boy or girl child nor even if a name were given it. Elizabeth buried her firstborn in the cold winter earth deep enough to protect the tiny body from the carnivorous wolves which roamed the area in those times.

The birth and death of the Bennett baby was therefore the first birth and death of a white person in Delaware County, Iowa. The exact year is not known but it was either 1837 or 1838.

Evidently Mr. William Eads of Galena, Illinois, the father of Elizabeth Bennett, was never altogether happy with his daughter's choice of a husband. For the 1838 William Eads and his family removed to Delaware County, Iowa, to settle near where his daughter was living. But William Bennett returned home shortly after and determined to have none of his disapproving father-in-law. So he took his wife and moved farther west.

William Eads and his family remained, however, seeing the futility of following the Bennetts, and suppressed his fatherly instincts. The Eads family settled in at the Bennett site and it then became known as Eads Grove. Not long after arriving there the Eads family were joined by another son-in-law, John Hinkle who settled nearby.

While the Bennetts, as we have noted, were the first settlers in Delaware County, the area had been visited by many white men in former times. It is thought that in 1833 an Indian trader who had built the first brick house and established the first hotel in Dubuque had visited the area. He didn't stay and may have returned to Dubuque the only significance of historical value to his visit being that he returned to Delaware County in 1840 as we shall see.

We are told that a Frenchman named Henry Teegarten lived near the Dubuque county line southeast of present-day Colesburg. He is said to have cleared four acres of land and many say he had done so a year or two earlier perhaps making him the first settler in the county. One way or another there seems to have been nothing permanent about his settlement for he shortly removed across the line back into Dubuque County.

Henry Teegarten is an enigma in northeast Iowa history and is found in several places at different times. An early letter reported that he had once been connected with the LeBeaux, a band of roving fur thieves, but that suspicion is chalked up to rumor only and is not verified by any empirical evidence or credible historians.

During the winter of 1836-1837 Lucius Kibbee settled on a site that was to become known as Rockville on the Delaware and Dubuque county line but he later moved over into Dubuque County.

**Hugh and James Livingston along with Hugh Rose arrived and settled** in the southeastern part of Delaware County in 1837 as a part of the Scottish migration from Canada. They and others had been driven from the Selkirk colony by the established gentry in that British dominion and were seeking new places to settle. Many Scotch immigrants from Canada had tried to establish themselves near Winnipeg and in the Red River Valley. Other opposition to their settling up there came from both the Indians and the fur traders. More will be related about the Scots later.

The Nicholson family were the first to settle in the Hopkinton area and they arrived in the fall or early winter of 1836-37. In any event, they were there in March of 1837 when Joel Bailey, along with Cyrus and John Keeler, arrived.

Joel Bailey had been in the area

*Joel Bailey*

before in 1836 and had selected a site near a rapidly flowing spring where he had envisioned settling and building a home. When he found the Nicholsons already there when he returned, he and the Keelers explored farther north into the Delaware county area and Joel Bailey eventually located on the Maquoketa River. The site he chose came to be known as Bailey's Ford. (Joel Bailey was a direct ancestor of Miss Belle Bailey who recorded so much of the county's history.)

Thomas Nicholson died a year after he arrived and his widow sold his land to Leroy Jackson, an Indian trader. Jackson was the one who had built the first brick house in Dubuque and had kept a hotel there and is the one we mentioned earlier who had probably been exploring Delaware County as early as 1833. In that year he was not only exploring the new land but trading with the local Indians. Jackson liked the area and when he was ready to remove elsewhere he returned and bought the Nicholson property.

With Henry Carter, Leroy Jackson founded the beautiful little town of Hopkinton.

A government land office was opened at Dubuque in 1838 and by November of that year those claiming land in Delaware County recorded their entries there. The first ones were for Abner Eads and Richard Barrett of Honey Creek Township. It is said that non-resident speculators in land often entered claims and that some of those who actually lived on the land had to wait several years until they could put together the $1.25 per acre cost of their properties.

Lucius Kibbee, as mentioned heretofore, came to within Delaware County in the winter of 1836-37 and remained a few years living on the west bank of the north fork of the Maquoketa River. In 1839 he was joined by Gilbert Dillon who built the first frame house in the county. They were soon followed by others and the village of Rockville was formed.

Rockville was on the road from Dubuque and therefore a stopping-off place for many travelers. The Kibbee house had come into the ownership of Oliver Olmstead and it was there that many travelers stayed overnight. Olmstead also built a saw mill and a grist mill on the river. Rockville became a very busy community due largely to its location. At one time it had three hotels among its other shops and businesses.

About 1838 the first settlement was established in what is today Bremen Township. John Flinn is regarded as the founder and he located on Bear Creek a little east of the center of the township. He was followed some years later by seven brothers name Bockenstedt which has become a well-known name in Delaware County and northeast Iowa.

It was also in 1838 that William Eads moved into the cabin originally built by his but then estranged son-in-law and daughter Elizabeth. That cabin was situated in Section 35 of Honey Creek Township. Eads later erected a much larger double cabin and travelers and potential settlers often stayed there while scouting for sites upon which they, too, could settle and build.

The son-in-law of William Eads, to whom we referred earlier, John Hinkle, settled in the northern part of Honey Creek Township. His location was that upon which the later village of York would take root.

Ox-drawn cart similar to a covered **wagon** but smaller is shown in this sketch. It was in this type of transportation that the Scottish immigrants came to Delaware County from Canada.

WE'RE PROUD OF
DELAWARE COUNTY'S LONG HISTORY

Always proud to be of service to you!

JOHNSON'S FEED MILL
Hopkinton, Iowa
(319) 926 - 2211

Eads Grove and York seemed to grow rapidly at first and both enjoyed beautiful locations on Honey Creek. But, as with Rockville, the eventual coming of the railroads and the halting of most overland travel caused them and small communities like them all over to enter into a decline.

The buildings began to disappear from non-use and neglect and the land upon which they once stood reverted to the farmer's tillage. Today little or no trace remains of the work, efforts and hopes of those early pioneers.

Thomas Nicholson was the first white adult to die in Delaware County, when he passed away in 1839. After Mrs. Nicholson sold the property to Jackson and to Carter she and her family moved away. Before their final departure they ordered a tombstone to mark the final resting place of Thomas Nicholson. However, the family left before the monument to the pioneer settler arrived. With the family gone no one was around to supervise the placement of the stone.

Some years later, as the story is told, Mr. Nicholson's then grown children returned to find their father's grave but there was no stone marking it. A search was begun that yielded nothing so the family left and many more years passed.

Finally it was discovered that the marker for Thomas Nicholson's grave was face-down in the local print shop and being used for ink rollers to ink the presses. It found its way to mark the final resting place of the pioneer.

Communities sprang up around Delaware County; some survived and some did not even as we have seen in the early years we've covered.

Delaware County, like many other counties, was to have its fights over the location of the seat of government. It would finally end up at Manchester, of course, but other towns were considered.

It seems that Delaware County had more than the average of small towns springing up and then dying out. Who today hears of Rockville, Yankee Settlement, York or Eads Grove? Or Golden Prairie, Barryville, Sand Springs, Compton, Forrestville, Hazel Green or Hartwick?

# Dircks LP Gas

We're Proud of Our History

HOPKINTON, IOWA
Phone 926 - 2071

*Very proud . . . .*
OF THE HISTORY OF HOPKINTON
AND OF DELAWARE COUNTY . . . . . .

# H. A. Gearhart, DO

Physician and Surgeon
Diplomate of the
American Osteopathic
Board of General Practice

HOPKINTON, IOWA

Office Telephone 926 - 2911

# Delaware County - 1838

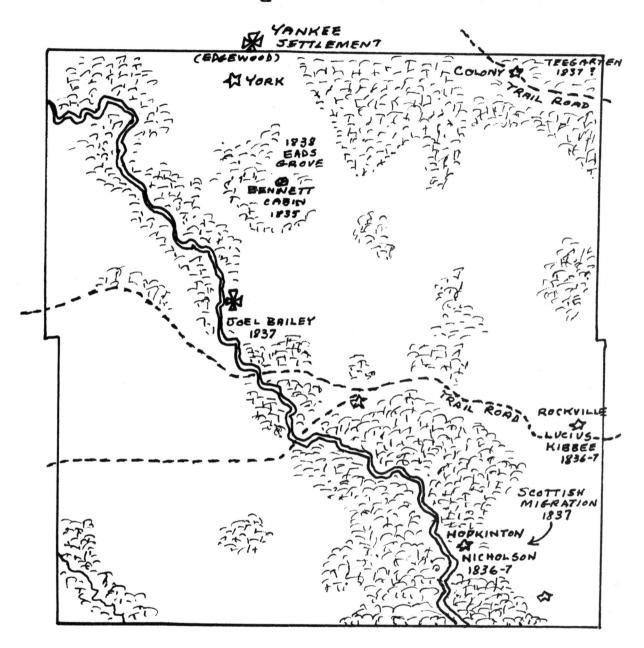

~~~~~~~~~ Denotes trails that, with immigration, were becoming roads.  Recall that trails were first used by animals, then Indians and then the pioneers. Many early "trails" are today's main arteries of transportation.

Denotes heavily forested areas some of which would be eventually cleared for agricultural use. Delaware County today retains  much wooded area.

# Preserving the history of Delaware County

Miss Arabelle Bailey, always known as "Belle," was born at Manchester, Delaware County, on 19 April 1869 the daughter of Clement J. and Julia Loomis Bailey.

The direct descendant of early pioneer settlers, she took an unusual interest in her ancestry and the history of Delaware County and recorded much of it. Belle Bailey was one of those rare individuals who, by her diligence in recording history and her dedication to it, has left valuable information and facts seldom found in the histories of some counties.

Miss Bailey was herself a granddaughter and a great-granddaughter of two of Delaware County's very early settlers, Joel Bailey (See picture, p. 305) and Clement Coffin both of whom have historic sites named for them. Her own interest was easily understandable and the results of her work will be treasured for all time.

Belle Bailey lived from 1869, when Delaware County was "officially" only 32 years from its creation. For much of her early life she knew personally many of the early settlers who related much of the very early history to her. She passed from this life in 1946 and left as her legacy writings from which we can all learn Delaware County's history almost first hand.

She was educated in the Manchester schools and at the (then) Iowa State Teachers College in Cedar Falls. She taught in the county's rural schools for five years and then was employed by the Manchester PRESS. She loved writing and only

# Miss Arabelle Bailey
# 1869 - 1946

## "Barley Green"

. . . . . IS SWEEPING THE COUNTRY AS AN ANSWER TO MANY NUTRITIONAL PROBLEMS.          GET YOURS TODAY!

You can "see and feel" the difference.

Free information. Send long (#10) S. A. S. E. to . . . . . .

## Golden Rule Sales

BOX 10 - RR #1
Colesburg, Iowa 52035
Ph. (319) 856 - 4345

Cassette available $ 3.00
Also   Miracle   Green   &   Legacy
Products available.

the failing health of her mother caused her to leave the paper to care for her parent.

In later years she devoted much time to the study of the county's history, much of which she had gleaned from the pioneers whom she recalled. Other material she gathered by diligent research. The result was that she eventually published two books, one in 1932 and another in 1935.

Miss Bailey was loved by all and was a special friend of young people, befriending many high school boys and girls by hiring them to help care for her beautiful lawns and gardens. She was an authority on birds and was active in the local garden clubs, her church and the Daughters of the American Revolution. She reportedly had a deep sense of humor, a keen wit and a smile for everyone.

Belle Bailey died in 1946 at the age of 77. At the time of her death the third book was in preparation.

The manuscript of that third volume was edited and prepared for publication by Mary Doolittle Maxfield who said: "It was with great anticipation that I undertook the task of editing the manuscript for this book, left by Belle Bailey at the time of her death in 1946. It had been stored in the public library since that time until the Delaware County Historical Society decided to edit and publish the book, prepared in the 1930s and 40s and many of the pioneer buildings and sites she mentions are not now in existence."

To Miss Belle Bailey and to Mary Doolittle Maxfield, the residents of Delaware County and the researchers of its proud history should be grateful for the work they have done in leaving and preparing such a quantity of valuable information to generations yet unborn.

--- D. L. K.

HOPKINTON, DELAWARE COUNTY --- The annual Hallowe'en parade by the young folk of the community. Dressed in their costumes grade school children parade through the town; this was 1987. (Photo by George Dircks)

# Chapter Twenty-One
# CEDAR COUNTY

Cedar County was another of the "inland" counties and got its name from the Cedar River.

Early histories tell us that Colonel George Davenport had one of his Indian trading posts in Cedar County above the mouth of Rock Creek between 1831 and 1835. The first permanent white settler made a claim in Cedar County in 1836.

David Walton was a resident of Indiana before removing to the west. In 1835 he helped a daughter move to Musquitine County (it was not yet a county, of course) and was impressed with the Iowa country.

David Walton made his claim on the east bank of Sugar Creek, built a cabin and broke the land. That was in 1835. In the fall he returned to Tippecanoe, Indiana, to his family and stayed the winter. In the spring of 1836 he and his family started to Iowa and his claimed land. They crossed the Mississippi on 1 May 1836 and arrived in the county on the 10th. They reportedly put 100 acres into corn and wheat that year. Mrs. Walton thereby became the first white woman to cook a meal in Cedar

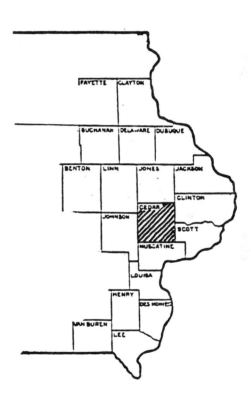

County; she was the first woman early pioneer settler. The Waltons were the first family to plant and harvest a crop in the county. They became the owners of much land and some of it remained in the family for many years.

Almost immediately after David Walton and his family settled on the east side of Sugar Creek, Andrew Crawford and his family arrived and established themselves on the west side. As soon as Crawford got settled he sent for his family who had remained at Fort Wayne, Indiana. Other than his wife there were three children to include Andrew, Jr., a daughter Phoebe and a baby, Charles, only a month old born in April 1836. (Charles would live to be 80 years old, living well into the 20th century.)

There is the story that Andrew Crawford once lost his way during a snow storm and walked all night in Sugar Creek to keep from freezing. By morning he found neighbors who nursed him back to health. He was so badly frostbitten

that all his toes fell off.

Another early pioneer settler to establish himself in Cedar County was Abner Stebbins although it is not claimed that he was necessarily the third one to do so. Born in New York in 1811 he came west while a young man and stopped at Chicago, then arrived in the area of Cedar Rapids. He left there and came to Pioneer Grove in northwest Cedar County where he staked his claim. The farm he developed would be his home for the rest of his life; it would have been about two miles northwest of the present community of Mechanicsville.

The story is that Abner Stebbins brought with him his own apple seeds from the east and when he founded his farm he planted them. They grew into a splendid orchard, we are told. Later a school was started west of the orchard and the apples were a delight to the pupils.

The area that was to become Cedar County and into which those early pioneer settlers sought homes and opportunity became a formal county 24 miles square bounded by Jones County on the north, Clinton and Scott on the east, Muscatine on the south with Johnson and Linn to the west.

The Cedar River enters the county on its west border and leaves it near the middle of its south line. The Wapsipinicon River flows through the northeast corner and at one time great stands of timber covered the banks of the rivers.

The Indian name for red cedar is Mosk-wah-wak-wah and we've read of the derivation of Wapsipinicon previously.

Before those early pioneers arrived and toward the end of the aegis of Col. Davenport in the area a portion of Cedar County had been part of a claim on a vast property made by him along with Antoine Le Claire, George L. Davenport, the colonel's son, Maj. William Gordon, Alexander W. McGregor, Louis Hebert and others. Their claims were mainly in Allen's Grove and Hickory Grove in Scott County but they entered into the future Cedar County area at Posten's Grove; they also took claim to all of Onion Grove.

Later there was question about who was really the first permanent white settler in Cedar County. Those claiming the honor were David Walton, Andrew Crawford, Enos Nyce and Robert G. Roberts. It was finally concluded "that Colonel

David W. Walton was that ubiquitous personage....."

Robert G. Roberts, mentioned before, was a Pennsylvania native who came to Iowa in July of 1836. He made a claim on what later became known as the Dillon farm. He didn't stay long and crossed the river into Muscatine County, actually "jumping" a claim of some people already there. The "claim law" which was an unwritten "understanding" was probably part of the Common Law of the day. It was people in a self-regulating situation whereby they protected the claims of each other.

Roberts's infraction of the "claim law" brought the "claim regulators" from the "Muscatine slough" down on him forcing him to quit the premises, as it were. Roberts thought the entire proceeding arbitrary, which it was, but true frontier justice prevailed and the intruder returned to the Cedar County area and settled in what became Iowa Township in August of 1836. He thereby became the first settler west of the Cedar River and his daughter Eliza was probably the first white woman to cross the river.

Other than the "claim jumping" Robert G. Roberts was an upright citizen and was later elected to the House of Representatives of the first Iowa Territorial Legislature representing Cedar, Linn, Jones and Johnson Counties.

In fact he earned the nickname of "Old Cedar" for his legislative efforts to be sure that Cedar County was included in any proposed legislation important to it. The account given us is that Roberts was prone to fall asleep easily and one day he was in "his somniferous repose" when a bill came before the House requiring a vote. When he was awakened he stood up and sleepily inquired: "Mr. Speaker! Mr. Speaker! is Cedar in that 'ere bill? Because if it is in that 'ere bill, I goes for it."

Enos Nyce came to Cedar County on 20 May 1836, shortly after the Waltons arrived. With him came his wife and two children. He made a claim but sold it that fall to Luke Billopp and removed to the west bank of the Cedar near the west branch of the Wapsinonock.

Meanwhile David Walton prospered because he arrived in the county with a nest-egg, had a gift as a blacksmith and farmed. He was given the rank of colonel of militia in the Black Hawk War by Governor Dodge and was always Col. Walton. Nor had he lighted upon his claim without knowledge of the entire area. We saw him here in 1835. He had come with his 15-year old son, George, and together they had explored most of what became Cedar County. The land he chose was among the best.

In June of 1836 we saw Andrew Crawford and his family arrive in the county. Around the same time he did George McCoy and Stephen Toney came on the 10th of June.

Ben Halliday, John Halliday and Samuel Hulick followed. Others who came in the month of June 1836 were Harvey Hatton, C. C. Dodge, Abram Stebbins, Alanson Pope and Peter Crampton.

July 1836 was when Robert G. Roberts came with a wife and six children. Aaron Porter, also with a wife and six young ones, arrived in July of that year as did William Baker and James Poston after whom Poston's Grove was named. (We have found the named spelled both Poston and Posten.)

In August 1836 Joseph Olds came with John Jones and his stepson John Barr. Other August settlers were the Sterrett family consisting of a mother who became known as "Granny" Sterrett and her three sons, Robert, William and Hector.

HECTOR STERRETT
In his later years.

In October came Richard C. Knott, John Roper, David Barras, Solomon Knott, Reuben Long, W. A. Rigby, James and John Burnside, James Leverich and possibly Jacob Turner.

In November the Rev. Morten Baker staked a claim the previous May but did not occupy it with his family until the 15th instant. John Scott arrived that month as did William M. Knott whose claim to fame was the building of the Goose Creek schooner named "Sally Acker."

The claim of William M. Knott covered the area that is now occup-ied by the City of Tipton.

Robert Miller is the only recorded pioneer settler to arrive in December of 1836. Those early settlers usually arrived during the better seasons when getting settled was easier.

Others who came to the county in 1836 but whose time of arrival is not known were Joshua King, James W. Potts, Jesse Potts, Elisha Edwards, James W. Tallman, H. B. Burnup and Isaac Dickey. Tallman became the first sheriff of Cedar County.

WASHINGTON A. RIGBY
And Mrs. Rigby, in their later years.

By 1837 the beauty of the area and the rich land that was being broken saw a great influx of pioneer settlers to Cedar County.

Cedar County is one of those counties that takes a unique pride in its history and much of it has been perserved by those interested in it. A publication by the Cedar County Historical Society has pictured many early pioneer settlers. The pictures, of course, were taken in the pioneers' later years but the fact that they have been preserved and published is a tremendous compliment to the history-minded folk of Cedar County.

Among those who spearheaded some of the effort was this author's late friend, the Honorable A. L. Mensing, among many others.

Among those early pioneer settlers whose later images have been preserved by the camera are those whose pictures are here.

### MR. & MRS. G. W. PARKS
The Parks family arrived in what is now Linn Township on 10 June 1837. His name was probably George Washington Parks as most whose initials were "G. W." were so named then.

### WILLIAM MAXSON
Ebenezer Gray and William Maxson settled in the north part of Iowa Township. (It was in the Maxson home that John Brown planned his raid and drilled his men for the later attack upon Harper's Ferry in faroff Virginia.) For many generations both Gray and Maxson descendants lived in Cedar County and may still.

### PRIOR SCOTT
He settled in Pioneer Township and became a large landholder northeast of Mechanicsville. He married twice and sired 13 children. His descendants still live in the area.

### MR. & MRS. SAMUEL YULE
They arrived in Red Oak Township in 1837 and finally had 16 children.

### EBENEZER GRAY
Mr. Gray came to Iowa Township with William Maxson and settled there permanently in 1839.

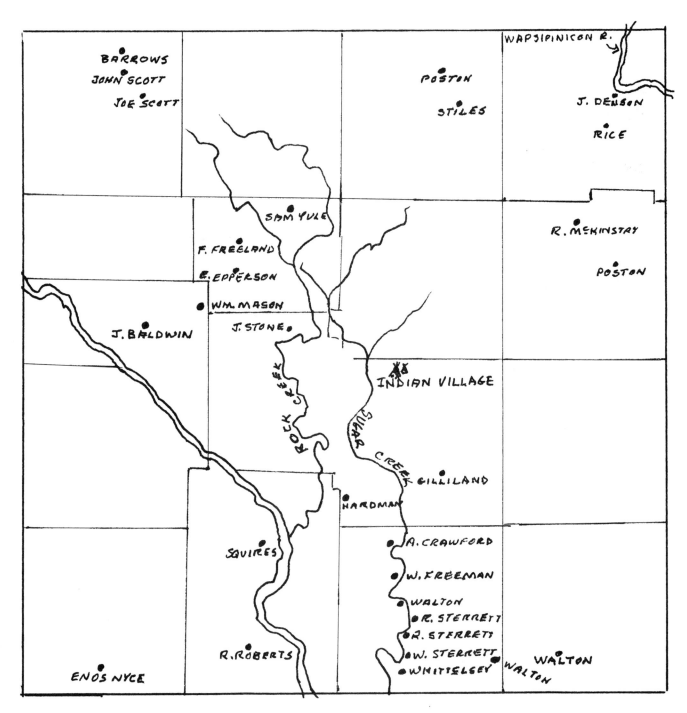

Sketch map of Cedar county after surveying in 1837 showing its irregular townships. They are much the same today; the county is not a dimeter quatrainthus. Note the Indian village located east of Sugar Creek in the center of the county. One of the Walton homesteads east of Sugar Creek would have been David's. Andrew Crawford's homestead is shown; he who froze his feet in Sugar Creek. Note also the location of the claims of other pioneer settlers about whom we've read. Three homesteads are located showing where "Granny" Sterrett's farmed their claims. Frontier legislator "Old Cedar" Roberts' home is at the bottom of the map. Many other names mentioned in the chapter are shown by the land they claimed.

# Chapter Twenty-Two
# LINN COUNTY

Linn County was created by the Wisconsin Territorial Legislature in 1837 from the large northeastern part of the Iowa lands that were, until then, Dubuque County. It was named for Lewis Field Linn who was a United States senator from Missouri. Senator Linn had been kindly disposed in his official functions toward the needs of the Wisconsin Territory and the area of Iowa in particular. He was therefore honored by having a county named for him.

When it was created it was an area of rich prairie, thickly wooded hills and transgressed by the Cedar River. A century and a half later Linn County boasts Iowa's second largest city and is the second largest county. Cedar Rapids is the largest commercial and industrial center located on the banks of the Cedar and takes an unusual pride in its growth and accomplishments.

William Abbe is considered by historians to have been the first settler in Linn County.

He was born in Connecticut on 19 April 1800 and married Olive Green in 1824 after which they became the parents of four children. Olive Abbe died in 1839 after settling in Iowa with her husband and living here about one year. In 1840 William Abbe married Mary Wolcott and to them

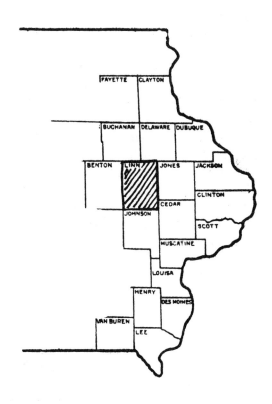

two sons were born when they lived near Marion. The sons were Augustus Wolcott Abbe and William Alden Abbe.

As early as the summer of 1836 William Abbe is supposed to have penetrated the area of Linn County even prior to its creation. He journeyed to Iowa from Elyria, Lorain County, Ohio, and came through Rock Island, Illinois. Abbe followed the

Red Cedar River, as it was known, upstream and explored the then wild and uninhabited lands as far northward as the area upon which the city of Mount Vernon now stands.

It was there that he found a site he liked and staked out a claim adjacent to a tiny rill that is still known as "Abbe's Creek." After establishing his claim, he returned to Ohio where his family had remained.

In Ohio he assembled his small family, gathered the belongings they chose to take and started toward Iowa. That was in the winter of 1837, probably in February or March. According to the record they crossed the Mississippi when it was yet frozen so solid that they could do so easily. Then they headed toward the staked-out land in Linn County.

It is reckoned that William Abbe built the first home in Linn County that April of 1837. It was 12 x 14 feet in area and covered with birch bark. It had a dirt floor as did most pioneer log cabins.

The rugged wilderness area was also the home of many Indians who dressed in animal skins, lived in tepees, rode their ponies, wore blankets, carried guns when they could obtain them and "took all they could from the government." Their way of life was rapidly changing as the white man came to settle in Iowa and Linn County.

William Abbe cleared some of his land and planted a crop that year of 1837 and, with his own resourcefulness and what was available to him, began a homestead. By the autumn of 1837 he was established to the extent that he was ready to build a larger and better home for his family. The next one was a large, double log house with three rooms and an upstairs which could be reached by the use of a wooden ladder, also of smaller logs.

The Abbe family would remain there for five years enjoying the frontier family life, getting along with thier Indian neighbors, clearing more and more land and generally improving their lot. Soon new neighbors settled closer and closer to them while their home was an early stopping-off point for pioneers heading farther westward. After that five years was up they moved to a 300 acre farm near Marion.

Many years later Susan Abbe who was by then Mrs. John Shields recalled the early intimacy of the white children with the Indian children. She recalled that they were all kind to her and that they were her first playmates. Mrs. Shields remembered their first winter in Iowa, that of 1837-38: "There were no white people here for a long time after we came here." She was seven at the time. Mrs. Shields, later of Vinton in Benton County, recalled Robert Ellis and Asher Edgerton.

William Abbe was a justice of the peace for a time and history had it that he assumed much responsibility for establishing and keeping the first "law and order" in Linn County.

Susan Abbe Shields later recalled how her father had once, for whatever reason, taken charge of two horse thieves and chained them together in one of the rooms of their home until they could be brought to trial.

(She also remembered that the first time she saw Marion there were but two houses and a jail---obviously after it had become the county seat.)

William Abbe was a member of the legislature when it decided to locate the capital at Iowa City. He was also a Mason and became the first Master of the Lodge early established at Marion.

Among his other entrepreneurial activities, William Abbe was evidently something of a "frontier banker" as we learn that he always had ready money with which he made loans. Along with Robert Ellis he became an agent for the government especially in supplying food and other goods to the Winnebago Indians at Fort Atkinson far north in the area that would eventually become Winneshiek County but which was at the time Fayette County. The distance between Marion and Fort Atkinson would have been considerable in the late 1830s.

In the winter of 1838-39 an act **was passed by the legislature to organize the County of Linn. The**

county had already been created and was a part of the map. But for taxation and judicial purposes it was reportedly "attached" to Johnson County. The legilslative act that provided for the organization of Linn County called for it to be so from the date of 10 June 1839.

Richard Knott, Lyman Dillon and Benjamin Nye were appointed the commissioners to "locate the seat of justice." The new commissioners met at the home of William Abbe on the first Monday in March.

When they met in the Abbe home Knott, Dillon and Nye agreed to establish the first Linn County "seat of justice" at Marion.

The first judicial records were kept in and for Linn County dated 26 October 1840.

As William Abbe was the first settler in Linn County and built the first home, it was natural that others would soon follow.

The first structure built in Cedar Rapids, the future city, was probably Shepherd's Tavern which was erected of logs on the site that is now the YMCA.

The second structure built on the site of the future Cedar Rapids was, or is said to have been, "Astor House," erected in 1839.

As the county gathered some settlers and some sizeable population growth began, the commissioners created three voting precincts which were Abbe's home at Sugar Grove, one in Marion and another at Michael Green's residence.

The commissioners appointed Ross McCloud as county surveyor and public lands within Linn County proper were not advertised for sale until January of 1840.

In the "Guide, Gazeteer and Directory" of the Dubuque and Sioux City Railroad, published in Dubuque in 1868, Railey and Wolfe write of Cedar Rapids: "The first settlement was in the year 1838 by William Stone, who erected a log cabin on the bank of the river in the rear of No. 1 Commercial Street. The same year Osgood Shepherd, a supposed leader of a band of outlaws, jumped Stone's claim and took possession of the cabin and held it until the year 1841........."

Apparently there is some dispute about who was first to come and who was first to build among the early pioneer settlers but that is usual in many counties.

Ed Crow, C. C. Haskins and others built temporary cabins and lived within the geographic limits of Linn County in its very early years.

John Henry built a small store which was not much more than a log cabin on and facing the river in "the squatter town of Westport" in 1838. It was 14 x 18' in size. Westport was about where the city of Ely is today but in its early years it was a larger settlement than Marion. It was also the site of the first election in the county according to historian Harold Ewoldt of Cedar Rapids.

The Shepherd Tavern mentioned earlier was not much more than a crude log cabin nor did it pretend to be. It evidently served its purpose.

But John Young's house, another crude log structure was given---by John Young himself!---

the illustrious name of "The Astor House" after the famous and elaborate real Astor House in New York City. Young's Astor House was Linn County's first hotel and it can be stated that rooms were added to it which made it literally a frontier hotel. "The Astor House" would have stood in the area of First Street and Fourth Avenue in today's Cedar Rapids.

G. R. Carroll later recalled the first log cabin erected by his father, Isaac Carroll, in 1839 and reported that it took about ten days to erect an ordinary log cabin.

From the pursuits of those early settlers Linn County and Cedar Rapids grew to the magnificent area it is today. An "inland county," Linn grew rapidly once it got its start. The reason for its early growth was that it was on the Cedar River which was once a great artery of commerce and trade in a day when river traffic afforded a community that advantage.

From 1838 the area grew and its future history and accomplishments brought it more renown as time went on.....and, as we shall see.

# Ernest Kosek of Linn County
# --- A part of history for
# over half a century......

For well over half a century the name of Ernest Kosek has been known not only in Linn County but throughout the state of Iowa and in national circles.

Sometimes in his quiet and persuasive manner he has been an influence upon historical trends and events from Cedar Rapids and Linn County in subtle but far-reaching ways. Other times as a public figure and a state official the name and influence of Ernest Kosek has come to the fore. His place in the history of Linn County and the State of Iowa is secure.

His activities have taken him from sitting on the Board of Education for Cedar Rapids to working with Mrs. Winthrop Rockefeller in national mental health activities. He is descended from the Czech immigrants who located in Cedar Rapids and Linn County and, like them, has made tremendous contributions to the culture, business, politics and life of that city and county.

Over the years, "Ernie," as he is popularly known, might have been sitting at the counter in the old Woolworth coffee shop next to the Merchants National Bank building on one morning and and visiting with the president of the F. W. Woolworth Company in New York City the next morning............or rubbing elbows with a President of the United States!

Ernie Kosek's vast experiences in life or his various influences on

Governor Terry Branstad, who wrote a forward to this book of history, is shown above with former Senator Kosek at a 1987 reception the two attended.

events may not have all been well known or well publicized. But his presence has always been known in circles far beyond his home city and his input into state and national events has been very real. Probably not obvious to all, but very real.

321

Ernest Kosek was born in Cedar Rapids, Linn County, Iowa, on 13 March 1907, the youngest son of the C. K. Koseks, Czech immigrants who ran a bakery.

The future Iowa lawmaker was graduated from Washington High School, attended Coe College and was graduated from the University of Iowa with the degree of bachelor of science in commercial engineering. In 1931 he was commissioned an officer in the engineer corps of the U. S. Army. That same year he entered the army in the flying cadets.

He entered the investment banking business in Cedar Rapids in 1932 and in 1934 organized Ernest Kosek and Company which eventually became the city's oldest and largest investment banking firm.

Kosek brothers Chuck and George are shown above during World War I. They served in the Rainbow Division commanded by then Brig. Gen. Douglas MacArthur.

The C. K. Kosek Bakery in Cedar Rapids, Linn County, Iowa, in 1906. It was in this building, in the upstairs residence, where Ernest Kosek and his older brothers, Charles, George and Otto, and sister Rose were born. The area where the bakery was is now known as "Czech Village." Ernest Kosek has long been a student of Cedar Rapids and Linn County history, especially that of the area's Czech culture. Sen. Kosek's views and recollections have recently been taped for posterity.

He married Vlasta Victoria Vondracek and to them were born two daughters and a son. They were Ann Jeanette who died in 1971, Karen and Ernest George who is now associated with his father in business.

Ernie Kosek's first venture into "politics" was when he ran for and was elected to the Cedar Rapids School Board in 1938. He served in that office until 1943 when he resigned to entered the United States Navy during World War II. His unique experiences in the business and financial world took him into similar work during his navy career for he was sent immediately to New York City where he became assistant disbursing officer for the Third Naval District there. While his wishes were for combat duty on one of the Navy's battleships his desires were turned down and the service kept him busy in his own field.

(Some years later Ernest Kosek was made an honorary admiral.)

When World War II was over he returned home to his family and Cedar Rapids where he continued his investment banking business and was elected to the Linn County School Board. Ernest Kosek eventually served as president of the Linn

Home on leave from the Navy during World War II, Ernie Kosek is shown above with daughters Karen and Ann Jeanette. Young Ernie was not born.

Former Senator and Mrs. Kosek are shown below at the Menger Hotel in San Antonio, Texas, where in 1986 they joined with others to observe the 55th anniversary of the Flying Cadets. Many who attended, and who had remained in the military, were generals.

County Board of Education as well as president of other groups and associations of which he was a part. He was president of the Iowa Investment Bankers, the Iowa Association for Mental Health and the Legislative "52" Club.

In business he has served on several boards of directors to include the local Roosevelt Hotel in Cedar Rapids, Iowa Business Investment Corporation and Iowa Fund, Inc.

The Koseks are members of the Presbyterian church and Ernie is a 32nd degree Mason and a Shriner. He is also a member of the American Legion, Kiwanis, the Chamber of Commerce, Odd Fellows, Farm Bureau, "T" Mens Club, Alpha Kappa Psi and Sokols. He was formerly very active in the Western Bohemian Fraternal Association.

Ernest Kosek entered politics on a larger scale after serving many years on the Cedar Rapids and the Linn County boards of education.

In 1948 he ran for and was elected to the Iowa House of Represenatives where he served with distinction for many years. He was once considered for Speaker of the House. He served on many legislative committees and subcommittees and was chairman of several of them. The legislature always made use of Kosek's financial genius and he is turn kept a close eye on the public treasury always working for efficiency in government.

State Rep. Kosek's service to the taxpayers of Linn County and Iowa won him re-election time after time to the extent that he served six consecutive terms in the Iowa House of Representatives.

Later he was elected to the Senate of the State of Iowa where he served with further excellence. Sen. Kosek was often mentioned in Republican circles for higher offices such as Governor or Lieutenant Governor but he never chose to seek them.

Kosek Avenue in Fairfax, Linn County, Iowa, is named in honor of the former senator.

Senator Kosek is pictured above in the Chair of the Iowa Senate. The lieutenant governor is president of the Senate but often other senators are chosen to preside.

During his 12 years in the Iowa House of Representatives, Rep. Kosek of Linn County worked with experts to try to make government more efficient and to save taxpayers dollars. Over 90% of the bills offered by Kosek became law. He served as chairman of the Cities and Towns Committee of the Iowa House. His expertise in the world of finance was invaluable to the Iowa legislature.

Ernest Kosek served a total of 23 years in civic work dedicating himself to education. He was for five years a member of the Cedar Rapids School Board resigning as noted to enter Naval service in World War II. He later served 18 years on the Linn County Board of Education during which he also served some years as its president.

As a member of the Iowa House of Representatives Ernest Kosek is shown at right shaking hands with President Dwight D. Eisenhower. The occasion was the National Corn Picking Contest held near Cedar Rapids in 1958. The author of this volume of history was also there and later wrote the nation's only complete biography about Mamie Doud Eisenhower. (I REMEMBER MAMIE by Donald L. Kimball, 1981.)

IN MILITARY SERVICE — Kosek served his country in the Navy during World War II. Prior to that time he had also seen service in the Army Air Corps and, the Army Engineers.

The Kosek home for 38 years is perched majestically upon a hill overlooking Indian Creek. It was built by Arthur Poe of Quaker Oats in 1917 and later owned by R. S. Sinclair and then Cedar Rapids capitalist Sutherland Dows. John Hamilton married a Spanish countess and they resided there until she persuaded her husband to buy "Lakeside" east of Marion. Hamilton then sold the the 18-room to Ernest Kosek. It was in and from this beautiful mansion that Senator Kosek conducted both political and financial affairs of historical note.

IN VOLUNTEER WORK — Immediate Past President of the Iowa Association for Mental Health, Kosek also served as a director and a member of the Legislative and Executive Committees of the National Association for Mental Health. The Kosek package of mental health bills saves Iowans millions of dollars . . . restores thousands of citizens to useful, happy lives.

# Clair Lensing --- An Iowa Success Story From Farm Boy to President of the Iowa Bankers Assocation

Iowa has always been called a land of opportunity and that "pioneer spirit" to which we referred in Chapter Six has remained to this day in the hearts and minds of most Iowans. It was endowed in Clair J. Lensing and it has served him, and Iowa, very well over the years.

Clair Lensing was born in Chickasaw County a hundred years after those first pioneer settlers forded the mighty Mississippi. In the past half century Clair Lensing has gone from feeding the animals on the farm, gathering eggs and harvesting corn to walking in the councils of the mighty in Des Moines and Washington, D. C. where he fights for the financial interests of Iowa's farmers, its small towns and the rural banking industry.

From farm boy to banker, from a rural neighborhood to becoming president of the Iowa Bankers Association, the Lensing story is an Iowa success story.

His job as president of the Iowa bankers will take Lensing away quite often. He has already been to Washington more than once. The job will require frequent trips to the IBA offices in Des Moines and maybe a half dozen more trips to Washington for various reasons to include lobbying. Since September of 1987 Clair Lensing has been exercising his high office.

He is president of the Farmers State Bank in Marion and the major stockholder in banks at Hazleton, Hawkeye and Maynard.

He has appointed a special IBA task force to decide the best moves to make plans and to implement them, seeking more effective organization for the banking industry.

He was born 1 September 1934 and when he went into banking didn't really intend to make a career of it. He attended the University of Iowa for "two short years," he says and then received an offer that turned him into a banker.

He has attended the Agricultural Credit School at Ames, the Illinois School of Banking and the Graduate School of Banking, Wisconsin.

# Chapter Twenty-Three
# FAYETTE COUNTY

Fayette County was one of the several counties created by the Wisconsin Territorial Legislature which met in Burlington, the temporary capital, in November of 1837. Des Moines County (Old Des Moines County) had been divided into several counties the year before. The creation of Fayette County was part of the division of (Old) Dubuque County.

When that Territorial Legislature created Fayette County the northern and western boundaries did not exist as they do today. The county went on and on forever, it seemed.

The county was named after Gilbert du Motier, the Marquis d'LaFayette, a Frenchman who had served with General George Washington in the War for American Independence. (At Washington's home, Mount Vernon in Virginia, one can still see the key to the Bastille given to Washington by LaFayette as a gesture recalling their close friendship.)

Fayette County extended northward to the Canadian border, the British dominions, to include all the lands west of the Mississippi River to its source and then to Canada; the western boundaries extended

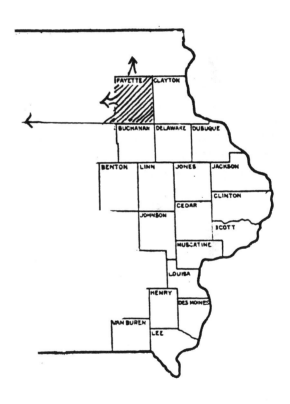

westward until they bordered upon the Missouri and the White Earth Rivers in North and South Dakota, a vast area, indeed, but all merely drawn on a map. The two northern tiers of Iowa counties as they are known to us today were also part of Fayette County, the District of Iowa, Territory of Wisconsin.

# Fayette County . . . . . . .
## *the largest county ever*

The above map shows Fayette County as it originally was. It was the largest county unit ever created in the history of world; that is, as counties go. Counties, as such, go way back to mediaeval times when they were, of course, ruled by counts. Fayette County had no population other than Indians when this map showed its existence. The new and largest county took up most of the two northern tiers of Iowa counties as we know them, all of Minnesota west of the Mississippi River to its source and to the Canadian border and a good portion of North and South Dakota east of the Missouri and White Earth Rivers. The Fayette County of that day was assigned to Clayton County for judicial and taxation purposes and the county seat of Clayton County was Prairie La Porte, now Guttenberg. While Fayette County as it is shown above was never more than a "paper county," laid out---created---but never organized.

We don't know who the first white man was who set foot on the soil of Fayette County before others did. It was probably James Langworthy who some years before employed a young Indian as guide and explored Jones and Delaware counties and journeyed north to the Turkey River.

In 1837 Chancy Edson and William Grant brought a party of workmen from Clayton County to the mouth of Otter Creek where they started to build a dam with the probable intention of opening a mill. the site they selected was at the place where John Sutter later built a home for his family.

The area was at the time part of the area called the Neutral Ground which was reserved for the Winnebago Indians and was off-limits to white men. It is speculated whether or not they realized this but assumptions are they did. When the local Indians learned of their activities they complained to the Indian agent who caused the white men to leave. The Indians then burned the half-built dam and also the log shelter the men had hastily erected. (Read more details of this event in Chapter XVIII, Clayton County.)

Thus Fayette County was not only on the "frontier" but perhaps a bit beyond it in 1838. What other white folk meandered into or out of the area we do not know. What we do know is that it would be 1840 before the first permanent white settler would make a claim, cut the logs and build the first cabin in Fayette County. that would be Franklin Wilcox whom we would find in Illinois in 1838 perhaps thinking about a westward migration with his family and a brother, Nathaniel.

## John Falb & Sons

"OLD RELIABLE"
Established in 1909
One of the oldest dealerships
in the entire United States
A History of Our Own . . . . .

CHEVROLET & BUICK

OVER THE YEARS Fayette County would take its place among the growing and developing areas of the State. It would relinquish its (paper) vastness to the borders it has today. Congressmen, others officials and outstanding people to include a governor for the State would emerge from Fayette County.

A noble and venerable institution of higher learning would find its roots there also. Upper Iowa University would educate and turn out into the world many leaders in all fields, even to include a Nobel Prize winner, and a famous football coach.

WE'RE PROUD OF OUR HISTORY

PRESCRIPTIONS
Registered Pharmacist
Always ready to help YOU

# Union Drug
"In the Mall"
WEST UNION, IOWA

WE TAKE PRIDE IN
THE HISTORY OF FAYETTE COUNTY

WE HAVE A PROUD
HISTORY OF SERVICE
TO OUR MANY CUSTOMERS

# West Union Co-Op
WEST UNION, IOWA

# OUT OF THE MIDWEST: A portrait
## 562-page Volume published by volunteers; some still available

As their Bicentennial project the Fayette County Helpers Club and Historical Society published a huge 562-page book entitled "OUT OF THE MIDWEST: A Portrait" all about Fayette County, Iowa. That was in 1976.

The tome was edited by Helen Moeller and the "Presentation," or introduction, was written by Mrs. John W. (Frances) Graham, prominent Fayette County historian. Assisting with the work were Mona Ladwig and Eleanor Baird who operate the county's headquarters and museum in West Union. There was input by many, many others too numerous to mention. Copies of the large book are still available. (See advertisement below.)

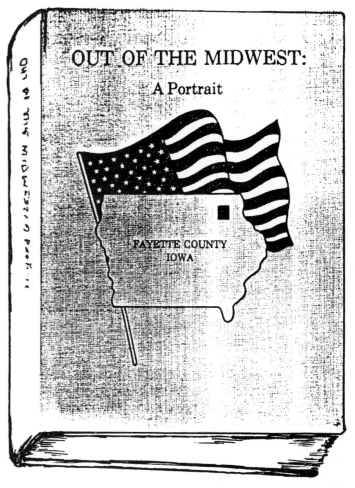

Actual size of the book is 8" x 11 1/4" and is nearly 1 1/2 inches thick containing its 562 pages.

====================================================

## To order.....
## OUT OF THE MIDWEST: A Portrait

Send $ 25.00 to the address below
and OUT OF THE MIDWEST: A Portrait
will be sent to you postpaid.
SEND TO:

Fayette County Historical Society
100 North Walnut
West Union, Iowa 52175

# Dynamic young president brings
# new life to ancient university

Upper Iowa University is 131 years old having been founded in 1857. Like all small colleges it has had its ups and downs over its century plus of existence.

In 1983 when Dr. James Rocheleau was elected to take the helm of the ancient university he brought with him a vigor and a forsight not seen in other Iowa college leaders. When he took over he wasted no time determining directions and re-establishing priorities.

Today, 1987, as a direct result of his leadership and actions Upper Iowa University is "in the black," on a sound financial basis, with a reorganized curriculum, a dedicated student body, the support of its alumni, a professional faculty and a future looking very bright.

Dr. Rocheleau was reared in Seattle, Washington, and after high school served in the U. S. Army where he was graduated from the Defense Language Institute and became a Russian translator in Berlin, Germany.

**DR. JAMES ROCHELEAU**
**President, Upper Iowa University**

Following his military service he returned to Washington state and worked as an account executive for a major newspaper in Spokane. From there he became a sales representative for RJR Nabisco and then decided to pursue a career in higher education.

He then entered the University of Idaho and was graduated with a B.A. and M.A. degrees in history, political science and the Russian language. He went on to receive a Ph.D. in

## *Speedy*
### MANUFACTURING DIVISION

Manufacturers of
FARM MACHINERY

UNITED FARM TOOLS, Inc.
Oelwein, Fayette County, Iowa

TRUSTWORTHY HARDWARE
"In the Mall"
Corner Hwys 18 & 150
West Union, Iowa          422-5646

# Almost 150 years of tomorrows

photo by Jerry Wadian

# Upper Iowa University
### Fayette, Iowa
## The right choice since 1857

Russian history, language and literature from Washington State University.

Pursuing his goal of becoming a college professor, Dr. Rocheleau was hired as an instructor at Buena Vista College at Sorm Lake, Iowa, being promoted later to assistant professor of history. When that college began an off-campus center for non-traditional students in Council Bluffs, Iowa, Dr. Rocheleau was chosen to be director of the program. He later became chief executive director for the Council Bluffs campus and dean of continuing education at Buena Vista College.

In 1984 Dr. Rocheleau became president of Upper Iowa University in Fayette and brought to the position a new vision, personal vigor, enthusiasm, innovation and a goal of guiding the ancient institution to a new and higher level of excellence.

Since becoming president Dr. Rocheleau has seen the student body more than double. Income to the private institution has increased by $1.7 million and annual giving has increased by 75% a year. Faculty raises have averaged an annual 45% increase and those for staff in excess of 25%.

Dr. Rocheleau currently serves as a consultant for the North Central Association accrediting agency and provides assistance to colleges establishing continuing education programs. He has served on several state education study committees and in September of 1987 accompanied U. S. Senator Charles E. Grassley, Iowa's senior senator, on a trade mission to South Korea, a country he has frequently visited.

Dr. Rocheleau and his wife, Meg, enjoy traveling and pursue a continued interest in the development of young people.

DAVE WHITE, president of LYA Industries, is a local garage owner who has brought outside business to his hometown. LYA Industries sells adjustable basketball equipment to school, colleges and other institutions all over America. He is pictures above with son, Seth, and his daughter, Martha. He is originally from Worthington.

WE SERVE A HISTORIC AREA
. . . . . . and are proud to do so.

BUMPER - TO - BUMPER STATIONS
General Petroleum Products

# Fauser Oil Co., Inc.
ELGIN, IOWA

We have a long history of
SERVING YOU
We're proud of our area's history
BOSTROM'S SUPER-VALU
West Union, Iowa

# Today.........
## ...... *in Fayette County*

# Frank Meighan pushes the "AA" Program in Northeast Iowa

Francis Leo Meighan is a highly decorated veteran of World War II; he was a "hero" then and he is a "hero" today.

In World War II he gave of himself to serve his country in fighting Hitler's Nazi control over Europe. In the allied effort to liberate France from the Nazi horrors, the tank upon which he was riding following the invasion of Europe was shelled and blown up under him.

Frank Meighan was nearly killed; he was severely wounded and spent over a year in a body cast at army hospitals in England and several places in America. Today he still has a bullet in his right arm testify-to the wounds he received. You can feel it, should you choose to do so.

Other than the Bronze Star Medal and the Purple Heart, he won other military decorations. But the wounds are the constant reminders of the ordeal he suffered fighting in France during the Second World War. The scars and wounds, however, are not the only reminders he has of his long-suffering and the results of it.

Like many veterans with the sordid experiences of war behind them, he lapsed into alcoholism which amounted to a "bout with the bottle" for several years.

In 1952 he got "sick and tired of being sick and tired" and joined the ranks of Alcoholics Anonymous.

He has been sober ever since and in November of 1988 he can boast of 36 years of continuous sobriety.

Frank Meighan makes no bones about his experiences nor is there anything "anonymous" about his dedication to "AA" and the principles it espouses. For, from the beginning, he has entered into the organization's work with all his heart.

Frank Meighan, camera-shy, stands in front of his home; those seeking his help cannot miss the name, address and the Irish shamrocks. He is the son of Jim Meighan pictured in the Chapter XVI, Clinton County. His telephone number is (319) 425-4056.

# TRULY ADJUSTABLE BASKETBALL GOALS

SHORT OR TALL — CAN SUCCEED AT BASKETBALL
Safe and Dependable - Any adult or child can easily adjust the unit up or down. Can be adjusted in seconds by means of a <u>long removable hand crank.</u>

## MODEL 150S390

## MODEL 280 ADJUSTABLE

Install on ceiling mounted swing down and other types of installations found in modern gymnasiums.

Manufactured under one or more of the following patents: 3,765,676; 4,395,040.

## Model 650 Portable
Many times the existing backboard can be installed on a newly purchased Adjusting Frame.

**WALL INSTALLATION**                    **OUTSIDE POLE**

Manufactured to Institutional Standards by
# LYA Industries, Inc.
ADJUSTABLE BASKETBALL GOALS
119 South Main Street – P. O. Box 506 – Fayette, Iowa 52142
Telephone (319) 425 - 4014

# Preserving the history . . . . .
### . . . . . of Fayette County

JAMES I. MEIGHAN, a native of Clinton County (See Chapter XVI, page 266), is shown above in his garden. He was born in 1886 when Grover Cleveland was president the first time. Until the last year he went deer hunting annually. The patriarch of a large family he is visited regularly by several generations of his offspring. He was born in Clinton County, farmed there and in Bremer and Allamakee Counties and is now a resident of Fayette County. He is considering retiring or "slowing down a bit."

PRESERVING THE HISTORY OF FAYETTE COUNTY are Mona Ladwig, left, and Eleanor Baird. They operate the Fayette County Historical Museum at the southeast corner across from the court house in West Union. Both work for no wages and come to work daily in the large, old building to preserve the history of their county. Eleanor Baird is a granddaughter of Lucien L. Ainsworth of West Union who served in the Congress of the United States around a century ago.

KISSIN' COUSINS - Mary E. Kimball (Mrs. Donald L.), is pictured at right chatting with a cousin who landed a federal government job in 1980. President Reagan once worked in Davenport, Scott County, and in Des Moines, Polk County. He has many Iowa cousins who include Mabel Kuper and Bessie McNulty of Oelwein, Frank H. Moore, Jr., of Cresco and Ruth Lentzkow, formerly of Independence.

# Chapter Twenty-Four
# BENTON & BUCHANAN

Benton and Buchanan Counties were two of the original counties. They were carved out of old Dubuque County which consisted in its ancient form of all the northern half of Iowa and including those wilderness areas yet hardly imagined of most of Minnesota and the eastern parts of North and South Dakota.

This volume takes the history of Iowa up to its becoming a territory in 1838. The rich soil that lay under the woods and prairie grasses of Benton and Buchanan Counties was to remain unbroken for a few years yet; i.e. a few years after Iowa became a Territory.

Unlike Dubuque, Des Moines, Lee, Scott, Clayton, Muscatine, Henry and some of the others, very little happened in Benton and Buchanan Counties. Yet before 1838 they were, indeed, counties. On the map. They were "paper" counties, if you please.

Remember, also, that there was a difference in a county being "created" and a county being populated and organized. New counties or uninhabited counties were always attached to their eastern neighbor counties for governmental reasons, mainly taxation and judicial.

The Cedar River flows south and easterly bisecting Benton County. Its rich soil would be turned

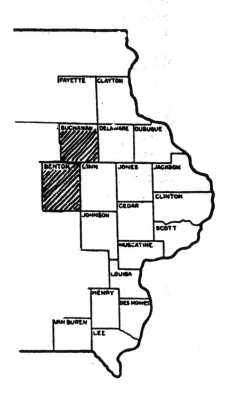

by settlers but the first wouldn't arrive until the spring of 1839. We'll meet Benton County's first settlers in Volume Two, "The Territory of Iowa."

Buchanan County was seemingly as far "westward" as Benton whose settlers came from or through Linn County. Buchanan's came from or through its sister county to the east, Delaware County.

And therein lies another tale

337

of unique history. Remember William and Elizabeth Bennett who were the first settlers in Delaware County? And recall Elizabeth's father coming to the county? William Bennett decided his in-laws were too close by then and in 1842 he and Elizabeth removed to Buchanan County. To what is now Quasqueton. He built a cabin on the east shore of the Wapsipinicon river.

William Bennett thereby became the first pioneer settler in Buchanan County. But, he also had that distinction in Delaware County. A first, perhaps?

## BENTON COUNTY HISTORICAL SOCIETY PUBLISHING NEW COUNTY HISTORY

The Benton County Historical Soceity is publishing a unique new history book for the county. Suggesting that residents "leave your thumbprint in time . . . if you don't, who will" the group asked everyone's cooperation in the project.

The History Book Committee is chaired by Yvonne Fischer on the overall project; Allegra Schueler and Ila Jean Krug are chairpersons for the Topical Committee; Margie Wyckoff is chairperson of genealogy; Alberta Reifenstahl is chairperson of publicity and promotion and Richard Hadley is the banker.

All Benton County residents were asked to send in their family histories, genealogies and pictures.

Copies of the gigantic book may be obtained for $ 49.95 plus $2 Iowa sales tax and $4 postage and handling. Total $ 55.95. Send orders to:

Benton County History Book
P. O. Box 147
Vinton, IOWA 52349

BUCHANAN COUNTY RESIDENTS TODAY of this 1951 graduating class of the (then) Stanley High School, located on the Buchanan-Fayette County line are identified. Front row, far left, Delores (Martin) Gerstenberger of Hazleton; third from left, Sharon (Duckett) Bearbower of Brandon; far right, front row, Mary Ann (Recker) Ryan of Fairbank. In the back row standing, third from left, La Verne Lentz of Aurora. This is a picture of the cast of the senior play, "STARDUST," directed by Mr. Arvid K. Stock, far right.

bettendorf public library
and information center

# Chapter Twenty-Five
# WASHINGTON & KEOKUK

Washington County probably bears the most noble name in the whole of American history, that of the Father of our Country.

Nor was Washington its original name. Instead of the Father of our Country, the area that became Washington County was once named Slaughter County. It didn't bear that name for long and the legislature changed it to Washington.

The county is inland but not far from the Mississippi River with only Louisa County between it and the mighty river. Therefore, it was destined to be one of the first inland counties to attract the early pioneer settlers. Yet in the period with which we deal in this volume, i.e. up to 1838, no great population settled there. Henry County, on its southern border, was filling with immigrants more rapidly. Louisa to its east and on the river didn't have all that many by 1838 possibly for lack of the better harbors. Johnson County lies to its north and wasn't created until late 1837 and it was expected to be the site of a "more central" state capital.

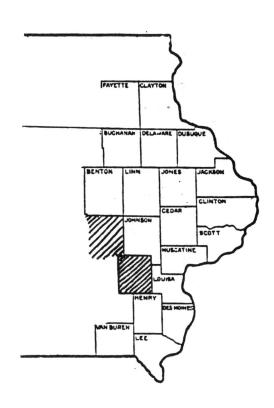

Adam Ritchie was the first permanent white pioneer settler in Washington County having arrived in the spring of 1836.

With Ritchie came his two brothers, Matthew and Thomas, and a man named Humphrey. Whether that was his first or last name, we do not know.    Ritchie and his group crossed the Mississippi River at a time when it was solid ice.

He came as far inland as what was to become Slaughter County and built a cabin of logs on the north side of Crooked Creek.

Later in 1836 he returned to Illinois, in May we are told, and stayed a while. When he returned he brought with him his 15-year old son, Matthew and a 13-year old daughter named Sarah.   Adam Ritchie planted the first corn by a white man in the county in 1836.

Adam Ritchie returned to Illinois late in the summer of 1836 and when he returned he brought with him the remainder of his family.   Earlier that year, in the spring of '36, he had found another settlement and thus it was not so difficult to leave his crops to return and bring back his family.      In the

pioneer family of the 1830s everyone in a family worked and it was logical to bring a 13-year old girl back who could work in the house and prepare the meals, sew and tend the garden. The boy of 15 would have been nearly grown and he would have shared in the men's chores such as breaking ground, tending the crops of grain, caring for livestock and probably cutting trees. And hunting, too!

The other group of early pioneer settlers found not far a way by Ritchie was headed by Richard Moore, the second white settler in Washington (Slaughter) County.   With Moore were two sons of his own; Amos and Thaddeus Moore and a son-in-law of Richard, John C. Maulsby.

After getting somewhat established Richard Moore returned to Illinois and came back with John Mosteller, George Baxter and William Hunter. Those men, too, became early pioneer settlers and they staked out claims on which they could start farming just southeast of the Moore settlement.

In the fall of 1836 one Thomas Baker settled close to the Indian line which was in the future county's area and it wasn't long before the Indians were complaining about Moore's livestock.   Their complaints continued and in April of 1837 Chief Wapello himself, accompanied by some braves, called at Baker's cabin and let it be known that he and his tribe wanted Baker's cattle removed forthwith.   Baker expressed his reluctance and nothing was done.

After demanding that Baker get rid of his cattle and his subsequent refusal, the Indians descended upon Baker's cabin the following day and drove him off the place and burned his buildings.

A week later the Indians made similar demands upon Richard Moore who couldn't seem to reason with them, so he took his family and left his new farm. Mr. and Mrs. John Maulsby thereupon left the settlement and moved to Henry County to the south where there was a larger population, fewer Indians and where they felt safer.

The vaguely outlined county was established by the Wisconsin Territorial Legislature and named Slaughter County. Its name would remain that until after Iowa itself became a Territory.

In 1837 new settlers came and established themselves in Oregon Township. They were David Gamble and his family and Oliver Sweet.

Also in 1837 Silas Washburne came and started a new settlement at Brighton. He was soon joined there, a few months later we are told, by Morgan Hart. Coming to join them in 1838 were S. Seneca Beach and John Beers.

Thus Slaughter County was being settled. It took some time and doing and some boundary disputes to settle into becoming the Washington County we know today. There is the story of the lost townships with

which we'll deal in detail in Volume Two. Iowa, meaning the land west of the Mississippi that was part of the Territory of Wisconsin in 1836, became a Territory in its own right by an Act of the Congress. When it did the Territorial Legislature acted and Slaughter County became Washington County on 25 January 1839.

From then on it began to grow and its history will become more colorful and have new life as we will see in Volume Two.

Keokuk County was one of the later of the earliest counties created and the most inland of them all. Being farther inland it was, of course, a later one to attract settlers.

And, of course, Keokuk County was named after Chief Keokuk about whom we've read so much in earlier chapters.

Keokuk County was attached to Johnson County for judicial purposes and wasn't organized as a county until several years later.

The two counties south and west of Johnson County, Washington and Keokuk, were little more than wilderness in 1838 as we have seen.

When Adam Ritchie and Richard Moore came to the county in 1836, huge flocks of wild turkeys such as these shown at the left abounded. They were hunted for food by the early pioneer settlers but never became extinct. The wild turkey lived all over eastern Iowa.

Cabins like the one above were built on the rich prairie soils of Washington and Keokuk Counties. There was plenty of timber in those counties although most of it, of course, was situated along the rivers and streams. The homestead started with a shelter, cropland and fences.

ANCIENT MAP of the new Territory of Iowa the date of which we do not know exactly. Note that the British Possessions are still "Brittish." The map appears to be quite accurate and would have to be 1838 or thereafter. Note that the Neutral Ground in northeast Iowa is identified but that was created in 1830. Somewhere in that vast wilderness shown in between the Missouri and the Mississippi Rivers are Washington and Keokuk Counties. Keokuk was to be a dimeter quatrainthus or a four townships by four townships county and Washington would be different.

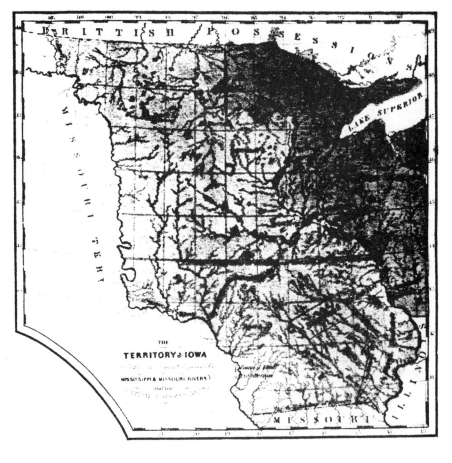

# Chapter Twenty-Six
# JOHNSON COUNTY

Johnson County was created by an Act of the Wisconsin Territorial Legislature which was approved on 21 December 1837.

Johnson County was the last of the original nineteen counties created prior to Iowa coming into its own as a Territory. The act which created Johnson County was passed at Burlington, Des Moines County, Iowa. As we have noted, when a county is created it is not necessarily organized.

Johnson County was later organized by enactment of the legislature again meeting at Burlington in June of 1838 to date from 3 July 1838. Iowa was to become a Territory on 4 July 1838.

(Upon being appointed governor of the new Territory of Iowa by President Van Buren, Robert Lucas, a former governor of Ohio, established the seat of government at Burlington in Des Moines County.)

Burlington had served as the capital for a time of the Territory of Wisconsin while a permanent capital was being created in Wisconsin proper. But Burlington was on the Mississippi River and on the eastern boundary of what was envisioned to become a state that would extend much farther westward, probably to the Missouri River. Therefore, it was the thinking of early Iowa leaders that a capital should be more centrally located.

It was also the thinking of the first Territorial Legislature that the

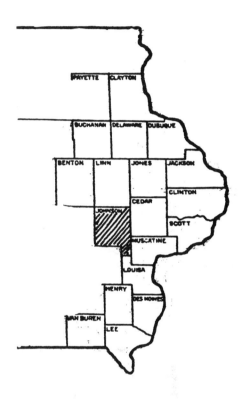

capital should be located "more centrally" and the new Johnson County seemed the choice. Finally three commissioners were selected by the lawmakers to choose a suitable site. The place to be decided upon was designated to be called Iowa City.

Johnson County, being what was regarded as "inland" was settled later than the river cities and counties. But white settlers began arriving in the area of Johnson County not long after the area was opened to settlement in 1833.

The first settlers had arrived, according to records, in 1836 and it was by 1839 that the future city had been designated as the location for the capitol of the Territory of Iowa and the State it would eventually become.

In the fall of 1836 Philip Clark and Eli Myers left Indiana and via Rock Island, Ills., they crossed the great river and journeyed as far as the site of what is Iowa City today. The area wasn't even a paper county at the time. They thus began the settlement of the area.

PHILIP CLARK

About that time a John Gilbert operated a trading post in the Indian country for the American Fur Company. Probably no longer happy with his employment, he fell in with Clark and Myers and led them to his trading post.

After claiming land in the area that would become the future site of Iowa City they returned to Indiana and made preparations to move to Iowa. The tracts they claimed were in Pleasant Valley Township near Morfordsville. It was the custom in those early days to move onto the land in the spring and to plant crops that would yield them food for the next winter. So the group left Indiana in the late winter of 1837 so they could arrive in Iowa in time for the spring planting.

In 1837 surveyors in the employ of the U. S. government were still laying out boundary lines and that made establishing claims somewhat difficult. That is in locating exact lines and often one man's claim went until it met with another's claim and settlers often became neighbors by some sort of general agreement.

In the spring of 1837 Pleasant Harris arrived in the area to join those already there and to make his claim and settle. He, too, was from Indiana. Along with Harris came his nephew James Massey who had a wife and one child. Both Harris and Massey claimed land across the river from Eli Myers.

After determining his claim, Pleasant Harris returned to Indiana for his own wife and children. When he returned to Iowa he also brought some other relatives and some friends.

Among the very early settlers in the county were Dr. I. N. Lesh, Bill Duvall, Tom Bradley, Eli Summy, William Wilson, Henry Felkner and C. S. Trowbridge. Other early settlers of Johnson County were Jacob, John and Henry Earhart along with the Walker brothers: Samuel, James, Joseph and Henry.

Henry Felkner and C. S. Trowbridge were later among the first county officers chosen.

About this same time other areas in the future Johnson County were were being settled. William Sturgis and G. W. Hawkins, along with their families, settled in the southern portion of the future county. The information was rapidly going eastward in 1836 and 1837 that rich farmland was to be claimed in this new land of "Iowa."

Later in 1837 there came to the area of Johnson County John Trout, E. Hilton and A. D. Stephens who later had established a claim on the county seat site. The names of Samuel Mulholland and John Knight appear on the land that was later to be set aside for the future capital of the coming Territory of Iowa.

The area that was to become the capital county was early made up of several former Indian tracts. A triangle of land at the east of the county had been part of the Black Hawk Purchase of 1832. Adjacent to it and to the southwest was a five-sided area that had been a part of the Keokuk Reserve and which was ceded to the United States in 1836. Almost all the remainder of the county's area was part of the large cession of 1837 and which comprised an estimated three-fourths of the land area. (See early map herein.)

An early community was laid out in 1837 on the banks of the Iowa River and on the site of "River Junction" but it never attracted a population and therefore didn't grow. Its Indian name was Sepe-nah-mo or an English spelling of Sepanamo. In 1912 a 92-year-old longtime Johnson County resident was interviewed who recalled that Sepanamo had been called "stump town" probably because it never grew and the trees from which logs had been cut had left that impression.

Eli Myers and Philip Clark and others took the traditional route to the area that was to become Johnson County. The immigrants into Iowa came usually through Rock Island, Rockingham or Bloomington which is now Muscatine. River cities enjoyed the term "ports" in those days and those communities were the "ports of

ELI MYERS

entry," so to speak.

It was their chance meeting with the trader John Gilbert that persuaded them to leave the river town and proceed farther west to the valley of the Iowa River. Both Myers and Clark became leaders in the new community and held several posts of distinction in Johnson County's establishment, organization and growth.

Around the time they arrived in the Iowa River valley that portion of land known as the Keokuk Reserve became a part of the area that was to be the new county.

When Clark and Myers made their original claims they were an estimated mile from the Indian lands. Clark retained his claim until 1838 when he exchanged it for land farther up the Iowa River.

The establishment of a town was in order but the early settlers did not at first agree upon where it should be. Some favored a site on the west bank and settled upon the name of Osceola for it. Another

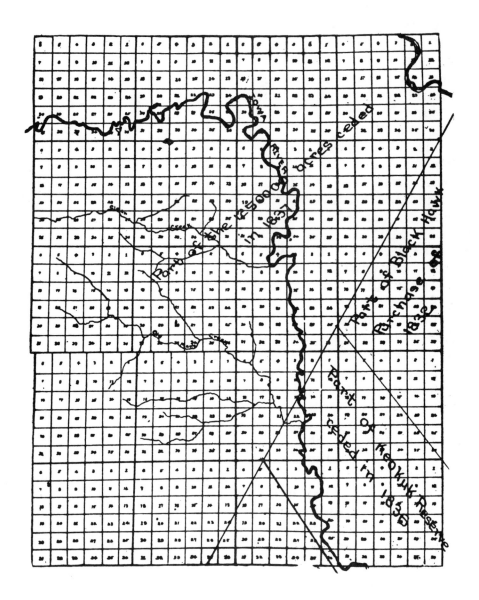

Map of Johnson County as it was
when originally established in 1837.
Note the tracts that were formerly
owned by the Indians.

group favored a community to be established on the east bank. John Gilbert and Philip Clark were leaders in the east bank party. The land they favored was Indian land located in what is now Section 22 in what is now East Lucas Township.

With the consent of the Indians they erected a small cabin and employed John Morford to reside in it thus establishing and holding thereby the claim for that time when the Indians would either sell or vacate the property.

It was following the treaty of 1837 that the land became government land and it was then that Philip Clark exchanged the farm he had claimed in 1836 for the "Morford claim." Clark then proceeded to lay out the town he had long envisioned.

The spreading knowledge that a new capital would be located in a "more central" place gave new interest in Johnson County and a new impetus for settlement. The location of a state capital or even a county seat goes with it the prospects of a market for goods and services that towns and cities without such governmental possibilites do not have. While a capital building and a capital city were but an idea, a dream, if you please, potential entrepreneurs with their minds set upon future business were exploring the area and envisioning the city.

Napoleon, down the Iowa River a few miles from the future site of Iowa City, was early designated the county seat for Johnson County temporarily for it would be natural to locate it in a place central to the county at some future date.

At the time there appeared to be good reason for the location of an "Iowa City" as a capital in Johnson County. The immense territory that comprised Iowa was in the undisputed

Pen and ink drawing of an early pioneer log house by Bertha Horack Shambaugh.

possession of the Indians. As established by the treaty with the Indians of 21 October 1837 the area of Johnson County was about as central as could then be made; the boundary line was just about immediately west of the city limits.

The commissioners were to select a 640 acre site to be laid out into a town that was directed to be called "Iowa City." That was done later, in 1839, but meanwhile the capital of the Territory of Iowa would remain at Burlington in Des Moines County.

Thus Johnson County was created. A little later than the other original counties but with great prospects for its future. It was established and organized more rapidly than most of the counties because of the avowed need to make it a "centrally located" capital. And so it did remain a capital for a few years after the seat of government was, indeed, moved there. But more importantly it would become the home of a great university.

# "Steamboat Bill"

# Preserving the history
## . . . . of Johnson County
## . . . . . and *IOWA*

No man in the history of the State of Iowa has had more to do with preserving the history of the state than has Dr. William J. Petersen who spent most of his life in Iowa City, Johnson County, Iowa.

Time and activity accorded him the nickname of "Steamboat Bill" for both his studies and knowledge of the great river Mississippi and for his many excursions on it.

From 1947 until recent years he was Superintendent of the State Historical Society of Iowa and during those same years an associate professor at the University of Iowa.

"Steamboat Bill" Petersen was born on the river, so to speak, in possibly Iowa's most historic city and county, Dubuque. From early childhood his interests centered around history. He was born in 1901 and was graduated from the Prescott School there in 1916; from the Dubuque High School in 1920.

In 1926 he was graduated from the University of Dubuque with a B.A. degree and was the given the Alumnus of Distinction Award from that college in 1963. In 1927 he received a Master of Arts degree from the University of Iowa and his Ph.D. from there in 1930. In 1958 he was awarded the honorary degree of Doctor of Laws by Iowa Wesleyan College and in 1966 the Honor Iowan Award from Buena Vista College at Storm Lake, Iowa.

Dr. Petersen is the author of 12 books under his own name and participated in the publication of 19 others in one way or another.

The books by Dr. Petersen are: True Tales of Iowa, 1932, joint authorship; Two Hundred Topics in Iowa History, 1932; Steamboating on the Upper Mississippi, 1937; Iowa: The Rivers of Her Valleys, 1941; A Reference Guide to Iowa History, 1942; Looking Backward on Hawkeyeland, 1947; Iowa History Reference Guide, 1952; The Story of Iowa (in two volumes), 1952; The Pageant of the Press, 1962; The Annals of Iowa, Volume One, 1964, and Mississippi River Panorama, 1967.

He is living in Dubuque today and is listed in Who's Who in America, Who's Who in the Midwest, the Author's and Writer's Who's Who.

# Chapter Twenty–Seven

# THE TERRITORY OF IOWA

From the first moment settlers staked claims and broke the Iowa soil it was presumed that Statehood was somewhere in the future. On the way to Statehood an area ordinarily went through Territorial status.

From becoming a part of the United States with the Louisiana Purchase of 1803 and through its various government "assignments" Iowa was part of the Michigan Territory (1834-1836) and then part of the Wisconsin Territory (1836-1838) and was sometimes designated the District of Iowa.

After the lands of the Black Hawk Purchase were open to settlement following 1 June 1833 the population began to increase. This was especially so after the reports of the rich soil in Iowa reached eastward. And those seeking opportunity headed for Iowa.

When the first census was taken of Du Buque and De Moine, the two vast counties, there were 10,531 persons excluding Indians. By 1838 there were 22,859 and the push for Territorial status increased.

Recall that concurrently with the first session of the Wisconsin Territorial Legislature that met in Iowa at Burlington there was a convention of the organized counties of the Iowa side of the big river advocating Territorial status.

THE NEW TERRITORY OF IOWA covered a vast area as is shown on this map of the central United States. Most of it, of course, was uninhabited except by Indians and was therefore unbroken prairie and wilderness.

Those Iowans wanting their area to become a Territory had a good friend in Congressional Delegate George W. Jones who strove with his mighty connections and influence in Washington to bring it about.

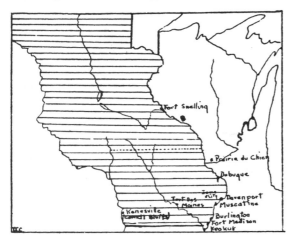

THE TERRITORY OF IOWA as it would have appeared on a map of the north central part of the United States.

The Congress eventually passed the act that Delegate Jones had been pushing for sometime. Both Presidents Jackson and Van Buren were close personal friends of Gen. Jones and their influence was helpful with the Congress.

It is related that Sen. Calhoun from South Carolina (a former vice president who resigned the office to become a senator) opposed the bill believing Iowa would eventually become a State opposing slavery. Gen. Jones maneuvered Calhoun out of the Senate chamber when the bill was to come up by urging the solon's daughter to call him from the floor. The bill passed and Sen. Calhoun felt tricked; it is suggested that Calhoun County, Iowa; was named for the daughter and not the senator!

The bill granting Iowa Territorial status was put on its final passage on 12 June 1838 to go into effect on 4 July 1838. President Van Buren quickly signed the act and Iowa was to be divided from Wisconsin with the natural border being the Mississippi River.

It would be a vast domain, indeed, if it could be called a domain, that would comprise the Territory. For all the inhabitants were located in a few counties and a few towns and villages not far west of the Mississippi River.

The capital building that Jeremiah Smith, Jr., had built with his own money had burned and so the new Territory of Iowa would almost start from scratch. The legislature would find quarters and the governor would arrive.

The new Territory took in all of Iowa, most of Minnesota and a good part of North and South Dakota as has been related heretofore.

Volume Two of this history will be entitled "The Territory of Iowa" and it will cover the years from 1838 to 1846.

ROBERT LUCAS, a former governor of Ohio, was appointed by President Van Buren to become the first governor of the Territory of Iowa. His would seemingly be a stormy term as the frontier Iowa legislators objected to the new governor's imperious nature.

# Who WAS Who in Iowa 1673 - 1838

ABBE, WILLIAM - 1st settler, Linn Co.

ANDROS, DR. FREDERICK - 1st settler Garnavillo area, Clayton County.

ARMSTRONG, JAMES - With Alexander Reed, 1st settler in Jackson County.

BAILEY, JOEL - Early pioneer settler, Delaware Co. Bailey's Ford.

BENNETT, ELIZABETH - 1st woman in Delaware Co. 1st permanent settler. Wf William Bennett; dau Wm.Eads.

BENNETT, WILLIAM - 1st to build cabin, Delaware Co. Soon left.

BLACK HAWK - Indian war chief after whom BH War and Purchase named.

BOWEN, HUGH - 1st settler, Jones Co. Bowen's Prairie.

BUELL, ELIJAH - 1st settler into Clinton Co.

CAMPBELL, ISAAC R. - Explored Des Moines Co. area 1821; later settler and landowner in Lee Co.

CHAPMAN, W. W. - Early leader in Dubuque Co. Later delegate to Congress. Held other offices.

CLARK, CAPT. BENJAMIN W. - Early settler, Scott Co. Founded Buffalo, Ia.

CLARK, PHILIP - With Eli Myers was first settler Iowa City area.

CRESAP, DR. ROGER N. - Early settler, landowner Bonaparte area, Van Buren County.

DAVENPORT, COL. GEORGE - Early comer to Rock Island; trader, Indian agent. City of is named for him.

DAVENPORT, GEORGE L. - Son of the colonel. Settler, capitalist, developer and a founder of Davenport, Ia.

DAWSON, JAMES - 1st permanent white settler in Henry County.

DOOLITTLE, AMZI - Early pioneer settler, Des Moines Co. With White and Tethro, the first ones.

DUBUQUE, JULIEN - 1st permanent white settler in Iowa from Sept. 1788. Mined lead; developed area. d. 1810.

EADS, WILLIAM - Early pioneer settler, Delaware Co. Father E. Bennett.

GOODENOW, JOHN - Pioneer settler, a founder, Maquoketa, Jackson Co.

GRIFFITH, JOHN W. - Apptd 1st sheriff Clayton Co. by Gov. Dodge, Wisc. Terr.

HEMPSTEAD, STEPHEN - Att'y in Dubuque 1836; later el. governor of Ia.

INGHRAM, ARTHUR B. - Des Moines Co. El. to Wisc. Terr. Legislative Council.

JACKSON, LEROY - Orig. Dubuque; to Delaware Co., a founder of Hopkinton.

JENKINS, BERRYMAN - School teacher Keokuk, 1829-30. Possibly 1st in Iowa.

JOHNSTONE, EDWARD - Early settler; attorney; with Francis Scott Key litigated the Half-breed Tract cases.

JOLIET, LOUIS - With Fr. Marquette arr. Iowa June 1673; made several shorings on way down river.

KEOKUK - Indian chief who treated with general government; a city and a county are named after him.

KIBBEE, LUCIUS - Early pioneer settler Delaware Co. at Rockville.

KING, JOHN - Published 1st newspaper in Iowa, The Du Buque VISITOR, 1836.

KNAPP, GEN. JOHN - Early promoter and developer of Ft. Madison, city.

KNAPP, NATHANIEL - Bro. Gen. John; early businessman, Ft. Madison. Murdered in Van Buren County.

LANGWORTHY, JAMES L. - Dubuque Co. Active in (new) Dubuque the city. Very prominent figure in Co. history.

LE CLAIRE, ANTOINE - Settler and founder Davenport, Scott Co. Indian friend. Le Claire named after him.

MANNING, EDWIN - Early settler, Van Buren Co., Keosauqua; Hotel Manning.

MARQUETTE, FR. JACQUES - With Joliet first white man to set foot on Ia. soil in Clayton Co. and elsewhere.

MASSEY, LOUISA - Of Dubuqe, Avenged murder of W. Massey.

County is named for her, Louisa Co.

MASSEY, WOODBURY - Early founder in Dubuque, city. Jury foreman; killed and death avenged by Louisa Massey.

MAXSON, WILLIAM - Early settler, Cedar Co. John Brown trained his men at Maxson's farm for his famous raid.

MAZZUCHELLI, FR. SAMUEL - Multi-talented early priest; served to establish Roman Catholic Church in Iowa.

McCARVER, MORTON M. - Early settler Des Moines Co. Businessman, Burlgtn.

McGREGOR, ALEXANDER - Crossed river in 1837 to found McGregor, Clayton County; Owned ferry service.

McKNIGHT, THOMAS - Early founder of (new) Dubuque. Terr. legislator.

MEEK, WILLIAM - Early pioneer settler Van Buren Co. Built Meek's Mills.

MORGAN, COL. WILLIAM - Prominent early pioneer settler, Des Moines Co.

MUIR, DR. SAMUEL C. - Army surgeon, 1st permanent white settler Lee Co.

MYERS, ELI - With P. Clark, first settler in Iowa City, Johnson Co. area.

NICHOLSON, THOMAS - Early settler in Hopkinton, Delaware Co. area.

NYE, BENJAMIN - 1st permanent white settler in Muscatine Co. Est. village.

QUIGLEY, PATRICK - Dubuque Co. In his home was held 1st Rom. Cath. mass, 1833. Frontier legislator; almost elected 1st governor of Iowa.

REED, ALEXANDER - With J. Armstrong, 1st settler in Jackson Co.

REYNOLDS, DR. ELI - Early pioneer settler Muscatine Co. Founded town of Geneva; Rep'd Old Des Moines Co. in Wisc. Terr. Legislature.

RITCHIE, ADAM - (Also sp. Ritchey) 1st settler, Washington County.

ROSS, WILLIAM R. - Early settler, Des Moines County, Burlinton area. Methodist leader; held many gov't offices.

SAUNDERS, ALVIN - Early settler Henry Co. Bro of Presley; Named Henry Co. Went to Nebraska, became governor and later U. S. senator,

SAUNDERS, PRESLEY - Early pioneer settler and founder, Mt. Pleasant, Henry Co. Merchant, trader.

SHAFF, HEMAN - Early settler Clinton Co. Successful farmer, landowner. Ancestor of prominent Shaff family.

SMITH, HIRAM - 1st pioneer white settler in Henry Co. Built 1st cabin.

SMITH, JEREMIAH, JR. - Early settler of Des Moines Co. Svd in Terr. Legislature (Wisc.), built temporary capital at Burlington which burned Dec. 1837.

TEAS, GEORGE W. - Early Des Moines County settler. Frontier legislator.

TETHRO, DAVID - (Also spelled Tothero in some accounts.) With A. Doolittle and S. S. White, the first settlers of Des Moines Co., Burlington area.

TIMEA - Indian chief, patriarch and law-giver of Fox tribe in Flint Hills.

TOOLE, WILLIAM - Early pioneer settler Louisa County. Founder of Toolesville.

VAN QUICKENBORNE, FR. CHARLES - Celebrated 1st Roman Catholic Mass in Iowa. Quigley's, Dubuque, 1833.

VARVEL, DANIEL - 1st pioneer settler in area that is now Monticello, Jones County, Iowa.

WALTON, COL. DAVID - 1st pioneer settler in Cedar County.

WAYMAN, WILLIAM W. - 1st permanent white settler in Clayton County 1833.

WHEELER, LORING - Early founder and settler (new) Dubuque. Wisconsin Territorial legislator.

WHITE, SIMPSON S. - With Doolittle and Tethro, first settlers in Burlington area, Des Moines County.

WILBOURNE, ZACHARIAH - Early settler built Henry Co.'s 1st grist mill.

WILSON, T. S. - Judge fr. Dubuque Co. Held 1st Ct. in Iowa Terr'y at Prairie La Porte, Clayton Co. Later on Sup. Ct.

WILLIAMS, BARTLETT - Early settler, Mt. Pleasant, with Saunders in Henry County, 1835.

YULE, SAMUEL - Early pioneer settler of Cedar County. Arrived in 1837 and sired 16 children.

# THE IOWA CONNECTION . . .

## . . . . . with American history

Those acquainted with American history have heard names such as the following all their life. What do they have to do with Iowa history? Names such as Ann Rutledge, Daniel Boone, Abraham Lincoln, Robert E. Lee, Zachary Taylor, Jefferson Davis, William Henry Harrison, John Brown, Sarah Bernhardt, Francis Scott Key, Betsy Ross, U. S. Grant, Zebulon Pike or Lewis and Clark. If you're wondering, here's their Iowa connection . . . .

ANN RUTLEDGE - Lincoln's alleged sweetheart; her mother is buried in Van Buren County.

DANIEL BOONE - At least one of his nephews was stationed in Lee County and another may have been an early pioneer settler.

ABRAHAM LINCOLN - For his service in the Black Hawk War he was granted farms in Tama and Crawford counties. He had other later connections.

ROBERT E. LEE - Army officer assigned duties in Iowa. Charted navigation on Mississippi. Le County may have been named for him or the Lee family.

WILLIAM HENRY HARRISON - Various connections. He engineered the infamous Indian treaty of 1804 that Black Hawk hated so much.

JEFFERSON DAVIS - Later president of the Confederacy. Stationed in Iowa more than once. By orders, raided settlers who anticipated crossing river.

ZACHARY TAYLOR - Later president. Commanded units in and about Iowa, especially at Ft. Crawford, Wisc. Defeated by Indians firing cannon.

JOHN BROWN - The abolitionist actually trained his men for the raid at Harper's Ferry, Virginia, at the William Maxson farm in Cedar County.

SARAH BERNHARDT - Famed actress. Her mother is buried in Cedar County.

FRANCIS SCOTT KEY - Composer of the "Star Spangled Banner." As a New York lawyer he came to Keokuk to enter the Half-breed Tract litigation.

ZEBULON M. PIKE - Explored the Mississippi River to source. Pike's Peak(s) in Clayton County, Iowa, and Colorado are named after him.

GENERAL WINFIELD SCOTT - Secured Black Hawk Purchase at site of Davenport in 1832. Commanded army 1841-1861. Whig pres'l candidate 1852.

LEWIS AND CLARK - Their famous expedition, order by Pres. Jefferson, traversed Missouri River and Western Iowa to explore Louisiana Purchase.

BETSY ROSS - Some of her descendants came to Iowa; her granddaughter is buried in a cemetary at Keokuk, Lee County, Iowa.

U. S. GRANT - Ulysses S. Grant, later general and president, roamed eastern Iowa often dealing in furs and peltries; he did some of that around Fairview (Anamosa) and Maquoketa. Once stayed at the historic Decker House in Maquoketa. (See Sponsor's adv. p. 270 this volume.)

# Honor Roll of Sponsors

This "Honor Roll of Sponsors" is published in appreciation to those who have supported this work in one way or another, mostly financially. As with many earlier histories their names will repose in public, high school, college libraries and in the homes of many individuals for generations. We urge you to thank them with your patronage.

A & D Management, Mt. Pleasant, Henry County

Banowetz Antiques, Maquoketa, Jackson County

Blue Bird Midwest, Mt. Pleasant, Henry County

Bostrom's Super-Valu, West Union, Fayette County

CECO Buildings Division, CECO Corp., Mt. Pleasant, Henry County

Coast-to-Coast Store, Mt. Pleasant, Henry County

CONTEL, General Offices, Mt. Pleasant, Henry County

Cornick Realty, Inc., Mt. Pleasant, Henry County

Decker House Inn, Maquoketa, Jackson County

Deere and Company, Dubuque Works, Dubuque, Dubuque County

Dircks LP Gas, Hopkinton, Delaware County

Dobson's Garage, Montrose, Lee County

Dohrer Investments, Elkader, Clayton County

Elvers Insurance and Real Estate, Elkader, Clayton County

Falb Motor Company, Elgin, Fayette County

Fauser Oil Company, Inc., Elgin, Fayette County

Finch, C. W., Author, Dubuque, Dubuque County

Garnavillo Mill, Garnavillo, Clayton County

Dr. H. A. Gearhart, DO, Hopkinton, Delaware County

Golden Rule Sales, Colesburg, Delaware County

Halvorson Insurance and Real Estate, Monona, Clayton County

Hawkeye Bank & Trust, Mt. Pleasant, Henry County

Heidelburg Haus Restaurant & Lounge, Mt. Pleasant, Henry County

Hoffmann-Schneider Funeral Home, Dubuque, Dubuque County

Home Furniture, Mt. Pleasant, Henry County

Hometown Partners Real Estate, Mt. Pleasant, Henry County

Interstate Federal Savings & Loan Association, McGregor, Clayton County

Iris City Antique Mall, Mt. Pleasant, Henry County

Iris City Real Estate, Mt. Pleasant, Henry County

Jerry's Restaurant & Lori's Loft, Mt. Pleasant, Henry County

Jessen's Super-Valu, Strawberry Point, Clayton County

Johnson's Feed Mill, Hopkinton, Delaware County

Kline's Super-Valu, Elkader, Clayton County

Little Switzerland Bed & Breakfast, McGregor, Clayton County

LYA Industries, Fayette, Fayette County

Mackay Envelope Corporation, Mt. Pleasant, Henry County

Marianne's Studio, Mt. Pleasant, Henry County

Main Street Frame and Art, Mt. Pleasant, Henry County

Maquoketa State Bank, Maquoketa, Jackson County

McWhirter Chevrolet, Mt. Pleasant, Henry County

Metromail Corporation, Mt. Pleasant, Henry County

Midwest Federal Savings & Loan, Mt. Pleasant, Henry County

Monona Co-operative Co., Monona, Clayton County

Monona Pharmacy, Monona, Clayton County

Motorola, Inc., Production Plant, Mt. Pleasant, Henry County

Osterhaus-Snyder Pharmacy, Maquoketa, Jackson County

Pioneer Hy-Bred Int'l, Production Plant, Mt. Pleasant, Henry County

Richard Realty & Auction, Mt. Pleasant, Henry County

H. Eugene Smith, General Contractor, Mt. Pleasant, Henry County

Speedy Division, United Farm Tools, Inc., Oelwein, Fayette County

Spirits & Things, Monona, Clayton County

Strawberry Point Drug, Strawberry Point, Clayton County

Trustworthy Hardware, West Union, Fayette County

Union Drug, West Union, Fayette County

Upper Iowa University, Fayette, Fayette County

Walker's Office Supply, Mt. Pleasant, Henry County

Weir Funeral Home, Mt. Pleasant, Henry County

West Union Co-operative Co., West Union, Fayette County

## Our Sponsors have their place in history . . . . . . . . . . .

# General Index

# Bibliography

BAILEY, Arabella, History of Delaware County, Mary Doolittle Maxfield, Editor, 1935.

CHRISTENSEN, Thomas P., The Story of Iowa, 1928, 1931, Self-published.

BUELL, Strong, The History of Clinton County, pub. @ 1931.

CHILDS, Chandler C., Newspaper Columns., Book, Robert F. Klein, Editor.

COLE, Cyrenus, IOWA - Through the Years, 1940, State Historical Society of Iowa, Iowa City, Iowa, Printed by Torch Press.

FAYETTE COUNTY HELPERS Club and Historical Society, OUT OF THE MIDWEST - A Portrait, Helen Moeller, Editor, Wlasworth Publishing Co., Marceline, Missouri.

GALLAGHER, Sr. Mary Kevin, BVM, Editor, SEED/HARVEST - A History of the Archdiocese of Dubuque, 1987, Archdiocese of Dubuque Press.

HARLAN, Edgar Rubey, The People of Iowa, A Narrative History, 1931, The American Historical Society, Inc., Chicago and New York.

HASKELL, Jonan, newspaper article, William Ross Helped Make North Hill Park Reality, The Burlington HAWK EYE, Midweek Gazette, 16 February 1988.

HOFFMANN, The Rev. Msgr. M. M., Antique Dubuque, 1934.

KIMBALL, Donald L., The Money and The Power, 1985, Trends & Events Publishing Co., Fayette, Iowa 52142.

MONTICELLO SESQUICENTENNIAL COMMITTEE, Monticello, Iowa - 1836 - 1986, C. L. "Gus" Norlin, Chmn; Leigh Clark, Ed. in Chf; Dr. L. C. Perkins, Co-Ed; C. J. "Jim" Matthiessen, Copy Ed; Monticello EXPRESS, Monticello, IA 52310

OWEN, F. E., Gazeteet and Directory of Jackson County, Iowa, 1878, Reprinted 1976 by Jackson County Bicentennial Committee. Orig. pub. by The Gazette Company, Davenport, IA. Reprinted by Walsworth, Marceline, MO.

PERCIVAL, C. S. & Elizabeth, the History of Buchanan County, 1881, Williams Brothers, Publishers, Cleveland, Ohio.

STATE HISTORICAL SOCIETY OF IOWA, The Annals of Iowa, 1863, Reprint of 1964, Economy Advertising Co., Iowa City, Iowa. (And other editions.)

WESTERN HISTORICAL SOCIETY, Histories of Individual Counties, 1878, 1881, Western Publishing Co., Chicago, Ills.

(AUTHOR'S NOTE: It is with apology that we can offer our readers but an incomplete bibliography. Due to the extreme heat of 1988 and the pull of electricity, a brief lapse in power caused the loss of the complete bibliographical information. There are many other sources not listed which should have credit but this is what could be re-assembled at press time. Volume Two will carry a more complete bibliography. There is little creative in writing history other than straightening out some information. No intention exists not to credit anyone and everyone with credit for their work whether it be pictures, text, maps, charts, information or data. DLK)